South Vietnam

U.S.-Communist
Confrontation in
Southeast Asia

Volume 3

1968

South
Vietnam

U.S.-Communist Confrontation in Southeast Asia

Volume 3

1968

Edited by Stanley Millet

FACTS ON FILE, INC.   NEW YORK, N.Y.

South Vietnam

U.S.-Communist Confrontation in Southeast Asia

Volume 3

1968

Library of Congress Card Catalog No. 66-23943
ISBN 0-87196-235-7

9 8 7 6 5 4 3 2 1
PRINTED IN
THE UNITED STATES OF AMERICA

Contents

Foreword

THIS IS THE 3D VOLUME IN THE FACTS ON FILE record of U.S. involvement in the war in Vietnam. It brings that history to the end of the year 1968. In the course of the year covered, one of the great turning points in the war occured: the policy of bombardment of North Vietnam, begun in 1965 under the Johnson Administration, was suspended. At the end of 1968, the U. S. was still involved in the war, and the controversy and conflict occasioned by the U. S. involvement was still in progress.

As in all FACTS ON FILE books, and corresponding especially with the 2 earlier volumes on Vietnam, the aim in this account of this one-year period has been to produce a journalistic narrative as accurate and as faithful to the sources as was possible. The major source was the weekly record compiled by FACTS ON FILE. All that was reported is here; what was not reported, of course, is missing. The full history of the war must await that future time when all the documents and accounts have been made public. Within these limits, it has been the aim of the editor to provide the reader with most complete and objective account he could.

1

1968

A powerful Tet offensive was launched by the Viet Cong in Feb. 1968; South Vietnamese cities and allied forces were badly mauled both in the initial assaults and in the ultimate counterattacks. Faced with growing domestic opposition to his policy in Vietnam, Lyndon B. Johnson withdrew as a candidate for reelection to the U.S. Presidency and ordered the cessation of the U.S. bombing of North Vietnam. Negotiations to end the war were opened in Paris after long preliminaries. The antiwar movement in the U.S. reached a peak of violent opposition in Chicago during the Democratic National Convention. Republican nominee Richard M. Nixon was elected U.S. President after a political campaign in which Vietnam was very much on the minds of the participants. 14,314 American, 20,482 South Vietnamese and 978 other allied military men were reported killed in combat in Vietnam during 1968, and Viet Cong/North Vietnamese combat deaths for the year were reported to total 35,774.

OPENING MOVES

Uneasy Truce, Many Truce Breaches

1967 closed and 1968 opened with what U.S. military authorities described as "the worst truce ever." The New Year's cease-
fire, aimed at suspending fighting between allied and Communist
forces in South Vietnam, was shattered by 170 enemy-initiated
violations, U.S. officials reported Jan. 2.

The worst breach of the cease-fire was a major Communist
attack Jan. 1-2 near Tayninh, 60 miles northwest of Saigon and
close to the Cambodian border. 355 North Vietnamese and Viet
Cong troops were killed and 5 captured. American losses were
listed as 23 killed and 153 wounded. The battle began 6 hours
before the end of the 36-hour allied cease-fire, which had started
6 p.m. Dec. 31, 1967, and one hour before the expiration of the
truce period announced by the Viet Cong, which had started at
1 a.m. Dec. 30. The fighting started shortly before midnight with
3 separate Communist mortar attacks on the 25th Infantry Division base camp. The North Vietnamese/Viet Cong force broke
contact at about 5:15 a.m. Jan. 2 after it was pounded heavily by
U.S. artillery and by armed helicopters and Air Force C-47s,
which flew 28 sorties against the attackers.

In what was described as another truce breach, attacking
Communist forces Jan. 1 killed 19 South Vietnamese marines and
wounded 49 near Mytho in the Mekong delta. A South Vietnamese government spokesman charged that U.S. commanders
had withheld a supporting air strike called by the beleaguered
government force on the ground that it would have constituted
a truce violation. A U.S. Air Force spokesman conceded Jan. 2
that an American plane called in to support the South Vietnamese
troops had dropped a flare but had not opened fire.

The U.S. command reported that 27 U.S. troops and 45
South Vietnamese soldiers had been killed during the truce; the
Communist death toll was listed as 553.

Fighting Sharpens

In the immediate aftermath of the truce, the early weeks of
January were marked by a sharp increase in military activity.
The American command reported Jan. 10 that as a result of the

increase in fighting, the Viet Cong and North Vietnamese had suffered a record weekly death loss Dec. 30-Jan. 6 of 2,968 killed (including those slain during the truce period).

The announcement of this increased level of casualties was highlighted by the figures claimed for 1967 in a report issued by the U.S. Defense Department Jan. 5. North Vietnamese and Viet Cong combat deaths for the entire year (totals since 1961 are given in parenthesis) were said to be 90,401 (249,145). Other combat deaths in 1967 cited by the report: U.S.—9,353 (15,997), South Vietnam—11,135 (53,137), other allied—189 (1,700). (The U.S. mission in Saigon at the same time reported that, in 1967, the Viet Cong had killed 3,820 civilians in South Vietnam [1966: 1,618] and had kidnaped 5,368 civilians, as compared with 3,507 in 1966.) The escalation in the conflict was also reflected in the announcement by the U.S. command Jan. 5 that the American troop build-up in South Vietnam had reached 486,000 men with the arrival the previous week of the 11th Light Infantry Brigade.

Among major encounters in the post–truce period:

• 241 attacking troops were reported killed Jan. 3 in North Vietnamese raids against 2 U.S. artillery bases in the Queson Valley south of Danang. The North Vietnamese killed 18 troops and wounded 100 men of the defending U.S. 3d Brigade, First Cavalry Division (Airmobile), and 198th Light Infantry Brigade. The raid on the artillery positions was coordinated with a rocket attack on the U.S. airbase at Danang and at least 10 attacks on 10 South Vietnamese outposts, district headquarters and combined U.S.–South Vietnamese units. In the Danang base raid, 3 planes were destroyed.

• Renewed fighting in the Queson Valley raised the North Vietnamese death toll to 359 Jan. 4 when First Cavalry Division troops repulsed an attack 11 miles southeast of Anhoa. 30 of the enemy were slain; one American was killed and 16 wounded. The U.S. toll in the 2-day battle: 19 killed and 151 wounded.

• A U.S. artillery base of the 196th Light Infantry Brigade near the Queson Valley district headquarters of Hiepduc (about 30 miles southwest of Danang) was attacked by North Vietnamese Jan. 6. 20 Americans were killed and 54 wounded. The Viet Cong, striking further south, attacked a district headquarters and a South Vietnamese regimental headquarters at Tanuyen, 20 miles north of Saigon. The positions were partly overrun before the Viet Cong broke off the attack, in which 8 South Vietnamese

militiamen were killed and 35 wounded.
- 16 U.S. Marines were killed and 46 wounded Jan. 7 in North Vietnamese attacks on the district headquarters town of Phuloc, 25 miles southeast of Hué, and on 5 surrounding Marine positions. The bodies of 51 enemy soldiers were found in the area later.
- 2 heavy engagements were fought in the vicinity of Saigon Jan. 8. Preceded by a rocket and mortar barrage, about 700 men of the 269th Viet Cong Battalion stormed into Khiemcuong, capital of Haunghia Province, raised their flag in the market place but withdrew from the town 3 hours later. The Viet Cong killed at least 26 South Vietnamese defenders; 27 were reported missing. 14 U.S. advisers were wounded. 26 of the attackers were reported killed. The Viet Cong also heavily damaged a camp for defectors in the town. The 2d clash took place 19 miles south of Saigon. In it U.S. 9th Infantry Division troops reportedly killed 26 men of a force of 300 guerrillas in a 10-hour engagement. 3 American helicopters, including one carrying U.S. wounded, were shot down.

War in Air Intensifies

During the post-truce period, U.S. concern over the apparent movement of men and materiel into the war zone led to an intensification of action in the air. The increase in the bombardment of North Vietnam and Laos resulted in a series of protests by Communist China and the Soviet Union.

U.S. planes were accused of bombing the Chinese Communist freighter *Hongqi 158* in the North Vietnamese port of Campha Jan. 3 and the Soviet freighter *Pereslavl-Zalessky* in Haiphong harbor Jan. 4. Peking charged Jan. 12 that American planes also had dropped bombs across the border in Yunnan Province, China and had killed or injured several Chinese.

A Soviet protest message Jan. 4 said that American planes that day had bombed the *Pereslavl-Zalessky* as it was unloading flour in Haiphong harbor. According to the Soviet account, U.S. jets, during a raid on Haiphong, had dropped 8 time bombs around the Soviet vessel; one of the bombs, exploding 25 minutes later, punctured the ship's hull, smashed the stern and damaged the engine room. The vessel was completely disabled. No casualties were reported. The other bombs were said to have exploded at intervals of 12 hours. Moscow warned that "appropriate Soviet agencies will be compelled to take measures to insure the safety of the Soviet vessels sailing for [North Vietnamese] port."

Soviet Amb.-to-U.S. Anatoly F.Dobrynin delivered a protest to State Secy. Dean Rusk Jan. 4. Meeting Dobrynin again Jan. 5, Rusk handed him a reply that said: "If any damage to international shipping in the Haiphong area was produced by ordnance dropped by United States aircraft, it was inadvertent and is regretted by the United States government." The Soviet Union charged Jan. 6 that the attack on the *Pereslavl-Zalessky* had been deliberate. The purpose of the attack, Moscow claimed, was "not to hit the ship directly. The idea was to drop delayed-action bombs all around the ship." The captain of the ship said 15 American planes had passed over the vessel several times before the bombs were dropped.

A U.S. State Department statement released Jan. 5 had said that an official investigation of the incident had "neither substantiated nor ruled out the possibility" that the U.S. was to blame. The department asserted that "careful precautions are and will continue to be taken" to avoid hitting foreign ships in North Vietnamese ports during American raids. But it was "impossible to eliminate completely the risk" taken by foreign ships entering the combat zone, the department said.

Peking charged Jan. 12 that "3 pirate planes of U.S. imperialism and its lackey Laotian rightists" had "intruded China's airspace [Jan. 7] from the direction of Laos and barbarously bombed and strafed the Miaochai area of Yunnan Province [which bordered Laos, Burma and North Vietnam], throwing and launching more than 20 bombs and rockets." The planes had "caused serious loss to life and property" but had been "powerfully rebuffed by the Chinese armed forces and people" and had "fled hurriedly in the direction of Laos," the Peking statement said. (The target of the alleged American attack was believed to have involved the Sibsong Panna Autonomous Region, adjoining Burma and Laos, which was inhabited by people of Lao and Thai stock.) Peking warned that China would take "all necessary measures to support the just struggle of the Laotian people" if the U.S. extended the Vietnam war into Laos. (The U.S. Defense Department said Jan. 12 that it had no confirmation of the alleged raid.)

A statement issued by the Chinese Foreign Ministry later Jan. 12 claimed that "pirate aircraft of United States imperialism, including Thailand-based B-52 bombers," were attacking rebel

Pathet Lao areas in Laos while Laotian government forces had "even started a massive military attack on the upper Laotian liberated areas bordering China and Vietnam."

(U.S. concern over the movement of materiel to North Vietnam by sea was reflected in a speech by Rep. Charles E. Chamberlain [R., Mich.], who reported to the U.S. House of Representatives Jan. 15, on the basis of U.S. Defense Department figures, that the number of free-world ships arriving in North Vietnam had increased from 74 in 1966 to 78 in 1967. Free-world nations whose ships were involved [number of arrivals in 1966 followed by number in 1967]: Britain, 50 and 67; Cyprus, 12 and 5; Malta, 4 and 3; Italy, 1 and 2; Lebanon, 0 and 1; Greece, 7 and 0. The number of Soviet ship arrivals in North Vietnam increased from 122 in 1966 to 185 in 1967. The number of Communist Chinese ship arrivals dropped from 138 to 93 in the same period, and the number of East European [non-USSR] arrivals declined from 45 to 31.)

Among other air-war developments:

• U.S. planes Jan. 12 bombed the Hoalac airbase (20 miles west of Hanoi) and the Caonung railroad yard 55 miles northeast of the capital. U.S. B-52s on bombing missions over the demilitarized zone (DMZ) were fired on by North Vietnamese missiles from sites 4 and 5 miles north of the DMZ. There were no hits. One of the targets struck in North Vietnam Jan. 15 was the Thainguyen steel plant, 38 miles north of Hanoi. The raid was the first on the complex since it had been reported destroyed in a raid in June 1967.

• U.S. plane losses in the war passed the 1,000 mark when 4 were downed over North Vietnam Jan. 5 after one had been lost in a bombing mission Jan. 4 over the South Vietnamese Central Highlands city of Banmethout. As of Jan. 5, U.S. plane losses over North Vietnam totaled 781 since the raids had started Feb. 7, 1965; and 220 U.S. planes had been shot down over South Vietnam. The North Vietnamese press agency had claimed Jan. 2 that 1,063 U.S. planes had been shot down over North Vietnam in 1967 and that the capture of American pilots that year had been "higher than in 1965 and 1966." According to the Communist claim, 176 of the American planes downed over the North in 1967 had been victims of Hanoi's air defenses.

Diplomatic   Offensive

Against this background, the U.S. was confronted with a diplomatic offensive launched by North Vietnam as 1968 opened.

North Vietnamese Foreign Min. Nguyen Duy Trinh said in a statement broadcast by Hanoi radio Jan. 1 that his government would start talks with the U.S. if the U.S. unconditionally halted attacks against North Vietnam. His declaration stirred international speculation that Hanoi might have eased its conditions for peace negotiations. Speaking Dec. 29, 1967, at a reception for a delegation to Hanoi from Mongolia, Trinh had said: "The American government never stops repeating that it wants talks with Hanoi but that Hanoi does not react by any sign. If the American government really wants conversations, as clearly stated in our declaration of Jan. 28, 1967, it must first unconditionally cease bombing and all other acts of war against the Democratic Republic of Vietnam [the DRV, or North Vietnam]. After the cessation of bombing and all other acts of war against the Democratic Republic of Vietnam, the DRV will start conversations with the United States on relevant problems."

Heretofore, North Vietnam had insisted that talks "could," rather than "will," be held after the U.S. ended hostilities. Other parts of Trinh's address dealt with Hanoi's previously stated belief that North Vietnam's "4 points" remained "the basis for the settlement of the Vietnamese question"* and that North Vietnam opposed UN Security Council consideration of the Vietnamese situation on the ground that the UN had no jurisdiction. Trinh assailed the U.S. for threatening "to extend the war to Cambodia and Laos."

---

*North Vietnamese Premier Pham Van Dong, in a speech to the North Vietnamese National Assembly Apr. 8, 1965, had enumerated these "4 points" as Hanoi's basic conditions for a peaceful settlement:

"(1) Recognition of the basic national rights of the Vietnamese people—peace, independence, sovereignty, unity and territorial integrity. In accordance with the Geneva Agreements, the U.S. government must withdraw from South Vietnam U.S. troops, military personnel and weapons of all kinds, dismantle all U.S. military bases there and cancel its military alliance with South Vietnam. It must end its policy of intervention and aggression in South Vietnam. In accordance with the Geneva Agreements, the U.S. government must stop its acts of war against North Vietnam and completely cease all encroachments on the territory and sovereignty of the Democratic Republic of Vietnam.

"(2) Pending the peaceful reunification of Vietnam, while Vietnam is still temporarily divided into 2 zones, the military provisions of the 1954 Geneva Agreements on Vietnam must be strictly respected. The 2 zones must refrain from joining any military alliance with foreign countries. There must be no foreign military bases, troops or military personnel in the respective territories.

"(3) The internal affairs of South Vietnam must be settled by the South Vietnamese people themselves, in accordance with the program of the National Front for the Liberation of South Vietnam [the Viet Cong's political arm], without any foreign interference.

"(4) The peaceful reunification of Vietnam is to be settled by the Vietnamese people in both zones, without any foreign interference. . . ."

A correspondent for the Westinghouse Broadcasting Corp., Bernard Redmont, reported in Paris Jan. 3 that a member of the North Vietnamese diplomatic mission in Paris had "confirmed more clearly than ever that Hanoi is willing to open peace talks at once if the bombing and all other acts of war against North Vietnam are halted." Redmont used the words "peace talks," but Trinh did not. The North Vietnamese diplomatic mission in Paris said Jan. 4 that one of its members, speaking to Redmont, had only confirmed Trinh's statement, but "as for the rest [of the interview], it is just pure invention."

Diplomatic sources in Saigon said Jan. 4 that North Vietnam had informed Indonesia in Dec. 1967 that "it would promptly enter into peace talks with the United States after an unconditional bombing cessation." And it was reported in Vientiane, Laos Jan. 4 that North Vietnam had asked Laos, Cambodia and Burma if their capitals were available for preliminary peace talks. North Vietnam's chargé d'affaires in Laos, Nguyen Chan, reportedly had forwarded the request Jan. 1.

These moves by the North Vietnamese apparently rested on an optimistic estimate of the situation then existing in Vietnam. North Vietnamese Pres. Ho Chi Minh Jan. 1, in a New Year's message, had predicted military victories for the Communist forces in 1968. He said: "This year the United States aggressors will find themselves less able than ever to take the initiative and will be more confused than ever, while our armed forces . . . will certainly win many more and still greater victories."

The North Vietnamese Communist Party newspaper *Nhan Dan* said editorially Jan. 1 that North Vietnam was militarily and politically stronger despite the American bombings of the North and the pressures of war. The editorial said: North Vietnam had become "stronger than ever"; "our communications lines remain open as ever"; "the political and moral unity of our people has strengthened."

U.S. & Saigon React

The Johnson Administration responded to Hanoi's "peace feelers" with caution and began a probe of North Vietnamese intentions.

U.S. State Secy. Dean Rusk declared Jan. 4 that the U.S. was using diplomatic channels in an effort to determine whether North Vietnamese Foreign Min. Trinh's statement that Hanoi "will" start talks—if the U.S. ended hostilities—constituted a genuine peace bid. Speaking at a news conference in Washington, Rusk said: Trinh's remarks were a "new formulation" that still "leaves a great many questions open." "I wouldn't want to characterize this statement today as either a peace feeler . . . or as purely a propaganda move." "Let's find out what this statement means as well as what it says and then . . . see whether there are any conclusions to be drawn from them."

Rusk restated U.S. policy as outlined by Pres. Lyndon B. Johnson in a speech in San Antonio Sept. 29, 1967. Rusk recalled that Johnson had said the U.S. was "willing to stop all aerial and naval bombardment of North Vietnam when this will lead promptly to productive discussions. We, of course, assume, he continued, that while discussions proceed, North Vietnam would not take advantage of the bombing cessation or limitation."

Asst. State Secy. (for Far Eastern affairs) William P. Bundy, in an NBC-TV interview (rebroadcast Jan. 7), expressed doubt as to whether a halt in U.S. bombing would result in genuine peace talks. "I am not sure that they are anywhere near the point of being ready to yield," he said. "There is no indication of when they would talk— . . . no mention of whether they themselves would exercise any kind of restraint." Bundy warned that an unconditional halt in American aerial attacks while negotiations started would not be conducive to arriving at a resolution of the conflict. He said: North Vietnam could "take advantage of things to pour down more divisions, and to play the thing as, what they call . . ., fighting while negotiating."

Trinh's statement prompted appeals in the U.S. for a halt in the bombing to test Hanoi's sincerity. Sen. Robert F. Kennedy (D., N.Y.) said in San Francisco Jan. 4: "It would make some sense to go to the negotiating table and see if we can resolve the conflict. It is possible we can go to the negotiating table and they will not be genuinely interested in finding a solution. . . . We have to at least take the first step."

Sen. John Sherman Cooper (R., Ky.) Jan. 5 lauded Johnson's decision to settle the dispute over the Cambodian border by diplomatic means rather than by dispatching American troops into Cambodia to seek out alleged Communist military bases. "I hope that [the President] will now take the step—with its risk—to stop the bombing of North Vietnam." Cooper said.

Chairman L. Mendel Rivers (D., S.C.) of the House Armed Services Committee urged Pres. Johnson Jan. 5 "to consider no cessation of bombing unless Hanoi agrees immediately to exchange of American prisoners, or, at very least, inspection of prisoners by International Red Cross."

In a further comment on Trinh's statement, Rusk said in San Francisco Jan. 12: "We have drawn no conclusion yet about the precise meaning of any statements from Hanoi. But we will know shortly whether it is a move toward peace or something else. If there is a genuine peace move, there will be no problem in the United States. If it is something else, we must try again to find some other basis for a peaceful settlement."

Confronted by the possibility of a political settlement between Hanoi and Washington, the Saigon regime moved to strengthen its position in any negotiations that might follow. South Vietnamese Pres. Nguyen Van Thieu Jan. 15 expressed "regret" that the U.S. had taken the lead in "peace efforts" in Vietnam. He said the South Vietnamese government "should have the central role in any developments relating to the events in Vietnam."

Speaking at a dinner of the Society of Vietnamese Newspaper Editors, Thieu said that to "overlook or to disregard" the "central role" of his government in Vietnamese affairs "is to give leeway to the Communist tendentious propaganda and damage the success of our common cause." Although not mentioning the U.S. by name, Thieu made clear he had Washington in mind. He cited the past efforts of "our allies" in "placing themselves at the center of peace efforts on Vietnam, for instance, by asking the United Nations or other governments to help solve the Vietnamese problem, while such a move should be made by the government of South Vietnam, as the principal party, with the support of all allied and friendly countries."

Thieu said the "Communists also use the stratagem of addressing themselves to the United States government only, while omitting the government of South Vietnam, to reverse the positions and place our allies in the role of aggressors and interventionists." Thieu denied that Trinh's Dec. 29, 1967 statement was a softening of Hanoi's position. Thieu pointed out that Trinh had emphasized acceptance of Hanoi's "4 points." He said this was "nothing less than a demand for our surrender to the

Communists." Thieu called for the continued bombing of North Vietnam as "an integral part of our system of defense against Communist aggression." He said: "The bombing of North Vietnam is measured and gradual. It is not destined to the destruction of North Vietnam but only to persuade the Communists to stop their aggression. . . . It constitutes the only incentive for Communist North Vietnam to make peace. Otherwise the Communists can continue guerrilla warfare indefinitely, at little cost, to disrupt our society and to wear us down."

Thieu emphasized the need to seek out Viet Cong/North Vietnamese troops operating on Cambodian soil "to launch attacks against us." "We respect the independence and the territorial integrity of Cambodia," Thieu said, "but we fully reserve the right of pursuit against the Communist aggressors if they continue to use staging areas in Cambodia."

Rusk assured Saigon Jan. 15 that "it goes without saying that the future of South Vietnam could not be decided without full participation of the legal and constitutional government of South Vietnam."

(In his first reaction to Trinh's peace bid, Thieu Jan. 3 had dismissed it as "not serious." Thieu restated Saigon's position that "there will never, never be a coalition government because we will never recognize the Communists.")

Thieu clarified his position Jan. 19, stating that "if the Communists want a bombing pause, they must first stop their infiltration and all aggressive actions." Asserting that there was no conflict in U.S. and South Vietnamese peace aims, Thieu said Pres. Johnson's stand on a halt in the bombing as expressed in his State-of-the-Union message was "categorical and clear."*

Thieu repeated his view on the bombing of the North in a speech Jan. 25 at a joint meeting of the South Vietnamese Senate and House of Representatives. Thieu said: The raids had been launched in "response to the whole apparatus of Communist

*Delivering his State-of-the-Union message Jan. 17 at a televised joint session of the U.S. Congress, Johnson said the U.S. position on a bombing halt had been stated in the address he had made in San Antonio Sept. 29, 1967. "The bombing would stop immediately," Johnson declared, "if talks would take place promptly and with reasonable hopes that they would be productive. And the other side must not take advantage of our restraint. . . . If a basis for peace talks can be established on the San Antonio foundations, . . . we would consult with our allies and the other side to see if a complete cessation—a really true ceasefire-can be made the first order of business."

aggressive activities, including Communist infiltration across the borders as well as guerrilla attacks, subversion, sabotage and terrorism." Thieu had "actively explored the avenues that may lead to fruitful negotiations" with North Vietnam. The conflict "should logically be discussed, in the first place, among" the officials of North and South Vietnam.

Thieu's insistence on talks between North and South Vietnam was reiterated Jan. 24 by South Vietnamese Foreign Min. Tran Van Do. Do said that peace proposals drawn up by the UN or any other 3d party "without the participation of South Vietnam would be nullified, and we will not recognize the decisions made" at such meetings.

Immediate peace negotiations and an indefinite truce were urged in a petition signed by 65 faculty members of South Vietnam's university system (reported Jan. 22). The statement said: The war was "seriously endangering the very existence of the Vietnamese people from both material and moral standpoints. The complex differences between the official positions [in the conflict] require subtle solutions that can only be reached after long deliberations and drawn-out negotiations."

The Saigon regime further clarified its peace terms in a resolution adopted by the House of Representatives Jan. 4. The resolution opposed (a) the formation of a coalition government that would include the National Liberation Front (NLF, the political arm of the Viet Cong) and (b) the holding of formal negotiations with the NLF. All 72 deputies of the 136-member house present approved the resolution.

In opposition to the stand taken by Pres. Thieu, the South Vietnamese Council of Roman Catholic Bishops, in a statement issued Jan. 8, called for a halt in the bombing of North Vietnam, a cessation of military activities in the North and South and peace negotiations. The council's 17 bishops, representing 1.8 million Catholics in South Vietnam, also criticized the South Vietnamese government by asking: "How can there be peace when those in responsible places mask their false promises behind rhetoric? How can there be peace if laziness, hypocrity and corruption prevail everywhere in society?"

International Reaction

Pope Paul VI Jan. 8 urged parties to the Vietnam war to

"take the chances for negotiations the moment they present themselves." The pope Jan. 1 had deplored what he called the "new, terrible obstacles" to the attainment of peace in Vietnam. Speaking in St. Peter's Basilica to an audience of 20,000 people who were marking his call for the proclamation of New Year's Day as a day of peace, the pontiff "exhort[ed] the powers involved in the conflict to attempt every possible means that could lead to an honorable solution of the sorrowful dispute. The same entreaty we place before international bodies that might be able to intervene." (The Vatican weekly *L'Osservatore della Domenica* Jan. 3 had expressed fear that the U.S. might seek a way out of its "impasse" in Vietnam by extending the war to Laos and Cambodia "with effects of unforeseeable scale, ill-omened for all." This kind of military escalation would undermine the U.S.' "moral and political" position, Federico Alessandri, editor of the weekly, asserted.) The pope, receiving Yugoslav Premier Mika Spiljak Jan. 10, expressed determination to continue to seek peace in Vietnam "in spite of the many difficulties and, sometimes, misunderstandings" he seemed to encounter.

UN Secy. Gen. U Thant urged Jan. 18 that the bombing of North Vietnam be ended as the first step towards peace. Asserting that a bombing halt should have first consideration, Thant said: "So long as that priority is not met, I do not see any way how the conflict can be shifted from the battlefield to the conference table." Thant suggested that it was preferable "to concentrate attention on the full implementation of the Geneva agreement of 1954" rather than to attempt a new approach toward negotiation. Thant criticized both sides in the war as "juvenile" for adopting the "simplistic" position that the other side was responsible for the conflict.

British Foreign Secy. George Brown had said, after conferring with State Secy. Dean Rusk in Washington Jan. 11, that he regarded Trinh's statement "a significant move" towards the holding of peace talks, despite some elements of the message that were "not so encouraging." Disclosing that he had discussed Trinh's speech with Rusk, Brown said: "It is important that we make sure as soon as we can how significant the speech was, and what part of it was significant."

North Vietnam Amplifies Proposal

The North Vietnamese, during the opening weeks of 1968,

continued their offensive to bring the U.S. to negotiations on terms acceptable to them. In an initial reaction to the American State Secretary's reception of Hanoi's proposal, North Vietnamese officials Jan. 7 called Rusk's remarks evasive. The Communist leaders said that Hanoi's linking of an unconditional bombing halt with talks was clear and that the resumption earlier in the week of heavy American raids on North Vietnam was untimely.

North Vietnamese diplomats in Paris Jan. 10 and 16 reaffirmed Hanoi's statement of Dec. 29, 1967 that North Vietnam "will" start talks with the U.S. if the U.S. unconditionally halted the bombing of North Vietnam and "all other acts of war." The latter statement, expressed Jan. 16 in Paris by Mai Van Bo, North Vietnam's chief representative in Western Europe, further elaborated the Dec. 29 bid for talks. It was reported in Paris Jan. 17 that Bo, who had been used previously for Hanoi trial balloons, had prepared his statement in consultation with his superiors in Hanoi.

North Vietnamese Foreign Min. Trinh's remarks had been regarded as a softening of Hanoi's conditions in contrast to his previous statement of Jan. 28, 1967, in which he had said that negotiations "could" start if the bombing stopped. Bo, interviewed by a French radio-TV reporter, said: "All political observers have underlined the change from the conditional to the future in the remarks of Dec. 29. It is obvious . . . that the declaration of Jan. 28, 1967 . . . has thus been made perfectly clear by his [Trinh's] remarks of Dec. 29."

The government-controlled French radio-TV network did not broadcast the Bo interview the day it was given. A member of the North Vietnamese mission in Paris, therefore, gave the text of the interview to the *N.Y. Times* and Agence France-Presse Jan. 16 and indicated that Hanoi wanted it published as soon as possible.

Bo asserted: "Following the unconditional cessation of bombing and all other acts of war against . . . [North Vietnam], the 2 parties will meet to reach agreement on such questions." The "conversations will begin after a suitable time following upon the cessation" of U.S. acts of war. The U.S. "can announce this unconditional cessation . . . by means of a declaration or any other procedure to prove its reality."

When questioned as to what he meant by "other acts of war," Bo replied: "all military action that violates the sovereignty and the territory" of North Vietnam. As for the U.S.' demand for North Vietnamese "reciprocal action," Bo asserted that the bombing of North Vietnam constituted a "deliberate aggression" that had to be "ended without any condition whatsoever." Bo criticized State Secy. Rusk's Jan. 4 reaction to Trinh's statement. Rusk Jan. 4 had repeated Pres. Johnson's policy statement of Sept. 29, 1967, and Bo called this a reaffirmation of the U.S. proposal of "a conditional cessation of bombing." Rusk had said the U.S. was interested in a clarification of Trinh's remarks, particularly in regard to (a) the time gap between a halt in the bombing and the holding of talks and (b) the issues that North Vietnam would be willing to discuss. Bo amplified the North Vietnamese position by saying that talks could take place at a "suitable time" after a cessation of the bombing and that the agenda would be subject to agreement by the 2 sides.

The earlier reaffirmation of Trinh's statement had been made public by the *Christian Science Monitor* Jan. 10. It had been reported by the newspaper's correspondent in Hong Kong, John Hughes, to whom the North Vietnamese Foreign Ministry had sent the reaffirmation in reply to an inquiry Hughes had made.

Both Sides Firm

Pres. Johnson made it clear in his State-of-the-Union message Jan. 17 that the U.S. rejected Hanoi's offer of peace talks based on the "unconditional" end of the bombing of North Vietnam. The North Vietnamese Communist Party newspaper *Nhan Dan* made it equally clear Jan. 21 that Hanoi rejected the "San Antonio formula" of Sept. 29, 1967, which Johnson had reaffirmed as the U.S. terms for peace talks.

Nhan Dan said: In his State-of-the-Union message, the President "only beat around the bush, repeating his San Antonio formula." "The so-called San Antonio formula is but a habitual trick of the United States to put on the same footing the aggressor and the victim of aggression and to force the Vietnamese people to give up struggling in the face of continued American aggression." The U.S. "must definitively [interpreted as meaning 'permanently'] and unconditionally" end the bombing of North Vietnam before peace talks could be held. The U.S. had "no right to ask for reciprocity" as a condition for halting the bombing since North Vietnam had "never encroached on the independence and sovereignty of the United States." *(Nhan Dan* said that "the Vietnam war is the main cause of the [U.S.'] political, economic and social difficulties. . . . The American people are stepping up their struggle against this war. . . . ")

Johnson had said in his San Antonio statement that the U.S. air strikes against North Vietnam would stop "when this will lead promptly to productive discussions. We, of course, assume that while discussions proceed, North Vietnam would not take advantage of the bombing cessation or limitation." Speculation had arisen that Johnson had stiffened his San Antonio statement when he said in his State-of-the-Union message that North Vietnam "must not take advantage of our restraint as they have [during bombing pauses] in the past." But U.S. Administration officials denied Jan. 18 that the stiffened wording in the President's statement basically changed the position he had stated in San Antonio.

State Secy. Rusk said Jan. 23 that *Nhan Dan*'s reaction to Johnson's Jan. 17 message was regarded as a rejection of the President's "San Antonio formula." Rusk, however, expressed hope that this was not North Vietnam's "last word."

The North Vietnamese press agency had said Jan. 18 that Foreign Min. Trinh's Dec. 29, 1967 statement did not represent a softening of Hanoi's position. The agency said acceptance of North Vietnam's 4-point plan and of the Viet Cong's political program remained "the basis for any solution to the Vietnam problem."

Debate in the U.S.

The debate in the U.S. Congress and among academic and citizens' groups over Administration policy in Vietnam intensified after Hanoi's statement at the end of 1967 that talks "will" be held if the U.S. stopped its bombing and other acts of war.

Calls for a bombing halt were renewed by Sens. John Sherman Cooper (R., Ky.) Jan. 13 and Senate majority leader Mike Mansfield (D., Mont.) Jan. 14. Both cited Hanoi's recent statement. In a speech Jan. 22, Mansfield warned that the war was "still expansive" and had "brought about a diversion of initiative, energy and public attention, not to speak of funds, from the pressing problems of the cities," which were approaching a "national disaster" because of such neglect.

Sen. Robert F. Kennedy (D., N.Y.) had said in San Francisco

Jan. 4 that the U.S. should respond to the apparent Hanoi offer: "It makes sense to go to the table and try to resolve the conflict. If we wait another year it will be far worse." Appearing with Sen. Gale McGee (D., Wyo.) Jan. 21 on a special CBS-TV program on Vietnam, Kennedy said the U.S. was "asking for unconditional surrender" as its terms for talks. Instead, he said, the bombing should be halted as an inducement to begin negotiations. McGee, who opposed a bombing halt, said it would be "totally irresponsible" to "go to any conference table strictly on a fishing expedition."

Sen. George D. Aiken (R., Vt.) also charged that the Administration was seeking "unconditional surrender." He said in the Senate Jan. 19 that the Administration was using "military strength" because of its "ineptitude" in devising a political solution. Actually, he said, "we are fighting nationalists first in Vietnam," and "to make out that the North Vietnamese and the Viet Cong . . . are integral parts of a unified and monolithic world communism is simply self-destructive fantasy." Because of the Administration's belief in this "fantasy," he said, "we must now produce a victory over an . . . almost indefinable enemy. The Administration has . . . become the prisoner of its own bad rhetoric" and "so trifled with words" as "to endanger the peace of the world and to embitter our society at home in a manner not seen in a century." "Is negotiation among the Vietnamese factions" the Administration's "present real objective?" he asked. "I feel all Americans should have an answer." Aiken said the issue was between those seeking to demilitarize U.S. policy to reduce the "unjustified costs" and those "who cling to the elusive hope of some kind of military victory." "It remains as true today as it was 2 years ago," he declared, that "only" the U.S., "by its own deliberate actions, can revive the possibility of a political resolution of the conflict."

In rebuttal, McGee told the Senate Jan. 23 that Pres. Johnson had repeatedly said "the military is not the solution in Southeast Asia" but one tactic to attain a resolution of the conflict. He appealed to Aiken "not to put words in the President's mouth . . . in an attempt to chew them up himself in order to have an argument." The real issue, he said, was "stability in all Eastern Asia."

A call for deescalation was also made by the Methodist Board of Missions Jan. 15. The board, meeting in Denver, Colo., stressed "the importance of deescalation—such as a halt in the bombing of North Vietnam—and a sincere search for a negotiated settlement."

Senate Republican leader Everett McKinley Dirksen (Ill.) Jan. 14 reaffirmed his support for Administration policy. "What are we going to do other than what the President is doing right now?" he queried. "We can't retreat, we can't pull out and we can't get the other side to negotiate." Assistant Senate GOP leader Thomas H. Kuchel (Calif.), in a Senate speech Jan. 22, warned: "We must not, in attempting to end the war in Vietnam, repeat the major oversight in the course of the American involvement. There must be support for our action on a broad international front." Kuchel said the U.S. should work toward a "new Geneva [peace conference]."

Another call for multilateral negotiations was made Jan. 22 by Sen. Wayne Morse (D., Ore.). "We must have others settle the war for us," he said.

The Administration side had been taken Jan. 15 by an 8-member committee made up of ex-Pres. Dwight D. Eisenhower; ex-Sen. Paul H. Douglas (D., Ill.), the organizer of the committee; Gen. Omar N. Bradley; Dr. James B. Conant; the Most Rev. Robert E. Lucey, Roman Catholic archbishop of San Antonio, Tex.; Mrs. Oswald B. Lord, ex-U.S. representative to the UN; ex-State Undersecy. Charles E. Saltzman and Princeton University Prof. Eugene P. Wigner. Their statement said that "the beginning of an extended bombing pause must be promptly followed by Hanoi's cessation of sending men and materials into the South and any firing from the North upon our fighting men."

The Johnson Administration policy on peace talks was further clarified by Clark M. Clifford before the Senate Armed Services Committee. (Clifford had been nominated by the President to succeed Robert McNamara as Defense Secretary and was unanimously confirmed by the Senate Jan. 30.) In testimony before the Senate committee Jan. 25, Clifford opposed a cessation of the bombing of North Vietnam under the current military and political circumstances. "It is my hope," Clifford said, "that the time will come, and the sooner the better, that the North Vietnamese will indicate some reciprocal action [in exchange for a bombing halt]. We have not asked for much. The President has placed it at almost an irreducible minimum. He has said, 'if you will agree to talk promptly, if you will agree also not to take advantage of the suspension, we will stop the bombing.' It seems to me this is a minimal requirement. They have chosen not to do it. . . . In my opinion, it [the bombing] can't stop with their [the North Vietnamese's] present wholly and completely intransigent attitude."

When asked if he would expect Hanoi to stop all military activities as a condition of a cessation in the bombing, Clifford said: "I do not expect them to stop their military activities. I would expect to follow the language of the President when he said that if they would agree to start negotiations promptly and not take advantage of the pause in the bombing."

Sen. Strom Thurmond (R., S.C.) then asked Clifford: "What do you mean by taking advantage if they continue their military activities?" Clifford replied: "Their military activity will continue in South Vietnam, I assume, until there is a cease-fire agreed upon. I assume that they will continue to transport the normal amount of goods, munitions, men, to South Vietnam. I assume that we will continue to maintain our forces and support our forces during that period. So what I am suggesting is, in the language of the President, that he would insist that they not take advantage of the suspension of the bombing."

Clifford told the committee: He was satisfied with the way the war was being conducted. The U.S.' "limited objective" in the war in Vietnam "is to assure to the South Vietnamese people the right of self-determination, give them the right to select the type of government they choose and to conduct it in the manner that they wish, without their being forced by the subjugation from within, or by application of force from without, to have another kind of life in their country. . . . It is not and certainly must not be our intention to acquire any territory of any sort. . . . We are fighting a limited war. We are not fighting to destroy our enemy. We are fighting to persuade our enemy to withdraw from South Vietnam and to leave it alone. . . . As far as talking about a military victory is concerned, I believe in a great respect we have already attained a type of victory in South Vietnam. I believe our successful presence there has many times justified the cost to us in our men and in our treasure, for as one travels in Southeast Asia he finds that this is the general attitude. They have no hope in the French. The British are withdrawing from Malaysia and Singapore. If it were not for the United States, there would be no hope there. . . . To me it is not a question of years, it is a question of weeks and months, if we weren't there, until Southeast Asia, nation by nation, succumbed, and that is not happening now, and it is not happening, in my opinion, because we are there, and because we have extended this shield, and I believe we must continue to do it."

Pressure on Cambodia

The American effort to make South Vietnam secure from what it called Communist invasion from the North led to continued pressure on Cambodia, which had severed relations with the U.S. May 3, 1965. In early 1968, the U.S. attempted through diplomatic means to end what it described as Cambodia's role in the war in Vietnam. At his news conference of Jan. 4, State Secy. Rusk had disclosed that U.S. Amb.-to-India Chester Bowles would go to Pnompenh to discuss with Cambodian officials measures to curb the alleged use of Cambodian territory by Viet Cong and North Vietnamese forces. When questioned as to whether the U.S., as had been reported, was considering "hot pursuit" of Communist forces into Cambodia, Rusk replied: "Our major objective . . . is to find a way to remove the presence of North Vietnamese and Viet Cong elements on Cambodian territory and therefore eliminate the problems. . . ."

North Vietnamese concern over U.S. intentions toward Cambodia had been expressed Jan. 1 in a government statement that declared that Hanoi's forces would prevent any U.S. invasion of Cambodia. It denied that North Vietnam used Cambodian territory in fighting the war.

Bowles began talks with Cambodian officials in Pnompenh Jan. 9. The major topic on the agenda was the possible "hot pursuit" by U.S. and allied forces chasing Viet Cong or North Vietnamese troops into Cambodia. Following a meeting with Bowles Jan. 10, Cambodian Chief of State Norodom Sihanouk said he and Bowles had agreed on the strengthening of the 3-nation International Control Commission (India, Poland and Canada) to police the Cambodian-South Vietnamese border to prevent incursions by foreign forces. Sihanouk said the U.S. had agreed not to pursue Communist forces into Cambodia. Instead, he said, the U.S. would inform Pnompenh of any Viet Cong/North Vienamese movement into Cambodia and thus enable Cambodian troops or ICC observers to check on the border violations. (An Indian government spokesman in New Delhi had noted Jan. 4 that the ICC's military components had been withdrawn from Cambodia and that it therefore was impossible for the ICC to supervise the border with South Vietnam. Meeting with Indian Prime Min. Indira Gandhi in New Delhi Jan. 1, Bowles had suggested that India take the lead in strengthening the ICC in Cambodia. Mrs. Gandhi reportedly told Bowles that her government would not commit itself until it consulted with Cambodia.)

Sihanouk said he would also accept information from the Chinese Communists or North Vietnamese on U.S. incursions into Cambodia. (The *Wall Street Journal* reported Jan. 10 that "some small American units have been crossing into Cambodia for years on secret raids." Such incursions had been widely reported for months.) Sihanouk said he would not publicly denounce the violation of his country's frontiers in order not to compromise Pnompenh's friendship with foreign powers "unless they install themselves in our country."

Sihanouk said he and Bowles disagreed on the general situation in Vietnam. "I asked for a halt to the bombing of North Vietnam," Sihanouk reported, "but the Americans demand in exchange a halt in the shipment of North Vietnamese reinforcements to the South. They forget that their aerial escalation has brought about the *de facto* reunification of Vietnam." Sihanouk said he had urged the Americans to support a neutralized, reunified Vietnam and to "attach importance to the program of the National Liberation Front."

In an interview published in the *N.Y. Times* Jan. 6, Sihanouk had said of Bowles' then impending visit: If Bowles brought U.S. "recognition of our present borders, we shall immediately reestablish diplomatic relations with the United States. If he does not, . . . Mr. Bowles' mission will at least permit, if Mr. Johnson is willing to prevent aggression against our country, a reduction in tension between the United States and Cambodia." Sihanouk reiterated his support for expansion of ICC powers to carry out surveillance of the Cambodian-South Vietnamese borders. But he noted that the Soviet Union, co-chairman of the Geneva Conference, and Poland opposed such expansion. If U.S. forces invaded Cambodia, Pnompenh would first call on Peking for "material aid," Sihanouk warned. "If American pressure became too strong," he said, his government would appeal for Chinese "volunteer combatants to be placed under Khmer [Cambodian] command [and] who would be subject to repatriation at any time." Sihanouk ruled out a request for volunteer soldiers from Vietnam because "we have learned from experience through the previous Viet Minh occupation, after the departure of the French in 1953."

Peking had warned Jan. 3 that it would "not look on with folded arms" if U.S. troops entered Cambodia in pursuit of Communist troops. The following day, Cambodia announced the receipt of 11 planes and antiaircraft guns from China. In accepting the equipment, Cambodian Premier Son Sann said the shipment from "our friend China" "has a great significance" in view of the "growing . . . threat of American intervention against our independence, our neutrality and our territorial integrity."

U.S.-Cambodian Agreements

The U.S. and Cambodia announced agreement Jan. 12 on means of preventing Cambodia from becoming involved in the Vietnam war. The accord was announced in a joint communiqué by U.S. Amb.-to-India Bowles and Cambodian Premier Son Sann. *Major points of the communique:*

• Bowles "renewed American assurances of respect for Cambodian sovereignty, neutrality and territorial integrity. He expressed hope that . . . the International Control Commission would avert violations of Cambodian territory and neutrality by forces operating in Vietnam. Moreover, he declared that the . . . United States . . . is prepared to provide material assistance to the International Control Commission to enable it to increase its ability to perform its mission."

• Sihanouk expressed "the desire to keep the war in Vietnam away from his borders" and to have Cambodia's territory and neutrality "respected by all countries, including the belligerents in Vietnam." Cambodia, therefore, was "exerting every effort to have the present frontiers of the kingdom recognized and respected."

• Bowles emphasized that the U.S. intended not to violate Cambodian territory and to "do everything possible to avoid acts of aggression against Cambodia as well as incidents and accidents which may cause losses and damage to the inhabitants of Cambodia."

• Sihanouk reiterated his 1961 suggestion that the ICC be strengthened "by the creation of mobile teams and by the establishment of fixed posts at various points in the country" "so that it may be able, within the framework of its competence as defined by the Geneva agreements of 1954, to investigate, confirm and report all incidents as well as all foreign infiltrations on Cambodian territory."

The agreement incorporated the differences between Cambodia and the U.S. without resolving them. These differences arose from the lack of confidence on the part of the U.S. in the ability—or the willingness—of Cambodia to deny the use of its territory to North Vietnam and the Viet Cong. The revival of the ICC machinery referred to in the communique was intended to solve this problem. But the 1954 Geneva agreements establishing the 3-nation ICC had not made clear whether ICC decisions required unanimous or only majority vote. Therefore, implementation of the U.S.-Cambodian agreement to expand ICC surveillance powers remained questionable. The Cambodian news agency reported that Sihanouk had been informed Jan. 11 by Soviet Amb.-to-Cambodia Sergei M. Kudryautsev and M. Mylicki, head of the Polish mission to the ICC, that widening the commission's authority required not only unanimous ICC consent but also the approval of all the participants of the Geneva Conference. The Soviet Union and Poland opposed the granting to ICC of wider powers in Cambodia. The U.S. held that ICC actions could be decided by a 2-vote majority.

Ultimately, the ICC was unable to fulfill the task that the U.S. had sought to confer on it. The issue of "hot pursuit" persisted in the aftermath of the Cambodian-American agreement until the breakdown of that agreement the following week.

U.S. spokesmen, however, insisted that the U.S. had a right to act in what it considered its self-defense. On returning to New Delhi Jan. 12, Bowles said he had not given Cambodia assurances against accidental intrusions. " 'Hot pursuit' is not our intention and should never be necessary," Bowles asserted. "We said flatly that 'hot pursuit' was not an issue. The whole issue was how he [Sihanouk] and we would cooperate to prevent Cambodia's neutrality from being infringed upon by anybody." But in commenting on the U.S.-Cambodian agreement, Assistant State Secy. (for Far Eastern affairs) William P. Bundy said in Washington Jan. 12 that Bowles had emphasized to Sihanouk that the U.S. maintained the right of self-defense, including the right to pursue Communist troops who might be launching attacks from Cambodia. "When you have a situation where Viet Cong and North Vietnamese troops are there [in Cambodia], there may arise a situation where American forces are faced with the necessity of taking action in what is called the right of defending yourself."

Cambodia's apparent effort to preserve neutrality in the face of mounting pressures and to implement its agreement with the U.S. as it interpreted it was expressed in a Cambodian news agency report Jan. 12 that Sihanouk would dispatch Cambodian troops "to request the Viet Cong to leave Cambodian territory" on receipt of evidence of infiltration. The U.S. would "inform Cambodia of all information she possesses of Communist Vietnamese infiltration [to] enable Cambodia to perform its duties as a neutral country," the agency said. North Vietnam was reported the same day to have agreed to come to Cambodia's aid in the event of U.S. aggression against Cambodia. The pledge was made in a joint Cambodian-North Vietnamese communiqué on 9 days of talks Cambodian Foreign Min. Prince Norodom Phourissara had held in Hanoi with North Vietnamese officials. Phourissara had left Hanoi Jan. 8 after conferring with Pres. Ho Chi Minh, Foreign Min. Nguyen Duy Trinh and Premier Pham Van Dong. The joint communiqué assailed the U.S. for fighting a "war of aggression" in South Vietnam and a "war of destruction" against North Vietnam for the purpose of transforming the area into American "neo-colonies and military bases." In the communiqué, Cambodia voiced "resolute support" of the South Vietnamese National Liberation Front.

The Soviet Union warned the U.S. Jan. 12 that Moscow would "not remain indifferent" to U.S. "attempts to violate Cambodia's territorial integrity, whatever the pretexts." The text of the Soviet note was made public Jan. 18 in Washington and Moscow. A similar protest had been delivered orally by Soviet Chargé d'Affaires Yuri N. Chernyakov Jan. 12 to U.S. Amb.-at-Large Averell Harriman in Washington. The USSR said: American claims of Viet Cong/North Vietnamese use of Cambodian territory were a pretext "to justify the spreading of military actions to . . . Cambodia and Laos, which is now being prepared." "Special anxiety is evoked by calls by American military leaders for actions that would mean a violation of the sovereignty and territorial integrity of Cambodia and Laos, up to and including a direct incursion of ground forces into . . . neutral Cambodia." U.S. calls for the strengthening of the ICC in Cambodia were "an attempt to find an excuse for hostile actions against that country and justify such actions in advance."

In disclosing the contents of the Soviet note, the State Department said Jan. 18 that Harriman had asked Chernyakov whether the Soviet Union had discussed with Hanoi the question of Viet Cong/North Vietnamese operations in Cambodia. The department again appealed to the Soviets to "turn their attention and influence to efforts to strengthen the International Control Commission and to assure the neutrality and territorial integrity of Cambodia."

A similar plea to the Soviets had been issued by the State Department Jan. 17 because of fears that Prince Sihanouk might have been changing his mind about his previous appeals for widening ICC surveillance powers. Sihanouk was quoted as having said at a news conference Jan. 16 that, when he had met with the Soviet ambassador to Cambodia, he had informed the Russian envoy "that I am not interested in a strengthening of the ICC personnel or power or otherwise and that I am interested precisely in what has been done by the Soviet Union to dissuade the Americans from launching aggression on us." The Soviet ambassador, Sihanouk stated, had "brought me the good news that the Soviet Union had taken further steps in Washington and New York and even in Moscow to persuade the Americans to fully respect Cambodia and its borders and to refrain from crossing them." Soviet support of Cambodia's cause, Sihanouk said, was "worth all the helicopters in the world that can be given to the ICC. It is the best deterrent possible to halt the aggression of the inveterate U.S. warmakers."

(British concern over the "hot pursuit" issue was reflected in a note sent to the Cambodian government Jan. 12. The note said London respected Cambodia's frontiers. Japan Jan. 12 sent Pnompenh a similar note expressing the view that it planned to recognize "the inviolability" of Cambodia's frontiers. Cambodia had warned Tokyo that unless it recognized its borders by Jan. 15, it faced the prospect of a break in Cambodian-Japanese diplomatic relations.)

Cambodia charged Jan. 19 that a combined U.S.-South Vietnamese force had clashed with Cambodian troops Jan. 18 after intruding 200 yards into Cambodian territory in Preyveng Province. The Pnompenh report said: 3 government soldiers had been killed and one seriously wounded in the allied attack on a government outpost at Peam Momtea; the allied force, supported by 4 fighter-bombers and a spotter reconnaissance plane, fled after 40 minutes. In a further report on the incident, the Cambodian government said Jan. 21 that abandoned equipment of the "American-South Vietnamese" force found on the battlefield, later shown to the International Control Commission, included paratroop commando scarves, a U.S. officer's helmet, weapons and radio sets. 15 of the attackers were killed and "several" wounded, according to the report.

The U.S. State Department said Jan. 18 that the penetration—which it described as 75 yard deep—was inadvertent. The statement said: "The [border] crossing took place without hostile intent. It was not planned. It occurred in the heat of battle . . . [in] an attempt by the U.S. and ARVN [South Vietnamese] forces to protect themselves." The Viet Cong force had been bombarded by allied guns in a Vietnamese village and then had fled across a river into Preyveng Province. The allied patrol crossed into Cambodia after being fired on by the guerrillas from there, and 2 U.S. and 4 South Vietnamese soldiers were killed in the operation. The department expressed "regrets" for any casualties suffered by Cambodians.

Norodom Sihanouk had charged Jan. 17 that the U.S. had violated its pledge to respect Cambodia's borders. Speaking at a dinner for Yugoslav Pres. Tito, who had arrived in Cambodia Jan. 17 for a 6-day state visit, Sihanouk said that U.S. government statements made after the Jan. 12 accord had been announced had (a) "cynically" proclaimed that "America is not bound by promises just made by the representative of Pres Johnson [U.S. Amb.-to-India Bowles]" and (b) affirmed the U.S.' "right to launch military operations up to 16 kilometers [10 miles] inside our territory." The U.S. State Department Jan. 18 denied that "any responsible United States official" had said that U.S. troops would, if necessary, push 10 miles into Cambodia. American assurances to respect Cambodia's borders were also conveyed Jan. 18 to Cambodian Premier Son Sann by the ambassador of Australia, which represented U.S. interests in Pnompenh. (The East German press agency reported Jan. 22 that, at the conclusion of Tito's visit to Cambodia, Tito and Sihanouk had expressed full support for the Viet Cong and the North Vietnamese in a joint communiqué. Tito had said at a rally in Pnompenh Jan. 20 that the Vietnam war was "a direct menace to neighboring countries.")

In a dispatch from Pnompenh Jan. 21, freelance British journalist Charles Reiss, who had accompanied a 24-member British peace group touring the Cambodian-South Vietnamese border, reported that the group had witnessed a shooting incident along the frontier in Soaireng Province Jan. 16. Reiss said 4 helicopters and an L-20 spotter plane, all without noticeable markings, had "fired machineguns and about 20 projectiles" at a clump of trees for 30 minutes. There was no return fire, Reiss said.

The Cambodian embassy in New Delhi said Jan. 18 that ICC observers Dec. 11, 1967 had visited the site of a reputed abandoned Viet Cong camp 4 miles inside Cambodia. The embassy said the commissioners had found no evidence to support AP and UPI reports of Nov. 19-20 that the guerrillas had a base of operations in the area. The Indian and Canadian members of the ICC declined to disclose the commission's findings.

The Cambodian ambassador to the UN, Huot Sambath, said in New York Jan. 22 that he had filed 851 protests against U.S./ South Vietnamese air, land and sea intrusions of Cambodian territory during May 1-Oct. 31, 1967. Sambath said 25 Cambodians had been killed and 49 wounded in that period. (Cambodia claimed Feb. 3 that a U.S.-South Vietnamese force had attacked a Cambodian government post Feb. 2 in Takeo Province [adjacent to South Vietnam's Chudoc Province], killing one Cambodian soldier and wounding 5 others.)

The Indian Foreign Ministry reported Feb. 6 that the International Control Commission in Cambodia had agreed unanimously to investigate "specific complaints" of violations of Cambodian border areas by allied or Communist forces fighting in nearby South Vietnam. The ICC had first met in Pnompenh Jan. 15 to consider Norodom Sihanouk's request for wider ICC powers to survey his country's frontiers. The Indian spokesman made clear that the ICC would not expand its operations but would investigate by "using whatever means it has at its disposal or by supplementing them." The commission, the spokesman said, had not yet decided to accept a U.S. offer of 2 helicopters.

(Australian recognition of Cambodia's border claims against Thailand and South Vietnam was announced Feb. 21 in a joint communiqué issued in Canberra by Cambodian Foreign Min. Prince Norodom Phurissara and Australian Foreign Min. Paul Hasluck. Phurissara said that the U.S. was the only major country that had not formally recognized Cambodia's borders.)

Pressure on Laos, Prelude to Tet Offensive

There was a general escalation of hostilities in the regions bordering on South Vietnam in the latter half of January. A flare-up of military activity in Laos was disclosed in reports Jan. 13-15 of major U.S. air strikes against the Ho Chi Minh Trail in the eastern part of the country, the capture by Pathet Lao rebel and North Vietnamese troops of the strategic Laotian center of Nambac and the reputed build-up of North Vietnamese troops in eastern Laos.

An AP dispatch from Saigon Jan. 13 said that increased movement of North Vietnamese troops and truck convoys along the Ho Chi Minh Trail in Laos had prompted the U.S. Air Force to temporarily shift most of its attention from targets in North and South Vietnam and to concentrate on this major North Vietnamese infiltration route to South Vietnam. An estimated 250 planes a day, more than 3 times the average daily rate, were said to be carrying out the strikes. U.S. military authorities estimated that American planes were destroying 25% of the trucks but that 75% were getting through. An estimated 6,000-8,000 vehicles were reported to have moved into the southern panhandle of North Vietnam and into Laos in Dec. 1967.

Laotian authorities reported Jan. 14 that North Vietnamese forces were attempting to extend the Ho Chi Minh Trail further westward in Laos because U.S. bombing in the previous 2 to 3 months had made the old route unusable. The North Vietnamese effort, according to Laotians, was concentrated west of Savane, where the North Vietnamese had captured 3 Laotian outposts in Dec. 1967. The purpose of this operation was to carve out a new infiltration route to the west around Savane.

A *N.Y. Times* dispatch from Saigon Jan. 16 quoted an informed source as saying that the North Vietnamese had massed a large force of men and materiel in eastern Laos and just over the border in South Vietnam for a possible onslaught against Khesanh, site of a U.S. Marine outpost. Khesanh was about 7 miles from the Laotian border and 18 miles south of the demilitarized zone (DMZ). North Vietnamese truck traffic was said to have increased at the Laotian town of Tchepone, regarded as the crossroads of the Ho Chi Minh Trail.

The fall of Nambac, which took place Jan. 13 and was reported by the Laotian government Jan. 15, was regarded as a major defeat inflicted by Pathet Lao and North Vietnamese forces. An estimated 2,000 government troops were reported missing in the final 36 hours of fighting for Nambac, a major government supply center 60 miles north of the royal capital of Luang Prabang. The government garrison had originally numbered 4,500 men. Finance Min. Sisouk Na Champassak, reporting on the Nambac battle, said: "Our forces had to reshuffle their defensive positions. We are ordering them to make a fighting retreat to the west." The retreating government troops left behind their heavy weapons, including 2 batteries of howitzers. The government garrison fled because it was outnumbered by the North Vietnamese. North Vietnamese planes had entered Laotian combat for the first time Jan. 12, when they bombed the Samneua Province town of Muong Yut. 2 of the 4 attacking planes were shot down and 3 North Vietnamese killed.

The commander of the Nambac garrison, Col. Bounchanh Savophaipha, had reported Jan. 8 that his forces had suffered 1,000 casualties since the fighting for the government-held enclave had started 10 months previously. U.S. C-123 transport planes had supplied the government base with ammunition and rice.

North Vietnam denied Jan. 19 that its troops were fighting in Laos and insisted that Pathet Lao troops alone had captured Nambac. Hanoi's statement charged that Laos and the U.S. had created the "myth" of a North Vietnamese military presence in Laos.

2 battalions of Laotian government troops were reported Jan. 22 to have set up a defensive line south of Nambac to prevent a possible Pathet Lao/North Vietnamese drive against Luang Prabang. More than 2,000 government troops of the original Nambac garrison were reported straggling back to Luang Prabang. A government battalion of 400 to 600 men, spotted in the hills north of Nambac by U.S. helicopters Jan. 19, was airlifted to safety.

Laotian Premier Souvanna Phouma said Jan. 23 that a North Vietnamese army division (the 315th) involved in the fighting for Nambac had withdrawn and recrossed the border into North Vietnam at Namou, near Dienbienphu.

Laotian military sources reported Jan. 25 that a North Vietnamese/Pathet Lao force Jan. 24 had captured a government outpost at Ban Houei Sane in southern Laos. The 300-man garrison fled into South Vietnam, about $2^1/_2$ miles away.

A Pathet Lao broadcast Jan. 26 asserted that recent attacks against Laotian government outposts had been in reaction to "new [U.S.] military plots in Laos." The rebel radio said the U.S. had ordered Laotian, Thai and South Vietnamese soldiers to carry out "mopping up" operations against the Pathet Lao in Laos. The broadcast said that operations of a 5,000-man force in the Nambac Valley were aimed at creating a "long-term war base for attacks on Communist-held areas in northern Laos."

U.S. Marines and South Vietnamese militiamen withdrew Jan. 22 from Khesanh (comprising 6 mountain villages) following a heavy 3-pronged North Vietnamese assault launched Jan. 21. Khesanh was situated just above the Ho Chi Minh Trail. The allied force of 3 platoons moved back into the U.S. Marine Corps' Khesanh base, just south of the Khesanh villages, while hundreds of village civilians were evacuated by helicopter to Danang, 110 miles to the southeast.

The assault on Khesanh was one of a series of Communist attacks across the 40-mile border area from Laos to the South China Sea first mounted Jan. 13. Unofficial accounts placed the U.S. Marine casualties during the period at 52 killed and 207 wounded. 18 Marines were killed and 40 wounded in the Khesanh operation. At least 25 Communist troops were reported slain. The North Vietnamese shelled the Marine base airstrip with rockets and mortars; one helicopter was destroyed and 4 damaged. The North Vietnamese also struck a hilltop outpost $2^1/_2$ miles north of the base. A Marine A-4 Skyhawk jet was shot down by North Vietnamese fire during a bombing mission in support of the hilltop defenders. The North Vietnamese also pounded a U.S. Special Forces Camp at Langvei, 4 miles southwest of Khesanh, near the Laotian border. 12 of the South Vietnamese defenders, mostly *montagnards*, were killed and 25 wounded. U.S. B-52s Jan. 21-22 bombed North Vietnamese supply routes leading to the Khesanh villages.

The U.S. Marine base of Camp Carroll, 20 miles northeast of Khesanh and just south of the DMZ, came under heavy North Vietnamese rocket attack, but no casualties were reported.

In another engagement in the area of the DMZ, U.S. Marines Jan. 18 had killed 162 North Vietnamese in a 6-hour fight 2 miles northeast of Conthien. Marine casualties totaled 8 killed and 39 wounded. The battle began when a 4th Marine Regiment company, on a routine patrol, came across an enemy force $1^1/_2$ miles south of the buffer area. North Vietnamese artillery across the DMZ opened fire in a vain attempt to interdict the arrival of 150 Marine reinforcements. The North Vietnamese finally withdrew from the area.

Among other military developments in this period:

● Heavy fighting erupted around Dakto Jan. 19–20 for the first time since Nov. 1967. 11 men of the U.S. 4th Infantry Division were killed and 52 wounded in a drive to clear North Vietnamese soldiers from a fortified hilltop 14 miles north-west of the village. The fighting started Jan. 19 when troops of the division's First Brigade came under fire while patrolling less than a mile from their artillery base at the top of Hill 849. Reinforced by 2 companies flown in Jan. 19, the Americans launched a drive Jan. 20 against the North Vietnamese, estimated at 500, but failed to dislodge the defenders. The U.S. attack halted to permit the softening up of the hill by air and artillery strikes, but the shelling was stopped by fog and rain Jan. 21.

● 21 South Vietnamese civilians were accidentally killed and 21 wounded Jan. 19 by U.S. artillery and air strikes in a Tayninh Province forest, about 60 miles northwest of Saigon. Reporting on the incident Jan. 22, a U S. military spokesman said the victims, all woodcutters, were working in a fire-free zone in violation of Vietnamese army regulations. Anyone in the restricted area, marked off as enemy territory, was regarded as a potential enemy.

● U.S. troops of the American Division Jan. 17 engaged a Viet Cong force 11 miles north of Quangngai (335 miles northeast of Saigon) and killed 80 guer-rillas. 2 Americans were wounded. The U.S. attack was aided by supportive fire from nearby artillery position and helicopter gunships. The Viet Cong withdrew after 6 hours.

● 2 U.S. convoys were attacked Jan. 15 in the Central Highlands, but the raiders were repelled with a loss of 37 killed and 40 captured. 24 North Viet-namese were slain and 13 American soldiers were wounded in the first incident, when Communist forces attacked 4th Infantry Division trucks carrying supplies from Kontum to the Dakto area. The 2d convoy, consisting of 40 vehicles, was first stopped between Ankhe and Pleiku by a mine; North Vietnamese troops on the side of the road then opened fire. 13 enemy soldiers were killed and 4 captured, and 10 Americans were wounded in the 2d attack.

● 46 Viet Cong were reported killed Jan. 11 in an all-day battle with about 800 troops of the U.S. 9th Infantry Division in the Mekong delta, near Caibe, 54 miles southwest of Saigon. 11 Americans were killed and 30 wounded.

TET OFFENSIVE

Viet Cong Begins Attacks

Viet Cong troops Jan. 30 launched the heaviest and most coordinated offensive of the war. Fierce assaults were mounted against major cities throughout South Vietnam. Widening their drive, Viet Cong forces, attacked 30 provincial capitals and a number of district towns and U.S. and South Vietnamese air-fields and bases. Increasing numbers of North Vietnamese troops participated in the offensive.

The Viet Cong attacks started on the first day of the Tet (lunar new year) truce, agreed to by the Communists and the allies. The U.S. and South Vietnam had canceled their 36-hour cease-fire Jan. 29 for the 5 northern provinces because of the heavy Communist build-up around Khesanh.

The bloodiest battles were centered in Saigon and Hué. The fighting in Saigon Jan. 31 was marked by the seizure for 6 hours of the U.S. embassy compound by a 19-man Viet Cong suicide squad. Other cities that came under sustained attack included Dalat, Pleiku, Danang, Quangtri, Kontum, Banmethout and the Mekong delta cities of Mytho and Cantho. Several of the centers that fell into Viet Cong hands were contested by counter-attacking U.S. and South Vietnamese troops. Among the cities taken by the Viet Cong were Hué, Dalat, Kontum and Quangtri.

It was believed that most of the 50,000 Viet Cong and North Vietnamese troops in South Vietnam, exclusive of those massed around the U.S. Marine base at Khesanh near the demilitarized zone, were committed to the offensive.

Record casualties were suffered by both sides: The U.S. command reported Feb. 6 that, 21,330 Viet Cong/North Vietnamese troops and 1,169 allied soldiers had been killed. American losses were listed as 546 dead and 6,075 wounded. South Vietnam reported that 993 government soldiers had been killed and 3,229 wounded. An Agence France-Presse report from Saigon Feb. 4 said that more than 500 civilians had been killed in the fighting in the capital. It was reported Feb. 5 that about 1,250 civilians had been slain and more than 3,000 wounded in the Mekong delta's 11 provincial cities. 80,000 to 120,000 were left homeless. An estimated 20,000 civilians fled their homes in Saigon. The total number of refugees in the battle area was estimated at more than 200,000.

The Viet Cong casualty figures had been supplied by the South Vietnamese. In view of the fact that the number of enemy weapons found on the battlegrounds was considerably less than the number of Viet Cong reported killed, some quarters suggested that the South Vietnamese had overestimated the Viet Cong toll.

A National Liberation Front communiqué claimed Feb. 4 that the Viet Cong forces had achieved "tremendous initial victories in close cooperation with the people." The communiqué asserted that Communist forces had seized Banmethout, Kontum, Quangtri, Bentre, Chaudoc, Mytho, Vinhlong, Soctrang, Travinh, Cantho, Mochoa, Tayninh, Bienhoa, Baria, Tudautmot, Baclieu and Longan. The NLF report claimed Viet Cong control of Hué, Dalat, Phanrang and Phanthiet and occupation of Danang. The

NLF urged the Vietnamese people to rally to the side of the Viet Cong in the drive against U.S. and South Vietnamese forces and called on allied soldiers to refuse to obey orders and to demand "repatriation and an end to this dirty aggressive war." The communiqué said the Saigon regime had "disintegrated" and that an "organization of all patriots" had been established.

Among the major actions in the fighting for the cities:

• In the initial attack on Saigon Jan. 31, a commando unit of 19 Viet Cong made their way into the compound of the U.S. embassy. The Marine guard inside the building bolted the doors, and an exchange of fire ensued. The raiders made their way into several buildings on the grounds but were unable to get into the embassy. The entire Viet Cong unit was wiped out in 6 hours of fighting. Most were killed by the U.S. guard unit inside the building, the rest by American reinforcements who shot their way into the area. 36 U.S. paratroopers landed by helicopter on the embassy roof, but most of the guerrillas had been killed before they arrived. 5 U.S. military policemen and 2 U.S. Marine guards were killed. Amb. Bunker had been removed to safety from his residence, which was 5 blocks away from the embassy. He returned to the embassy 2 hours after the Communist force had been defeated.

Other Viet Cong Jan. 31 fought their way onto the grounds of the Presidential Palace and were attacked by rocketfiring helicopters and machineguns. Pres. Thieu and Vice Pres. Nguyen Cao Ky were not in the building at the time. Other targets that came under attack were an American officers' billet, the Tansonnhut air base on the edge of the city, the compound of the South Vietnamese General Staff, adjoining the airport, and the Buddhist An Quang pagoda.

Heavy fighting continued in Saigon and suburbs through Feb. 5. Major action was centered in the Cholon district. South Vietnamese artillerymen Feb. 5 shelled a densely populated part of the city in an effort to dislodge the Viet Cong. Despite the shelling, the guerrillas overran a police station. A defending force of about 60 policemen was said to have been helicoptered to safety. An estimated 11,000 U.S. and South Vietnamese troops supported by armor and artillery, were committed to the battle for Saigon. As many as 1,000 Viet Cong were believed to have infiltrated into the city.

According to a government statement, the An Quang pagoda,

headquarters of the militant Buddhists, had been the Viet Cong command post for the attack on Saigon. After the guerrillas were ousted from the pagoda, Brig. Gen. Nguyen Ngoc Loan, the police chief, shot a prisoner to death Feb. 1 in front of the building. Vice Pres. Nguyen Cao Ky Feb. 5 said the executed man was "a very high-ranking Viet Cong officer." Although Ky would not identify the man by name, he said he was a "civilian, a political officer." Ky said he had given orders against carrying out "such brutal acts," "but when you see your friends die, it is hard to control your reactions."

In a letter to Gen. Earle G. Wheeler, chairman of the Joint Chiefs of Staff, U. S. Rep. Henry Reuss (D., Wis.) deplored the execution of the Viet Cong prisoner by Gen. Loan. Reuss said that such an act "carries the terrible risk that our prisoners in the hands of the North Vietnamese and Viet Cong will be exposed to retaliatory brutality." Wheeler, in a reply Feb. 5, expressed a "sense of revulsion at barbarous acts and summary executions." But he said the incident in front of the An Quang pagoda had taken place "more in a flash of ourtage" than in cold blood.

● Counter-attacking U.S. and South Vietnamese troops, supported by artillery, were encountering fierce resistance in efforts to recapture Hué. The Viet Cong were reported still in control of the major part of the city Feb. 6. Many of them were holding out in the walled, inner city known as the Citadel, while fighting raged in other parts of Hué,

A U.S. Marine unit of 500 men had broken into Hué Jan. 31 to reinforce the beleaguered allied garrison there. 10 Marines were killed in the break-through operation, and 20 to 30 were wounded. The Americans reported killing 50 Viet Cong.

On first smashing their way into Hué, the Viet Cong had stormed the Thuathien Province jail and released all 2,500 prisoners, most of them Viet Cong. North Vietnamese troops also were fighting in Hué, and the total Communist force there was estimated at 12,000 men.

● North Vietnamese troops also were active in the Central Highlands and were reported Feb. 3 to be firmly in control of sections of the city of Kontum. Civilians had been evacuated from the city Feb. 1 as U.S. troops battled to wrest control of Kontum from the Communists.

● The Viet Cong launched attacks in the Mekong delta Feb. 1. The heaviest fighting raged in the principal cities of Mytho,

Cantho, Bentre and Soctrang. Mytho (population 70,000) was half destroyed, most of the damage having been caused by U.S. and South Vietnamese bombs, artillery and rockets. The majority of the 1,250 civilian fatalities in the delta occurred in Cantho, where about 1,000 civilians were killed and 1,500 wounded.

Hanoi & NLF Explain Attacks

In a statement made Jan. 30 on the opening of the offensive, North Vietnam announced that the attacks against South Vietnamese cities had been carried out "to punish the United States aggressors and their henchmen for unilaterally cancelling their own cease-fire" and for having "slighted the traditional new year festival of the Vietnamese people." The attacks, Hanoi said, also were in reprisal for U.S. air strikes on "Vietnamese people in many parts of the country."

The Viet Cong statement of the aims of the offensive was couched in stronger and more ambitious terms. In a broadcast over the clandestine "Liberation Radio," the National Liberation Front announced that its offensive was aimed at overthrowing the "Thieu-Ky puppet administration" in Saigon. The announcement appealed to government troops to join the Communist side by providing the Viet Cong with arms and ammunition. The Viet Cong appeal was broadcast in the name of the South Vietnam Revolutionary Armed Forces Command. The Communist broadcast said:

Compatriots: the revolution we waited and yearned for has broken out. ... We have been leading an ignominious and shameful life for years because a group of Vietnamese traitors has been exploiting and oppressing us. ... We must rise up to wrest back power and restore independence, peace, freedom, and a clean and comfortable life.

The Alliance of National & Peace Forces has set forth the following goals: (1) To overthrow the Thieu-Ky puppet regime and set up an administrative power that really represents the various strata of the South Vietnamese people. (2) To recover national independence and sovereignty, demanding that the United States put an end to the Vietnam war and withdraw its troops and those of its satellites from South Vietnam. (3) To restore peace and build an independent, democratic, peaceful and neutral South Vietnam. (4) To negotiate with the National Liberation Front of South Vietnam in order to achieve together the above-mentioned goals.

Compatriots: the hour ... to liberate ourselves has come. Everybody must stand up and launch attacks against the hideouts of the Thieu-Ky clique and topple the traitorous and country-selling government in various areas. We must set up at once a revolutionary government, . . . punish and arrest all the cruel lackeys of the Thieu-Ky clique and foreign nations. ...

We exhort the officers, soldiers and the police forces of the Saigon regime to side with the ranks of the people and to give their arms and ammunition to the revolutionary armed forces.

We exhort all those who have been going astray to quickly wake up. Those who recognize their faults and are willing to accomplish and exploit will be forgiven by the revolution. Those who willingly resist the revolution will be duly punished.

We exhort the American troops and their allied troops to put an end to their military activities and not to interfere in the internal affairs of South Vietnam. We exhort the American people . . . to side with the South Vietnam revolution. . . .

No matter who the enemy of the revolution is or the means he uses to oppress us . . . , we will not be shaken and will not retreat. We prefer to die than to return to the slave regime.

Let us go forward together! . . . Long live an independent, democratic, peaceful and neutral South Vietnam!

Allied Reaction

South Vietnamese Pres. Nguyen Van Thieu Feb. 1 declared a nationwide state of martial law to cope with the crisis. Public gatherings and demonstrations were banned, and places of entertainment were closed. A 2 p.m.–8 a.m. curfew was imposed in Saigon. Thieu declared: "All activities harmful to public order and all political movement aimed at helping the Communists through the so-called 'peace and coalition government' will be severely punished."

In his first public statement on the Viet Cong attacks, Thieu said Feb. 2 that the South Vietnamese armed forces had "broken the back of the enemy offensive." Thieu called for an escalation of the bombing of North Vietnam as a "punishment" for the Viet Cong drive.

Gen. William C. Westmoreland, commander of U.S. forces in Vietnam, said Feb. 1 that he expected the Viet Cong offensive to continue for several days but that there were signs that it was "about to run out of steam." Westmoreland warned, however, that the 20,000 to 40,000 Communist troops facing the 5,000 U.S. Marines protecting their base at Khesanh had the "capability of attacking in force at any time." The Communist offensive, Westmoreland said, was "a diversionary effort to take attention away from the northern part of the country." Westmoreland and other U.S. commanders had said that they had anticipated the Viet Cong assault on Saigon and that U.S. and South Vietnamese forces were alerted. An unidentified senior officer with the U.S. high command, however, was quoted Feb. 3 as saying:

"There's no denying it. This has been a week of surprises. It was a very successful offensive, surprisingly well coordinated, intensive and audacious."

The U.S. high command in Saigon Feb. 2 issued a communiqué that said: "Although the enemy raided numerous cities and towns throughout the republic and achieved some temporary successes, they have failed to take and hold any major installations or localities. Although some enemy units are still occupying positions in a few cities, they are rapidly being driven out."

U.S. Amb.-to-South Vietnam Ellsworth Bunker Feb. 2 denied a Viet Cong radio claim that U.S. forces were "cooperating with the Viet Cong forces" in Saigon to help establish a coalition government for South Vietnam. The Viet Cong claim, Bunker said, was "a desperate and shameful effort to compensate for the Viet Cong failure to destroy law and order in the Republic of Vietnam during the last few days."

Speaking at his news conference Feb. 2, Pres. Johnson asserted that the Viet Cong's offensive was "a complete failure," militarily and psychologically. Johnson said the Communist drive was the first phase of a campaign to be followed by "a massive attack across the frontiers of South Vietnam by North Vietnamese units" against the U.S. Marine base at Khesanh, just below the demilitarized zone. The attack had been "anticipated, prepared for and met," he said. (In the "Pentagon papers" published by the *N.Y. Times* in 1971, however, an anonymous Pentagon analyst was quoted July 4, 1971 as saying that the Tet offensive took the White House and Chief of Staff "by surprise, and its strength, length and intensity prolonged this shock.") Asserting that "we have known for several months, now, that the Communists planned a massive winter-spring offensive," Johnson expressed confidence that U.S. and South Vietnamese troops would give "a good account of themselves." The Viet Cong onslaught against South Vietnamese cities, the President said, was aimed at "overthrowing the constitutional government in Saigon" and at creating "a situation in which we and the South Vietnamese would be willing to accept the Communist-dominated coalition government." Johnson disclosed that in attacks on U.S. airfields throughout South Vietnam, 15 planes and 23 helicopters had been destroyed and "a good many more" damaged. He said, however, that he had been told by Defense Secy. Robert S. McNamara, Gen. Westmoreland and the Joint Chiefs of Staff that "they do not think that our military operations will be seriously affected."

In his first public reaction to the Viet Cong offensive, Johnson had stated Feb. 1 that "the enemy will fail and fail again" because "we Americans will never yield." He pledged to continue the bombing of North Vietnam "with a very precise restraint" until there were "some better signs than what these last few days have provided." Johnson advised the critics of his bombing policy to "answer this question: What would the North Vietnamese be doing if we stopped the bombing and let them alone?" The answer, Johnson said, would be an increased Communist force in the South, better equipped and harder to defeat; "and of one thing you can be sure: it would cost many more American lives."

State Secy. Dean Rusk said Feb. 4 that the Communist drive in South Vietnam was, in effect, a rejection of U.S. efforts in the past month to find a basis for peace talks. Rusk, appearing on the NBC-TV program "Meet the Press" with Defense Secy. Mc-Namara, disclosed that "we have exercised some restraint in our bombing in North Vietnam during this period of exploration, particularly in the immediate vicinity of Hanoi and Haiphong." (There had been no bombing near the 2 cities since Jan. 18.) The purpose of shunning raids in that sector, Rusk explained, was "to make it somewhat easier to carry forward these [peace] explorations so that particularly difficult incidents would not interrupt them." In view of Hanoi's awareness of U.S. peace soundings and Washington's hopes of converting the Tet truce "into a more productive dialogue," Rusk declared, "it would be foolish not to draw a political conclusion" from the launching of the Viet Cong offensive that Hanoi was "not seriously interested at the present time in talking" about peace. Rusk said that "we have known for some months that they were going to launch a winter-spring offensive . . . , which they anticipated would trigger off . . . a popular uprising." But considering the "widespread sense of outrage" against the Viet Cong "campaign of terror," Rusk said, he saw "very little prospect or evidence of that popular uprising."

The *N.Y. Times* Mar. 21, however, published excerpts from a year-end classified report on the situation in Vietnam. Sent to Washington by Westmoreland Jan. 1, this optimistic assessment had predicted nothing approximating the Tet offensive and had, until the offensive, apparently formed the basis of U.S. policy on Vietnam. *Among major statements made in Westmoreland's report:*

• Allied forces would achieve more military victories in 1968 "through careful exploitation of the enemy's vulnerabilities and application of our superior firepower and mobility." The Communists had not won "a major battle in Vietnam in 1967" because U.S. troops had been able "to detect impending major objectives and to mount spoiling attacks."
• Allied strategy in 1968 would be based on 2 principal objectives: (1) to "search out and destroy Communist forces and infrastructure in South Vietnam by offensive military operations"; (2) to "extend the secure areas of South Vietnam by coordinated civil-military operations and assist the GVN [government of South Vietnam] in building an independent, viable non-Communist society."
• Viet Cong/North Vietnamese troops in 1968 would be forced "to place greater reliance on sanctuaries in Cambodia, Laos and the northern DMZ" as allied forces inflicted greater casualties on them and destroyed and neutralized their bases in South Vietnam through continuous naval and air bombardment and direct ground combat. Enemy strength would be further weakened by sickness, desertions, lower morale and "acceleration of our . . . pacification efforts." (Communist defections had totaled 18,076 during Jan.-June 1967 but had dropped to 9,102 in the July-Dec. 1967 period and a low of 904 in December. Communist desertions had continued at a low rate of about 1,000 a month in January and February 1968.)
• 1968 military planning was based on an anticipated increase in enemy defections to 60,000 for the year. There should be an additional 340,000 new refugees in the combat areas. (The Tet offensive had left 350,000 Vietnamese civilians homeless; these were added to the 800,000 refugees who had been living in temporary camps or were without minimum shelter at the end of 1967.)

(In its initial response to the Tet offensive, U.S. public opinion had rallied to the support of the American war effort. A Harris Survey conducted Feb. 3-4 and published Feb. 12 reported a rise in support of the war by the public from 61% in Dec. 1967 to 74% in Feb. 1968. But a Gallup Poll Feb. 13 reported a decline in public approval of Pres. Johnson's handling of the war from 39% in January to 35%. A Gallup Poll published Mar. 10 reported that 49% of those interviewed thought the U.S. had made a mistake in sending troops to fight in Vietnam. Another Gallup Poll revealed Mar. 12 that a majority of both "hawks" and "doves" interviewed favored a plan to train and draft South Vietnamese to take over the fighting and permit withdrawal of U.S. troops. Public approval of the plan had increased to 69%—from 58% in Dec. 1966.)

Battle for the Cities

By the end of the first week in February, U.S. and South Vietnamese soldiers were reported to have driven the Viet Cong and North Vietnamese troops from most of the cities they had invaded at the start of the offensive. Heavy fighting continued, however, in Saigon and Hué, and the Communists maintained pressure against U.S. troops in the Khesanh region just below the demilitarized zone by capturing the nearby U.S. Special Forces camp at Langvei Feb. 7.

The North Vietnamese Communist Party newspaper *Nhan Dan* said Feb. 7 that American forces had suffered "great military disaster" and "extremely heavy political defeats" in the Viet Cong offensive. The Communist onslaught, the newspaper said, "has enabled the whole world to see the very obvious situation of defeat of the American aggressor as well as the the pitiful impotence of their army and the decomposition of the puppet administration and army—that is, to say, the failure of the neo-colonialist war."

Casualties suffered by both sides since the start of the offensive, as reported by U.S. officials Feb. 11: Viet Cong/North Vietnamese—30,795 killed; U.S.—973 killed, 4,874 wounded; South Vietnam—2,119 killed, 7,718 wounded. (Commenting on the validity of reports of Communist casualties, U.S. Defense Secy. Robert S. McNamara had noted Feb. 4 that "to some degree they may be overstated, but we know there are many understatements.") More than 500,000 civilians were reported to have been left homeless in the wake of the fighting; 217,000 of them were in Saigon and the surrounding area. (The U.S. high command Feb. 8 had reported a record weekly loss suffered by U.S. troops Jan. 28–Feb. 3—416 killed and 2,757 wounded. Other casualty figures for Jan. 28–Feb. 3: Communists—15,515 killed; South Vietnam—784 killed and 2,230 wounded.)

Lt. Gen. William B. Rosson, U.S. commander of troops in the Central Highlands' II Corps area, reported Feb. 7 that of the 8,000 Communist troops who had carried out 14 powerful attacks in that sector, 4,661 had been killed and 599 captured. Allied casualties there, Rosson said, were 460 killed and 1,531 wounded, including 90 U.S. soldiers slain and 430 wounded. Kontum, a major city in the highlands, had been cleared of the last Communist soldiers Feb. 5. Of the more than 3,000 North Vietnamese troops committed to the Kontum battle, 758 had been killed, Col. James P. Cahill, senior U.S. officer in the area, said. American troops, who had carried the major burden of the defense of Kontum, had suffered 12 killed and 151 wounded. South Vietnamese losses were 17 killed and 86 wounded.

In Saigon, fighting was concentrated in Cholon, the south-western section of the city (3 miles from midtown), while the rest of the capital was reported to be returning to normal. Most clashes were in the vicinity of the Phutho Race Track, where an estimated 300 Viet Cong troops held out against allied counter-assaults, including air and artillery strikes. U.S. officials estimated the entire guerrilla force in Saigon and its environs at 700-1,000 men. An estimated 13-17 American battalions of about 700 men each were committed to the defense of Saigon. But most of this force was posted outside the city in Giadinh Province, 5 to 15 miles northwest of the center of Saigon, with the mission of preventing new guerrilla infiltration and of killing Viet Cong fleeing the city. U.S. 25th Infantry Division troops were reported Feb. 9 to have killed 278 Viet Cong in 2 engagements in Giadinh's Hocmon district.

4,000 men of the U.S. 199th Light Brigade were brought into Saigon Feb. 9. Part of the force, 200 men, was helicoptered to the Phutho Race Track to engage the Viet Cong force there, and U.S. troops were reported to have killed 303 Viet Cong Feb. 9 in 3 engagements 7 miles northeast of Saigon's Tansonnhut airfield.

In the Mekong delta Feb. 9, 2 Viet Cong battalions assaulted Tanan, the capital of Longnan Province, and the headquarters of the 3d Brigade of the 9th Infantry Division nearby. According to South Vietnamese authorities, 122 guerrillas were killed when the raid was repulsed. Allied casualties: 8 South Vietnamese policemen, 3 militiamen and 4 Americans killed. 49 Americans were wounded.

It was reported Feb. 7 that at least 1,000 civilians had been killed and 1,500 wounded when allied air and artillery bombing destroyed Bentre, capital of the Mekong delta province of Kienhoa (30 miles south of Saigon), in an effort to dislodge the 2,500 Viet Cong soldiers who had seized the city of 50,000 Jan. 31. Bentre came under heavy allied fire Feb. I, and by Feb. 2 the fighting had subsided.

(South Vietnamese Vice Pres. Nguyen Cao Ky had announced Feb. 5 that the government would give arms to loyal South Vietnamese the following week and train them for protection against Viet Cong attacks. Ky said emphasis would be placed on distributing the arms to the rural areas, where the threat was greatest. Weapons also would be handed out in other places where "we are sure the people are anti-Communist nationalists," Ky promised.)

Sharp, sporadic clashes flared outside Saigon Feb. 11. The heaviest fighting occurred in the Go Vap district, where 2 South Vietnamese airborne battalions, assisted by U.S. and South Vietnamese air strikes, were locked in battle with 400 Viet Cong near an ammunition dump along the Bencat River, 4 miles north of the capital. The South Vietnamese reported that the guerrillas had overrun the dump earlier but had been thrown back with a loss of 107 lives. South Vietnamese casualites in that engagement were 9 killed and 22 wounded.

The U.S. and South Vietnamese counter-drive aimed at ousting the North Vietnamese from Hue made steady progress, and by Feb. 11 U.S. Marines penetrated the 2-square-mile walled Citadel. 2 companies of Marines landed above the Citadel the night of Feb. 11 after being transported up the Huong River by naval landing craft. The American reinforcements brought to about 1,000 the total Marine force fighting in and around Hué. The mayor of Hué, Lt. Col. Phan Van Khoa, said Feb. 11 that the Viet Cong had executed 300 South Vietnamese civilians Feb. 9 and had buried them in a common grave several miles from the city. Khoa said those slain included government officials, civil servants and technicians.

The U.S. Special Forces camp at Langvei, about $3^1/_2$ miles southwest of Khesanh, was captured by North Vietnamese troops Feb. 7 after an 18-hour siege. U.S. officials reported that the North Vietnamese had used 9 PT-76 light tanks, the latest Soviet model, in the assault and that 5 had been destroyed. South Vietnamese military headquarters reported Feb. 7 that 316 allied defenders of Langvei, including 8 American advisers, had been killed or were missing. The camp's personnel was made up of South Vietnamese irregular militia and *montagnard* tribesmen. About 200 irregulars and 12 Americans escaped and made their way to the U.S. Marine base at Khesanh. Also arriving at Khesanh were 5,000 to 6,000 refugees, including about 2,000 Laotian soldiers and their families (who had fled to Langvei in January after their outpost in Laos had been overrun by North Vietnamese) and Brou mountain tribesmen. The South Vietnamese and Laotian soldiers were disarmed as they came into Khesanh for fear that they had been infiltrated by the Viet Cong. The escapees were flown to Danang Feb. 9 for transfer to refugee camps.

56 U.S. Marines were killed and 123 wounded in a series of actions in the northernmost provinces Feb. 8. The heaviest

engagement was fought 2 miles north of Khesanh on a hill position protecting the base. 21 Marines were killed and 27 wounded. 127 Communists were reported slain.

Focus on Khesanh

In the early weeks of the Tet offensive, the U.S. military command centered its concern on the U.S. Marine base at Khesanh, which had been reoccupied by the U.S. late in January. Defense Secy. McNamara, in making his estimate of the situation Feb.2, had said that the Viet Cong/North Vietnamese had failed in 2 military objectives: (a) to divert U.S. and South Vietnamese troops "from the probable offensive action of the Viet Cong and North Vietnamese around Khesanh" and (b) "to penetrate and hold one or more district or provincial capitals." In its initial response to the Viet Cong/North Vietnamese effort, American strategy concentrated on holding Khesanh and other U.S. positions just below the demilitarized zone, as well as resecuring the cities of South Vietnam.

These positions had come under sporadic North Vietnamese infantry and artillery attack since late in January as both sides massed troops in the sector for an expected major battle. Gen. Vo Nguyen Giap, North Vietnamese defense minister, reportedly was personally directing the battle preparations from Hanoi.

It was reported Jan. 23 that Marine reinforcements had been flown into the region and that the number of U.S. troops there exceeded 5,000. The Americans were backed up by several hundred South Vietnamese militia and a Special Forces unit. Tons of supplies had been flown into the American base Jan. 21-23. A senior U.S. officer in Saigon Jan. 25 said 2 North Vietnamese battalions totaling 16,000 to 20,000 troops had been "positively identified" in western Quangtri Province, 10 miles from Khesanh. Other reports placed the Communist force in the area as high as 40,000 men.

Among actions around Khesanh:

● 3 U.S. planes flying support missions for Marines in the area were shot down by North Vietnamese gunners Jan. 22, 23 and 24.

● U.S. air and artillery strikes were reported to have killed 61 Communist troops Jan. 23. U.S. planes Jan. 24-25 flew 301 support missions, a record for a 24-hour period.

● The Marine base came under heavy North Vietnamese shelling Jan. 24. 7 Marines were killed and 77 wounded in 2 separate barrages.

● 8 Marines were killed and 44 wounded Jan. 25 when North Vietnamese troops ambushed a convoy carrying ammunition to an artillery base near Khesanh. The convoy had come from Camp Carroll, an artillery base 15 miles from Khesanh. Heavy fog and clouds prevented American planes from aiding the beleaguered U.S. force.

● A 500-man Marine force, on a search-and-destroy mission, encountered entrenched North Vietnamese troops north of Camp Carroll Jan. 27. Supported by air and artillery strikes, the Marines routed the enemy and killed 150 of them. American casualties totaled 19 killed and 90 wounded. The fighting was along Route 9, the only supply road available to the Marines in the northern region.

● North Vietnamese mortars pounded the Khesanh base Jan. 28 and cut the air strip in several places. The damage to the runway forced a delay in incoming supply transports for several hours.

● Hill 861, the U.S. strongpoint northeast of the Khesanh base, came under heavy North Vietnamese infantry and artillery attack Feb. 5. The attackers broke through an outer ring of barbed wire but were repulsed by an American counter-thrust. The U.S. base was simultaneously hit by artillery, mortar and rocket shells.

● The South Vietnamese military headquarters in Saigon reported Feb. 7 that a South Vietnamese Special Forces camp at Langvei, 6 miles west of Khesanh, had been overrun and occupied by North Vietnamese troops that day. According to the report, the Communist troops had used tanks and armored cars for the first time. A South Vietnamese spokesman said that 7 tanks and armored vehicles, coming from the direction of Laos, were involved in the fighting and that 4 tanks had been destroyed. The Langvei camp was said to be garrisoned by 500 men, including about 40 U.S. advisers. The camp was also occupied by about 300 Laotian soldiers and their families, who had taken refuge there after North Vietnamese and Pathet Lao forces Jan. 24 had captured a Laotian government outpost at Ban Houei Sane, just over the border.

The North Vietnamese Communist Party newspaper *Nhan Dan* asserted Feb. 10 that the Communists' capture of the Langvei camp presented American forces at Khesanh with another Dienbienphu (the French defeat in Dienbienphu in 1954 ended France's struggle for Indochina). The journal said that if Pres. Johnson and his military advisers "think Khesanh is like Dienbienphu, then the battle of Langvei is really a repetition of the battle of Independence Hill." With the capture of the hill in May 1954 after a 55-day siege, the newspaper said, the French troops "had to get ready to raise the white flag. With Langvei razed, how can the Americans hold Khesanh?" As a result of the capture of Langvei, "the Americans living in Khesanh are cornered even more tightly, in dismay and fear," *Nhan Dan* said.

The U.S. Defense Department had said Feb. 4 that the Joint Chiefs of Staff had reported to Johnson that the U.S. Marine base at Khesanh "could and should be defended." The Joint Chiefs expressed their view in a memo signed by Gen. Earle G. Wheeler, chairman, after discussing the situation with Gen. William C. Westmoreland, U. S. commander in South Vietnam.

A U.S. military spokesman in Saigon reported Feb. 10 that 2 or 3 Soviet-built IL-28 jet bombers had been sighted at the Phucyen airbase 18 miles northwest of Hanoi. The base was within striking distance of Khesanh. The IL-28s, first built in 1950, were considered obsolete. A U.S. officer expressed fear that the North Vietnamese had transported enough steel matting into eastern Laos to build a runway for MiG-21s within 100 miles of Khesanh. He said U.S. reconnaissance planes were probing the area to determine whether the North Vietnamese were building an airstrip there.

Johnson Feb. 16 denied that the use of nuclear weapons in the Vietnam war had been recommended to him or was under consideration. "It is reasonably apparent and known to all that it is very much against the national interest to carry on discussions about the deployment of nuclear weapons," the President said. "So far as I am aware, they [the Secretaries of State and Defense and the Joint Chiefs of Staff] have at no time ever considered or made a recommendation in any respect to the employment of unclear weapons. They [A-weapons] are on our planes on training missions from time to time."

Public speculation on the possible use of nuclear arms in Vietnam, specifically in defense of Khesanh, had broken out after an anonymous phone call Feb. 5 to the Senate Foreign Relations Committee. The caller suggested an inquiry into why a tactical nuclear weapons expert, Prof. Richard L. Garwin of Columbia University, had been sent to South Vietnam by the Defense Department. The Defense Department said Feb. 6 that Garwin and other scientists had gone to appraise "the effectiveness of new weapons" that had "no relationship whatsoever to atomic or nuclear systems." The subject, however, was broached at a Senate Foreign Relations Committee meeting Feb. 7, when the defense of Khesanh was mentioned. Committee Chairman J. William Fulbright (D., Ark.) Feb. 8 sent to State Secy. Dean Rusk a letter asking whether nuclear weapons were being introduced into South Vietnam. Rusk's reply to Fulbright, made public by the State Department Feb. 15, said the purpose of Garwin's trip was to discuss "technical matters of a nonnuclear nature."

Sen. Eugene J. McCarthy (D., Minn.) had been asked by a reporter in Boston Feb. 8 whether he was concerned that setbacks in Vietnam might bring demands for the use of tactical nuclear weapons there. He replied that "there have been some demands already." McCarthy's remark was denounced Feb. 9 by White House Press Secy. George Christian as "false" and "unfair to the armed services." Christian said: "Decisions of this nature rest with the President. The President has considered no decision of this nature. I might add that irresponsible discussion and speculation are a disservice to the country."

In his reply to Fulbright, Rusk quoted Christian's statement about "irresponsible discussion and speculation" being "a disservice to the country." Fulbright later Feb. 15 rejected the "implication" about disservice to the nation. "I believe," he said, "it would be a grave disservice to our country, in truth a disaster, if our leadership should so expose our troops in Vietnam as to require nuclear weapons to prevent their destruction."

Gen. Wheeler, chairman of the Joint Chiefs, was asked by a newsman Feb. 14 whether nuclear weapons might be used if Khesanh were overrun. Wheeler said he "refused to speculate any further." He added later that "I do not think that nuclear weapons will be required to defend Khesanh."

Offensive Blunted

By the end of the 2d week in February, the tactics of the National Liberation Front were manifesting a change. Viet Cong forces Feb. 18 began coordinated rocket and mortar attacks on U.S. and South Vietnamese military installations and cities from the Central Highlands to the Mekong delta. In most cases the shelling was not followed by a general ground assault. The initial thrust of the offensive thus appeared to have been contained by the U. S. and South Vietnamese forces.

During this phase of the offensive, one of the major targets hit was the Tansonnhut airbase, 6 miles from the center of Saigon. In sporadic firing on the U.S. base, 6 Americans were killed and 67 wounded by Feb. 19. 4 planes were set on fire, the base chapel destroyed and the control tower and several buildings damaged. The American airbase at Bienhoa, 14 miles northeast of Saigon, was also shelled. Several planes were reported damaged. U. S. Army headquarters at nearby Longbinh was hit by shells, and a big fire was started.

In one of the few ground attacks that followed the shelling, about 500 Viet Cong troops Feb. 18 stormed into Phanthiet, the capital of Binhthuan Province, 90 miles east of Saigon. The invaders captured the jail, released 500 prisoners and took over the provincial hospital. U.S. and South Vietnamese airborne troops were rushed into the city to drive out the Viet Cong. By late Feb. 18 the allied troops had recaptured the jail and retaken some prisoners.

Other targets of Communist shelling were Kontum, Quangduc and Dalat in the Central Highlands; Longbinh, Laikhe and Phuloi in the III Corps area around Saigon; and Mytho, Cantho, Chauphu, Soctrang, Rachgia, Bentre and Vinhlong in the Mekong delta.

The Viet Cong shelling had been preceded by sharp allied-Communist clashes throughout South Vietnam Feb. 13-17. The fighting was marked by the continuing battle for Hué, where a North Vietnamese force held the Citadel despite U.S. artillery, air and naval strikes. A Viet Cong communiqué Feb. 14 claimed that Viet Cong forces controlled 4 provincial capitals south of Saigon and partially controlled 2 more. The cities under claimed Viet Cong control were Vinhlong, Travinh, Soctrang and Baclieu. Part control was claimed for Camau and Rachgia.

In the battle for Hué, the entrenched North Vietnamese/Viet Cong force, believed to total about 800 men, was confined to the southern part of the Citadel, facing the Huong River. Another possible escape route was blocked by the U.S. First Cavalry Division (Airmobile). (The allies also confronted a 600-700 man Communist force outside the Citadel on the south side of the Huong River.) The Communist troops in the Citadel were pounded by air, naval and artillery shelling Feb. 14-16. Despite the barrage, Communist rocket, mortar and sniper fire thwarted the allied advance. U.S. and South Vietnamese troops were attempting to move in from opposite sides of the Citadel. 6 U.S. naval craft landing supplies and troop reinforcements for Hué were struck in the Huong River by a rocket and mortar barrage Feb. 17. One ship was sunk and the other 5 disabled.

Among other military actions in South Vietnam during this period:

● 350 troops of the 11th Light Infantry Brigade killed 78 Viet Cong Feb. 12 in a 2-hour fight near the northern coastal town of Quangngai. One American was killed and 4 wounded.

● 13 Americans were killed in 3 separate engagements Feb. 13 in Saigon's suburbs. During the day's fighting U.S. B-52 bombers, on a support mission, mistakenly dropped 50 tons of bombs outside a target zone along the Saigon River 10 miles north of Saigon; 42-44 persons were killed, 57-59 injured.

● Fighting inside Saigon centered south of the Phutho Race Track area, where 700 to 1,000 Viet Cong remained entrenched. In sharp skirmishes in that sector Feb. 12-13, 49 enemy troops were killed. American casualties; 6 killed and 13 wounded.

● A U.S. Marine company was ambushed Feb. 14 south of Camp Carroll near the demilitarized zone. 12 men were killed and 107 wounded.

● U.S. planes continued to bomb and strafe the area around Khesanh in an effort to break up the heavy concentration of Communist troops surrounding the American Marine base. The U.S. command reported Feb. 16 that 2 North Vietnamese divisions were slowly moving into position for an attack.

● U.S. troops were reported Feb. 16 to have made their deepest penetration into the Mekong delta. They killed about 54 Communist troops near Cantho.

U.S. officials reported Feb. 16 that the Viet Cong offensive had created 350,000 new refugees so far. These refugees were in addition to the 800,000 who were officially listed as refugees before the outbreak of the Viet Cong attacks Jan. 30. U.S. Amb.-to-South Vietnam Ellsworth Bunker said in a CBS-TV broadcast ("Face the Nation") recorded in Saigon Feb. 16 that South Vietnamese troops had "turned in an excellent performance" in the fighting and had gained some respect from the people. He said the enemy had lost the people's respect because of their violation of Tet.

The situation was reflected in a modification of Viet Cong goals based on an assessment of the military effects of the first weeks of the offensive. The National Liberation Front announced in an article published in 2 Hanoi newspapers Feb. 19 that the aim of the current Viet Cong offensive was to destroy large quantities of American war equipment, to disrupt communications and to smash the South Vietnamese army and government. The NLF statement, appearing in the Communist Party newspaper *Nhan Dan* and the army journal *Quan Doi Nhan Dan*, said the goals of the military drive were stated in a report that had been adopted by the Presidium of the NLF's Central Committee at a meeting held in South Vietnam Feb. 11-12. The special session had been called to study the effects of the offensive. The meeting had been attended by representatives of political parties in the NLF and by Thich Thie Hao, a Buddhist monk. The statement added: "In 2 weeks we have completely upset the enemy's combat arrangements and taken over the complete initiative. Not only are we masters of the mountainous regions, but we are attacking inside the cities and big bases." U.S. military plans were "dead stillborn," and the "pacification program was a shambles," The U.S. was giving out false Viet Cong casualty figures, "multiplying the real losses 10 times over."

Major blow by the Tet off.

√*Pacification Program Disrupted*

It was reported by Feb. 13 that the Tet offensive had resulted in a virtual suspension of the South Vietnamese pacification program—the program to wrest the countryside from Communist control and secure it for the South Vietnamese government. The suspension was brought about by the forced withdrawal of pacification teams and government troops that protected them from the rural areas into the cities and towns that came under Communist attack. It was reported that the government Feb. 12 had advised administrative chiefs in the country's 44 provinces to get the pacification teams back to their posts by Feb. 28.

(Pacification teams operated in hamlets on a 6-month basis. They performed such tasks as training local residents, building farms and dispensaries and establishing links between the villagers and the Saigon government.)

The U.S. mission in Saigon admitted Feb. 24, for the first time, that the Communist offensive had dealt a major blow to the pacification program. A high U.S. official, who asked not to be identified, said at a Saigon news conference that the program had suffered "a loss of momentum, there has been some withdrawal [of security troops] from the countryside, there has been a significant psychological setback both on the part of the pacification people themselves and the local population." The major problem, the official said, was "who will fill the vacuum in the countryside. It depends on how fast the South Vietnamese government moves in and how aggressive and how fast the enemy will be."

About 8,000 government troops protecting pacification workers in the rural areas had withdrawn to the cities to cope with the attacks. About half of the 555 pacification teams in the hamlets had been shifted to larger provincial or district towns to provide security for inhabitants in those areas. The Viet Cong/North Vietnamese offensive had resulted in the killing of 79 of the 29,000 pacification workers; 111 were wounded, and 845 were missing.

The 1968 phase of the pacification program was to have begun about the time the Viet Cong launched the offensive, the American official disclosed. As a result, the program faced "a major re-examination" and would have to be "significantly modified," he said. The U.S. official added: "The hardest thing to measure is the psychological impact on the pacifiers and the rural population in looking at the vacuum that's developing in significant parts of the country. You have to consider that the Viet Cong suffered very heavy losses, too."

It was reported Mar. 2 that in response to the Feb. 12 government order, pacification teams had begun to return to the hamlets they had abandoned at the start of the Tet offensive. Although the directive had set Mar. 1 as the deadline, the shift was far from completed. *Developments in some South Vietnamese areas involving a resumption of pacification operations by Mar. 2:*

• All relief workers had returned to their posts in Quangtri and Quangtin Provinces in the northern part of the country.

• About 30% of the pacification teams had gone back to hamlets in Quangnam and Quangngai Provinces in the north.

• Very little progress was reported in Thuathien Province, which surrounded devastated Hué.

• 8% of the government teams had resumed their assignments in the Central Highlands and in the central coast areas.

• In Giadinh Province around Saigon, 70% of the pacification workers were back on the job.

• 2 provinces in the Mekong delta reported that all of the pacification workers had resumed operations. 80% were reported back at work in other delta provinces.

• Few pacification teams had taken up their posts again in Phongdinh, Kiengiang and Kienphong Provinces.

South Vietnam Mobilizes

South Vietnam Feb. 11 began to mobilize an additional 65,000 troops. The build-up, proposed by Pres. Nguyen Van Thieu, was intended to raise the strength of South Vietnam's forces by 10% to 765,000 men. In an address at a joint session of the National Assembly Feb. 9, Thieu had requested that the extra troops be called up because the Tet offensive had "enabled us to realize even more clearly the urgent problems that must be resolved." Thieu asked for authority to rule by decree for a year on economic and financial matters. His proposals included the curtailment of military deferments, the immediate drafting of 18- and 19-year olds, the abolition of military discharges except for medical reasons and the recall of veterans with less than 5 years of service. Thieu said all government officials under age 45 would be given military training and armed.

Thieu's mobilization action was, in effect, an implementation and acceleration of a decree he had issued in Oct. 1967 but had not put into effect because of public protest against its restrictions.

Reporting on the Tet offensive against South Vietnamese cities, Thieu said that 3,071 civilians had been killed, 7,945 wounded and 196,000 made homeless by attacks in 31 of the country's 44 provinces. Nearly 22,000 homes had been heavily damaged and "many others" partly damaged, Thieu said. Thieu charged that the casualties suffered by civilians had resulted from their use by Communist troops as shields while "we . . . took great pains to spare the lives of the people."

U.S. Sends Reinforcements

Pres. Johnson visited Pope Air Force Base, N.C. and El Toro Calif.) Marine Corps Naval Air Station Feb. 17 to give a personal send-off to combat troops newly ordered to Vietnam. The departing men were part of a new deployment of 10,500 combat troops to the war area requested by Gen. William C. Westmoreland the previous week after the Tet offensive. Under the previous troop build-up schedule, 25,000 more men were to have been sent to the war area by July to raise the total number of U.S. troops there to the authorized level of 525,000. But it had been planned originally to send support troops, not combat troops. The new deployment of combat-ready forces would raise the number of U.S. troops in Vietnam to 510,500.

The new deployment included units of the 82d Airborne Infantry Division from Fort Bragg (adjacent to Pope Air Force Base) and units of the 5th Marine Division at El Toro. Accompanied by Gen. Harold K. Johnson, Army chief of staff, and Lt. Gen. Lewis W. Walt, deputy commandant of the Marine Corps, the President told the 82d Airborne troops the enemy was trying to win in Vietnam "now and this year" by shaking the Saigon government "to its foundation" and destroying the confidence of its people and the will of the Americans to continue.

(The authors of the so-called "Pentagon papers"—a secret U.S. Defense Department history of the development of U.S. policy in Vietnam, published in 1971—regarded this experience of Johnson as his personal turning point. According to one of the analysts: "The experience proved for him to be one of the most profoundly moving and troubling of the entire Vietnam war. The men, most of whom had only recently returned from Vietnam, were grim. They were not young men going off to adventure but seasoned veterans returning to an ugly conflict from which they knew some would not return. The film clips of the President shaking hands with the solemn but determined paratroopers on the ramps of their aircraft revealed a deeply troubled leader. He was confronting the men he was asking to make the sacrifice and they displayed no enthusiasm.")

After an overnight stay aboard the aircraft carrier *Constellation*, at sea about 15 miles from San Diego, Johnson flew to Palm Desert, Calif. Feb. 18 for a 3-hour talk and a game of golf with ex-Pres. Dwight D. Eisenhower before returning to Washington. Addressing the men aboard the *Constellation* Feb. 18, Johnson said: "Men may debate—men may dissent—men may disagree, and God forbid that a time should come when men of this land may not. But there does come a time when men must stand. And for America, that time has now come. . . . So we have taken our stand. We shall do . . . all that is asked, all that may be required."

Johnson told reporters Feb. 18 that U.S. strategists thought the enemy strategy had changed from "a hit-and-run thing" to one of "going for broke." Johnson reportedly told Eisenhower that the enemy was believed to have been badly hurt in recent fighting. (Eisenhower was given a briefing on the war by Gen. Walt and Johnson's special assistant, Walt W. Rostow, who also briefed newsmen Feb. 18 and reported that a 2d enemy attack on Vietnamese cities was expected. Walt said: The enemy had "committed his blue chips" in the urban assaults and had lost an estimated 40,000 men of a force of 60,000 sent into the attack. Some 12,000 enemy weapons had been captured; it added up to a "real defeat.")

(None of the other governments supporting the U.S. effort in Vietnam sent additional troops in response to the crisis created by the Tet offensive. Australian Prime Min. John G. Gorton announced Feb. 2 that his government had no plans to increase the 8,000-man Australian force in South Vietnam. He said neither the U.S. nor South Vietnam had asked for more Australian aid.)

Hué   Recaptured

South Vietnamese troops Feb. 24 captured the Imperial Palace in the walled Citadel of Hué. Allied forces thus virtually completed their battle to reoccupy the city. The government troops encountered no resistance in the palace; most of the North Vietnamese who had occupied the building for 24 days had withdrawn, apparently the previous night. Sporadic fighting continued, however, both in the Citadel and in the Chinese quarter of Hué and in the southwestern sections of the city, both inside and outside the walled section. U.S. Marines reportedly engaged in sharp fighting with North Vietnamese troops less than 3 miles from Hué.

Lt. Gen. Hoang Xuan Lam, commander of the I Corps area (which included Hué), was reported Feb. 21 to have ordered military trials for an estimated 200 suspected Communist agents seized during the fighting for the city. The mayor, who had warned Feb. 20 that executions would be necessary to restore order, said Feb. 21 that on the basis of Lam's orders, no one would be shot without trial. Hanoi radio Feb. 22 said the Viet Cong Revolutionary Committee in Hué had warned Feb. 21 that American captives would be shot if Viet Cong prisoners were executed.

Developments during the fighting for Hué:

● 4 U.S. Marine A–4 Skyhawk bombers, raided North Vietnamese positions Feb. 21 on a strip of land 100 to 150 yards wide between the southern Citadel wall and the Huong River. North Vietnamese gunners later in the day struck a fuel-laden U.S. naval craft in the Huong River. 4 crewmen jumped overboard and were rescued.

● Lt. Gen. Robert E. Cushman Jr., commander of U.S. Marines in Vietnam, said Feb. 21 that American reinforcements were needed for Hué because the fierce house-to-house fighting had "cut the fighting power" of the U.S. force there. Speaking at a news conference in Danang, Cushman added: "I think the troops have gotten tired and the casualties are bound to have an effect. The steam has gone out." A company of U.S. Marine reinforcements were flown to Hue by helicopter Feb. 21.

● U.S. Marines reached the south wall of the Citadel Feb. 22. The American force thus completed a phase of their drive aimed at clearing 1/3 of the walled sector of North Vietnamese troops. Counter-attacking North Vietnamese troops threw back a South Vietnamese government force near a small airstrip that bisected the northern part of the Citadel. The following night most of the defenders withdrew through the southwestern section of the Citadel area.

South Vietnamese Pres. Nguyen Van Thieu visited Hué Feb. 25. He was informed by Lt. Col. Phan Van Khoa, the mayor and provincial chief, that 70% of civilian homes were destroyed and 300 government officials were killed or missing. 113,000 of the city's 145,000 residents were refugees, and the entire population faced a severe food shortage.

South Vietnamese military losses in the fighting for the city exceeded 2,000, of whom 1/4 were listed as killed. U.S. casualties, mostly Marines, were about 100 dead and 900 wounded. Communist fatalities in the battle for Hué were listed at more than 5,000; 131 were captured. The civilian death toll in Hué was estimated at more than 1,000; more than 3,000 civilians were reported wounded, many of them seriously.

A 230-vehicle supply convoy arrived in Hué from Danang Mar. 2. It marked the reopening of the 60-mile coastal road for the first time since the Communists had cut the north-south highway at the start of their offensive. The Communists had blown up the road's bridges, had ambushed allied traffic on the highway and thus had forced the allies to supply Hué by boat along coastal routes or by air.

Fighting in Saigon & Khesanh, Air Raids on North

Hostilities also focused on Saigon and the U.S. Marine base at Khesanh. The Saigon area fighting was marked by almost continuous shelling of the U.S. airbase at Tansonnhut. A number of U.S. service men were killed and many others wounded in the attacks. *Among the major actions in the Saigon sector:*

● Viet Cong troops Feb. 20 seized the village of Tanthoit, $2^1/_2$ miles north of Tansonnhut. The Communist force was driven out 8 hours later by national police and South Vietnamese army units. 4 hours prior to the attack, a Viet Cong rocket had hit Tansonnhut's civilian air terminal, killing 4 Americans and wounding 61.

● The South Vietnamese military command reported Feb. 20 that allied bombers that day had pounded a Viet Cong held area 2 miles south of Tansonnhut's runways to thwart an enemy attempt to set up antiaircraft guns there. The Communist move to install the guns had been spotted by air observers, the command reported.

● U.S. troops clashed Feb. 20 with a 500-man Viet Cong force 6 miles northeast of Saigon. 123 Viet Cong troops were reported killed in the 3-hour engagament. American losses: 15 killed and 11 wounded.

● American troops reportedly killed 158 Communist troops in 2 clashes in the Saigon area Feb. 22. 128 of the guerrillas were slain in a 5-hour engagement 7 miles west of the capital. Fighting broke out 4 hours later one mile to the east, and about 30 Viet Cong troops were killed.

● The Tansonnhut airbase was subjected to another rocket-mortar attack Feb. 24. 4 U.S. servicemen were killed and 21 wounded. 11 Vietnamese civilians were killed and 4 wounded in the shelling of a group of homes about 2 blocks from the base.

● A U.S. artillery post in Dinhthuong Province, 42 miles southwest of Saigon, was attacked Feb. 25 by a Viet Cong force of 500 men. Striking with rockets and mortars, the stormed into the post and seized a 155-mm. artillery piece before being driven off by U.S. air strikes. Before retreating, they destroyed 17 armored vehicles, killed at least 20 American soldiers and wounded 65. 94 Viet Cong bodies were left behind.

• U.S. troops Feb. 26 sighted 3 Communist armored vehicles 50 miles northwest of Saigon. Such equipment had never before been seen so close to the South Vietnamese capital. In the engagement that ensued, one of the vehicles was reported destroyed. About 400 Communist troops were engaged in the clash, and 30 were killed before the survivors fled west, presumably into Cambodia, the U.S. command reported.

In the Khesanh fighting, a Viet Cong/North Vietnamese force Feb. 23 carried out a major probe of the base's defense perimeter, which was manned by a South Vietnamese army ranger battalion. (The rangers were the only South Vietnamese troops at the base.) The attack had been preceded by a heavy Communist barrage on the base itself.

A U.S. Marine patrol came under heavy North Vietnamese attack Feb. 26 about 800 yards outside the Khesanh base. A Marine rescue platoon was also heavily mauled. Exact American casualty figures were withheld under a new directive announced by the U.S. command earlier Feb. 26. The U.S. command said that the restrictions on the news of battle reports was designed to hold back information that might be "of intelligence to the enemy." "If the tactical situation dictates," the command explained, it would withhold such information as casualty figures, reports of damage to installations and equipment and the number of enemy artillery rounds directed at specific targets. The Defense Department said that the new censorship rules would not affect the overall casualty figures released by the department. (The U.S. command had reported Feb. 22 that U.S. forces had suffered a record weekly fatality loss of 543 men in the period Feb. 11-17. 2,547 were wounded, and 1,247 of them required hospitalizauon.")

An AP report from Khesanh Feb. 27 said North Vietnamese troops were inching closer to the base by digging fortified, zigzag trenches and tunnels outside the defense perimeter. One trench was only 100 yards from Khesanh's barbed wire, according to spotter plane observation.

The U.S. intensified the air bombardment of North Vietnam. In one of the biggest raids in 6 weeks, U.S. jets Feb. 14 pounded the Canal des Rapides bridge, about 3 miles outside Hanoi. Other American aircraft bombed the Phucyen airbase, 18 miles northwest of the capital, and the Hoalac air base, 20 miles to the west. Hanoi radio said the U.S. planes had dropped rockets and bombs on a populated area of Hanoi. The broadcast claimed the downing of 6 U.S. planes—3 over Hanoi and 3 over Vinh, between Hanoi and the DMZ.

The U.S. command reported Feb. 22 that Navy Intruder planes had bombed a radio transmitter at Bachmai, $3^1/_2$ miles from the center of Hanoi. The station was regarded as the most powerful in East Asia. A Reuters dispatch said that Hanoi radio continued to broadcast to Southeast Asia after the attack on Bachmai and made no mention of the raid on the radio station.

The North Vietnamese press agency charged Feb. 25 that U.S. bombing of the center of Hanoi Feb. 24 had killed 12 persons and wounded 16 in a working-class district. The agency said that the attack on the Haibathung district had lasted 20 minutes and that "several" time-action bombs had been dropped.

A railroad yard 1.7 miles from the center of Hanoi came under U.S. air attack Feb. 25 for the first time since Dec. 15, 1967. The U.S. command reported that Navy A-6 Intruder bombers had hit the yard, which was along the main rail line from Haiphong to Hanoi.

Peking complained Feb. 2 that U.S. planes had bombed 2 Chinese freighters in North Vietnamese ports—one at Hongay Jan. 20 and the other at Campha Jan. 27. The Chinese Foreign Ministry described the attacks as "deliberate provocations by United States imperialism against the Chinese people." Peking had claimed Jan. 31 that U.S. planes that day had violated China's airspace over Hainan Island and Kwangtung Province, near North Vietnam. The U.S. State Department Jan. 31 conceded that a U.S. Navy plane had inadvertently flown within 7 miles of Hainan.

Pressure Sustained

During late February and early March major fighting flared throughout South Vietnam as Viet Cong/North Vietnamese troops continued to maintain strong pressure against U.S. and South Vietnamese forces. Sharp, sporadic engagements centered largely around Saigon and the U.S. Marine base at Khesanh, just below the demilitarized zone. The Tansonnhut airbase outside Saigon came under frequent mortar and rocket attacks, and the area was the scene of ground clashes. Allied firepower in the Saigon and Khesanh sectors reportedly had taken a heavy toll of enemy troops. Major Communist attacks also were carried out in the Mekong delta and Central Highlands.

The Communist attacks were coupled with intelligence reports that the Viet Cong was massing forces for a possible major thrust against Saigon. An alert was issued Mar. 2 in preparation for expected onslaughts against the capital Mar. 3. The alert was based on a report that the Viet Cong 5th Division was moving toward the city again. The division had withdrawn to the northeast after attacking Bienhoa airbase 15 miles northeast of Saigon and the U.S. supply base and headquarters at nearby Longbinh. A further intelligence report Mar. 4 said an 8,000-10,000-man Viet Cong force was within 15 miles of Saigon.

Among major military actions:

• U.S. military authorities reported Feb. 28 that American troops had killed 70 North Vietnamese soldiers around Dakto Feb. 26–27. The action was the heaviest in the Central Highlands since allied and Communist forces had fought a major battle around Dakto in Nov. 1967. In a Feb. 27 operation, about 400 soldiers of the U.S. 4th Infantry Division were reported to have repelled a North Vietnamese attack within a few yards of their bunkers west of Dakto. One American was reported killed and 9 wounded in the 2-day battle. The fighting had started when 2 companies of U.S. troops landed by helicopter in the area on a search-and-destroy mission.

• The U.S. command reported that North Vietnamese gunners Feb. 28 had shot down a Marine CH-46 transport helicopter 11 miles northeast of Khesanh. 22 men were killed and one injured. Since mid-January Communist fire near the DMZ had downed 3 fighter-bombers, a C-130 transport and about 10 helicopters and light observation planes.

• The U.S. command reported Feb. 29 the completion of the emergency deployment of the 4,000-man 3d Brigade of the 82d Airborne Division to Vietnam from the U.S. The troops, assigned to the Americal Division at Chulai, were among 10,500 soldiers whose deployment to Vietnam had been advanced by Pres. Johnson Feb. 17 in the wake of the Tet offensive. As of Feb. 21, U.S. strength in Vietnam had totaled 495,000 men—325,000 Army; 79,000 Marines; 33,000 Navy; 57,000 Air Force; 1,200 Coast Guard. Other allied forces numbered 61,000, South Vietnamese about 600,000.

• Communist rockets Feb. 28 hit the allied airbase at Bienhoa, 20 miles northeast of Saigon. The AP reported 14 persons killed and 20 wounded in the 20-round barrage. Damage to planes and the installation was reported to be light.

• Americal Division troops were reported Feb. 28 to have killed 148 enemy soldiers in a 4-hour battle in Tamky, capital of the northermost province of Quangtri.

• South Vietnamese troops, assisted by B-52 air strikes, repulsed an attack by about 500 Communist troops against the outer defenses of the Khesanh base Mar. 1. The planes dropped tons of explosives only 750 yards from the base's ring of barded wire. B-52s Mar. 2 pounded enemy tunnels and bunkers 1,000 yards from the defense perimeter. 31,000 tons of bombs and napalm were reported dropped in the area from mid-January to mid-February in an effort to thwart assault against the surrounded American base. 22 Marines were killed and 87 wounded Mar. 2 at the eastern end of the demilitarized zone in a day-

long clash. They were slain during a search of Maixthai, a village 5 miles south of the DMZ, following the Communist shelling of a Marine forward headquarters and airstrip at Dongha, 4 miles to the south.
● At least 20 engagements were fought in the northern suburbs of Saigon Mar. 1–2. 56 Communists were reported killed in 2 separate clashes with South Vietnamese and U.S. troops in the capital area Mar. 1. South Vietnamese reported killing 35 enemy soldiers at the eastern edge of the Tansonnhut airbase, while 15 miles to the northeast American troops ambushed a 150-man Viet Cong force near the northern perimeter of the Bienhoa base and killed 21.
● 48 U.S. troops were killed and 28 wounded 4 miles north of Tansonnhut Mar. 2 in what was described as one of the costliest ambushes of the war. In the attack, a 150-man company of the 25th Division was gunned down as it was moving along a road that ran between parallel canals several yards apart. Most of the Americans were slain in an 8-minute burst of fire from machine-guns, automatic rifles, mortars and rocket launchers positioned along the canal banks. 20 of an estimated 150 attackers were killed.
● U.S. air, artillery and naval fire Mar. 3 reportedly killed nearly 300 North Vietnamese troops in South Vietnam's 2 northernmost provinces—Quangtri and Thuatien. In one assault, Marines at Conthien called for air and artillery strikes after sighting 2 large groups of North Vietnamese troops at the southern edge of the DMZ. The ensuing bombardment resulted in the killing of 153 Communist troops, a U.S. spokeman said. 2 Marines were killed and 8 wounded. 3 companies of North Vietnamese troops spotted by an aerial observer 14 miles southeast of the city of Quangtri were fired on by an American destroyer and a Coast Guard cutter. 84 of the enemy were said to have been killed. 60 Communist troops were reported killed by fighterbomber raid within 5 miles of Hue.
● Communist rocket and mortar attacks Mar. 4 were directed at more than 20 cities and villages and allied military bases and airstrips throughout South Vietnam. Damage was reported light. In the most serious attack, on Ducduc (345 miles northeast of Saigon), 24 persons were killed and 84 wounded; 150 homes were destroyed.
● Communist mortar attacks were directed Mar. 5 against 5 provincial capitals in the Mekong delta—Cantho, Mytho, Caoinh, Bentre and Cahudoc.
● 206 Communist troops were reported slain in daylong fighting with U.S. and South Vietnamese troops at Tuyhoa, a provincial capital 230 miles northeast of Saigon. 5 American troops were killed and 16 wounded.

Repercussions in Laos & Cambodia

As the Tet offensive unfolded, fighting intensified in both Laos and Cambodia. The U.S. State Department Feb. 17 expressed concern about increased attacks by North Vietnamese and Pathet Lao forces in Laos, adjacent to the Central Highlands of South Vietnam. The department cited what it described as a 3-pronged assault that "may be a drive toward low-lying points of Laos" on the Mekong River bordering Thailand. It was believed that the purpose of the offensive was to extend westward North Vietnamese control of the infiltration routes into South Vietnam, to set the stage for a build-up around the South Vietnamese Central Highlands town of Dakto, or to create a diversion in Laos and thus further stretch U.S. military power.

Laotian Premier Souvanna Phouma charged Feb. 22 that North Vietnam had a force of 40,000 men in Laos. In an interview with the French newspaper *Le Monde*, Souvanna said that "as long as the Vietnam problem is not settled the problem of Laos will not be settled either." Souvanna Phouma charged Mar. 1 that the conquest of Laos was part of a Communist "master plan for Asian and world conquest and domination." In an address appealing for international aid for Laos' 600,000 war refugees, Souvanna rejected Pathet Lao claims that their war was "a revolution of the people against the yoke of a tyrannical dictatorship." Souvanna added: "The Pathet Lao brought this war of aggression to Laos, making false promises to the people of peace, justice and property. But they have done the opposite of what they promised and instead brought chaos, bloody and terrible war and death and the ruination of our beloved country."

The areas in which the Communists were reported operating: (1) The Mekong River town of Paksane, about 80 miles east of the administrative capital of Vientiane; Pathet Lao forces the previous week had captured the Laotian government positions at the nearby towns of Saladendin and Thathom. (2) The provincial capital of Attopeu, near the Cambodian and Vietnamese borders, reportedly under attack by about 1,000 Pathet Lao and North Vietnamese troops. (3) The Saravane area, about 80 miles north of Attopeu and parallel to Danang and South Vietnam's Central Highlands.

A Laotion government complaint that Saravane, encircled by North Vietnamese and Pathet Lao troops since January, was threatened with an attack was investigated Feb. 21 by the Canadian and Indian members of the International Control Commission. The commissioners said they had found no evidence of a Communist threat to the town. (The ICC's Polish delegation had refused to join the probe.) Vientiane sources reported Feb. 23, however, that government troops that day had repulsed attacks on Saravane and Attopeu.

In fighting 25 miles to the southwest of Saravane, North Vietnamese soldiers Feb. 23 overran a government outpost at Ban Nao

Ngam, which was recaptured by Laotian government troops Feb. 24. A government source said about 200 troops of both sides were killed; the dead included 80 North Vietnamese. The government outpost at Thathom had been seized by 3 Communist battalions Feb. 21. It was the last government stronghold defending the approach to Paksane. Fighting was reported Feb. 25 at the Saladendin Pass, 50 miles north of Paksane, between government troops and a Pathet Lao/North Vietnamese force. The pass faced the northeastern Thai border.

Laotian government military positions came under increasing attack Mar. 1–15. Military barracks near Saravane were hit by a North Vietnamese rocket barrage Mar. 1. Gen. Udone Sananikone, Laotian chief of staff, said Mar. 2 that it was the first time that North Vietnamese forces had used 140-mm. rockets in Laos. He said 8 soldiers were injured in the 30-round barrage. The government stronghold at Attopeu was attacked by North Vietnamese and Pathet Lao rockets, it was reported Mar. 8; 15 civilians and an undisclosed number of soldiers were wounded. A government communiqué Mar. 9 claimed that Laotian government air force raids in the northern part of the country had recently killed 67 Pathet Lao and North Vietnamese troops and wounded 100.

The Laotian Defense Ministry reported Mar. 12 that Communist forces were advancing from 3 directions on Mekong River town of Thakhek, in central Laos, opposite a U.S. Air Force base at Makhon Phanom in Thailand. The Communists Mar. 15 captured 2 villages north of Thakhek—Na Ngou and Ok Tong—and seized the last remaining road leading to the city. As a result, the Laotian government could only supply Thakhek by air or by boat along the Mekong River.

Because of the fighting in Laos, the Thai government Mar. 12 had closed the border with Laos in the northeastern province of Nakhon Phanom. Thai government troops in the province were put on the alert as refugees displaced by the Laotian fighting moved into Thailand.

Laotian military authorities in Vientiane had conceded Mar. 11 that Pathet Lao and North Vietnamese military gains since Jan. 1 had weakened the government's military position. The tactics employed against the government, similar to those used by the Viet Cong and North Vietnamese troops in Vietnam, had forced Laotian government soliders and their U.S. advisers to abandon the countryside for the cities, according to Laotian sources. More than 1,000 Laotian troops had been reported killed missing in recent fighting. About 400 Communist troops were-reported killed.

Pressures on Cambodia also continued to build. In early February, Cambodia was reported to be fighting, a Communist guerrilla movement.

Chief of State Norodom Sihanouk said Feb. 9 that the Communist military operations had been suppressed, but subsequent reports by him and the government indicated that the guerrilla activities were increasing. Sihanouk reported that government forces had virtually thwarted the Communist drive in Rattanakiri Province, bordering South Vietnam, and in Battambang Province, on Thailand's frontier. He denied French newspaper reports that the villagers in these provinces had been receptive to Communist propaganda because they had been mistreated by the Cambodian army. Sihanouk had charged previously that Cambodian hill tribes had been armed by Viet Cong and North Vietnamese forces and that Peking had given them equipment and propaganda materials.

Sihanouk Feb. 11 described the Communist movement in his country as "Viet Minh" (the term used for the Communist-supported guerrillas who had defeated the French in Indochina in 1954) and claimed that they were attempting to gain control of sections of Cambodia. The Cambodian rebels had recently forced residents of several Battambang Province villages to abandon their homes and flee into the forest, he said. In a letter published Mar. 7 in the French newspaper *Le Monde*, Sihanouk charged that Asian Communists were using Cambodian rebels to overthrow his government. Sihanouk said: "The rebellion in Battambang is basically political and launched from outside the country. Evidence of this abounds: discovery of propaganda pamphlets in Siamese printed in Peking and carrying the portrait of Mao. This is material handed out by the Thai Patriotic Front—which is subservient to the Chinese—which operates in neighboring Thai provinces and which supplies our rebels with arms and equipment."

The Cambodian government had reported Mar. 2 that at least 5 Cambodian areas had been placed on "a war footing" to cope with the spreading Communist encroachments. Fighting had been reported for the first time in Koh Kong, Kompong Speu and Kampot Provinces and in 2 other areas in the west and southwest. Sihanouk reported Mar. 8 that the Cambodian navy had captured a vessel carrying arms and ammunition for the Cambodian guerrillas in the southwest. The boat, he said, had been operated by 3 North Vietnamese and 2 Cambodians.

Offensive Assessed

The U.S. and North Vietnam each published assessments of the course of the offensive before February ended. Gen. William C. Westmoreland, U.S. commander, asserted Feb. 25 that the Viet Cong/North Vietnamese forces had "suffered a military defeat" in the Tet offensive despite "some temporary psychological advantage." He said he did not believe North Vietnam "can hold up under a long war," and he conceded that the Communist attack "does not seem to be a go-for-broke effort." But Westmoreland said he probably would need "additional troops" in order to "more effectively deny the enemy his objectives, capitalize on his recent defeats . . . and clearly demonstrate to Hanoi our firm determination to prevent him from taking over any part of South Vietnam." *Among other statements made by Westmoreland in written answers to questions submitted by AP:*

● Although the Communist offensive had made it "expedient and desirable" to shift some U.S. troops to the cities, basic strategy remained unchanged. "Friendly forces still must find, fix, fight and destroy the enemy and concurrently provide the necessary security for the population."

● The Communists ability to infiltrate South Vietnamese cities in large numbers had been underestimated. "The use of public roads and civilian disguise made it very difficult to detect the infiltrators." Many rode "public buses and bicycles in civilian clothes." But the success of the infiltrators did not mean that the Viet Cong had "more sympathizers than we believed." "It only takes a few collaborators to aid infiltrators entering into a populated area."

● The movement of the enemy force from "his jungle camps" to the cities made him "more vulnerable and gave us an opportunity to hurt him severely. That is why over 40,000 of the enemy have been killed in less than one month, which is over 40% of all the enemy killed in 1967."

● "One of the great distortions of the war had been the allegation that casualties inflicted on the enemy are padded. "There had been some duplication in reporting enemy fatalities, and sometimes civilians had been mistakenly listed. But these inaccuracies were more than offset "by enemy deaths that we do not know about."

● It was too soon to determine the effect of the Viet Cong/North Vietnamese offensive on the pacification program. "In the areas where there was a setback, certainly it will take months in some instances to restore the effort to its former level . . . "

● The Communist offensive was partially motivated by a desire to reverse his "deterioration in morale." Prior to the attacks, "extraordinary steps were taken to propagandize" the Viet Cong/North Vietnamese officers and troops. Despite this indoctrination, "many [Communist troops] fought half-heartedly, a number surrendered, and in several cases small units gave themselves up." On the other hand, South Vietnamese army troops had "performed well indeed." As an example, all 11 of the Vietnamese division commanders were at their posts at the time of the attack and commanded their units effectively.

• The massing of a large North Vietnamese force around the U.S. Marine base at Khesanh did not indicate a failure of the U.S. bombing of North Vietnam. "One has to judge the bombing program based on the problems it has created for . . . Hanoi and its present posture in the South compared to what would have happened had there been no interdiction of his lines of communication."

Gen. Earle G. Wheeler, chairman of the Joint Chiefs of Staff, visited South Vietnam Feb. 23–25 to confer with Gen. Westmoreland and inspect battle areas. Before boarding a plane for Washington Feb. 25, Wheeler said: "I see no easy end to this war. We must expect hard fighting to continue. The enemy retains substantial uncommitted resources. However, the major defeats inflicted on the enemy and the major losses he has sustained offer us opportunities for the future. Allied forces in Vietnam are continually alert to these opportunities." (According to the secret "Pentagon paper," published by the *N.Y. Times* in 1971, Wheeler reported to the President Feb. 27: The Tet drive had gained the intiative for the enemy. The South vietnamese forces had been forced into "a defensive posture around towns and cities" while the Viet Cong was "operating with relative freedom in the countryside." To hold the northern provinces, Westmoreland had been forced to send half the U.S. maneuver battalions, "stripping the rest of the country of adequate reserves" and robbing himself of "an offensive capability.")

The North Vietnamese army newspaper *Quan Doi Nhan Dan* said in an editorial Feb. 28 that the Tet offensive had achieved "military success which will have an important strategic significance." The editorial, "Big Victories, Firm Step Forward," called the North Vietnamese/Viet Cong drive "an unprecedentedly big victory for the southern revolution" and a major setback for U.S. and allied forces. The editorial, distributed Mar. 4 at the U.S. mission in Saigon, also said:

• The Communist assault constituted "a new step forward in controlling the battlefield" and presaged the beginning of a "new situation," politically, as well as militarily.

• As a result of the attacks, "the United States imperialists are now at the turning point and are doomed to failure. They have been witnessing a series

of contradictions that are developing at a critical stage and cannot be solved: the contadictions between the United States global strategy and the local war that they are waging in Vietnam; between the strategy of fighting and occupying areas quickly and the realities that compel them to lengthen the war with vague hopes.''
● The allied-held peaceful rear areas had been turned into ''terrible battlefields,'' and the allies had been forced to set up defenses in the center of cities and military bases. The allied forces had ''been upset'' by the onslaught and were in ''a state of chaos.'' ''They have to maneuver their forces to defend themselves everywhere. Their 2 prong search and-destory and pacification strategy has deteriorated.''
● Communist strategy was to ''attack the enemy everywhere, conduct concerted large-scale attacks throughout the country, foil the enemy's strategy, compel him to be continuously on the defensive.''
● ''Our rear has become much stronger, our reserve in manpower and material more abundant, our revolutionary organizations and their abilities and room to maneuver much wider, and the conditions for the development of the people's war more favorable. The tactics of encircling and cutting up enemy forces have become stronger and the attack springboard of the revolutionary army forces more and more strengthened.''

(In a report published by the U.S. government Apr. 6, 1969, Westmoreland conceded that the Tet offensive had taken him and his aides by surprise. Westmoreland explained that ''those of us who had been in Vietnam for a long time found it hard to believe that the enemy would expose his forces to almost certain decimation by engaging us frontally at great distances from his base areas and border sanctuaries. However, . . . this is exactly what he did, and in doing it he lost the cream of his army.'')

Offensive Contained

Military action in South Vietnam began to slacken by early March. The North Vietnamese, however, maintained heavy pressure on the U.S. Marine base at Khesanh and on other American strongholds in the northern part of South Vietnam just below the demilitarized zone (DMZ). Khesanh came under daily shelling between Mar. 5 and Mar. 11. In the Saigon area and in the Mekong delta region, heavy fighting continued to rage. It thus appeared that the Tet offensive, after more than a month of sustained combat throughout South Vietnam, had been contained by the forces of the U.S. and the Saigon regime.

Among developments in the DMZ area:
● U.S. planes and artillery Mar. 6 pounded an area near Khesanh where a column of 600 North Vietnamese had been spotted. 18 of the enemy reportedly were killed.

● A U.S. C-123 transport was shot down by North Vietnamese gunners Mar. 6 as it approached for a landing at Khesanh. All 44 Marine reinforcements, on a flight from Phubai, and 5 crewmen were killed. This was the 3d American transport shot down at the surrounded Marine base, which could be supplied only by air. In ground action that day, U.S. Marines reported killing 81 North Vietnamese 3 miles northeast of their base at Conthien, to the east of Khesanh and just below the DMZ. Marine losses were listed at 14 killed and 29 wounded.

● South Vietnamese troops killed 138 North Vietnamese troops Mar. 7 in a 7-hour battle near Dongha (7 miles south of the DMZ), headquarters of the U.S. 3d Marine Division. In a clash in the same area Mar. 8, South Vietnamese troops reportedly killed 50 North Vietnamese soldiers, 9 South Vietnamese soldiers were killed and 6 wounded. U.S. Marines also were involved in the 2 days of fighting around Dongha; 16 were killed and 116 wounded, 83 of them seriously enough to be evacuated.

● North Vietnamese troops Mar. 7 broke into a camp garrisoned by U.S. Marines and South Vietnamese troops 6 miles west of the Danang base. By the time reinforcements arrived, the attackers had fled, leaving the camp totally destroyed. U.S. and South Vietnamese losses were described as heavy. The North Vietnamese removed most of their dead and wounded; only 7 bodies were left behind.

● A North Vietnamese column of about 100 men, emerging Mar. 8 from one of many tunnels encircling Khesanh, came under attack by South Vietnamese troops guarding the base's defensive perimeter. 27 of the North Vietnamese were reported killed.

● U.S. American Division troops Mar. 9 killed 129 Communist troops in an engagement fought 9 miles Northwest of Tamky in Quangtin Province. American casualties were reported to be only 18 wounded.

● Several U.S. outposts just south of the DMZ were the target of heavy North Vietnamese artillery attacks Mar. 10–11. Tons of ammunition and supplies were destroyed. A supply base at the mouth of the Cua Viet, an estuary leading to the Marine base at Dongha, was hardest hit, (Cua Viet was a major shipping point for most supplies headed for Khesanh and other strongpoints along the DMZ.) A mortar shell struck the middle of an ammunition pile at Cua Viet and set off explosions. A gasoline storage area at Dongha was blown up by a mortar barrage, which also struck a nearby village. Khesanh and parts of the U.S. base at Danang were also pounded by artillery, mortar and rockets.

Among developments in the Saigon area:

Mar. 8—Guerrillas ambushed 5 trucks near Thuduc in Giadinh Province on the northeastern outskirts of the capital; they destroyed one vehicle and damaged another. South Vietnamese troops clashed with an enemy force near Tanuyen, 27 miles northeast of Saigon, and killed 49 in a 4-hour fight. A South Vietnamese army battalion ammunition dump in Bienhoa Province was destroyed when it was struck by Viet Cong mortar fire.

Mar. 9—The Viet Cong carried out 7 coordinated attacks in the southern outskirts of Saigon. One target was the district police headquarters and the militia post of Caykho, about 3 miles from the capital; the garrison repelled the assault. A 30-minute mortar and rocket barrage was directed at 2 police substations and a housing development about 1$^{1}/_{2}$ miles from the U.S. embassy.

Shells also hit Nhabe, an important petroleum storage area on the Saigon River about 4 miles southeast of the city.

The big U.S. supply and air base at Camranh Bay had been hit by Viet Cong fire for the first time Mar. 4. American authorities said that the base, on the South China Sea coast 175 miles northeast of Saigon, had been hit by 10-14 rounds of rocket fire, that the runway had been damaged but that air operations were unimpeded. The shelling was one of several mortar and rocket attacks on a dozen allied bases Mar. 4 and 5. Other targets hit included Cantho, Bentre, Mytho and Chaudoc in the Mekong delta, Banmethout in the Central Highlands and several installations around Danang.

The heaviest fighting in the Mekong delta in this period was waged Mar. 5 in Anxuyen Province's capital, Quanlong (formerly Camau). A force of about 500 Viet Cong, identified as the U Minh II Battalion, stormed into the city of 6,000-8,000, seized a hospital and carried out heavy attacks on the American compound, the provincial headquarters and a military air strip. Allied reinforcements were rushed into Quanlong, and several hours later the allied command in Saigon reported that the Viet Cong were "well clear of the city." The Viet Cong, however, continued sporadic shelling of Quanlong through Mar. 7. In the one-day battle for Quanlong 250-275 Communists were reported killed. Government losses were listed at 10 killed and 41 wounded. At least 20 civilians were said to have been slain and 50 wounded. More than 1,000 homes were destroyed.

The U.S. continued intensified air operations over North Vietnam. *Among developments reported:*

● U.S. jets Mar. 4 bombed a boat yard 6 miles southwest of Hanoi for the first time. Other American jets pounded a surface-to-air missile site 10 miles from Hanoi.

● During a 70-mission attack Mar. 5, U.S. planes hit army barracks 31 miles northeast of Haiphong and a boat yard 23 miles northeast of the city. The Hadong shipyard, 6 miles southwest of Hanoi, also came under attack.

● U.S. fighter-bombers Mar. 6 hit the Phucyen airfield 18 miles northwest of Hanoi.

● The Hanoi-Haiphong area was pounded heavily in an 83-mission attack Mar. 7. U.S. planes hit river-barge facilities less than 2 miles from the center of the capital and railroad yards and industrial facilities near Hanoi and Haiphong. Roads and military storage areas throughout North Vietnam also were hit.

● American planes Mar. 8 carried out the heaviest raids against North Vietnam in more than a month. During a 109-mission attack, the U.S. jets struck a military radio station 10 miles southeast of Hanoi and 9 surface-to-air missile sites and radar positions near Hanoi and Haiphong. In the area south of Hanoi, 30 supply trucks were reported destroyed or damaged. The Vinh airfield and an industrial complex at Ninhgiang, near Haiphong, was also hit.

Shake-Up in Saigon & U.S. Commands

The strains of the Tet offensive led both the U.S. and Saigon to reconstruct their military commands in South Vietnam.

The South Vietnamese Joint General Staff Feb. 27 confirmed the replacement of 2 of the country's 4 corps commanders. Maj. Gen. Nguyen Van Manh, commander of the IV Corps (Mekong delta), was succeeded by Maj. Gen. Nguyen Duc Thang, ex-deputy chief of staff in charge of pacification. Lt. Gen. Vinh Loc, commander of the II Corps (Central Highlands and lowlands), was replaced by Maj. Gen. Lu Lan. Loc had been widely described as a "warlord" who frequently ignored Saigon policy. He had buit up a network of local leaders considered loyal to him personally rather than to Saigon and had been under frequent criticism for corruption and lack of aggressiveness since his appointment to the II Corps command in 1965.

Pres. Nguyen Van Thieu Mar. 1 signed an executive order depriving South Vietnam's 4 military corps commanders of their civilian powers. The new law was aimed at providing the government with direct communications with province chiefs.

Vice Pres. Nguyen Cao Ky had resigned Feb. 20 as chairman of the Emergency Recovery Committee. The committee had been established 3 weeks previously to cope with the crisis caused by the Tet offensive. Maj. Gen. Nguyen Duc Thang, ex-deputy chief of staff for armed pacification forces, also resigned from the committee. In handing over the chairmanship of the committee to Pres. Nguyen Van Thieu Feb. 21, Ky said that he had withdrawn from the post because he had accomplished the 2 tasks he had undertaken as head of the agency—to provide emergency relief for refugees and to bring the country back to a state of normality (It was reported later that the true reason Ky and Thang had resigned was the reduction of their authority by Thieu.)

A new U.S. command was established in the I Corps area in South Vietnam's 2 northern-most provinces of Quangtri and Thuathien to cope with a Communist build-up there. The creation of the new command, designated "Provisional Corps, Vietnam," was announced Mar. 8 by Gen. William C. Westmoreland, U.S.

commander.

Lt. Gen. William B. Rosson, 49, of the U.S. Army, who had commanded the central area just south of I Corps, was named commander of the Provisional Corps, with headquarters in Phubai. The staff consisted of Army, Navy and Marine officers. The I Corps area previously had been the sole jurisdiction of the Marine Corps. Lt. Gen. Robert E. Cushman of the Marine Corps retained over-all command of I Corps. Gen. Creighton W. Abrams, Westmoreland's deputy, who had been sent to Phubai in February to establish a northern forward command, was shifted back to Saigon, where he was to help train South Vietnamese troops. The units directly under Rosson's command were the 3d Marine Division and elements of the Army's 101st Airborne Division.

In a statement made in Phubai Mar. 10, the day the new command began operations, Westmoreland predicted "very, very heavy fighting" in Quangtri and Thuathien Provinces. Westmoreland held that it was North Vietnam's "intent to dominate by military force these 2 provinces," which, he said, Hanoi regarded as part of its territory. "The enemy has failed to date, but he has not yet given up," Westmoreland declared. "I expect him to continue these efforts."

Westmoreland Mar. 6 had deplored news reports that, he said, had "interpreted" the impending restructuring of the northern command "as a reflection against the U.S. Marine Corps and the 3d Marine Amphibious Force." "Contrary to these speculative news stories," Westmoreland said, "I wish to make it absolutely clear that these arrangements are based on tactical considerations and have nothing to do with the performance of the Marines, which is, and always has been, excellent."

High Casualty Toll; Red Strength Reevaluated

The ferocity of the fighting and the destructiveness of the month-long Tet offensive were indicated in casualty statistics published by the U.S. government. U.S. military authorities said Mar. 6 that 50,000 North Vietnamese and Viet Cong troops had been killed since the start of the offensive Jan. 30. U.S. fatalities during that period were 2,000, South Vietnamese 4,000. The U.S. mission had reported Mar. 5 that 32 American civilians—11 employed by the U.S. government—had been killed during the offensive. 18 others were known to have been captured by the

Communists, and 7 others were listed as missing. The U. S. command reported Mar. 14 that casualties suffered by Americans since Jan. 1, 1961 had totaled 139,801 by Mar. 9 and exceeded the 3-year total of the Korean War (in which 136,914 U.S. soldiers were killed or wounded). U.S. combat deaths in Vietnam totaled 19,670; 33,629 Americans had died in Korea.

The South Vietnamese government reported July 3 that 7,424 civilians had been killed and another 15,434 had been wounded during the Tet offensive. (The U.S. embassy had reported Mar. 9 that, since Jan. 1, the Communists had killed 5,831 civilians and kidnaped 2,783; more than 5,000 were missing.)

The U. S. command Mar. 14 estimated Viet Cong/North Vietnamese strength in South Vietnam at 207,000 to 220,000, not including 100,000 to 150,000 irregulars, self-defense militia and political cadres. This was a 16,000-18,000 drop from the estimate of the previous week. The U.S. command had reported Mar. 13 that North Vietnamese infiltration in South Vietnam in February had totaled 6,000 men. This was a drop from the 20,000 North Vietnamese who had poured into the northern part of South Vietnam just below the DMZ in January for the siege of the U.S. Marine base at Khesanh.

The "severe losses" suffered by the Communists during their Tet offensive had been offset by the conscription of replacements, Maj. Gen. Nguyen Duc Thang, South Vietnamese commander of the IV Corps (Mekong delta), said Mar. 9. Thang said the Communists were able to carry out their recruitment drive in hamlets and villages when the government's rural pacification teams and accompanying defensive troops were forced to withdraw from the rural areas to help fight the attacks on the cities. "But the quality of these replacements is very poor," Thang said. Some were kidnaped and thus may prove unreliable to the Viet Cong, while others were 12, 13 and 14 years old, he explained.

A senior U.S. military command officer in Saigon had said Mar. 6 that he believed the Communists' next major attack would be directed at Hué, rather than at the U.S. Marine Corps base at Khesanh. Although he did not rule out a full-scale assault on Khesanh, the officer said U.S. air strikes against enemy positions around Khesanh had disrupted enemy supply routes and lessened the possibility of an immediate attack on the American stronghold. But more than a division of North Vietnamese and Viet Cong troops (about 10,000 men) had moved into the Hué area from the demilitarized zone, making it likely that the city would be "his next objective," the officer said.

U.S. officials had underestimated Communist military strength in South Vietnam prior to the Tet offensive, according to the U.S. Central Intelligence Agency. It was reported Mar. 18 that the CIA assessment, sent to the White House and the State and Defense Departments earlier in March, had placed the Viet Cong/North Vietnamese force at 515,000 to 600,000 at the start of the drive. The U.S. national intelligence had estimated the Communist force in Nov. 1967 at 448,000 to 483,000 men. This figure was still being used in January, although it was modified by the inclusion of another 15,000 North Vietnamese troops believed to have infiltrated into the South in December. (The national intelligence was the term applied to the consensus arrived at by various U.S. intelligence groups: the CIA, the Defense Intelligence Agency, the State Department's Bureau of Intelligence and Research, the Intelligence Branch of the Atomic Energy Commission, the National Security Agency and the FBI.)

The CIA's estimate of the strength of the Communist force's 5 distinct groups (national intelligence calculations in parentheses): North Vietnamese and main Viet Cong units—160,000, about equally divided (54,000 North Vietnamese, 64,000 Viet Cong); village guerrilla platoons and squads—100,000 to 120,000 (70,000-90,000); administrative and logistic apparatus—75,000 (35,000-40,000); political cadres—80,000-120,000 (75,000-85,000); irregulars, or self-defense militia—100,000 (150,000).

During his visit to Washington in Nov. 1967, Gen. William C. Westmoreland had reported Communist strengh as of that month at 242,000, a drop from 285,000 in the fall of 1966. Westmoreland's 1967 figures, however, did not include the political apparatus and irregulars; the 285,000 figure did. The inclusion of the 2 Communist units would have brought the Viet Cong/North Vietnamese total to the 448,000-483,000 level calculated by the national intelligence.

The higher CIA estimate of Communist strength was believed largely attributable to improved intelligence and the appearance of more of the Viet Cong's apparatus during the Tet offensive. The remaining increase was the result of an actual enlargement of the Communist force between November and January. And Washington intelligence officials were reported to have disputed U.S. military estimates that 50,000 Communist troops had been slain by allied forces in the Tet offensive.

ALLIED RALLY

Counter-Thrusts by U.S. & Saigon Forces

The U.S. and Saigon began to recover the military initiative in South Vietnam by the middle of March.

Allied military authorities reported Mar. 15 that about 50,000 U.S. and South Vietnames troops Mar. 11 had launched the largest offensive of the war against an estimated 8,000 to 1,0000 Viet Cong and North Vietnamese troops in the Saigon area. A U.S. spokesman said the purpose of the widespread coordinated attacks, extending to the Cambodian border, was to eliminate the Communist threat to the capital that had persisted since the Viet Cong/ North Vietnamese force had been driven from Saigon after its Tet offensive.

The allied drive, Operation Quyet Thang ("determined to win"), was being carried out in the 5 provinces surrounding Saigon —Binhduong, Longan, Haunghia, Giadinh and Bienhoa. A U.S. military spokesman reported that in the fighting through Mar. 17 more than 800 Communist and 30 American troops had been killed. 248 Americans were wounded. South Vietnamese casualties were described as light.

During fighting Mar. 15, South Vietnamese troops killed 60 Communists in 2 clashes 18 miles northwest of Saigon, and a combined U.S.-Vietnamese force killed 81 Communist troops about 15 miles west of the capital. 136 Communist soldiers were reported slain Mar. 16 in a $6^1/_2$-hour clash with South Vietnamese rangers and U.S. troops 16 miles northwest of Saigon.

As the allies sought to break up the enemy force around Saigon, heavy fighting continued in the northern provinces of Quangtri and Thuathien below the demilitarized zone (DMZ) and to the south in the Mekong delta. The fighting around the DMZ was centered near the U.S. Marine Corps base at Khesanh, where Communist troops continued to maintain heavy pressure.

In the north, a South Vietnamese regiment was reported Mar. 11 to have killed 102 North Vietnamese soldiers during an 8-hour battle 5 miles north of Dongha, headquarters of the U.S. 3d Marine Division. Allied casualties were listed as 3 killed and 7 wounded. The South Vietnamese attacked the outnumbered Communist force with the support of artillery and helicopters.

U.S. and South Vietnamese soldiers reported killing 288 Communist troops in 3 clashes near the DMZ Mar. 12. The heaviest outbreak occurred near the Cua Viet estuary, site of a 3d Marine Division supply base. 2 South Vietnamese battalions killed 194 North Vietnamese troops, while suffering 4 killed and 24 wounded. (South Vietnamese troops had killed 102 enemy soldiers in the same area Mar. 10.) In the other clash, U.S. Marines killed 35 enemy soldiers. American losses were 10 killed and 23 wounded.

U.S. planes Mar. 11-12 carried out one of the heaviest series of raids against entrenched North Vietnamese troops surrounding the American base at Khesanh. Jet fighter-bombers flew at least 250 individual raids while B-52 bombers also bombed enemy positions in the area.

A North Vietnamese force trapped in a U.S. pincer movement 6 miles northeast of Quangngai Mar. 16 lost 128 soldiers killed in a day-long battle. An American spokesman reported 2 U.S. soldiers killed and 10 wounded. The fighting had started when a force of about 150 Americal Division troops encountered the North Vietnamese. A 2d Americal Division company was airdropped 2 miles to the northeast, and it closed in on the beleaguered Communist force. The area had been pounded by artillery and air strikes before the ground operation got under way.

About 83 North Vietnamese troops were reported killed Mar. 16 in a clash with U.S. Marines at the eastern end of the DMZ. 2 Marines were killed and 26 wounded in the day-long fighting. The battle had started 2 miles west of the U.S. outpost at Giolinh when a 350-man American force engaged a Communist battalion of 600 men. During the fighting, the Marines came under heavy Communist artillery shelling from inside the DMZ. Khesanh also was attacked with a 120-round artillery barrage. The artillery shelling continued into Mar. 17, blowing up an ammunition dump and badly damaging phone antennas. South Vietnamese guarding the base's defense perimeter repulsed a North Vietnamese attempt to blow up the barbed wire that guarded the stronghold. 2 North Vietnamese were reported killed.

It was disclosed Mar. 13 that U.S./South Vietnamese forces had launched a combined operation Mar. 7 in the Mekong delta. The search-and-destroy operation, centered near Mytho (about 45 miles southwest of Saigon), thus far had resulted in the reported killing of 139 Viet Cong troops. U.S. 9th Infantry Division casualties were 18 killed and 107 wounded. It was reported Mar. 14 that North Vietnamese troops had been sighted in the Mekong delta for the first time. According to allied intelligence officers, a 300-man unit (identified as D-402) had been seen in Kienphong Province earlier in the week but had not been committed to combat.

U.S. planes Mar. 11 carried out a 76-mission attack over North Vietnam. They hit targets ranging from the Yenbai airfield 78 miles northwest to just above the DMZ. An Air Force F-4 Phantom was shot down during the raids, and 2 crewmen were missing.

U.S. planes Mar. 12 carried out their first daylight raids against the Hanoi region since Jan. 29. 4 radar stations were struck around the capital, and a missile installation near the Kep airfield (35 miles northeast of Hanoi) came under attack. In raids around Haiphong during the day, American pilots claimed to have knocked out 5 missile sites and 6 antiaircaft installations. The North Vietnamese claimed Mar. 13 that 28 persons had been killed and 56 wounded Mar. 12 in a U.S. aerial attack on the market town of Donthu, 20 miles south of Hanoi. U.S. planes Mar. 13 flew 94 missions, attacking 2 bridges and airfields in the Haiphong area and Hanoi's port facilities. Other targets attacked there and in other parts of North Vietnam included railroad yards, storage areas and army barracks. Similar targets were pounded in the Hanoi-Haiphong area again Mar. 14 during an 86-mission raid. Troops and artillery concentrations just north of the DMZ and an airfield at Donghoi also were struck. The U. S. command reported Mar. 15 that since Jan. 1, 1961 2,007 U.S. planes and 1,480 helicopters had been lost to Communist fire, accidents and other causes. Of this number, 809 combat planes had been downed over North Vietnam and 238 had been shot down in South Vietnam.

Saigon Threatens to Invade North

The South Vietnamese government said Mar. 13 that it was making plans to invade North Vietnam with a Vietnamese volunteer guerrilla unit led by retired generals. The announcement, made by Information Director Gen. Nguyen Ngoc Linh, said that the new group would be called the North Vietnam Liberation

Army and that its military leaders would be drawn from the anti-Communist Hoa Hao and Cao Dai religious sects. Although the unit would not be part of the South Vietnamese army, the Saigon government would supply it with arms and ammunition, Linh said. The volunteers, Linh said, would be chosen from Vietnamese who were "sick and tired of those people who want to 'liberate' South Vietnam."

Vice Pres. Nguyen Cao Ky Mar. 14 expressed support for the proposed invasion army and he said would join the guerrilla force. Speaking to a group of Vietnamese Roman Catholics near Saigon, Ky pledged arms to any anti-Communist who could fire them. "If necessary, I will be first, I will sacrifice myself," he said.

The U.S. State Department cautioned the South Vietnamese government Mar. 14 against invading the North. The statement reminded Ky of this statement in the Oct. 1966 Manila Conference communiqué (subscribed to by Ky, then premier): "The South Vietnamese people have no desire to threaten or harm the people of the North, or invade the country." The department insisted that American policy "remains as expressed in this communiqué and specifically with this quotation."

The South Vietnamese army newspaper *Tien Tuyen* Mar. 1 had called editorially for an invasion of North Vietnam as "the best solution to safeguard peace." The editorial said; "We suffer from devastation and deaths caused by the war, but we would suffer more if such a plight were forced upon us indefinitely." To "drain this abcess," the newspaper urged "landing in North Vietnam, bombing the Red River embankments, and if necessary attacking up to the border of Communist China."

It was reported in Saigon Mar. 15 that the government had distributed firearms to more than 5,000 civilians, mostly civil servants. The guns were given out as part of the "People Under Arms" program, which had been announced in the wake of the Communists' Tet offensive. As of Mar. 5, 22,000 civilians, including the 5,000 under arms, were reported to have been organized into defense groups to give South Vietnam greater security.

U.S. Reinforcements Move North

It was reported Mar. 30 that a Communist build-up of 50,000 troops in Quangtri and Thuathien—South Vietnam's 2 northernmost provinces—had prompted the U.S. to send more troops into the area and to 2 adjacent provinces. The dispatch of 30,000 more U.S. soldiers to the I Corps area since early January had raised the total U.S. force there to 170,000 men. According to American intelligence sources, the Communists were in a position to launch an onslaught against Khesanh or any other American installation just below the DMZ in division force 72 hours after deciding to attack.

U.S. Defense Department officials reported Apr. 1 that 15,000 to 20,000 of the original North Vietnamese force that had surrounded Khesanh had withdrawn. One unit, identified as the 325C Division, was believed to have moved into Laos, while elements of a 2d North Vietnamese division also were said to have left. It was estimated that the North Vietnamese pullback would reduce the number of Communist forces surrounding Khesanh within 10 miles to fewer than 10,000 men.

A U.S. military spokesman in Saigon, Brig. Gen. Winant Sidle, had said Mar. 21 that "there has been no significant movement of North Vietnamese troops either way [in the Khesanh area]—pulling out or reinforcing."

Saigon Sweep & Other Fighting

U.S. and South Vietnamese troops Mar. 25 killed 284 Viet Cong near Trangbang, 28 miles northwest of Saigon. The battle was the fiercest of Operation Quyet Thang, launched by allied forces to eliminate a threat by several thousand Viet Cong troops believed positioned in the 5 provinces around Saigon.

The Communists suffered additional losses in further fighting around Trangbang Mar. 27, and the estimate of their fatalities since the start of Quyet Thang rose to 1,842. U.S. combat deaths in the same period were listed at 69, South Vietnamese fatalities at 92. The Allied failure to make contact with the Communists' main force in the area was due to the withdrawal of 13,000 Viet Cong to base camps near the Cambodian border, according to a report by a U.S. officer Mar. 20. The Trangbang fighting had started when Viet Cong forces launched 2 coordinated attacks against government outposts 6 miles west and 5 miles east of the town. U.S. 25th Infantry Division and South Vietnamese troops, assisted by air strikes, rushed to the aid of the beleaguered garrisons and fought the Communists throughout the day. American casualties totaled 10 killed and 71 wounded.

In an engagement 4 miles northeast of Trangbang Mar. 27, a force of about 350 25th Infantry Division troops was fired on by entrenched Viet Cong. Strikes by U.S. artillery and helicopter gunships were said to have accounted for most of the 99 Viet Cong listed as killed in the ensuing action. U.S. casualties were 2 killed and 38 wounded.

South Vietnamese troops Mar. 19 had uncovered a cache of Viet Cong arms and ammunition on the banks of the Saigon River within firing range of the Tansonnhut Air Base. Described by an American officer as "the most significant find around Saigon in a long time," the weapons included 80 122-mm. rockets and 1,200 mortar rounds and recoilless rifles.

U.S. and South Vietnamese troops killed 142 Communist troops 15 miles west of Saigon Mar. 20. Tansonnhut came under Communist shelling Mar. 21 for the first time in 3 weeks. Damage was reported light.

Operation Quyet Thang was reported ended Apr. 5. Since the offensive had started Mar. 11, 2,658 North Vietnamese and Viet Cong were reported killed. American losses were 105 killed and 920 wounded. South Vietnamese casualties: 200 killed and 496 wounded. 63 South Vietnamese civilians were reported Apr. 5 to have been accidentally killed or wounded during 2 separate Quyet Thang operations: 10 civilians were killed and 40 wounded when a 500-pound bomb and a napalm bomb were dropped during a raid near Xuanloc, 39 miles east-northeast of Saigon; and when 2 U.S. Army helicopters attacked sampans on a canal 4 miles south of the capital, 6 civilians were killed and 7 wounded.

Fighting continued around the U.S. Marine base at Khesanh, and clashes took place in the Mekong delta and in the Central Highlands.

A Central Highlands struggle Mar. 26 was marked by a heavy North Vietnamese assault on an American artillery base 19 miles west of Kontum. Armed with flame-throwers, grenades and machineguns, a North Vietnamese force, identified as the 209th Regiment, smashed through the outpost's barbed wire perimeter under cover of darkness, but withdrew shortly after dawn as it was pounded by air strikes and ground counterattacks by nearly 700 troops, more than $1/_2$ of whom were reinforcements. 135 North Vietnamese and 19 Americans were reported killed.

The fighting around Khesanh during the period Mar. 18-25 was marked by intense Communist shelling of the American strongpoint and equally intense air strikes against North Vietnamese surrounding the base. *Among those developments and other actions just south Khesanh:*

• A 4th Marine Regiment company on patrol near Dongha (8 miles south of the DMZ) Mar. 18 came under attack by entrenched Communist troops. In the ensuing 5-hour clash, 67 Communists were reported slain, many by artillery, helicopter gunships and tactical fighters. Most of the Marines' 12 fatalities were suffered in the initial burst of Communist fire.

• B-52s bombed North Vietnamese troops around Khesanh Mar. 19 and 20. The base was shelled heavily Mar. 22-23 (more than 160 rounds were fired each day), but casualties among the defenders were reported to be light. A U.S. retaliatory strike for the Mar. 23 shelling was carried out by 6 waves of B-52s and nearly 400 fighterbombers and tons of artillery shells.

• 31 North Vietnamese were reported killed Mar. 25 in a clash with South Vietnamese rangers 2 miles northwest of Khesanh. A Marine helicopter was shot down, but the crew was rescued.

• In the biggest battle since Khesanh came under siege in January, U.S. troops Mar. 30 killed an estimated 115 North Vietnamese soldiers in their trenches and bunkers a mile from the stronghold. A reinforced company of 200 to 250 men pushed out from Khesanh and quickly came under attack by an estimated 500 Communist troops. Following a supportive artillery barrage and an exchange of fire with the Communist force, the Americans withdrew to the Khesanh base. 9 Americans were reported killed and 71 wounded in the engagement.

In the Mekong delta, U.S. helicopters Mar. 24 bombed Viet Cong sampans near the Cambodian border; 164 boats were reported destroyed or damaged. The boats were carrying rice and other food. The attacks followed reports of increased Communist arms shipments to the delta. A Viet Cong force clashed with South Vietnamese troops in the delta's Baxuyen Province Mar. 26. The South Vietnamese, supported by American artillery and helicopter gunships, killed 98 Communist troops. Their own losses totaled 5 killed.

Bombing of North

U.S. jets bombed the Hanoi-Haiphong areas Mar. 31 in raids carried out the day before a partial bombing halt ordered by Pres. Johnson went into effect. Navy jets hit the Catbi airfield (4 miles southeast of Haiphong) and Hanoi's radio-communications station (10 miles southeast of the capital). Other targets struck included a chemical plant 19 miles northeast of Haiphong, the Langgiai railroad yard, 18 miles from the Chinese border, and other rail targets further south. *Among other developments in the bombing of the North:*

• 2 U.S. Air Force F-111 fighterbombers were lost during missions over North Vietnam Mar. 28 and 30, only a week after the new planes were first committed to combat. The first F-111 was reported missing following attacks with other F-111s on truck parks in the vicinity of Donghoi, in North Vietnam's southern panhandle. Hanoi radio said the plane had been downed by ground fire in Hatinh Province, adjacent to the Laotian border, 100 miles north of the DMZ. The 2d F-111, according to a U.S. report, crashed in Thailand Mar. 30 "after an inflight emergency" and was "not downed due to enemy action." 6 F-111s had arrived at Thailand's Ta Khli airbase (north of Bangkok) Mar. 17 and had gone into combat for the first time Mar. 22. (The F-111 had been the subject of sharp interservice controversy, as the TFX project, under ex-Defense Secy. Robert S. McNamara.)

• U.S. planes Mar. 20 carried out 119 attacks in the heaviest raid in more than a month. A 125-truck convoy on Route 15A, north of the Mugia Pass near the Laotian border, was pounded, and 65 vehicles were knocked out. Another convoy between Vinh and Donghoi, believed to be carrying supplies for North Vietnamese troops around Khesanh, was struck and 55 vehicles were badly damaged. Other planes bombed the Hongay power plant, 27 miles east of Haiphong, and sank 20 supply barges near Thanhhoa.

• The Baithuong, Kienan and Vinh airfields were struck during a 119-mission raid Mar. 21. The main runway at the Baithuong base, 22 miles northwest of Thanhhoa, was reported cut. Other planes knocked out 25 trucks and an armored car south of Vinh.

• During an 80-mission raid Mar. 22, U.S. Navy pilots for the first time bombed the Haiguong chemical plant, between Hanoi and Haiphong. Other targets struck that day included the Baithuong airfield, the Uongbi power plant, 15 miles north of Haiphong, and several supply trucks in the southern part of the country. Other U.S. planes bombed rail lines linking Hanoi with Communist China. The Langdang rail yard, 18 miles from the Chinese border, was struck, as were the Dongcuong siding and the Somtra yard on the rail line to the northwest.

• The Catbi airfield, 3 miles southeast of Haiphong, was bombed by U.S. planes Mar. 23 during a 93-mission raid. Also struck were the Hadong military barracks, 8 miles southwest of Hanoi, and the Baithuong airfield.

• The Hanoi area was bombed in 2 separate raids Mar. 24. The 2d attack, the heavier, was concentrated on the Red River area on the southeast edge of the city.

● The Langgiai rail yard, 18 miles from the Chinese border, was pounded by U.S. Air Force jets Mar. 27. The yard, 70 miles northeast of Hanoi, was on the main northeast railroad supply route from China.

POW Exchanges

The U.S. Mar. 29 released 3 North Vietnamese soldiers who had been captured during naval action in the Gulf of Tonkin in July 1966. The release of the men had been arranged in a series of talks that had started the previous week between U.S. and North Vietnamese officials in the U.S. embassy in Vientiane, Laos. The talks had been held below the ambassadorial level.

The U.S. government said the North Vietnamese sailors had been set free in response to North Vietnam's release Feb. 16 of 3 U.S. pilots who had been captured in the fall of 1967 after they had been shot down in raids over North Vietnam. The released airmen, the first American captives freed by North Vietnam, were Maj. Norris Overly, 38, of Detroit, Capt. Jon D. Black, 30, of Johnson City, Tenn. and Lt. David P. Matheny, 23, of South Bend, Ind. Overly had been downed Sept. 11, Black Oct. 27 and Matheny Oct. 5.

The Americans had been handed over in Hanoi to the Rev. Daniel J. Berrigan and Howard Zinn, representatives of a U.S. peace group—the American Mobilization Committee against the Vietnam War. All 5 flew to Vientiane, Laos in an International Control Commission plane. From there the 3 airmen were flown to the U.S. airbase at Udon, Thailand and returned to the U.S. Feb. 17.

North Vietnam had announced Jan. 27 that it would free the American captives as a humanitarian gesture in honor of Tet, the lunar new year. Hanoi Jan. 28 had told David Dellinger, head of the Mobilization Committee, to send a representative to the North Vietnamese capital to receive the U.S. airmen.

(On arriving in New York Feb. 18, Berrigan and Zinn charged that the U.S. had jeopardized future prisoner releases by the North Vietnamese when U.S. Amb.-to-Laos William H. Sullivan had insisted in Vientiane that the freed Americans be flown from Laos to the U.S. in an American military plane instead of a commercial airliner, as requested by Hanoi under the release agreement. Sullivan was quoted as having said that the order for the use of a military plane had come from the White House.)

The release of 2 American women captured by the Viet Cong during the Tet offensive was reported by a U.S. spokesman Apr. 1. The women were Sandra Johnson, a teacher of the International Volunteer Services, and Dr. Marjorie Nelson who was visiting Mrs. Johnson.

Khesanh Relieved

A 30,000-man U.S. and South Vietnamese force Apr. 1 launched a drive (Operation Pegasus) to relieve the U.S. Marine base at Khesanh, surrounded by North Vietnamese troops since January. By Apr. 5 the siege was officially declared lifted. Most of the troops of Operation Pegasus were supplied by the First Cavalry Division (Airmobile), whose commander, Maj. Gen. John J. Tolson, was in command of the operation.

The relief column, making its way from Calu (15 miles to the east), moved along Route 9, the only overland supply road to the base, and encountered little enemy resistance in reaching the stronghold. More than half of the original 20,000-man North Vietnamese force surrounding Khesanh was believed to have withdrawn into neighboring Laos before the allied drive had started. Nearly 1,000 U.S. relief troops were flown into Khesanh by U.S. Army helicopters Apr. 6 as advance elements of an infantry column moved within 500 yards of the base's defense perimeter. The main relief column arrived at Khesanh Apr. 8.

As the allied force advanced toward Khesanh, armed helicopters carried out attacks against North Vietnamese in forward positions. 20 Communist troops were killed in one such raid 2 miles from Khesanh Apr. 4, and 53 were slain in a similar bombing mission 3¹/₂ miles south of the outpost Apr. 5. Only scattered ground clashes occurred during the allied march from Catu to Khesanh. 40 to 50 North Vietnamese were killed in one clash Apr. 6. American casualties were light. Route 9 came under constant North Vietnamese shelling during the allied advance. 6 Americans were killed and 14 wounded when the North Vietnamese fired 25 shells Apr. 3 at a landing zone 10 miles east of Khesanh that was used as a base for Operation Pegasus.

Pres. Johnson Apr. 7 sent a congratulatory message to U.S. troops in Vietnam on the occasion of the lifting of the siege of

Khesanh. The statement, published by the White House Apr. 8, "expressed the pride and confidence I feel in those who are carrying forward the nation's struggle against aggression in Southeast Asia." Johnson praised the troops for having "taken the full initial weight of the enemy's winter-spring offensive" and for preventing the capture of the Khesanh base. Despite these successes, the President warned, "the fighting in South Vietnam is not yet at an end. The enemy may throw new forces in the battle." But "the time of peace" had been brought nearer, the President said, "by your gallant and skillful support for the brave people and armed forces of South Vietnam." The President added: "As we seek now to find through negotiations an honorable peace in Vietnam, I wish you to know that we are grateful for what you have already accomplished and will be counting on you more than ever, until the blessed day when the guns fall silent."

With the siege of Khesanh lifted, South Vietnamese paratroops Apr. 8 launched a drive to recapture the Langvei Special Forces Camp ($3^1/_2$ miles southwest of Khesanh), which had been overrun by the North Vietnamese Feb. 7. In their first encounter with the Communist force in the area, the South Vietnamese killed 80. Government losses in the 4-hour battle were put at 11 killed and 12 wounded.

Westmoreland Replaced

Gen. Westmoreland was relieved as commander of U.S. forces in South Vietnam after the Tet offensive had ended. Pres. Johnson announced at a news conference Mar. 22 the appointment of Westmoreland as Army chief of staff. Johnson said the Westmoreland appointment had been recommended by ex-Defense Secy. Robert S. McNamara and current Defense Secy. Clark Clifford. The President praised Westmoreland as a "very talented and very able officer." In reply to a question as to whether the move implied "any change of search-and-destroy strategy with which his name has been associated or any other tactical adjustment in Vietnam," Johnson said "the strategy and the tactical operations have nothing to do with the appoinments as such."

(Westmoreland said in a U.S. government report published Apr. 6, 1969 that on ending his tour of duty in Vietnam, "I took with me the conviction that the enemy not only failed to attain [his] objectives, but in each case they lay farther from his grasp than at any time since the dark days of 1965, when the United States intervened in strength.")

Westmoreland conferred with Johnson at the White House Apr. 6-7 in the first of a series of meetings. The general briefed the president on the war, and the 2 men discussed American moves to promote peace talks with North Vietnam. White House Press Secy. George Christian said Apr. 6 that at their meeting that day, Johnson and Westmoreland had discussed: the appointment of a new commander to replace Westmoreland when he vacated his Vietnam post July 2, the President's decision (announced Mar. 31) to restrict the bombing of North Vietnam and Hanoi's reaction to it.

After his 2d day of talks, Westmoreland said at a news conference Apr. 7: He had informed the President that "militarily, we have never been in a better relative position in South Vietnam." "The spirit of the offensive is now prevalent throughout Vietnam with advantage being taken of the enemy's weakened military position." "Despite the initial psychological impact of the enemy's Tet offensive, the enemy failed to achieve a public uprising by the people of South Vietnam, to bring about the defeat of the Vietnamese armed forces, or to achieve his military objectives."

Westmoreland praised South Vietnam for having increased its armed forces by 135,000 men and said that "in general," South Vietnamese troops in recent months had "fought bravely and well."

BATTLE FOR 'NEGOTIATIONS'

U.S. Peace Counteroffensive

In the days immediately before the opening of the Tet offensive, the U.S. answered the diplomatic initiatives with which Hanoi had begun the year. Washington was reported Jan. 29 to have informed Hanoi through private diplomatic channels during the previous 2 weeks that it would be willing to halt the bombing of North Vietnam and enter into peace negotiations if North Vietnam would "not take advantage" of the raid suspension and would hold the infiltration of men and supplies into South Vietnam to "normal" levels. The U.S. State Department insisted that the Administration's latest reported position did not represent a relaxation of American conditions for peace talks, that it was consistent with Pres. Johnson's Sept. 29, 1967 San Antonio formula for ending the war.

The North Vietnamese Communist Party newspaper *Nhan Dan* Feb. 5 reiterated Hanoi's rejection of American demands for reciprocity in an exchange for a halt in the bombing of the North. The Communist Party journal said that Johnson, at his news conference Feb. 2, had shown that the U.S. was not interested in peace. *Nhan Dan* referred to the President's assertion that in probing Hanoi's intentions he had not "found anything that would give an impartial judge reason to be encouraged."

Agence France-Presse quoted North Vietnamese political sources Feb. 5 as saying that "despite Pres. Johnson's negative attitude toward the signs we have made him, the door remains open for the talks and the path to them is well marked."

It was reported in Washington Feb. 6 that the current round of American peace soundings dated back to Aug. 25, 1967, when the U.S. sent to Hanoi what was described as the first substantive message on peace prospects. It was also reported that this contact was subsequently followed by brief, periodic suspensions of the bombing of targets in the Hanoi and Haiphong areas in an effort to facilitate the diplomatic maneuvers.

The U.S. State Department Feb. 6 made public remarks delivered by State Secy. Dean Rusk Feb. 2 before college newspaper editors relating to the possibility of a renewal of Hanoi peace feelers if the current Viet Cong offensive against South Vietnamese cities was blunted. Rusk said: "There are indications that the Viet Cong and the North Vietnamese forces are making an effort at the moment which they cannot sustain over any protracted period of time, and what they will do when this effort is thrown back, we don't know yet. But I think we are seeing a lunge, rather than a sustained new phase of war." The U.S. could not halt the bombing of the North while the Communists "go ahead with these massive offensives of theirs across the demilitarized zone and through Laos."

North Vietnamese Foreign Min. Nguyen Duy Trinh Feb. 8 restated Hanoi's assertion that it was ready to start talks "as soon as the United States has proved that it has really stopped unconditionally the bombings and all other acts of war" against North Vietnam. When an Agence France-Presse interviewer asked

what he meant by his Dec. 29, 1967 statement that "relevant problems" could be discussed at negotiations, Trinh replied: "questions
related to a settlement of the Vietnam problem on the basis of
the 1954 Geneva agreements on Vietnam" and "other questions
which could be raised by either side." Trinh was asked what Hanoi
meant when it said that negotiations could begin "after an appropriate time following" an end to the bombing and "other acts of
war" against North Vietnam. "The talks will begin as soon as the
United States has proved it has really stopped unconditionally the
bombings and all other acts of war," Trinh answered.

Trinh charged that U.S. government claims that it was
probing Hanoi's intentions for peace was "a maneuver to soothe
public opinion and cover up its attempts for continued escalation
of the aggressive war in South Vietnam." Trinh said the Viet
Cong's then current offensive against South Vietnam's major
cities had dealt a serious blow to the South Vietnamese government: "The administrative apparatus of the puppet regime is col-
lapsing, and the puppet army is disintegrating by big chunks."

U.S. government officials confirmed Feb. 12 that Pres. Johnson
had sent a foreign envoy to Hanoi in January to determine North
Vietnam's conditions for starting negotiations but that the emissary
had left without receiving an acceptable response. Administration
sources refused to identify the envoy's name or his nationality.
Government officials confirmed the mission after it had been disclosed earlier Feb. 12 by Rep. Roman C. Pucinski (D., Ill.).
Pucinski said the U.S. had "actually suspended bombing of Hanoi
in order to give this emissary of ours a chance to get in without
any hazard." Pucinski said "the emissary's mission was to explain"
Johnson's San Antonio formula "and to make clear that we needed
some assurances that Hanoi would not pour 6 or 8 or 10 divisions
into South Vietnam during the pause in bombing."

Rep. Hugh L. Carey (D., N.Y.) said Feb. 13 that the mission
to Hanoi had first been disclosed by State Secy. Rusk at a closed
briefing with more than 100 Congressmen Feb. 7. Carey quoted
Rusk as having said that the envoy was in the North Vietnamese
capital "in possession of our stipulated and conciliatory conditions for negotiation at the very time that Hanoi had initiated
their escalation offensive in the South." Carey said that when he
asked Rusk "why we did not 'tell this to the world so our friends
and foes may know where the fault lies' in the failure to achieve
negotiations in good faith," Rusk had replied: "We would do

nothing that might impair any possible chance of negotiations even after the latest rebuff by Hanoi."

UN diplomats had reported Feb. 7 that U.S. Amb.-to-Poland John Gronouski had conferred Jan. 26 with a North Vietnamese envoy in Warsaw, but U.S. Administration sources said they knew of no such meeting.

Rusk said Feb. 14 that "all explorations to date have resulted" in North Vietnam's rejection of the U.S.' proposals for starting negotiations to end the war in Vietnam. In a prepared statement released by the State Department, Rusk said all American proposals to end the war "continue to be valid," particularly the "San Antonio formula" outlined by Pres. Johnson in Sept. 1967. But, Rusk charged, American efforts for peace had been answered by North Vietnam with intensified military attacks. "Repeated periods of bombing cessation or reduction in North Vietnam" and ceasefires in the ground fighting in South Vietnam, Rusk said, had been used by the Communists to build up their forces and to launch the Tet military drive. Although North Vietnam was aware of intensified U.S. peace explorations, which were accompained by a reduction in the bombing of the Hanoi and Haiphong areas, Rusk declared, the Communists' "reply was a major offensive through South Vietnam to bring the war to the civilian population in most of the cities." North Vietnam's lack of interest in peace, Rusk charged, was further evidenced by its refusal to recognize the territorial integrity and neutrality of Cambodia, by its "illegal infiltration through Laos into South Vietnam" and by its "contempt" for "the demilitarized character of the DMZ between North and South Vietnam." Rusk added: "We are not interested in propaganda gestures whose purpose is to mislead and confuse; we will be interested in a serious move toward peace when Hanoi comes to the conclusion that it is ready to move in that direction."

Pres. Johnson told newsmen Feb. 16 that he did not think North Vietnam was more ready to negotiate currently than it had been one, 2 or 3 years ago—and "I don't think it has been [more ready] at any time during any of that period." He said recent Administration probes and offers for negotiations had gone "as far as honorable men could go" and had been answered by the enemy attack on innocent civilians during a sacred holiday. Johnson made the comments during an impromptu news conference. (In a wreath-laying ceremony at the Lincoln Memorial Feb. 12, Johnson had compared the Civil War ordeal with the American ordeal in Vietnam. He said: Abraham Lincoln "heard the charges that the war was long and wrong; he saw Americans die . . . ; he saw dissent, riot and rebellion"; yet Lincoln "was sad but steady—always convinced of his cause—. . . stuck it out," and "sad but steady so will we"; "most Americans repudiate moral isolationism"; "we are sometimes forced by an adversary to back our belief with steel, just as Lincoln did, and we must stick it out, as Lincoln did.")

International Pressure on U.S.

The prospect of peace in Vietnam was the major topic of discussion in a tour of Asia and Europe made by UN Secy. Gen. U Thant in February. He visited India Feb. 7-9 and conferred in New Delhi Feb. 8 with Nguyen Hoa, the North Vietnamese consul general. Thant met with Soviet officials in Moscow Feb. 11-12. Prior to Thant's arrival Feb. 11, Soviet Pres. Nikolai V. Podgorny had conferred with Dang Quang Minh, chief representative in Moscow of the National Liberation Front, and Podgorny renewed the USSR's pledge to continue to provide the South Vietnamese "patriots" with "brotherly aid."

Thant conferred in London Feb. 13 with Prime Min. Harold Wilson, Foreign Secy. George Brown and other British officials. Thant reportedly expressed the belief that if the U.S. unconditionally halted the bombing of North Vietnam for about 2 weeks, Hanoi would start meaningful peace talks. In a visit to Paris Feb. 14, Thant held separate talks with French Pres. Charles de Gaulle and Mai Van Bo, Hanoi's chief representative in Europe. French officials expressed the view that peace prospects were less favorable than they had been at the beginning of 1967. They cited the escalation by both sides and the U.S. decision to resume the bombing of Hanoi and Haiphong and to dispatch 10,500 more troops to Vietnam in response to the Viet Cong offensive.

Thant discussed his diplomatic findings with U.S. Amb. Arthur J. Goldberg on returning to New York Feb. 15.

During these weeks, the Italian government also tried to act as a go-between. An Italian Foreign Ministry communiqué said Feb. 14 that "2 qualified representatives" of North Vietnam had met with Italian Foreign Min. Amintore Fanfani in Rome Feb. 4-6 on the request of the Hanoi representatives. The communiqué said the results of the talks had been communicated to Washington. U Thant predicted Feb. 24 that if the U.S. stopped bombing North Vietnam, "meaningful talks" to end the Vietnamese war "will take place much earlier than is generally supposed, even perhaps within a matter of a few days."

Thant made his prediction in a written report based on his tour. Thant said that in his meeting in New Delhi with Nguyen Hoa, the Hanoi representative had "affirmed that his government 'would hold talks with Washington on all relevant matters at an appropriate time after the unconditional cessation of bombing and all other acts of war' " against North Vietnam. Thant said he had received "a further clarification of Hanoi's position concerning discussions with Washington" from Mai Van Bo. Thant said Bo had transmitted the North Vietnamese message to him in Paris Feb. 14 in response to a query he had submitted Feb. 8 while in New Delhi. Thant reported that the reply, dated Feb. 13, said: North Vietnam "would hold talks with the United States at the appropriate time, that is, as soon as the unconditional cessation of the bombing and of all other acts of war against the Democratic Republic of Vietnam became effective."

Thant said: He "was further informed that, at the talks, the United States could bring up any matters for discussions in the same way as the Democratic Republic of Vietnam could bring up any other." Bo, in response to Thant's inquiry, "stated that the question of the reduction in the fighting in South Vietnam, the question of the reconvening of the Geneva Conference and any other question could be brought up at the talks."

Thant, who had discussed his mission with Pres. Johnson and State Secy. Rusk in Washington Feb. 21, said the President had "reaffirmed his continued desire to achieve a peaceful settlement and the continued validity of the San Antonio formula. Both the President and the Secretary of State stressed the no-military-advantage provision of that formula."

Thant said his meetings with world leaders on his tour "reinforced my conviction" that the question of Vietnam was "essentially a political problem which cannot be solved through the application of military force. . . . If the Vietnam question is seen as a contest of unyielding will, there can be no solution."

Thant chided the U.S. and the Soviet Union for attempts "to prevent the defeat of the side which each supports. If such a trend continues, . . . there will be continued intensification and escalation of the conflict. . . ."

Thant said that if the U.S. unconditionally halted the bombing of the North, "it can reasonably be assumed" that discussions on ending the ground fighting in the South "will be dealt with in good faith." The South Vietnamese government and the National Liberation Front should participate in all discussions, Thant declared.

In response to Thant's report, the Johnson Administration said in a statement issued through the American mission at the UN Feb. 24 that the U.S. "would welcome confirmation from Hanoi that talks would start promptly in circumstances where we could reasonably assume that North Vietnam would not take military advantage of the bombing cessation."

A French government statement Feb. 28 said Paris had "specific information" supporting Thant's contention that a halt in American bombing of North Vietnam was a "necessary and sufficient" condition for starting negotiations. The declaration was issued by Information Min. Georges Gorse after a cabinet meeting and reportedly was authorized by Pres. de Gaulle.

Johnson Limits Bombing, Quits Election Race

Pres. Johnson announced in a surprise TV speech Mar. 31 that he would not seek nor accept nomination for another term as President and that he had ordered—"unilaterally"—a halt to air and naval bombardment of North Vietnam "except in the area north of the demilitarized zone where the continuing enemy build-up directly threatens allied forward positions and where the movement of their troops and supplies are clearly related to that threat."

"The area in which we are stopping our attacks includes almost 90% of North Vietnam's population and most of its territory," Johnson said. "Thus, there will be no attacks around the principal populated areas, or in the food-producing areas of North Vietnam." He asserted that "even this very limited bombing of the North could come to an early end—if our restraint is matched by restraint in Hanoi." The President called on North Vietnamese Pres. Ho Chi Minh "to respond positively and favorably to this new step toward peace."

(This U.S. policy action was discussed in the "Pentagon papers" published by the *N.Y. Times* in 1971. According to this

secret account of discussions in Washington, as reported in the
Times July 4, 1971, "a fork in the road had been reached" following the 1968 Tet offensive. There was a bitter policy debate
over the demands of the Joint Chiefs of Staff and Gen. William
C. Westmoreland for a national mobilization to achieve victory
in Vietnam. The military pressed for a "full-scale call-up of reserves" and for "putting the country economically on a semiwar
footing," but the service chiefs were overruled. Before Tet, the
Pentagon papers indicated, Johnson had tended to discount "negative analyses" of U.S. strategy in the war offered by top civilian
advisers in 1967. The study said he had embraced "optimistic
reports" such as a year-end assessment offered by Westmoreland
Jan. 27, 1968, just 4 days before the first Tet attack. Westmoreland had said: "The year ended with the enemy increasingly re-
sorting to desperation tactics in attempting to achieve military/
psychological victory; and he has experienced only failure in these
attempts." After Tet, Westmoreland was relieved of his command,
the military received only about 10% of the additional troops they
had requested for Vietnam, and Johnson made his Mar. 31 announcement of the limited bombing halt and of his decision not
to seek reelection.)

Johnson's 40-minute address Mar. 31 was devoted almost
entirely to the war in Vietnam. In the speech he announced that
he was sending 13,500 more U.S. troops to Vietnam. Some would
be members of Reserve units he was ordering to duty. Further
defense expenditures—2^1/_2$ billion in fiscal 1968 and $2.6 billion
in fiscal 1969—were also requested by the President to meet the
costs of the troop build-ups and military supplies since the beginning of the year and the cost of re-equipping the South Vietnamese forces and of meeting "our responsibilities in Korea."

Before announcing his withdrawal from the Presidential race,
Johnson called for unity within the nation and stated his conviction "that I should not permit the Presidency to become involved in the partisan divisions that are developing in this political
year." Throughout his 37 years of public service, Johnson said,
"I have followed the personal philosophy that I am a free man, an
American, a public servant—always and only. . . . I have put the
unity of the people first. I have put it ahead of any divisive partisanship. And in these times, as in times before, it is true that a
house divided against itself . . . is a house that cannot stand. There
is division in the American house now. There is divisiveness among

us all tonight. . . . I cannot disregard the peril of the progress of the American people and the hope and the prospect of peace for all peoples, so I would ask all Americans whatever their personal interest or concern to guard against divisiveness and all of its ugly consequences. . . . What we won when all of our people united just must not now be lost in suspicion and distrust and selfishness and politics among any of our people."

"With American sons in the fields far away," the President said, with America's future under challenge right here at home, with our hopes and the world's hopes for peace in the balance every day, I do not believe that I should devote an hour or a day of my time to any personal partisan causes or to any duties other than the awesome duties of this office—the Presidency of your country. . . . But let men everywhere know, however, that a strong and a confident and a vigilant America stands ready tonight to seek an honorable peace; and stands ready tonight to defend an honored cause, whatever the price, whatever the burden, whatever the sacrifice that duty may require."

(Political commentators pointed out that Johnson had apparently made his decisions under the heavy pressure of widespread domestic attacks on his Vietnam policy and growing opposition within his own party to his renomination. Sen. Eugene J. McCarthy [Minn.], a leading Democratic foe of the Johnson Administration's Vietnam policy, had received a surprisingly big vote in the New Hampshire Democratic Presidential primary Mar. 12 in a campaign stressing opposition to Johnson on the Vietnam issue. And an even presumably stronger contender for the nomination, Sen. Robert F. Kennedy [N.Y.], perhaps the most potent Democratic opponent of the President's Vietnam policy at that time, had announced his candidacy Mar. 16.

(The Pentagon analysts who prepared the "Pentagon papers" also noted that "large and growing elements" of the U.S. public were dissatisfied with the Vietnam situation. The study gave this summary of what the analysts believed had led Johnson to his Mar. 31 announcement: "The political reality which faced Pres. Johnson was that 'more of the same' in South Vietnam, with an increased commitment of American lives and money and its consequent impact on the country, accompanied by no guarantee of military victory in the near future, had become unacceptable to these elements of the American public. The optimistic military reports of progress in the war no longer rang true after the shock of the Tet offensive. Thus, the President's decision to seek a new strategy and a new road to peace was based upon 2 major considerations: (1) The conviction of his principal civilian advisers, particularly Secretary of Defense [Clark] Clifford, that the troops requested by Gen. Westmoreland would not make a military victory any more likely; and (2) a deeply felt conviction of the need to restore unity to the American nation.")

In his Mar. 31 address, Johnson preceded his announcement of bombing restrictions with a new call for Hanoi to enter into peace talks. "We are prepared to move immediately toward peace through negotiations," he said. "So tonight, in the hope that this action will lead to early talks, I am taking the first step to de-escalate the conflict." "Our purpose in this action," said, "is to bring about a reduction in the level of violence that now exists. ... It is to permit the contending forces to move closer to a political settlement." He reaffirmed his pledge "to withdraw our forces from South Vietnam as the other side withdraws its forces to the North, stops the infiltration, and the level of violence thus subsides."

The President appealed to the Soviet Union and Britain, as co-chairmen of the Geneva conferences and as permanent members of the UN Security Council, "to do all they can to move" his proposal "toward genuine peace." He designated Amb.-at-Large W. Averell Harriman as his personal representative "to any forum, at any time, to discuss the means of bringing this ugly war to an end." Amb.-to-USSR Llewellyn Thompson was on call to join Harriman "at Geneva or any other suitable place just as soon as Hanoi agrees to a conference," Johnson said.

"It is our fervent hope that North Vietnam, after years of fighting that has left the issue unresolved, will now cease its efforts to achieve a military victory and will join with us in moving toward the peace table," Johnson declared. Hanoi "should be in no doubt of our intentions. It must not miscalculate the pressures within our democracy in this election year. . . . The United States will never accept a fake solution to this long and arduous struggle and call it peace."

The President said "the precise terms of an eventual settlement" could not be foretold, but a settlement could be based on "political conditions that permit the South Vietnamese—all the South Vietnamese—to chart their course free of any outside domination or interferences, from us or from anyone else."

Johnson said there was a need for further effort by the South Vietnamese, who must carry "the main burden of preserving their freedom" themselves. Although "substantial progress" had been made in the past 3 years, he said, the South Vietnamese must still expand their armed forces, "move back into the countryside as quickly as possible," increase taxes, "select the very best men they have for civil and military responsibility," "achieve a new unity within their constitutional government and . . . include in the national effort all those groups who wish to preserve South Vietnam's control over its own destiny." Johnson promised that the U.S. would "accelerate the re-equipment of South Vietnam's armed forces" and thus "enable them progressively to undertake a large share of combat operations against the Communist invaders."

(The Pentagon papers disclosed that before Johnson spoke, the State Department Mar. 31 had sent the U.S. ambassadors in Australia, New Zealand, Thailand, Laos, the Philippines and South Korea a cablegram revealing the contents of the forthcoming address. "You should make clear," the cablegram said, "that Hanoi is most likely to denounce the project [the bombing limitation] and thus free our hand after a short period. Nonetheless, we might wish to continue the limitation even after a formal denunciation, in order to reinforce its sincerity and put the monkey firmly on Hanoi's back for whatever follows. . . . With or without denunciation, Hanoi might well feel limited in conducting any major offenive at least in the northern areas. If they did so, this could ease the pressure where it is most potentially serious. If they did not, then this would give us a clear field for whatever actions were then required. . . . In view of weather limitations, bombing north of the 20th Parallel will in any event be limited at least for the next 4 weeks or so—which we tentatively envisage as a maximum testing period in any event. Hence, we are not giving up anything really serious in this time frame. Moreover, air power now used north of the 20th can probably be used in Laos . . . and in SVN [South Vietnam]. . . . Insofar as our announcement foreshadows any possibility of a complete bombing stoppage, in the event Hanoi really exercises reciprocal restraints, we regard this an unlikely. . . .")

Air Raids Bring Dispute on Bombing Curb

The bombing limitation announced by Pres. Johnson went

into effect Apr. 1. But U.S. air strikes carried out that day ranged as far as 205 miles north of the demilitarized zone (DMZ), where a radar site was struck near Thanhhoa, 81 miles south of Hanoi. As a result of these air strikes deep in North Vietnamese territory, Johnson was criticized in Congress and elsewhere for misleading the public in his announcement of bombing restraint.

Following the outcry, the Administration explained Apr. 2 that the bombing limitation meant that there would be no raids north of the 20th Parallel, which was 225 miles north of the DMZ.

After the Apr. 1 raid near Thanhhoa, a Defense Department official had insisted that the attack had not constituted a breach of the terms of the bombing limitation order. He said: "Any raids that have been conducted since the President's speech are obviously within the framework of the President's speech."

In reply to newsmen's questions as to whether the 20th Parallel and the target near Thanhhoa were intended to be included in the bombable "area north of the demilitarized zone," as defined in the President's speech, White House Press Secy. George Christian said Apr. 2 that "this was the intent" of the President's statement and order.

The Defense Deparment said in a more detailed explanation later Apr. 2: In accordance with Johnson's "purpose ... to take a unilateral step to reduce significantly the level of violence," attacks "have halted in the area of North Vietnam containing almost 90% of its population and 3/4 of its land. Attacks are continuing in the remaining southern quarter of North Vietnam ... , the area in which, in the President's words, 'the movement of their troops and supplies are clearly related' to the threat against allied forward positions. This area ... is the funnel through which enemy troops and supplies flow directly to the battlefront. ... Pursuant to the President's purpose, bombing since Sunday night has been directed primarily against targets in the southernmost areas of the panhandle. 90% of the sorties have been within 60 miles of of the DMZ while only 2.3% were against targets in the Thanhhoa area. Thanhhoa is a well authenticated transshipment point for military personnel and supplies moving south. . . . As the President said, 'Even this very limited bombing of the North could come to a early end if our restraint is matched by restraint in Hanoi.' ... "

The actions announced in Pres. Johnson's Mar. 31 speech had been praised in both chambers of Congress Apr. 1 before

criticism was resumed Apr. 2 when the limited nature of the bombing "halt" become clear.

A major critic of Administration policy in Vietnam, Chairman J. W. Fulbright (D., Ark.) of the Senate Foreign Relations
Committee, told newsmen Apr. 1 that Johnson's withdrawal from
the political race gave "great credence" to his offer to de-escalate
the war. It was "a very significant move that should be received
very seriously" by Hanoi, he said. Sen. John Sherman Cooper
(R., Ky.) agreed and said the President's action "supports the
sincerity of his purpose of bringing the war to an honorable close."
On the Senate floor Apr. 1, Sen. Albert Gore (D., Tenn.) praised
Johnson's "courage, generosity and patriotism" and said he had
"made a contribution toward unity of our country and a possible
peace." Senate Democratic leader Mike Mansfield (Mont.) said
"the President has indeed made a great sacrifice, and I hope there
will be no question raised in this country about the credibility of
Lyndon B. Johnson." Asst. Republican leader Thomas H. Kuchel
(Calif.) said that the President, by "his worthy act, has lent an
enormous credibility to his entreaties for peace."

The Congressional attack on Johnson's bombing policy was
spearheaded by Fulbright in a speech on the Senate floor Apr. 2.
Fulbright said it appeared that the President's bombing restriction
order "was not a significant change at all." "In other words," he
said, "we have done again what we have done before—refrained
from bombing Hanoi, Haiphong and the docks. . . . This is not
going to be a significant inducement to bring about a cease-fire
and a conference." Fulbright said he had been "mistaken" in
believing that Mr. Johnson "would in a significant way stop the
bombing in an effort to end the war." Fulbright, disclosing that
he had discussed the matter with an ambassador of a Communist
country, said he was certain there would have been a significant
response from North Vietnam if the bombings were restricted to
the DMZ area.

Mansfield said Apr. 2 that in discussion with Johnson Mar. 27,
the President had brought up "the cessation of bombing above the
20th Parallel and the need below the 20th Parallel to protect the
Marines and our troops stationed along the DMZ. . . ." Mansfield
acknowledged that "the inexact language" in the President's
speech on the bombing limitation "could give rise to questions."
Johnson "did not lie," he said. "Technically he is correct." Mansfield disclosed that the President wanted to make reference to the

20th Parallel in the text of his address but that he was persuaded "by his diplomatic colleagues . . . not to put that in because it would, in effect, furnish a signal over which a safe area could be created."

Sen. Richard B. Russell (D., Ga.) also disclosed Apr. 2 that the President had discussed the speech with him beforehand and that Russell had been apprised of a specific reference in the text to the fact "that there would be no more bombing above the 20th Parallel." "I do not know why it was taken out," he said.

Sen. Cooper said Apr. 2 that he had considered Johnson's statement to be "an order for an unconditional cessation of bombing, except in the area contiguous and adjacent to the demilitarized zone. I believe that must have been the impression in this country and throughout the world."

Hanoi Attacks U.S. Move but Agrees to Meet

Hanoi's initial reaction to the U.S.' move was to attack it as "fraudulent." The North Vietnamese army newspaper *Quan Doi Nhan Dan* asserted that the bombing limitation was an attempt to deceive world opinion, that the U.S. still failed to comply with North Vietnam's demand for a complete and unconditional bombing halt. The North Vietnamese Communist Party newspaper *Nhan Dan* charged that the U.S. was "planning a new plot to maintain its new colonialism and increasing its troops to reconstruct the South Vietnamese puppet regime and troops. The United States is attempting to increase the bombing of North Vietnam, and the so-called fraudulent proposal for peace talks is aimed at getting rid of isolation from the people of the world."

Despite the agreement to hold preliminary talks on negotiations, the bombardment of North Vietnam continued to be an issue. The North Vietnamese Communist Party newspaper *Nhan Dan* charged Apr. 5 that the U.S.' decision "to limit bombings is insufficient proof that the United States sincerely wants to put an end to the war and peacefully settle the Vietnamese problem on the basis of guaranteed independence, sovereignty and territorial integrity for Vietnam." Since Johnson's announcement of a limitation of the air strikes, "savage bombings" of the North continued and U.S. ground troops were intensifying the war in the South, the Communist journal stated. The newspaper noted that a North Vietnamese communiqué Apr. 4 had claimed that U.S.

planes that day had dropped 50 bombs on a "populated area" in Laichau Province, about 140 miles above the 20th Parallel, which had been designated by the U.S. as the northernmost limit of the area of North Vietnam that would be bombed. "It is clear that the declaration by Johnson of a halt of aerial and navy bombardments" of North Vietnam "is insufficient and that the American war of destruction against North Vietnam is still continuing," *Nhan Dan* charged. (U.S. Defense Secy. Clark Clifford said Apr. 8 that a Defense Department investigation of North Vietnam's charges had shown that there had been no U.S. "attacks north of the 20th Parallel since the President's speech 8 days ago." "The North Vietnamese are in error," he declared.)

The U.S. bombing curb was attacked Apr. 5 by North Vietnamese Foreign Min. Nguyen Duy Trinh. In an interview with CBS chief foreign correspondent Charles Collingwood (excerpts of the interview were published Apr. 8), Trinh charged that "over the past few days, U.S. aircraft have committed new crimes in North Vietnam and bombed many places in a 300-kilometer-long area from the 17th Parallel to the 20th Parallel." He insisted that the U.S. "must prove by words and deeds that it really wants serious contacts and talks—that is, it must unconditionally stop" all acts of war against North Vietnam. Trinh rejected Johnson's suggestion that "even this limited bombing of the North could come to an early end if our restraint is matched by restraint in Hanoi." "To ask for 'reciprocity' as a condition, or 'restraint' as a price, is nothing but a trick to blur the distinction between the aggressor and the victim of aggression," Trinh declared. Trinh also said:

● Johnson's statement that the Communists' Tet offensive in South Vietnam had failed was "falsely optimistic." The Communist drive had "dealt a telling blow at the U.S. machine of aggressive war, brought about the disintegration and decay of the prop of U.S. neo-colonialism—the puppet army and administration [of South Vietnam]."
● The Thieu-Ky government of South Vietnam "will be overthrown by the people of South Vietnam" and should be replaced by "a broad coalition government representing the aspirations of all patriotic social strata."

U.S. sources in Saigon reported Apr. 8 that Johnson had ordered further restrictions on the bombing of North Vietnam. He limited air strikes to the area from the demilitarized zone to the 19th Parallel, a distance of about 170 miles. The Saigon sources explained that the new orders had not been made public in order to give the President the option to resume the air strikes up to the 20th Parallel, the northernmost limits of his original bomb-curb order. A White House statement Apr. 7, however, had denied that the U.S. had ordered a cessation of raids between the 19th and 20th Parallels. Asst. Press Secy. Tom Johnson said Pres. Johnson's Mar. 31 order for a limited halt to the bombing of North Vietnam remained "exactly as we have given it to you publicly." Despite the White House's denial of the reputed new bombing restrictions, the U.S. command reported Apr. 9 that American pilots that day had restricted their air srikes to the area between the DMZ and the 19th Parallel for the 5th consecutive day.

(During the 2d day of the restrictive bombing missions, U.S. planes Apr. 2 had struck one mile south of the 20th Parallel. The target hit was a railroad siding 12 miles north-northeast of Thanhhoa. The Thanhhoa area was struck again by U.S. Navy planes Apr. 3. Targets included the Baithoung airfield, 22 miles northwest of Thanhhoa. Other planes hit truck parks and storage areas near Mugia Pass, a principal infiltration route.)

(The Soviet press agency Tass Apr. 1 had attacked Johnson for not ordering a complete halt to the air raids. "Refusing to fully stop the barbaric bombing of the Democratic Republic of Vietnam, the United States, as before, ignores the lawful demand of the DRV [North Vietnamese] government and all the world public insisting on a full and unconditional end to the bombing and all acts of war against the Vietnamese people," Tass said. The statement complained that the President "did not mention any period for the cutback in the attacks." A Moscow radio statement later Apr. 1 reiterated the Soviet view that Johnson's decision on the bombing had failed to meet North Vietnamese damands for a total and unconditional halt in the air strikes as a precondition for peace talks. The broadcast assailed the President's decision not to seek renomination as a "pre-election maneuver.")

Within 3 days of Johnson's speech, however, the North Vietnamese government Apr. 3 "declared its readiness" to arrange for a meeting with a U.S. representative "with a view to determining . . . the unconditional cessation of the U.S. bombing raids and all other acts of war against the Democratic Republic of Vietnam so that talks may start."

The North Vietnamese acceptance of Johnson's peace overture came at the end of a government message broadcast by Hanoi radio. The statement said Johnson had been forced to limit the bombing of North Vietnam because of U.S. and allied military setbacks in South Vietnam "and in face of ever stronger pressure from world public opinion and from progressive American opinion." The statement assailed the President's action as "a perfidious trick . . . to appease public opinion" since Washington "keeps sending more U.S. troops to South Vietnam" and "continues to bomb an important part of the Democratic Republic of Vietnam from the 17th to the 20th Parallel" and "refuses to stop unconditionally the bombing raids and all other acts of war on the whole territory" of North Vietnam. The statement reiterated that Hanoi's 4-point plan and the National Liberation Front's program remained "the correct basis for a political settlement of the Vietnam problem."

In his initial public response to Hanoi's message, Johnson told a group of news editors Apr. 3 that "we are very interested in it. If it says what some people think it says, we're very interested." Johnson said he could not limit the bombing further without sacrificing "the lives of our boys and our security." But "we would like to stop it all" if North Vietnam pledged not to "take advantage of it," he declared. Describing his decision to reduce the bombing of the North as "one positive step" toward peace, Johnson said that if North Vietnam accepted this view, other measures would be carried out "until maybe we would find some way to end this terrible war."

Johnson later Apr. 3 issued a statement in which he mentioned only the paragraph in Hanoi's message dealing with its suggestion that talks be held to bring the American bombing to a total halt. The President reiterated his desire to send a delegation "to any forum at any time to discuss the means of bringing this war to an end." "Accordingly," he announced, "we will establish contact with representatives of North Vietnam. Consultations with the government of South Vietnam and our other allies are now taking place."

Johnson said he would go to Honolulu Apr. 4 for a weekend of preparatory strategy meetings with U.S. diplomatic and military leaders stationed in South Vietnam. But the President canceled the trip after the assassination Apr. 4 of the Rev. Dr. Martin Luther King Jr. and the resultant domestic riots. Johnson, instead, conducted the strategy talks at the White House. The first of the sessions was held Apr. 6 with Gen. Westmoreland, U. S. commander in Vietnam.

After receiving Hanoi's acceptance of his proposal for peace talks, Johnson later Apr. 3 had suggested in a message delivered to the North Vietnamese embassy in Vientiane, Laos that ambassadorial meetings be held in Geneva or some other place. A North Vietnamese reply, received by the President Apr. 8, proposed that the ambassadors of the 2 countries meet in Pnompenh, Cambodia or any other site agreed to by both sides. The message, relayed through the U.S. embassy in Vientiane, reiterated Hanoi's view that the ambassadorial parley should deal with fixing a date for the "unconditional" stoppage of all bombing of North Vietnam and other acts of war against it. The "formal talks" that would follow the preliminary meetings should be conducted with the view towards arranging a political settlement, including a "broad national democratic coalition government" for South Vietnam, the North Vietnamese statement said.

The Southeast Asia Treaty Qrganization [SEATO] held its 13th annual Ministerial Council meeting in Wellington, New Zealand Apr. 2-3. A communiqué issued at the conclusion of the parley Apr. 3 indorsed the limitation of the bombing of North Vietnam but warned that Communist aggression in Southeast Asia must be halted. In a speech at a closed meeting of the Council Apr. 2, U.S. State Secy. Dean Rusk had voiced opposition to the establishment of a coalition government in South Vietnam and the neutralization of the country. He said this would be no solution to the war. Rusk cited the failure of the Laotion coalition government as devised by the 1962 Geneva conference. [The conference had established a neutralized Laos to be governed by a merger of rightists, neutralists and leftists. But the leftwing Pathet Lao withdrew and was currently in revolt against the Vientiane regime.] In an address at an open meeting of the Council later Apr. 2, Rusk said that Johnson's decision to restrict the bombing of North Vietnam was "as fair as any reasonable man could ask." He warned that "if Hanoi does not respond, more hard fighting lies ahead."

The Soviet Union Apr. 5 expressed full support of North Vietnam's agreement to begin talks with the U.S. on ending the bombing of the North. A Moscow statement said the USSR believed that Hanoi's acceptance "indicates a realistic way to end the war in Vietnam, to a political setteelement in the interests of the Vietnamese people, in the interests of restoring a normal situation throughout Southeast Asia." But "a good basis for a lasting settlement in Vietnam" can be achieved only if the U.S. unconditionally halted all bombings and other acts of war against

North Vietnam and if the U.S. "takes a positive view" of Hanoi's and the National Liberation Front's programs for settling the conflict, the Soviet statement said.

(In its first official reaction to the partial U.S. bombing halt, Communist China charged Apr. 6 that it was a cover-up for further intensified U.S. military action. "Peace will return to Vietnam only after the Vietnamese people win victories in the battlefield and drive the U.S. aggressors out," the Peking statement asserted. The partial bombing halt, China alleged, was "a new trick intended to force the Vietnamese people to their knees and surrender to the aggressors."

(UN Secy. Gen. U Thant Apr. 3 had expressed "gratification" at the prospects of U.S.-North Vietnamese contacts and Johnson's "initiative . . . in deescalating the war." Thant reiterated his "long-held conviction that meaningful talks will take place even perhaps within a matter of a few days once all bombing and other acts of war against North Vietnam are ended."

(Johnson's limiting of the bombing of North Vietnam had been welcomed Apr. 3 by French Pres. Charles de Gaulle as "an act of reason and political courage." The fact that Johnson "publicly prescribes the halt of the bombings of North Vietnam, even though this halt is not yet either general or unconditional, seems to be a first step in the direction of peace," de Gaulle said.

(Canadian Prime Min. Lester B. Pearson Apr. 1 had hailed Johnson's order to limit the bombing. He said: "It is now strictly up to the Communist side to reciprocate and show their desire to end the war by negotiation rather than by force."

(But South Korean reservations about impending peace talks were expressed Apr. 10 by Lt. Gen. Chae Myung Shin, commander of ROK forces in Vietnam. In an interview in Seoul after consulting with Pres. Park, Chae asserted that "another patch-up settlement in dealing with the Communists [similar to the Korean armistice agreement] will eventually lead to a 2d Vietnam elsewhere." Chae added: "It was shocking to me, as it was to the Republic of Vietnam people, that Washington-Hanoi contacts for peace talks came at a time when only a little more push is needed to win the war.")

Site Dispute Delays Talks

Preliminary U.S.-North Vietnamese peace talks on an ambassadorial level were delayed by a dispute over where the projected conference was to be held. The site for the proposed parley was taken up in private discussions by U.S. and North Vietnamese representatives, who met almost daily in Vientiane, Laos starting Mar. 31, and in a public exchange of notes between Hanoi and Washington.

North Vietnam had rejected the U.S.' suggestion for Geneva as the site for the talks. The North Vietnamese Apr. 8 recommended Pnompenh, Cambodia. Pres. Johnson Apr. 9 opposed Pnompenh and proposed 4 other cities: New Delhi, Rangoon, Jakarta and Vientiane.

Hanoi proposed Apr. 11 that the preliminary talks be held in Warsaw. But the U.S. opposed Warsaw and continued to insist on a "neutral" location. The proposal to hold the conference in the Polish capital was first disclosed in an English language dispatch by Tass, the Soviet press agency, and was later relayed to the U.S. through diplomatic channels. Chiding the U.S. for refusing to accept Pnompenh, Tass said the decision "cannot but cause wonder, because the United States has repeatedly expressed willingness to send its representatives to any point of the globe to establish contact with a representative" of North Vietnam. "It is believed in Hanoi's authoritative circles," Tass added, "that the U.S.' refusal to accept Pnompenh as the meeting place may be taken to indicate that the United States delays the solution of the question." Tass quoted North Vietnamese officials as saying: "Having declined Pnompenh, the U.S. motivated its refusal to meet by the absence of the necessary conditions. But Warsaw does have an American embassy, a staff of correspondents and means of communications"; "Warsaw has been the site, for over 10 years now, of contacts between the U.S." and Communist China.

The U.S. response, issued Apr. 11 through White House Press Secy. George Christian, rejected Warsaw as a meeting site and criticized Tass for publicizing the proposal before it was relayed through diplomatic channels. Christian said: The U.S. had "proposed a number of neutral countries as possible sites for contacts, and we have not yet had any response to this proposal. On serious matters of this kind, it is important to conduct talks in a neutral atmosphere, fair to both sides." "The selection of an appropriate site in neutral territory, with adequate communication facilities, should be achieved promptly through mutual agreement, and those acting in good faith will not seek to make this a matter of propaganda."

An American note delivered to North Vietnam Apr. 11 restated the U.S. view that the preliminary talks should be held in a "neutral" city. The message, transmitted through the U.S. embassy in Vientiane, asked Hanoi to reconsider Jakarta, Rangoon, New Delhi and Vientiane and to propose a mutually acceptable site if it objected to the 4 Asian capitals. The note stressed that the talks should be held in a city where both sides had diplomatic missions and adequate communication facilities to send and receive confidential messages. American officials had explained that the 4 Asian sites picked by Washington had American diplomatic missions, while Pnompenh had none.

North Vietnam Apr. 13 rejected all sites proposed by the U.S. because they were not "adequate." A statement issued by the Foreign Ministry charged that the U.S. "attitude in the choice of the place of preliminary contacts" between the U.S.'s and Hanoi's representatives was "in complete contradiction with the statements made by the U.S. government so far." The statement recalled that Pres. Johnson and other U.S. officials had "time and again stated that they desire 'prompt talks' with North Vietnamese officials" and "that they are 'ready to go anywhere, at any time' for talks." "It is clear," the North Vietnamese statement asserted, that the U.S. was "deliberately trying to delay the preliminary contacts" it had agreed to. "If the United States government really wants talks" with North Vietnam, "it must stop creating difficulties in the choice of a place for preliminary contacts, which only delay the talks between the 2 sides," the Foreign Ministry declared. The North Vietnamese statement again assailed the U.S. for increasing its air attacks on North Vietnam and for intensifying the war in the South while preparations for peace talks were under way.

North Vietnam was urged by Johnson Apr. 15 to agree to hold ambassadorial talks in a neutral capital where both countries had diplomatic missions and adequate communication facilities. Johnson made the statement in Honolulu, where he had arrived that day to confer with South Korean Pres. Chung Hee Park and with American officials on the political and military aspects of the situation in Southeast Asia. Johnson said the U.S. had explained to North Vietnam why Pnompenh and Warsaw were "not suitable" places for talks. "As of now, we have had no response or comment from Hanoi, other than radio statements, about one of the locations we have suggested." "What is needed now," Mr. Johnson said, "is an equally serious and considered reply, reacting to our proposals for neutral sites, or offering additional suggestions or neutral capitals, where both of us have representatives and communications." He pointed out that Vientiane, Rangoon, Jakarta and New Delhi were all located in the region which has the most direct and vital interest in the achievement of a stable peace." The President added: "We are eager to get on with the task of peacemaking. Precious time is being lost."

(A further report on the situation in Southeast Asia had been made to Johnson at Camp David, Md. Apr. 9 by U.S. Amb.-to-South Vietnam Ellsworth Bunker and Adm. U.S. Grant Sharp, commander-in-chief of Pacific forces. In a statement made after the talks, Bunker called the Tet offensive "a psychological and political defeat" as well as "a resounding military defeat for the Communists." Despite the physical damage incurred by the Communist attacks, the South Vietnamese had become stronger and had developed "a new sense of danger, urgency and patriotism," Bunker said. He added: "I am very much encouraged about what's happened, and I look to the future with a good deal of confidence." As for the South Vietnamese government's attitude toward negotiations, Bunker said: "I do not think they are disturbed by it. Their position is similar to ours." Among other Administration officials attending the Camp David meeting were State Secy. Dean Rusk, Defense Secy. Clark Clifford and Amb.-at-Large W. Averell Harriman.

(But South Vietnamese government concern over peace talks were expressed by Foreign Min. Tran Van Do and Vice Pres. Nguyen Cao Ky. Do said Apr. 12: "I feel no qualms [about the future] as long as the fighting continues"; but "I look forward to negotiations with serious misgivings." In addressing the South Vietnamese Senate Foreign Relations Committee Apr. 10, Do had said that even if the Communists "agreed completely to all our peace terms by stopping the aggression and withdrawing Hanoi's troops to the North," South Vietnam's problems would not be over. The Viet Cong's infrastructure would remain intact, Do said, and the Communists would seek a majority in the future National Assembly by posing as members of other parties. He warned that a Communist-dominated Assembly would declare South and North Vietnam united under Hanoi rule. Ky had asserted Apr. 3 that

South Vietnam would oppose a coalition government with the Viet Cong as a price for peace. "To accept coalition under American pressure," he said, "means we are going to die in the next 5 or 6 months, or at least lose the country. So it is better to lose it fighting.")

Air Raids Stepped Up

Hanoi radio charged Apr. 12 that U.S. jets had carried out missions 19 miles northwest of the North Vietnamese capital and over 3 provinces north of the 20th Parallel, but it did not specify whether they were bombing or reconnaissance flights. The charge coincided with a report by U.S. military sources that American reconnaissance flights had been resumed up to and above the 20th Parallel to inform U.S. ground commanders of North Vietnamese movements that might jeopardize their troops.

The North Vietnamese press agency claimed Apr. 15 that an American plane had been shot down that day 37 miles southwest of the capital of Ninhbinh Province, between the 20th and 21st Parallels.

Among major U.S. air strikes:

● A railroad siding 22 miles north-northwest of Vinh was hit Apr. 9 during a 131-mission raid. Other American planes struck airfields, trucks, highways and antiaircraft sites throughout the southern panhandle just north of the demilitarized zone.

● U.S. planes Apr. 11 ranged as far north as 8 miles below the 19th Parallel. Among the targets hit in the 105 missions were lines of communications and storage tanks. 8 military storge structures were reported destroyed.

● U.S. planes flew 143 missions Apr. 14 in the 2d heaviest attack of 1968. During raids Apr. 15, American jets bombed 2 bridges 169 miles north of the DMZ. 14 other spans also were struck, as were trucks, sampans, supply dumps and artillery positions.

U.S. planes carried out intensified attacks on targets in North Vietnam's southern panhandle the following week:

● During an 80-mission raid Apr. 15, 4 U.S. planes were lost. 2 Air Force F-105 Thunderchiefs were shot down near Donghoi, and 2 Navy F-4 Phantom jets collided and crashed south of Vinh. All escaped except the pilot of one of the Thunderchiefs, who was reported missing. The anti-aircraft fire was reported to be the heaviest since the limited bombing had begun Mar. 31. U.S. military sources speculated that the North Vietnamese had moved some of their anti-aircraft weapons from the Hanoi-Haiphong area, where the raids had been suspended, to the southern panhandle, where American attacks were concentrated. During the day's raids, U.S. jets pounded a bridge and a surface-to-air missile site near Donghoi.

● U.S. planes Apr. 18 carried out the heaviest raids of 1968 as flying conditions improved. Pilots attacked trucks, bridges, cargo craft, anti-aircraft sites and storage centers in a 145-mission attack. North Vietnam was pounded by another record flight of American planes for the 2d consecutive day Apr. 19. Pilots flying 160 missions reported destroying or damaging in the Vinh-Donghoi area 28 trucks, 26 supply boats, 10 bridges, 24 fortifications and 7 buildings.

• North Vietnam claimed Apr. 24 that 2 U.S. F-4 planes had been shot down Apr. 22 in Quangbinh Province, just north of the DMZ. Hanoi claimed that another U.S. plane, a reconnaissance aircraft, had been downed at Haiphong Apr. 23.

• U.S. planes carried out a 155-mission attack Apr. 23 and a 111-mission raid Apr. 24. A U.S. spokesman said that the pilots reported destroying or damaging 19 supply craft, 6 trucks, 4 bunkers and several antiairaft and artillery positions in the Apr. 23 strikes.

• U.S. Thailand-based F-111A jets Apr. 26 resumed raids against North Vietnam. Their missions had been suspended Apr. 22 after a 3d F-111A had been lost in the first month of F-111A combat operations. (Previously, F-111 combat missions had been suspended after 2 were lost Mar. 28 and 30, but the flights were resumed Apr. 12 following replacement of the 2 F-111s.) The F-111A air strikes Apr. 26 were directed at highways and communication and supply lines in the area around Donghoi, about 35 miles north of the demilitarized zone.

• Hanoi radio claimed Apr. 28 that 2 U.S. pilots had been captured that day when their plane was shot down over Quangbinh Province just north of the DMZ.

LBJ Goes to Honolulu

Pres. Johnson conferred in Honolulu Apr. 16 with U.S. military commanders in South Vietnam and Apr. 17 with South Korean Pres. Chung Hee Park.

Johnson's discussions with the American officers dealt with the deployment of Communist and allied forces since the start of moves to arrange preliminary peace talks with North Vietnam. Johnson was briefed by Adm. U.S. Grant Sharp, commander of Pacific forces. Among other officers reporting to the President was Adm. John S. McCain Jr. (who replaced Sharp July 2). The President was accompanied by Gen. Earle G. Wheeler, chairman of the Joint Chiefs of Staff, special consultant Cyrus Vance and Asst. State Secy. (for Far Eastern and Pacific affairs) William P. Bundy.

Johnson's meeting with Pres. Park Apr. 17 was aimed at assuring the South Korean leader that his country's interests would not be compromised by a Vietnamese peace agreement and at reaffirming the American military commitment to Seoul. A joint statement issued after the talks said that Johnson and Park had discussed "the serious threat to the security" of South Korea

and "to peace in East Asia resulting from the increasingly belligerent actions of the North Korean Communists during the past
18 months. . . ." Johnson explained the U.S.' preliminary peace
contacts with North Vietnam and reaffirmed American intentions
to "consult fully with the Republic of Korea and other allies
concerning negotiating developments and positions to be taken
on the allied side at each stage."

En route back to his ranch in Texas, Johnson discussed with
newsmen the background to his decision Mar. 31 to reduce the
bombing of North Vietnam and to offer Hanoi peace talks. Johnson said that the U.S. had communicated with North Vietnam
about 30 times in the past few years. In leading up to the Mar.
31 decision, he said, "we searched our minds to be sure we were
not being too inflexible or too rigid, that we were opening our
minds to all possible avenues."

Impasse in Talks

The talks, held in Vientiane, Laos, had reached the first in a
series of impasses by mid-April. The ostensible issue was still the
choice of a site for the preliminary talks. A North Vietnamese
Foreign Ministry statement, reviewing the exchange on the matter
since Mar. 31, charged Apr. 19 that the U.S. government's "attitude is not at all serious." It recalled that after rejecting Hanoi's
suggested designation of Pnompenh, the U.S. had "set one condition" for selection of a site: "that there should be representations
of the 2 sides at the site of the preliminary contacts." After opposing Warsaw as a meeting place, the U.S. then raised its require-
ments to " 'minimum standards,' " the ministry said: "the contacts
should be held in a neutral country, in a place where the 2 parties
have representations and adequate means of communications."
Now, it said, Pres. Johnson had set 2 new conditions: " 'a place
where other governments aiding Vietnam [in the war] . . . have
their representatives' " and " 'a suitable, mutually agreeable place
without psychological advantage for either side.' " Thus "within
3 weeks only, the United States, which at first did not set any
conditions, . . . has come to pile up extremely absurd and in-
solent conditions.

The North Vietnamese statement contended that 10 new
sites suggested by State Secy. Dean Rusk Apr. 18 had failed "to
meet even the conditions posed" by the U.S. "Many of the

countries proposed by Rusk," Hanoi held, were "not neutral," while others were "support-bases for the U.S. war of aggression." The 10 sites proposed by Rusk Apr. 18 were Ceylon, Japan, Afghanistan, Pakistan, Nepal, Malaysia, Italy, Belgium, Finland and Austria. These were in addition to Geneva, New Delhi, Rangoon, Jakarta and Vientiane, all proposed by the U.S. previously. "Any of these 15 suggested locations would . . . offer an atmosphere conducive to serious negotiations," Rusk said. Alluding to the U.S.' objection to the cities proposed by North Vietnam, Rusk said "negotiations must take place in a setting fair to both sides. . . . We would not recommend sites such as Washington, Seoul or Canberra—and we could not accept such sites as Hanoi, Peking or Moscow."

The State Department Apr. 20 deplored North Vietnam's rejection of the U.S.-proposed sites and questioned whether Hanoi was serious about the matter. The department also issued a statement denying that "there was a difference between . . . Rusk and the White House about a site for contacts with Hanoi." The statement was in reference to an Apr. 19 *N.Y. Times* dispatch, which had said that "top echelons in the State Department, apparently including Secretary of State Dean Rusk," were opposed to the addition of 10 more possible sites. The article said the officials had privately expressed fears that the new suggestion "means that the White House has decided for the time being to match Hanoi in a propaganda battle that will be difficult to resolve without the aid of 3d parties."

Defense Secy. Clark Clifford Apr. 20 predicted that North Vietnam eventually would agree to the holding of preliminary peace talks despite the fact that it was "attempting to extract as much propaganda value" as it could from the "kind of jockeying you go through in this sort of negotiation." Clifford said that Johnson's repeated assertions that he would "go any place at any time" to participate in peace negotiations really meant "any reasonable time." "It did not occur to me, for example, that he would go to Hanoi," Clifford said.

Johnson said Apr. 24: "We don't know if it is just a ploy. We talked today and we talked yesterday. There are some who think that, if they were serious, they wouldn't have suggested Warsaw."

UN Secy. Gen. U Thant had disclosed Apr. 13 that he was using his good offices in an effort to end the impasse. Thant said he had proposed Paris and several other sites to U.S. and North

Vietnamese representatives. Thant warned that "any further delay in the agreement on the venue would be most unfortunate in view of the fact that massive destruction of life and property is still going on" in Vietnam. Thant repeated his suggestion of Paris and "other possible sites" during a meeting Apr. 16 with U.S. Amb.-to-UN Arthur J. Goldberg and U.S. Asst. State Secy. (for international organization affairs) Joseph J. Sisco.

The U.S. Apr. 16 expressed willingness to accept the intercession of "some 3d parties" to "come up with a site which both sides can agree to without anybody losing face." An Administration official said: "We're not trying to save face. We're trying to save South Vietnam."

The announced appointment Apr. 16 of 2 North Vietnamese to high-level governmental posts raised diplomatic speculation that the designees were Hanoi's probable chief delegates to the proposed peace talks. The appointees, as announced by the North Vietnamese press agency, were ex-Foreign Min. (1963-5) Xuan Thuy, 55, given the rank of minister, and Tran Quang Huy, 46, appointed chairman of the Cultural & Educational Board of the premier's office. Thuy had served as deputy chairman of the North Vietnamese delegation to the 1961 Geneva conference on Laos.

U.S. and North Vietnamese representatives conferred again in Vientiane Apr. 25, 27 and 28. The Apr. 25 and 27 talks were held by U.S. Amb.-to-Laos Willian H. Sullivan and Nguyen Chan, the North Vietnamese chargé d'affaires. The Apr. 28 meeting was conducted by 2 North Vietnamese embassy officials and Robert C. Hurwich, counselor of the U.S. embassy. State Department sources Apr. 27 quoted Chan as having denounced the U.S. embassy in Laos for allegedly violating a pledge not to make public the U.S.-North Vietnamese contacts. Chan was said to have asserted: "Vientiane is the only place we are having private exchanges, and we mutually agreed to keep them secret. The Americans are the ones who gave out the news."

The U.S., heretofore, had not rejected Warsaw and Pnompenh outright and had only stated its objections to those 2 cities. But the Johnson Administration appeared definitely to turn down the Polish or Cambodian capitals as possible meeting sites when Asst. State Secy. (for Far Eastern affairs) William P. Bundy asserted Apr. 28 that the U.S. had made it "quite clear that we simply don't regard Pnompenh or Warsaw as suitable for the kind of contacts that are now clearly envisaged on both sides." The North

Vietnamese Foreign Ministry Apr. 29 accused Bundy of delaying the talks.

The U.S. did not regard a North Vietnamese oral message delivered to Amb. Sullivan at the Apr. 25 meeting in Vientiane as a reply to Washington's latest note on the subject of a conference site, sent to the North Vietnamese embassy in Vientiane Apr. 22. The dispatch of the note was disclosed by the State Department Apr. 24, but its contents were not made public. U.S. officials said that it had proposed no new locales for talks but had suggested a new approach to ending the deadlock.

UN Secy. Gen. U Thant Apr. 24 had issued another appeal to the U.S. and North Vietnam "to agree without further delay on a venue for preliminary talks." Considering the conditions posed by both sides for a meeting place, the selection of a spot "has now narrowed down to a few cities. Among these . . . , Warsaw and Paris could be regarded as suitable sites," he said. Thant deplored the fact that while negotiations on a site for talks continued, "the war in Vietnam has been raging unabated."

It was reported in Warsaw Apr. 24 that Polish Deputy Foreign Min. Jozef Winiewicz had met the previous week with 6 ambassadors to Poland—from the Soviet Union, Japan, Britain, Canada, France and India—and had urged them to use their good offices to bring the preliminary talks to Warsaw. The ambassadors reportedly were asked to exert their influence on the U.S. government.

A compromise on a meeting site was reported Apr. 26 to have been advanced by Soviet Amb.-to-France Valerian A. Zorin and his embassy staff aides in Paris. Zorin was said to have suggested that the talks could be held in 2 parts—starting in Warsaw and continuing in Paris.

South Vietnamese Pres. Nguyen Van Thieu said Apr. 26 that he advocated a cease-fire during negotiations. But he insisted that a truce must be coupled with a guarantee of a halt in infiltration from North Vietnam. He suggested that safeguards against infiltration could be provided by stationing troops along South Vietnam's borders and along the DMZ. (South Vietnamese Foreign Min. Tran Van Do had disclosed Apr. 23 that the South Vietnamese government and "allied forces" fighting in Vietnam had warned the U.S. not to restrict the bombing of North Vietnam indefinitely. Do said that any prolonged limitation of the air strikes would permit an increase of North Vietnamese infiltration of the South. Do would not disclose which allied governments had made such representations to the U.S.)

Paris Picked as Talks Site

The U.S. and North Vietnam agreed May 3 on Paris as the site for their preliminary talks on Vietnam. The parley, Hanoi said, would start May 10 or shortly thereafter. The agreement on a talks site climaxed 34 days of U.S.-North Vietnamese discussions.

North Vietnamese acceptance of the French capital as a meeting place, as previously suggested by U Thant and others, had been disclosed in a message delivered May 2 to the U.S. embassy in Vientiane.

Pres. Johnson agreed to the arrangements in a return message and announced his decision May 3 at a previously scheduled news conference. The President said that France was "a country where all parties" to the negotiations "could receive fair and impartial treatment." He expressed "hope that this agreement on initial contacts will prove a step forward and can represent a mutual and serious movement by all parties toward peace in Southeast Asia." Johnson cautioned, however, that "this is only the very first step, and there are many, many hazards and difficulties ahead." "I assume that each side will present its viewpoint in these contacts," he added.

Hanoi's acceptance of Paris was announced at the end of a North Vietnamese Foreign Ministry statement that reviewed U.S. and North Vietnamese discussions of the matter and accused Washington of having "deliberately resorted to dilatory maneuvers." The statement then said that North Vietnam "welcomes the French government's willingness to offer Paris as a site for the talks." It cited the suggestion as having been advanced Apr. 18 by French Foreign Min. Maurice Couve de Murville. The statement said that the North Vietnamese government considered Paris "a suitable place."

The Foreign Ministry disclosed that ex-Foreign Min. Xuan Thuy would head the North Vietnamese delegation at the talks. It restated Hanoi's view that the purpose of the discussions was to "determine with the U.S. side the unconditional cessation of the U.S. bombing raids and all other acts of war against" North Vietnam "and then to hold talks on other problems of concern to the 2 sides."

(The U.S. May 1 had disclosed its acceptance of an Indonesian suggestion advanced 2 weeks earlier that the meetings be held aboard an Indonesian cruiser in the Gulf of Tonkin. The North Vietnamese embassy in Vientiane May 2 termed the proposal "unacceptable" on the grounds that "Indonesia is not neutral." Pope Paul VI said May 5 that he had proposed that the talks be held in the Vatican. It was presumed that the offer had been relayed to the U.S. through the apostolic delegate in Washington and to North Vietnam through the papal embassy in Paris.)

A South Vietnamese Foreign Ministry statement May 4 said the Saigon regime had no objection to the selection of Paris but expressed reservations about the negotiations in general. The statement warned: The Communists might "take advantage of talks for propaganda purposes, foster dissension between the Republic of Vietnam's allies, raise a certain number of nonrelevant issues" and attempt to bring about "more confusion." "At the same time, the Viet Cong may increase the tempo of the war . . . to strengthen their position at the negotiations table."

Foreign Min. Tran Van Do was one of the few South Vietnamese officials to comment publicly on the agreement to negotiate in Paris. He said May 3 that the French capital "would be acceptable." Do said a South Vietnamese liaison team would be sent to Paris to maintain contacts with the U.S. delegation during the preliminary discussions but "would only enter the talks when actual negotiations begin."

Negotiating Positions Stated

The U.S. and North Vietnam May 4 restated their conditions for ending the fighting.

State Secy. Dean Rusk, in an address at the University of Georgia in Athens, asserted that the U.S. regarded a stop to Communist infiltration of South Vietnam as well as of neighboring Laos, Thailand, Cambodia and Burma as vital for "an honorable peace in Southeast Asia." The U.S., Rusk stated, sought "a negotiated settlement of the Vietnamese conflict in the hope that we can convince North Vietnam that its better future lies in development of the entire Southeast Asian region, rather than in a costly and wasteful effort to overcome the South by force." Rusk held that in accordance with the 1962 Geneva accords, North Vietnam

should cease its infiltration of Laos, recognize the Laotian government's authority throughout the country and grant "access to all
parts of the country by the International Control Commission."
Rusk added: Thailand was "entitled to live at peace without the
infiltration of arms and agents trained outside its own borders."
Cambodia and Burma were "entitled to live at peace without the
same kind of interference."

The North Vietnamese Communist Party newspaper *Nhan Dan*
declared that Hanoi's decision to agree to meet with the U.S. in
Paris reflected its willingness "to bring an end to the war in
Vietnam on the basis of the guarantee for the basic rights of the
Vietnamese people." The newspaper restated the North Vietnamese view that Hanoi's 4-point plan and the National Liberation Front's political program remained "the correct basis for a
political solution of the Vietnam problem."

The North Vietnamese Fatherland Front indicated May 4
that Hanoi would not oppose the inclusion of non-Communist
elements in a South Vietnamese coalition government. A statement made by the front's presidium said "all Vietnamese patriots
irrespective of social class, political tendency, nationality and
religious belief have realized the necessity to stand shoulder to
shoulder in the struggle against the common enemy—the United
States imperialist aggressors and the Vietnamese traitors." The
Fatherland Front's statement praised the anti-South Vietnamese
government Alliance of National, Democratic & Peace Forces in
Vietnam (ANDPF) as "a new development in the great national
united bloc for national salvation" in Vietnam.

George W. Ball, U.S. ambassador-designate to the UN, May
5 linked the current increase of Communist infiltration of South
Vietnam and of the fresh assaults launched by the Communists
throughout South Vietnam with Hanoi's attempts to improve its
bargaining power at the forthcoming talks. Speaking on the NBC-
TV program "Meet the Press," Ball warned that if the North
Vietnamese "think on the 5th of May, before the talks start on
the 10th of May, that this kind of a military operation is going
to result in improving their bargaining position, I think they
gravely misconceive the attitude of the United States, the power
position of the United States or the determination of the United
States to see an honorable settlement."

State Secy. Rusk had warned May 2, at a hearing of the
House Foreign Affairs Committee, that if the Communists launch-

ed a major drive in the South, it would result in "a big setback for the possibility of talks."

COUNTEROFFENSIVE

In the ground war in South Vietnam, U.S. and associated forces had succeeded in blunting the Viet Cong/North Vietnamese offensive early in March. By early April, the pressure had been reduced sufficiently to allow the U.S. and South Vietnam to organize and launch a series of counteroffensives.

The U.S. military command disclosed May 26 that a secret directive, prepared in April and sent to all U.S. field commanders May 6, had called for an "all-out" drive to defeat Communist forces in Vietnam. A command spokesman said, however, that no order had been issued by the U.S. Military Assistance Command "which ties the prosecution of the war in Vietnam to the peace talks, or which states that the war must be won within the next 3 months or in any other specified period of time." This statement was in denial of a *Chicago Daily News* report that the directive had called on American officers to attempt to win the conflict in 3 months and that the aim of the drive was to break a military stalemate to strengthen the position of the American negotiators in Paris. The command official said that the directive, whose text he refused to divulge "was a kind of a pep talk . . . that gets sent out about every 6 months or so. It said we had to make an all-out effort to keep the counteroffensive going—that is, the counteroffensive that began after the enemy's Tet offensive."

Saigon Area Sweep

The allied effort opened with an attempt to resecure Saigon and the provinces immediately surrounding it. A force of 100,000 men Apr. 8 began the biggest drive of the war to eliminate Viet Cong and North Vietnamese forces throughout the 11 provinces in the III Corps tactical zone around Saigon. News of the offensive, Operation Complete Victory, was not made public until Apr. 11 for security reasons.

The offensive was carried out in the same area as the recently-concluded Operation Quyet Thang. As in Operation Quyet Thang, the new drive by U. S., South Vietnamese, Australian, New Zea-

land and Thai troops failed to make contact with the main force
of an estimated 18,000-20,000 North Vietnamese and Viet Cong
soldiers believed operating in the area. By Apr. 13 only 120 Viet
Cong or North Vietnamese were reported killed; U.S. losses were
16 killed and 47 wounded. Many of the casualties were incurred
in a 5-hour clash Apr. 12 when a Viet Cong force attacked an
artillery base of the U.S. 25th Infantry Division northwest of
Dautieng, about 40 miles northwest of Saigon. In repelling the
onslaught, the U.S. troops killed 60 Viet Cong; at least 14 Americans were slain and 47 wounded.

The fighting in the capital area, however, continued to intensify during April. U. S. and South Vietnamese forces killed 46
Viet Cong in 2 separate engagements in the Saigon area Apr. 20
and 21. At least 31 Viet Cong troops were slain in the Apr. 20
clash near Thuduc, 10 miles northwest of the capital. A U. S. adviser with a South Vietnamese unit was slain. The fighting had
started when a U.S. First Infantry Division company patrol came
under attack. In the Apr. 21 clash, U.S. 101st Airborne Division
troops repelled an enemy attack on a company defensive position
39 miles north of Saigon. 15 Viet Cong and one American were
slain.

South Vietnamese army and national police units were placed
on the alert in Saigon Apr. 21-23 to cope with a possible attack
on the capital. Other government troops in the 11 provinces
around Saigon were alerted Apr. 22. A U.S. spokesman said Apr.
22 that no such "warning had been issued to American personnel." The alert order had followed the defection Apr. 20 of a
North Vietnamese colonel, who turned over to allied authorities
documents that told of Viet Cong plans for a "2d wave" of
attacks on Saigon similar to the Tet offensive. The plans reportedly called for the use of 10,000 troops. The defector was identified as Col. Tran Van Dac, a political commissar attached to the
Viet Cong's 9th Division. Officials said Dac was in his early 40s
and had also been known as Tam Ha in the Communist Party.
He had turned up in Binhduong Province, about 50 miles north
of Saigon. A South Vietnamese national police communiqué
warned Apr. 27 that "the Viet Cong are preparing to recommence
in the capital the terrorist acts they perpetrated" during the Tet
offensive. The statement asserted that the Viet Cong were "now
employing all means to transport arms, ammunition and explosives
into Saigon.")

A delayed report Apr. 24 said South Vietnamese troops had killed 132 Viet Cong in 2 days of fighting just west of Gocong, to the south of the capital. U.S. troops Apr. 24 killed 33 North Vietnamese troops after encountering the force in a bunker complex near Hieuliem, about 30 miles northeast of Saigon. 8 Americans were killed and 33 wounded in the 4-hour fight.

Following the fresh outbreak of fighting around Saigon, U.S. B-52 bombers carried out heavy raids in the vicinity of the capital Apr. 26-27. The bombers Apr. 26 attacked bunker concentrations near Bencat, 20 miles northwest of Saigon. The planes Apr. 27 dropped bombs on suspected Viet Cong base camps, tunnels and caves in Haunghia Province, 24 miles northwest of Saigon, and in Tayninh Province, about 10 miles beyond Haunghia.

Outlying Provinces

In the northern provinces, the U.S. sought to secure the area against North Vietnamese operating there. U.S. forces near the demilitarized zone continued to press Operation Pegasus, the offensive that had led to the lifting of the North Vietnamese siege of the American Marine base at Khesanh. Fighting centered Apr. 10-12 on the Special Forces Camp at Langvei, $3^1/_2$ miles southwest of Khesanh. U.S. troops Apr. 10 moved into one section of the camp, called New Langvei, without encountering the enemy. The American force withdrew for the night to a neighboring camp, Old Langvei, 700 yards away. About 100 North Vietnamese troops reoccupied New Langvei during the night and clashed with the returning Americans Apr. 11. The U.S. troops recaptured the camp Apr. 12 but found only 7 bodies in the rubble. The camp had been bombed and shelled repeatedly since it was first captured by the North Vietnamese in February. Hanoi radio then claimed Apr. 16 that North Vietnamese troops had driven out U.S. and South Vietnamese soldiers from the Langvei camp.

North Vietnamese forces resumed the shelling of the American base at Khesanh. The stronghold was struck by 250 to 300 artillery shells Apr. 16-17 and by more than 240 rockets, mortar and artillery shells Apr. 18. Sharp but sporadic ground fighting also flared around Khesanh despite the fact that the bulk of the North Vietnamese force that had surrounded the American stronghold prior to the lifting of the siege Apr. 5 was believed to have headed South and infiltrated northern Thuathien Province's

Ashau Valley. A senior U.S. officer said that the resumed shelling of Khesanh did not mean that the North Vietnamese were again advancing on the base to resume the siege. The officer said the firing probably had emanated from long-range artillery pieces emplaced in Laos and above the DMZ.

A report issued by the North Vietnamese press agency Apr. 18 said that heavy fighting continued around Khesanh. The agency claimed that 850 Americans had been put out of action in combat around the base Apr. 17 and that 5 helicopters on the base's air strip had been destroyed.

In one ground engagement 4 miles north of Khesanh Apr. 17, 19 American Marines were killed and 56 wounded in a 4-hour clash. About 20 of 25 entrenched North Vietnamese troops were reported killed. In another action near the base Apr. 16, 17 Americans had been slain after a Marine patrol encountered an enemy force in bunkers. At least 7 North Vietnamese troops were killed.

North Vietnamese artillery and mortar shells Apr. 27 struck 2 U.S. bases—Camp Carroll, an artillery position 12 miles east of Khesanh, and Quangtri airfield to the south. U.S. Marines just below the DMZ were reported to have killed 72 North Vietnamese in an engagement one mile west of Conthien. 9 Marines were slain and 17 wounded. U.S. Marines found near Camp Carroll a grave that contained the bodies of 56 North Vietnamese soldiers, believed to have been killed by artillery or air strikes.

Meanwhile, fighting continued further south. Early in April intelligence reports had led the U.S. command to believe that North Vietnamese from the Khesanh area were infiltrating the Ashau Valley around Hué and in the Central Highlands further south. To counter the movement, U.S. B-52s carried out heavy raids Apr. 8-13 on suspected troop concentrations and bunkers near the Cambodian border west of Dakto and Kontum, and a ground sweep was launched Apr. 1 to clear the coastal plain from Hué to Quangtri. The ground operation, first announced Apr. 14, resulted in the killing of 503 North Vietnamese troops as of Apr. 13, the U.S. command reported. American fatalities during the period totaled 57. In one clash in the Hué area, 27 U.S. Marines were killed and 27 wounded Apr. 14 in an attack on a fortified North Vietnamese village. The North Vietnamese lost 62 men killed before they quit the 9-hour battle.

According to preliminary U.S. intelligence reports made public Apr. 10, North Vietnamese troops and equipment had continued to infiltrate into South Vietnam on an unabated scale during the 10 days since the U.S. had announced a partial bombing halt against North Vietnam. A U.S. general said Apr. 10 that if the influx continued at the current rate, the Communists' fighting peak that had existed prior to their Tet offensive would be reached by early June.

By mid-April American forces were reported to have started a major effort to retake the Ashau Valley. A U.S. command spokesman reported Apr. 19 that U.S. B-52 bombers had made the Ashau Valley a "priority" target. The American aircraft carried out 61 raids Apr. 1-19 against suspected concentrations of Communist troops, trucks, bulldozers, tanks, armored cars and arms and ammunition. More than 9,000 tons of bombs were dropped in the 18-day period in a valley area 30 miles southwest of Hué. One of the heaviest raids occurred Apr. 18, when B-52s dropped 1,600 tons of bombs in the valley.

U.S. troops Apr. 19 launched a major offensive—Operation Delaware—against what was believed to be a large North Vietnamese force in the Ashau Valley. News of the drive was not disclosed by U.S. military authorities until Apr. 28, and then only details of the first 3 days of the operation were released. In fighting Apr. 19, it was reported that 10 U.S. helicopters had been shot down and several others damaged by North Vietnamese antiaircraft fire. 20 U.S. soldiers were reported killed that day, while the North Vietnamese were said to have lost 50 men.

Maj. Gen. John R. Tolson, commander of the First Cavalry Division (Airmobile), which spearheaded the sweep, said Apr. 28 that the Ashau Valley was one of the North Vietnamese army's "top logistical support bases, as important to him as Camranh Bay is to us." (The First Cavalry had played a major role in the lifting of the siege of Khesanh Apr. 5.)

The Ashau Valley, it was reported, had been under complete North Vietnamese control since North Vietnamese forces had overrun a U.S. Special Forces camp in the southern part in Mar. 1966. Repeated bombing raids by U.S. B-52s had failed to impede the Communists' supply and troop build-up in the area. Infiltration of the valley accelerated since the lifting of the Khesanh siege. The Ashau Valley was said to be held by an estimated 5,000 to 6,000 North Vietnamese troops.

American forces were active, as well, in the deep south. The U.S. command disclosed Apr. 11 that an offensive launched in the

Mekong delta Mar. 7 had resulted thus far in the killing of 1,371 Viet Cong and the capture of 855. U.S. losses: 53 killed and 347 wounded. South Vietnamese casualties: 214 killed and 915 wounded.

Pacification Program Reconstructed

Alongside the military effort, the U.S. undertook the reconstruction of the pacification program, designed to keep South Vietnam out of Communist hands.

The program was "generally back on the track and moving again" after the Saigon government had lost control of 1.? million people as a result of the Tet offensive, it was reported Apr. 18 by Robert Komer, the U.S. official in charge of pacification. Komer said at a Saigon news conference that 61% of South Vietnam's 17.2 million people were under allied control, while the Viet Cong wielded authority over 18.3%; the remaining population lived in contested villages and hamlets. Komer reported that prior to the Tet drive, in early January, the Viet Cong had controlled 16.3% of the population, the allies had controlled 67.3% and the rest of the inhabitants were in "relatively secure" areas. Currently, Komer reported, 4,559 hamlets were "relatively secure" (under general government control), 4,093 were controlled by the Viet Cong and 4,084 were contested. This compared to the situation in January with 5,331 hamlets relatively secure, 3,593 contested and 3,838 in Viet Cong hands, he said. The number of relatively secure hamlets in late February, one month after the Tet offensive, had been 4,472, Komer disclosed. The National Liberation Front, as the South Vietnamese government had done, had tightened their positions in recent weeks and were in control of 50 more hamlets than they had been at the end of February.

Komer conceded that the pacification drive "may not be as far along at the end of 1968, if the war continues until then, as we had planned to be." The program "is just not going to be susceptible to dramatic movement like the siege or the relief of Khesanh. But we're back on the offensive."

(The *N.Y. Times* reports on the "Pentagon papers," published in 1971, indicated that the pacification program had never recovered from the Tet offensive. A U.S. report Apr. 10. 1968 said that the Tet offensive had cost $173,633,000 in property damage. Structures destroyed or damaged included private homes, business establishments, warehouses and industrial and government build-ings. 115,276 homes [18,507 of them in the Saigon area] were damaged or destroyed.)

U.S. & North Vietnamese Build-Up

The intensification of the fighting led both the major contest-ants to mobilize additional troops. U.S. Defense Secy. Clark M. Clifford Apr. 11 announced a call-up of 24,500 military reservists to be used in Vietnam and to replenish the Army's Strategic Reserve.

According to the announcement, made at Clifford's first Pen-tagon press conference since he became Defense Secretary, 10,000 of the reservists would go to Vietnam in units as support forces for the 11,000 combat troops dispatched in February in response to the Tet offensive. The call-up, involving 88 units from 34 states, was for 2 years of service less any previous time spent on active duty. Clifford also announced a new troop ceiling of 549,500 for U.S. strength in Vietnam. He characterized it as a ceiling beyond which the Administration currently did not intend to go.

Clifford said that Administration policy was to transfer gradually to South Vietnam the major responsibility for the war effort.

In a speech in New York Apr. 22 at the annual AP luncheon, Clifford said that the South Vietnamese had "acquired the capac-ity to begin to insure their own security through their own efforts" and that "they are going to take over more and more of the fighting." "We have concluded," he said, "that Americans will not need always to do more and more but rather that the in-creased effectiveness of the South Vietnamese government and the South Vietnamese forces will now permit us to level off our effort and in due time to begin the gradual process of reduction." (This appeared to be the first public intimation of what was to become Nixon Administration policy in 1969 for getting the U.S. out of Vietnam by "Vietnamizing the war.") Clifford said that the U.S. was accelerating the delivery of equipment to the South Vietnamese forces so that all their combat troops would have the modern M-16 rifles by July.

Relating the war effort to the effort to begin peace negotia-tions, Clifford said: "If Hanoi would rather fight than talk, or elects both to talk and fight, the record of the success we have already achieved shows that military victory in South Vietnam is beyond Hanoi's reach."

(Sen. Eugene J. McCarthy disputed Clifford's statement that the South Vietnamese were ready to take over more of the fighting. He said in New York Apr. 23 that the statement was not consistent with the recent U.S. call-up and dispatch of more troops to Vietnam.)

Hanoi had called Apr. 15 for a build-up of North Vietnamese forces in view of what it called the "new situation." (This was an apparent reference to U.S. and North Vietnamese efforts to arrange preliminary peace talks). The army newspaper *Quan Doi Nhan Dan* said that the "new situation is a process of creating opportunities and favorable conditions, of maintaining and developing strongly our mastery in the battlefield, of simultaneously fighting the enemy and striving to strengthen our own forces."

A U.S. intelligence report asserted Apr. 27 that North Vietnam had sharply increased its infiltration of South Vietnam since the U.S.' limitations on bombing raids against the North had gone into effect Mar. 31. In the period Apr. 1–25, aerial reconnaissance was said to have observed an estimated 10,000 supply trucks (2,000 more than in March) moving along infiltration routes from North Vietnam, through Laos and into South Vietnam. All of the sightings were said to have been made in Laos.

Fighting in Laos

The intensity of the conflict in South Vietnam was reflected in renewed hostilities in neighboring Laos.

U.S. officials in Vientiane reported Apr. 13 that a new North Vietnamese/Pathet Lao offensive in southern Laos had resulted in the virtual encirclement of the 2 provincial capitals of Saravane and Attopeu and the district town of Lao Ngam. The American account said that the combined force had apparently embarked on a new strategy of "attacking towns and taking terrain, they are willing to accept and inflict . . . a lot of casualties, and they have brought in a whole range of new weapons, 140-mm. rockets, 120-mm. mortars, antitank weapons [and] B-40 rockets." A U.S. official said the offensive had succeeded in keeping the Laotian government and the U.S. mission in Laos "off balance."

North Vietnam's total military force in Laos reportedly had increased by 5,000 since Jan. 1. The increase raised the total

North Vietnamese force there to about 45,000 men. The rebel Pathet Lao troops numbered about 30,000, Laotian government soldiers 70,000.

The Indian and Canadian members of the International Control Commission (ICC) had flown to southern Laos Apr. 12 to investigate government claims of shelling of the Attopeu airport. The ICC's Polish delegate refused to join the inquiry because it had not been requested or approved by the Pathet Lao.

The North Vietnamese news agency reported Apr. 30 that the Pathet Lao had protested to Britain and the Soviet Union (as co-chairmen of the Geneva Conference on Laos) that U.S. planes during a $2^1/_2$-month period had sprayed toxic chemicals over 3 Pathet Lao-held towns and that 200 civilians had died. The towns allegedly raided were Van Loumboum and Ban Houi Sane, in Savannakhet Province, and Thanhinyek, in Attopeu Province.

A Chinese Foreign Ministry statement Mar. 29 had charged that U.S. bombing raids Mar. 21 and 22 had heavily damaged the Chinese economic and cultural mission buildings in Khang Khay, Laos, 100 miles northeast of Vientiane. The statement claimed the raids also had caused casualties in the town.

Hue Massacre

The U.S. embassy in Saigon reported Apr. 30 that the North Vietnamese and Viet Cong had killed more than 1,000 South Vietnamese government workers, civilians, priests and non-Vietnamese in Hué during the Tet offensive. The report was based on investigations by South Vietnamese police and military, and U.S. military and civilian advisers. It said evidence indicatad that many of the victims, found in 19 mass graves, had been beaten to death, shot or beheaded. Nearly half were apparently buried alive. A U.S. embassy, report Mar. 9 had said that the contents of the mass graves included the bodies of women and childern.

(A North Vietnamese document captured Apr. 25, 1968 and made public Nov. 24, 1969 reported that in Hué, "we eliminated 1,892 administrative personnel, 38 policemen, 790 tyrants, 6 captains, 2 first lieutenants, 20 2d lieutenants and many noncommissioned officers." Bodies of 2,737 persons reportedly slain by the North Vietnamese in Hué were recovered by Nov. 1969. The discovery of new mass graves in the area was reported as late as Nov. 7, 1969.)

The Tang Quang Tu Pagoda was the site of 13 graves in which 67 victims were found shot. The U.S. report said a Buddhist monk in the pagoda had "heard nightly executions by pistol and rifle shots in a plowed fields behind the pagoda during the first 2 weeks of February." The 2 largest graves were near Hué's imperial tombs, where 201 bodies were discovered, and at a slope near the Huong River, where 200 bodies were unearthed, 40-50 of them women.

One of those executed was identified as Nguyen Ngoc Ky, a leader of the splinter Vietnam Nationalist Party, described as anti-U.S. but also anti-Communist. Among the non-Vietnamese found slain were 2 French priests from a nearby Benedictine mission at Thienan—Father Urbain, 52, and Father Guy, 48; also 3 Koreans, a Hong Kong Chinese, a British citizen and 4 German members of Hué's university medical faculty.

NEW COMMUNIST OFFENSIVE

By the end of April the Viet Cong, supported by the North Vietnamese, had regrouped, and they were able to launch a 2d offensive early in May. Again, the center of the thrust was largely Viet Cong-manned and was aimed at Saigon.

2d Battle of Saigon

The 2d battle for Saigon began with a major Viet Cong ground attack inside the capital city May 5. The assault was coordinated with simultaneous shelling of major cities throughout South Vietnam. Heavy fighting continued in the capital city through May 7. At the start of the onslaught May 5, Brig. Gen. Winant Sidle, chief spokesman for the U.S. command, said the attacks were "a far cry from the Tet offensive" launched at the end of January.

A National Liberation Front broadcast May 5 called on the people of Saigon to "annihilate the United States aggressors and overthrow the barbarous rule" of the Saigon regime. Hanoi radio claimed May 5 that the Viet Cong had achieved "brilliant victories."

In the initial assault May 5, the Viet Cong and North Vietnamese shelled 119 towns and military barracks throughout South

Vietnam. Only about a dozen of the targets struck by rockets or mortar shells, including Saigon, came under ground assault. The U.S. command reported that in 2 days of fighting May 5-6, 537 Viet Cong soldiers were killed in provinces surrounding Saigon and 177 were slain inside the city. A total of 15,000 civilians were said to have been left homeless as a result of the Saigon fighting. Among the major cities attacked, in addition to Saigon, were Danang, Huê and Quangtri in the northern provinces, Banmethout and Pleiku in the Central Highlands and Cantho, Mytho, Bentre and Vinhlong in the Mekong Delta. 3 airfields and 3 American compounds came under Communist shelling. The attack on one of the U.S. strongpoints, the Marine base near Dongha, in Quangtri Province, left 10 Marines killed and 64 wounded.

The heaviest fighting was centered on and around Saigon. In the May 5 clashes, Brig. Gen. Nguyen Ngoc Loan, South Vietnamese national police chief, was shot and seriously wounded. 4 foreign newsmen and Baron Hasso Rüdt von Collenberg, first secretary of the West German embassy, were shot to death. Von Collenberg was found with a blindfold over his eyes, and it was assumed that he had been executed. The 4 newsmen were killed while riding in an open car in the Cholon district of Saigon, where heavy fighting was in progress. They were identified as John L. Cantwell, 30, an Australian correspondent for *Time* magazine, Bruce S. Pigott, 22, an Australian assistant bureau chief of Reuters, Ronald B. Laramy, 30, British-born Reuters correspondent, and Michael Y. Birch, 23, a correspondent for the Australian Associated Press. A 5th newsman was shot to death May 6 near Saigon's Tansonnhut Airbase. He was UPI photographer Charles R. Eggleston, 23, of the U.S. 3 other photographers were wounded.

The attack on Saigon had started May 5 with mortar rounds fired on several buildings in the center of the city. The fighting spread quickly to Cholon, the Tansonnhut airbase and the Phutho Race Track. U.S. helicopter gunships fired on suspected Viet Cong sniper positions on the outskirts of Cholon. Sporadic firing raged one block from the U.S. embassy. An old French military cemetery on the southwest fringe of Tansonnhut was the scene of sharp clashes between entrenched Viet Cong and South Vietnamese government forces. At least 28 Viet Cong were slain in the initial encounter May 6. South Vietnamese reinforcements were rushed into Cholon May 7 as fighting there intensified.

Combined U.S. and South Vietnamese forces had routed Viet Cong troops in several battles in the Saigon area May 3. In the fiercest encounter, government soldiers, assisted by U.S. helicopter gunships, killed 194 Viet Cong in a daylong clash in the Mekong Delta, 28 miles southwest of the capital. In other action May 3, U.S. soldiers engaged a force of about 500 Viet Cong troops 18 miles northwest of Saigon and killed 39, according to initial reports. An additional 48 Viet Cong were slain by American troops in 2 separate actions in the same general area.

Among major actions in the Saigon fighting:

May 7—A fresh outbreak of fighting in Saigon's southern and western sectors set entire blocks ablaze and forced thousands of civilians to flee to the center of the city. 2 battalions of Viet Cong troops were pinned down near the Phutho Race Track in the Cholon district by machinegun and rocket fire from South Vietnamese planes and U.S. helicopters. Other planes and 'copters attacked the Y Bridge (which linked Saigon with a southbound road to Gocong in the Mekong delta), where a Viet Cong company was entrenched. At least 30 to 40 civilians were reported killed in the crossfire.

At a smaller bridge to the west, South Vietnamese rangers, reinforced by armored personnel carriers, pushed a force of Viet Cong troops away from the span into a nearby factory building. An estimated 35 Communists were slain in several hours of fighting. Battling on a lesser scale raged at a French military cemetery near Tansonnhut airbase in the Govap district northwest of Saigon and at the Phanthangian Bridge on the Bienhoa highway.

May 8—Viet Cong forces intensified their attacks in the Cholon district, firing on 3 police stations and sniping at military vehicles. The Viet Cong seized a pagoda, a make-shift refugee center, and held it for 3 hours. Misdirected fire by a U.S. helicopter struck the pagoda and killed at least 5 refugees. The government placed Cholon and the surrounding area—about half of the city—under 24-hour curfew.

May 9—Fighting broke out again in Cholon. Resulting fires raged through 4 blocks of houses. Hundreds of refugees were forced to flee their homes. Col. Tran Van Hai, commander of the South Vietnamese rangers, estimated that 1,000 Viet Cong troops were operating in the western fringes of Cholon.

Fighting shifted later in the day to the Khanhhoi area, across the Benghe Canal from central Saigon. An estimated 1,200 to 1,500 Viet Cong troops were involved in operations in the district, but their attacks were stopped by South Vietnamese fighter planes and allied troops rushed in to reinforce national police patrols.

May 10—Viet Cong troops entrenched in the slum district around the Y Bridge were heavily pounded by allied jets, helicopters and artillery crews. Enemy resistance in the remainder of Saigon was reported to be virtually at an end.

May 11—Sporadic enemy resistance flared again in the Cholon area and around the Y Bridge. The heaviest action, however, raged in the outskirts of Saigon, largely to the south and the west. The largest of 4 battles fought there centered 4 miles southwest of the Phutho race track. South Vietnamese marines reported killing 11 Viet Cong and capturing 26. The Y Bridge area was pounded heavily by South Vietnamese fighter-bombers.

May 12—U.S. jets shattered the final Viet Cong resistance around the Y Bridge, pounding the area with high-explosive and napalm bombs. The raids paved the way for U.S. infantry assaults on the final stronghold of the enemy. During the night the Viet Cong force apparently withdrew. (South Vietnamese rangers May 13 discovered the bodies of 287 Viet Cong troops in a sweep 4 miles beyond the bridge.)

Saigon residents who had left Saigon during the fighting May 5-13 began returning May 14 to the city and to their homes, many of which had been destroyed or badly damaged. Preliminary figures for casualties suffered by civilians in the fighting were 118 killed and 2,768 wounded, of whom 1,068 remained hospitalized.

Viet Cong forces again shelled the center of Saigon May 19 but did not follow up the attack with a ground assault. Officials said that at least 12 rocket and mortar shells had killed 11 civilians and wounded 51. 151 homes were reported destroyed.

By the 2d week of May, the U.S. and the Saigon regime had regained enough control of the city to justify optimistic statements. The U.S. and South Vietnamese military commands claimed May 13 that allied troops had overcome the main thrust of the Viet Cong/North Vietnamese offensive. A joint statement issued by Lt. Gen. Fred C. Weyand, commander of U.S. forces in the 11 provinces around Saigon, and Lt. Gen. Le Nguyen Khang, commander of South Vietnamese forces in the same area, said: "Although isolated small attacks, terrorism and harassment by fire, including rockets, are still possible, a large number of the enemy have been attempting to withdraw from the battlefield for the past 48 hours, many being intercepted in the process."

According to the allied statement: 5,270 North Vietnamese and Viet Cong had been killed in the offensive, compared with 154 American and 362 South Vietnamese soldiers slain. The Saigon attacks had left 104,000 civilians homeless in the city and its suburbs and had resulted in the destruction of 10,700 homes. The civilian casualty toll was incomplete. It was known that 114 civilians had died in hospitals and that 2,702 had been admitted with injuries. But many others were said to have been killed outright.

North Vietnam, however, claimed May 13 that the Saigon offensive was a successful follow-up to the Tet drive. According to the North Vietnamese army newspaper *Quai Doi Nhan Dan*, South Vietnamese troops had been beaten despite the early intervention of U.S. military forces. The newspaper said the latest attacks had definitely shifted the fighting to the towns of South

Vietnam, while the rear areas had been made dangerous for the allies.

Fighting in the Provinces

Heavy battles also were fought in the demilitarized zone (DMZ) area and in the Central Highlands.

Allied forces secured complete control of the Ashau Valley May 10 in their Operation Delaware drive against the North Vietnamese supply stronghold, the U.S. command reported May 11. The North Vietnamese final setback came when allied soldiers in the valley linked up with American paratroopers along roads connecting the Ashau area with Hué. A further report on the operation by the command May 17 did not disclose for security reasons whether the U.S. and South Vietnamese troops had left the valley or were remaining. The command said that 132 U.S. and South Vietnamese troops had been killed in the operation and 662 wounded. North Vietnamese fatalities totaled 726. A large quantity of North Vietnamese equipment and supplies had been destroyed or captured, including heavy weapons, ammunition, trucks, bulldozers, explosives, rice and other foodstuffs.

Among reports on other major actions:

● U.S. and South Vietnamese troops killed an estimated 586 North Vietnamese in fighting Apr. 30-May 4 near the American Marine base at Dongha, just below the DMZ. The fighting began Apr. 30 with a North Vietnamese attack on an outnumbered U.S. Marine company. U.S. and South Vietnamese reinforcements were rushed in, raising the allied force committed to the battle to more than 1,000 men. The Dongha battle was marked by a savage fight for the village of Daido, 2 miles from the Marine base. The village changed hands 3 times before an American force took final possession of it May 4. Daido was virtually destroyed by U.S. artillery and air strikes directed at North Vietnamese soldiers entrenched in bunkers and tunnels. U.S. Marine casualties in the 4 days of fighting totaled 68 killed and 323 wounded.

● North Vietnamese forces were said to have suffered heavy losses Apr. 30-May 1 in fighting 4 miles west of Hue. U.S. and South Vietnamese troops reportedly killed 352 North Vietnamese and captured 95. Allied losses were 8 killed and 37 wounded.

● In the Central Highlands, a North Vietnamese attack Apr. 29 on an American infantry position 26 miles west of Kontum was repulsed with a loss of 46 lives. U.S. casualties totaled 2 killed and 20 wounded.

● In air action, U.S. authorities reported, 2 jets were downed in raids over Vinh, North Vietnam Apr. 28. North Vietnam claimed that 3 American planes had been shot down over the North Apr. 28; 2 of the planes were downed over Hatinh Province, and one over Vinh, the North Vietnamese press agency claimed.

● A force of about 5,000 North Vietnamese May 10 attacked a U.S. Special Forces camp at Khamduc, in the Central Highlands, about 350 miles northeast of Saigon. After fierce fighting, Gen. William C. Westmoreland ordered the camp abandoned; the base's 1,600 to 1,700 South Vietnamese defenders and their families were flown out by May 12. The U.S. command reported that the Khamduc camp had been abandoned "to avoid encirclement and to enable tactical aircraft and B-52s to strike the sizeable enemy force uninhibited by friendly elements in the area."

The battle had started May 10 with a North Vietnamese assault on one of Khamduc's outposts. During the weekend, a 600-man battalion of the U.S. 196th Light Infantry Brigade was flown in to reinforce the garrison. Despite the camp's expanded force, the North Vietnamese troops May 12 overran the Khamduc outposts, entrenched themselves at the eastern end of the base and were attacking to the northeast with an apparent intention to storm the garrison. It was then that the U.S. withdrawal airlift began. One of the evacuation planes, a C-130 transport, carrying an estimated 150 civilians and 6 American crewmen, was shot down by North Vietnamese groundfire. All aboard were killed. In addition to the C-130, the U.S. lost 8 other planes during the Khamduc battle. American casualties in the 3-day fight (excluding the 6 crewmen killed) were 19 slain and 125 wounded. The U.S. command reported that 300 North Vietnamese had been killed in the ground fighting and that many more had died in air strikes.

● A U.S. Special Forces camp 55 miles northwest of Saigon came under Viet Cong attack May 13, but the onslaught was repulsed. The Viet Cong forces managed to penetrate part of the camp's defense perimeter but were thrown back with a loss of 25 killed. U.S. casualties totaled 19 killed and 24 wounded; 2 South Vietnamese civilians also were killed.

● U.S. Marines around Khesanh May 19 killed 109 North Vietnamese in 2 separate engagements. In the first incident, a Marine company camped 3 miles from the base came under 2 probing attacks by a force of about 150 North Vietnamese. The Marines repulsed the attack with the aid of artillery fire from howitzers inside the Khesanh post. The North Vietnamese then withdrew, leaving 43 bodies behind. Marine casualties totaled 8 wounded. In the 2d attack, a Marine force was checking for mines along Route 9 leading to Khesanh when it was ambushed. In the ensuing 11-hour fight, 66 North Vietnamese and 8 Marines were killed. The attacking forces in both engagements were believed to have belonged to the 304th North Vietnamese Army Division, one of the 2 divisions that had besieged Khesanh during January-April.

High Casualties

The intensity of the fighting during these weeks was reflected in the uncommonly high level of casualties reported. A record 562 Americans were killed in the Vietnam fighting May 5-11, the U.S. command reported May 16. This was the highest number of U.S. fatalities for a single week of the war. 2,153 U.S. troops were wounded seriously enough to require hospital treatment; another 1,072 were wounded but did not require hospitalization.

The May 5-11 fatalities brought to 22,951 the total number of Americans slain in Vietnam since Jan. 1, 1961. North Vietnamese and Viet Cong deaths for May 5-11 were listed at 5,552.

An American command spokesman said most of the U.S.' May 5-11 casualties had been incurred in fighting in the 5 northern provinces, particularly around the 3d Marine Division's headquarters at Dongha, 11 miles south of the demilitarized zone. Marine Lt. Gen. Robert E. Cushman, U.S. commander in the northern sector, had reported May 11 that the North Vietnamese force in the Dongha area had been routed and that the Communists had also failed in a drive to block the Cauviet River supply route, which led from the coast to the Marine base at Dongha. More than 1,500 North Vietnamese troops had been slain in that area since Apr. 29, Cushman said. In the previous 24 hours, he disclosed, 142 North Vietnamese had been slain in 5 engagements in the Dongha region. American losses in those clashes totaled 24 killed and 54 wounded.

Prisoners Released

The South Vietnamese government announced May 15 that it had freed 2 Viet Cong prisoners from a camp in northern Quangngai Province. The captives were released in exchange for 2 U.S. prisoners who had been set free by the Communists in Quangtin Province Jan. 23. The 2 Americans were identified as Cpl. José Agosto Santos of the Marines and Pfc. Luis Ortiz-Rivera of the Army.

The releases appeared in part to represent a response to the concern expressed by the Viet Cong to the treatment their prisoners had received from the Saigon regime. The National Liberation Front (NLF) Apr. 10 had claimed the right "to take appropriate measures" against U.S. or South Vietnamese captives in retaliation for future killings of Communist prisoners.

The warning was based on an NLF charge that 2 Viet Cong leaders had been "massacred" in Saigon Jan. 31, at the start of the Tet offensive. The 2 were identified as Tran Van Kieu, a member of the central committee of the Federated Unions for the Liberation of Vietnam and vice president of the Trade Union Federation of the Saigon-Giadinh Region, who had been arrested in 1967, and Le Thi Rieng, a woman leader of the NLF.

The NLF statement reasserted the front's "unswerving humane policy toward the enemy detained by the NLF." But it threatened to take retaliatory action against allied captives if "the U.S. imperialists and their puppet administration continue . . . stealthily murdering South Vietnamese patriots or illegally trying them."

3d Battle for Saigon

The Viet Cong launched a 3d attack on Saigon in the period May 25-June 4, and fierce battles were reported in and around the city. The Viet Cong infiltrated the capital in large numbers and carried out heavy shelling attacks. U.S. and South Vietnamese counter-fire, including fire from planes and tanks, resulted in heavy damage to homes and caused thousands of civilians to flee to the center of the city. The fighting centered largely in the Cholon district and was particulary intense June 1-3. U.S. authorities estimated that about 1,000 Viet Cong had been killed. The U.S. command held that the attack did not represent a major challenge to Saigon, that its purpose was merely to harass allied forces in order to influence the talks in Paris.

During the first day of operation, sharp sporadic fighting broke out May 25 just north of the capital as South Vietnamese government forces battled with entrenched Viet Cong troops. A 24-hour curfew was imposed in Giadinh Province to the northeast, where an estimated 600 Viet Cong were believed to be on the move. Fighting flared later in the day just 2 miles from the center of Saigon.

South Vietnamese marines, conducting a house-to-house search of enemy troops in an area 2 miles northeast of downtown Saigon, came on an enemy force May 26 and killed 24. U.S. armed helicopters aided the operation by firing rockets and machineguns at the fleeing enemy. 3 South Vietnamese soldiers were slain. U.S. helicopters came to the aid of American troops fighting 5 miles south of the center of Saigon. 5 Americans were killed and 11 wounded when their unit of tanks and armored cars was attacked in an encampment 6 miles northwest of central Saigon.

Fighting in Saigon ebbed May 28-29 but increased in intensity May 30 as more Viet Cong squads infiltrated the city. The fighting raged in the heart of Cholon and at the northeast fringes of Saigon. 2 blocks in Cholon were burned out June 1 by fires ignited by Viet Cong rockets and allied recoilless rifle fire and grenades.

During a tour of the battlefront in Saigon June 2, 7 high-ranking South Vietnamese government officials were killed by a misdirected U.S. helicopter rocket. The mayor of Saigon, Col. Van Van Cua, was seriously injured. The dead were: Lt. Col. Nguyen Van Luan, Saigon police chief; Lt. Col. Pho Quoc Chu, brother-in-law of Vice Pres. Nguyen Cao Ky; Col. Tran Van Phan, chief of staff of the national police force; Lt. Col. Le Ngoc Tru, police commander for the Cholon district; Lt. Col. Nguyen Van Phuoc, commander of the 5th Ranger Group; Maj. Nguyen Ngoc Xinh, chief of the combined security section of the national police; Maj. Nguyen Bao Thuy, chief of the mayor's cabinet. An aide to Mayor Cua also was killed. Wounded with the mayor were Col. Nguyen Van Giam, deputy chief of the Saigon military district, and a Maj. Tho, commander of the 5th Combat Battalion for the police in Saigon.

Most of those slain or injured were political allies of Vice Pres. Ky, who had been struggling to maintain control of the Saigon military district and the III Corps, which surrounded Saigon.

The South Vietnamese victims were in a school used as a command post when it was ripped by an explosion. The U.S. mission in Saigon conceded June 4 that an American helicopter was responsible. According to the mission's statement: "The local commander called for a strike by a United States helicopter against an enemy target some distance away, from which friendly forces had been receiving rocket and small arms fire." The helicopter fired 3 rockets; 2 were on target, and the 3d "malfunctioned."

In addition to the helicopters, fighterbombers and tanks were called in to dislodge enemy troops entrenched in the Cholon area and on the outskirts of the city, but the Viet Cong held their ground. Some U.S. Army helicopters had dropped tear gas on Viet Cong positions in Cholon in a move to spare further destruction to homes and shops. But South Vietnamese soldiers resumed pounding the enemy strongpoints with mortars, tank guns and machinegun fire as the Viet Cong contiued sniping.

Saigon and the surrounding areas were struck by 40 Viet Cong rockets June 4. Among the targets hit were positions of a company of the U.S. 9th Infantry Divison, 5 miles south of the center of the city, the perimeter of Tansonnhut airbase, the dock areas and a hospital. 10 civilians were injured.

South Vietnamese officials had reported June 3 that fighting in Saigon in May had created 125,000 refugees. The U.S. embassy reported that fighting in the Saigon area between May 5 and early June had left 386 South Vietnamese civilians killed and 3,498 wounded. 16,242 homes were destroyed in that period, the report said.

(The U.S. May 28 made public a captured Viet Cong directive that linked the current Communist offensive in Saigon with the Paris peace talks. Principal points of the Communist document: The "objective of our diplomatic struggle . . . is intended to bolster the military and political struggles and not to substitute for them"; "unless a major military victory is achieved, nothing can be expected from the diplomatic struggles"; "we must respond to and support our diplomatic struggle by fighting harder in order to achieve more striking and more decisive victories.")

Northern Provinces

As the battle raged in Saigon, the North Vietnamese attacked in other parts of South Vietnam. Their assaults were particularly heavy in the area of the demilitarized zone. *Among major actions:*

• South Vietnamese troops May 21 reported killing 170 North Vietnamese soldiers in 2 separate engagements near Danang and Quangtri. The heaviest action was fought 12 miles south of Danang, the command center for the 5 northernmost provinces, where 92 North Vietnamese were slain and 3 taken prisoner.

• 3 major American installations came under rocket and mortar fire in the northern provinces May 21. 2 of them were a few miles southeast of Hue; the other was further to the north between Hue and Quangtri. The most serious clash occurred at the headquarters of the 101st Airborne Division at Camp Eagle, 6 miles southeast of Hue. The North Vietnamese stormed the camp's defense perimeter after firing about 300 shells. The Americans repulsed the attack, killing 54 North Vietnamese; American losses totaled 13 killed and 68 wounded.

• The U.S. command May 21 announced the start of 2 offensives to safeguard Quangtri and Hue from North Vietnamese attack. The largest of the operations was being carried out near Hué, where about 1,500 men of the 101st Airborne were seeking out 2 North Vietnamese divisions totaling about 20,000 men. 92 North Vietnamese were reported killed in the 2 drives so far.

• The announcement of the Hue area sweep was followed by a report May 23 that there was strong evidence that the North Vietnamese had reinfiltrated the Ashau Valley, 30 miles southwest of Hue. The reappearance of the North Vietnamese in Ashau was confirmed by aerial sightings reportedly detecting road construction workers in the area.

• The U.S. command disclosed May 25 that American Marines had opened an offensive May 20 to drive North Vietnamese troops from the vicinity of Danang. In the 5 days since the operation had begun, 24 miles away from the

city, 76 North Vietnamese and 12 Marines were killed. In 2 other engagements in the Danang area, reported May 26, 139 North Vietnamese were said to have been slain.
• U.S. troops killed 203 North Vietnamese in a savage fight May 22-23 2 miles northeast of Conthien, a Marine base just below the demilitarized zone. In fighting off an 800-man attack, the Marines lost 23 killed and 86 wounded.
• Elsewhere in the DMZ area, U.S. and South Vietnamese troops May 25 killed 363 North Vietnamese just north of the U.S. 3d Marine Division head-quarters at Dongha. In another clash in the same sector May 26, South Viet-namese forces killed 95 North Vietnamese.
• Heavy fighting broke out May 29 2 miles southeast of the U.S. Marine base at Khesanh as about 600 North Vietnamese attacked the American troops in a night defensive position. The Marine company, reinforced by another com-pany and aided by tanks and planes, repulsed the assault, killing 230 of the enemy. U.S. losses were listed as 13 killed and 44 wounded.

Pressure on Cambodia

Cambodia protested to the U.S. and South Vietnam June 8 against what it charged were a series of violations of Cambodia's borders. A Cambodian protest June 5 had charged that 2 Cam-bodians had been killed and 4 wounded in U.S.-South Vietnamese air raids on villages the previous week. The most recent attack allegedly had occurred June 2.

Chief of State Prince Sihanouk June 10 released 2 U.S. Army soldiers who had been captured May 25 aboard a Philippine tug intercepted on the Mekong River one miles inside Cambodia. 8 Filipino crewmen had been freed June 8. Sihanouk had been re-ported June 2 to have rejected a request by U.S. Amb.-to-India Chester Bowles for the release of the 2 Americans. The U.S., pro-testing the detention of the Americans, had claimed that the boat had penetrated Cambodian territory inadvertently. Announcing the release of the 2 Americans June 10, Sihanouk said he made the move as a gesture of respect for the late Sen. Robert F. Kennedy. (Kennedy had been assassinated June 5.)

Offensive Recedes

The Viet Cong offensive seemed to have spent its force by early June. The Viet Cong in general avoided battle and concen-trated their efforts in mortar and rocket attacks. The fighting June 3-15 centered in and around Saigon, where Viet Cong rock-ets continued to inflict heavy civilian casualties.

The South Vietnamese government reported June 11 that

since May 5, when the Communists had launched their renewed assault on Saigon, 433 civilians had been killed and 3,660 wounded in the city. South Vietnamese troops during that period had killed 2,880 Communists and captured 328. Allied forces, principally American, had slain 2,436 of the enemy and captured 105, the report said. South Vietnamese troop losses totaled 261 killed and 1,032 wounded.

Civilian targets, such as homes, churches and hospitals, as well as military installations, were hit by the rockets. In one attack June 7, 25 civilians were killed. Ground clashes inside the city were sporadic. But a force of about 25 allied battalions swept the fringes of Saigon in an effort to find and destroy the Communist rocket sites. In 2 of the heaviest clashes, South Vietnamese troops killed 30 Communist soldiers June 15 and another 52 June 16.

Gen. Creighton W. Abrams, commander of U.S. forces in South Vietnam, said June 17 that "we are going to put a stop to the attacks" on Saigon "because we have to stop them and we have the means to stop them."

It was reported June 13 that South Vietnamese legislators and Saigon newspapers were demanding that the U.S. resume the bombing of Hanoi if the Communists continued to shell Saigon. A resolution adopted by the Senate called on the Saigon government "to make use of all effective means to stop the Communists' savage shellings and to warn North Vietnam that appropriate measures will be taken."

Few clashes were reported by the end of June. Fighting in the Saigon region was marked by the downing of 5 U.S. Army helicopters June 24 and 25. The dead included 19 Americans, 16 Thai soldiers and a Vietnamese interpreter. Most of the fatalities occurred June 25 when 2 helicopters, carrying troops for an operation 16 miles east of Saigon, collided. The collision set off an explosion, sending out fragments that struck and brought down a 3d 'copter. All 29 persons aboard the 3d aircraft were killed. Another helicopter crashed June 24 into the Nhabe River, 9 miles southeast of the capital. 5 of the 8 soldiers aboard were killed. A 5th 'copter was shot down by Viet Cong gunners June 24, 19 miles southwest of Saigon. The pilot and passenger were found shot to death.

In ground action around Saigon, government forces June 22 suffered one of their worst defeats in several weeks when Viet

Cong troops ambushed a 400-man government battalion on a highway 60 miles northeast of the capital. 44 men were killed and 71 wounded. The attackers withdrew after 2 government battalions were flown in by helicopter to reinforce the besieged unit. The enemy left 41 dead behind.

South Vietnamese forces patrolling the Saigon area discovered huge quantities of rockets and other weapons and ammunition June 27 and 29. It was believed that capture of the materiel had blunted Viet Cong plans to launch further assaults on Saigon. The first find was made in rice paddies 13 miles northwest of the capital. It included 126 rockets, rocket grenades and machine guns. The 2d cache was unearthed June 29 near Mochoa, about 50 miles west of Saigon. It included 20 tons of TNT and nearly 300,000 rounds of ammunition for AK-47 rifles.

A Viet Cong force of about 75 men June 28 destroyed the village of Sontra (17 miles north of Quangngai) during an attack on a U.S.-Vietnamese military unit camped nearby. Military authorities reported the slaying of 88 civilians—73 villagers and 15 armed government pacification workers—and the wounding of 103. The enemy force lost 5 men killed before being driven off. The village had a population of about 4,000. No casualties were reported among the 44-man allied unit, a Combined Action Platoon composed of U.S. Marines and government Popular Forces (militia). At least 85% of Sontra's buildings were destroyed by Viet Cong grenades hurled into shelters beneath the homes of villagers, according to Vietnamese military sources. A U.S. military mission spokesman in Saigon said June 29 that "this may well be the worst Viet Cong atrocity against civilians of the war."

Vietnamese civilians had suffered heavy casualties in another incident June 22 on Highway 1, 240 miles north of Saigon. 33 were killed when a bus in which they were riding was blown up by a land mine.

In the northern region, the pressure of the North Vietnamese continued.

The U.S. command in South Vietnam comfirmed June 27 that U.S. Marines had begun to withdraw from the military base at Khesanh, the strongpoint once regarded as vital to American defense positions below the demilitarized zone (DMZ) separating North and South Vietnam.

The withdrawal was attributed to a change in the military situation, marked by strong North Vietnamese pressure. A U.S.

command statement said: "There have been 2 significant changes in the military situation in Vietnam since early this year—an increase in friendly strength, mobility and firepower and an increase in the enemy's threat due to both a greater flow of replacements and a change of tactics." To cope with the increase in North Vietnamese strength and activity in the DMZ area, "we have decided to continue the mobile posture we adopted in western Quangtri Province with Operation Pegasus in April," the drive which had broken the 77-day North Vietnamese siege of the base. This "makes operation of the base at Khesanh unnecessary."

The command reported that the North Vietnamese force in the I Corps area near the DMZ had increased from 6 divisions in January to 8 divisions currently.

With the abandonment of Khesanh, the U.S. base system in the area apparently was shifted to Landing Zone Stud, about 10 miles to the east along Route 9. The landing zone had been used to support the 8 battalions operating around Khesanh since the lifting of the siege.

The decision to quit Khesanh had first been reported June 24 by *Baltimore Sun* correspondent John S. Carroll. The U.S. military command June 26 disaccredited Carroll indefinitely on the ground that he had violated security regulations, which forbade reporting troop movements in advance of their official disclosure. Carroll, writing from Khesanh, had reported that one of the reasons for withdrawing the garrison was to remove it from the range of North Vietnamese artillery located across the nearby Laotian border. Commenting on his report June 26, Carroll said: "The Marine privates knew about it [the withdrawal], the North Vietnamese knew about it and the only ones who didn't know about it were the people in the United States."

White House press secretary George Christian said June 27 that the evacuation of Khesanh was a military decision and had not been made by Pres. Johnson.

Nguyen Thanh Le, spokesman for the North Vietnamese peace-negotiating team in Paris, June 28 described the American pullback from Khesanh as the "gravest tactical and strategic defeat" for the U.S. in the war. The Americans, he claimed, had been "forced to retreat" from the base.

Sporadic but sharp fighting had occurred in the Khesanh area prior to the announcement of the withdrawal. U.S. Marines killed

186 Communist troops just south of the base June 15 and killed another 128 in the same area June 18. In another engagement, 3 miles south of Khesanh, the Marines, supported by artillery and planes, killed 157 North Vietnamese July 1.

The North Vietnamese had taken heavy casualties in fighting elsewhere along the DMZ June 26. A South Vietnamese government unit came upon a North Vietnamese force 5 miles east of Quangtri and reported killing 148 and capturing 10 of the enemy. Government losses totaled 26 killed and 72 wounded. In another clash, 11 miles east of the U.S. Marine base at Dongha, First Cavalry Division troops fought a Communist force of 200 men and reported killing 152.

Radar sightings suspected to be of North Vietnamese helicopters operating over the DMZ June 16-19 were discounted by U.S. military sources June 21. The authorities said that radar operators probably had misinterpreted sightings of a mistaken attack by U.S. planes and artillery on allied ships. (The Australian destroyer *Hobart*, the U.S. cruiser *Boston* and 2 other American craft had been fired on off the coast near the DMZ. 2 men on the *Hobart* were killed June 16 by 3 missiles fired by an American jet.) In its first statement on the radar findings, the U.S. command had said June 17 that the "low-flying aircraft were suspected to be enemy helicopters and were taken under fire by naval vessels and United States aircraft."

Casualties & Other Costs

The U.S. command had reported June 20 that American combat deaths in Vietnam had risen to more than 25,000. The command said 25,068 Americans had been slain since Jan. 1, 1961. The weekly casualties reported June 28 brought total combat deaths to 25,367 and the number of seriously wounded to 82,972. (The U.S. command's June 20 report said that 1,000 more American troops had reached Vietnam the previous week, raising U.S. forces in the country to 534,000. Communist forces were said to number 282,000 to 307,000 troops and political cadres.)

U.S. combat deaths during the first half of 1968 exceeded the toll for the full year of 1967. The U.S. command in Saigon reported July 4 that 187 Americans had died in combat in Vietnam during the week ended June 29. While the weekly figure was the lowest listed since Jan. 6, it raised total U.S. combat deaths in

1968 to 9,557, or 138 more than the 9,419 men reported killed in all of 1967. (U.S. officials in Saigon reported July 13 that 47,411 South Vietnamese civilians had been treated in hospitals during the first 5 months of 1968. This figure compared with 49,037 reported treated in all of 1967.)

U.S. planes had continued to bomb the southern panhandle of North Vietnam. One jet was reported downed June 23, a day in which 126 missions were launched against the north. The loss brought the total downed over the North to 857. The U.S. Senate Republican Policy Committee June 20 issued Defense Department figures showing that 3,940 American aircraft had been downed over North and South Vietnam between Jan. 1, 1961 and June 10, 1968. Losses during the May 7-June 10 period totaled 186, of which 130 were helicopters.

The strains imposed by the accelerated fighting in South Vietnam were also visible in the U.S. budget. Pres. Johnson had asked Congress May 21 for a supplemental $3.9 billion in new obligational authority for the Vietnam war in fiscal 1968. This sum would have increased the year's defense commitments from $73.4 billion to $77.3 billion. The fund commitment for Vietnamese and Korean operations would have been increased from $23.8 billion to $27.7 billion. Congress voted July 2 to appropriate $3,750,950,000 in supplemental funds for military operations in Southeast Asia and to release $2.345 billion in frozen funds for the same purpose.

Westmoreland's Assessments

Gen. William C. Westmoreland, U.S. commander in South Vietnam, reported to Pres. Johnson May 30 that Communist troops appear "to be approaching a point of desperation" as their forces were "deteriorating in strength and quality." Discussing with newsmen a formal briefing paper he had presented to the President at his ranch in Texas, Westmoreland said he anticipated more heavy fighting in the northern provinces of South Vietnam, in the Central Highlands near Cambodia and in the Saigon area, but that "time is on our side."

Westmoreland said the Communists' new military policy of terror and attack was instituted after North Vietnamese officials realized the futility of their previous strategy of "protracted war." The foe's exaggerated claims of battle victories were partially due to the receipt of "false reports from his field commanders," Westmoreland said. Westmoreland noted that about 8% of South Vietnam's population had lost its "excellent security status" because of Communist attacks and that only $1/_3$ of this loss had been recovered. The Communist attacks on the cities, Westmoreland said, had created more refugees and civilian casualties. The purpose of the raids, he said, was to draw allied counterfire and cause more material destruction that might result in civilian demonstrations against the Saigon government.

Since Jan. 1, Westmoreland reported, more than 100,000 Communist troops had been killed. The enemy fatalities exceeded the total suffered by the foe in all of 1967. Communist recruitment in the South had dropped to 3,000 a month, but Communist infiltration of South Vietnam was up to more than 15,000 a month, according to Westmoreland. The American commander foresaw a continuance of this infiltration through the summer and suggested that "the war is destined to become increasingly more and more of a North Vietnamese invasion of the South." The number of North Vietnamese troops in the South had reached 90,000, he estimated.

But Westmoreland said June 10 that the American policy of "not expanding the war in Vietnam" made impossible the achievement of a military victory "in a classic sense." The Communists' strength, however, could be sapped through attrition, making continued fighting "intolerable to the enemy," Westmoreland said. Westmoreland's statement was made at a Saigon news conference the day he turned over command of U.S. forces in Vietnam to Gen. Creighton W. Abrams. (Westmoreland left for the U.S. June 11 to assume his duties as Army chief of staff.)

Westmoreland made clear that there was no contradiction between his current assessment of the military situation and his previous statements, particularly his May 30 remarks. He reiterated that the allies had defeated the Communists in every major action in 1967 and that "current trends are favorable." But Westmoreland said that Washington's current ban on ground attacks to interdict Communist infiltration via Laos permitted the enemy to go on with the war as long as he was willing to pay the price. "You cannot cut a surface line of communication with other than ground operations. You can harass it and disrupt it but you cannot cut it," he said.

Denying that the military situation was stalemated, Westmoreland added: "At this time our military strength is at its height since our commitment. We are now capable of bringing major military pressure on the enemy," and this was "beginning to show the effects. The Vietnamese armed forces are growing in size and effectiveness. . . . Trends are favorable, but it is unrealistic to expect a quick and early defeat of the Hanoi-led enemy."

NEGOTIATIONS I

Paris Conference Opens in May

Discussions between the U.S. and the North Vietnamese began in Paris May 10 against the background of the 2d Viet Cong offensive then taking place in South Vietnam. The talks were held in the French government's Center for International Conferences near the Arc de Triomphe. Formerly the Hotel Majestic, the building had served as the offices of the French Information Ministry at the start of World War II and was later taken over by the Gestapo during the German occupation of Paris.

The members of the 2 delegations were:

U.S.—Amb.-at-Large W. Averell Harriman, 76, delegation chief; Cyrus R. Vance, 51, deputy chief of delegation; Lt. Gen. Andrew J. Goodpaster Jr., military adviser; Deputy Asst. State Secy. (for East Asian affairs) Philip C. Habib, 48, adviser on Vietnamese affairs; William J. Jorden, 45, official spokesman for the delegation, White House specialist on Vietnamese affairs; Daniel I. Davidson, 31, special assistant to Harriman and specialist on Vietnamese affairs.

North Vietnam—Minister of State Xuan Thuy, 55, a secretary of the Central Committee of the North Vietnamese Communist Party, chief delegate; Col. Ha Van Lau, adviser to the chief delegate, who had served as liaison officer with the International Control Commission for Vietnam; Nguyen Minh Vy, adviser and spokesman for the delegation, deputy editor of the Communist Party newspaper *Nhan Dan*; Phan Hien, adviser to the minister of state, director of the North American section of the Foreign Ministry.

On arriving in Paris May 9, Harriman and Thuy had expressed hope that the talks would bring about a settlement of the war. Harriman repeated a week-old statement of Pres. Johnson's that he hoped the talks would prove "a mutual and serious movement by all parties toward peace in Southeast Asia." Thuy said his delegation would do its "utmost . . . to achieve the desire of the Vietnamese people and the wish of the American people and of all peoples of the world" "to see an early end to the war unleashed by the U.S. government."

At the request of the North Vietnamese delegation, the opening conference May 10 was restricted to preparatory matters. The session, as was the following day's, was handled by the delegations' deputies—Cyrus R. Vance for the U.S. and Col. Ha Van Lau for North Vietnam. The procedural points discussed May 10 included seating arrangements, delegation size and languages to be used. The 2 sides agreed on English and Vietnamese as the "official languages" of the talks and French as a "working language." May 13 was agreed on as the date to start substantive discussions.

The procedural arrangements for the formal peace talks were completed May 11. It was agreed that the meetings should be restricted, at least temporarily, to the U.S. and North Vietnam; the South Vietnamese and National Liberation Front representative thereby were barred from the initial phase of the conference. (The South Vietnamese government had a delegation of observers, headed by Amb.-to-U.S. Bui Diem, at the talks.) The 2 sides reportedly had agreed in principle to meet daily. But an American spokesman said sessions would be arranged as the talks proceeded. It was decided that the parley would be designated "official conversations."

Early Positions Taken

The substantive talks began May 13. Lengthy prepared statements were presented by Xuan Thuy, the chief negotiator for North Vietnam, and W. Averell Harriman, who spoke for the U.S. In this initial presentation, each side laid out its conditions to begin negotiations to end the conflict in Vietnam.

Reviewing Vietnam's recent history, Thuy charged that the U.S. had "resorted to many maneuvers to prevent the free general elections and the reunification of our country" as provided by the 1954 Geneva agreements. Thuy said: The U.S. had supported Ngo Dinh Diem by bringing him back to Saigon from the U.S. "to set up a puppet administration and a 200,000-strong army to fight as mercenaries for the United States and to suppress the South Vietnamese people." The U.S. had "directed the Lao

rightwing in sabotaging the 1962 Geneva agreements on Laos,"
and its planes had "daily showered bombs on Laos." The U.S.
had sought "to threaten the independence and neutrality" of
Cambodia.

Thuy noted the opposition to Washington's Vietnam policy
inside the U.S. and cited such prominent critics as the late Dr.
Martin Luther King Jr. and Sens. Robert F. Kennedy (D., N. Y.)
and J. William Fulbright (D., Ark.). Thuy declared that the U.S.'
demand for "mutual de-escalation" as a prerequisite for peace
was "unacceptable." He added: "Since the U.S.A. has unleashed
the war of aggression, the U.S.A. must stop it. Since the U.S.A. has
continually escalated the war, the U.S.A. must deescalate it. We
Vietnamese have been so far always on our own soil. . . . For the
sake of our country, we have the right to defend it."

Thuy repeated the position that North Vietnam's 4-point
program and the National Liberation Front's political program
"constitute the basis for a correct political settlement of the Vietnam problem." He said: "Since the U.S. government has unleashed the war of destruction against the Democratic Republic
of Vietnam, the U.S. has to definitively and unconditionally cease
its bombing raids and all other acts of war on the whole territory
of the Democratic Republic of Vietnam. That is the primordial
and most pressing legitimate demand" of North Vietnam and the
Vietnamese people. "We, therefore, wish to obtain a clear and
positive answer in this connection from . . . the U.S. government
during these official conversations."

Harriman, in his statement, declared that the U.S.' purpose
in Vietnam was "to preserve the right of the South Vietnamese
people to determine their own future without outside interference
or coercion." Harriman reviewed the steps leading to Pres. Johnson's decision Mar. 31 to limit the bombing of North Vietnam
and cited the President's belief "that even this limited bombing
could come to an early end—if our restraint is matched by restraint
on the other side." But Harriman expressed concern over a lack
of North Vietnamese reciprocation. Since Mar. 31, he said, North
Vietnam had "chosen to move substantial and increasing numbers
of troops and supplies from the North to the South. Moreover,
your forces have continued to fire on our forces from and across
the demilitarized zone."

Noting that North Vietnamese forces continually violated the
demilitarized zone by crossing it to attack U.S. and South Viet-

namese troops and by firing artillery across the line, Harriman stressed the need to reestablish the zone "as a genuine buffer" between the opposing forces. He suggested first "pulling apart the contending forces as a step toward broader measures of de-escalation. Restoring the demilitarized zone to its proper and original status can be an important test of good faith on each side."

Harriman assailed North Vietnam's violation of the Geneva conference accords by its infiltration of saboteurs into South Vietnam, starting in the early 1950s, and by its more recent "aggression" that had taken "the form of overt invasion" of the South. With this in mind, Harriman suggested a strengthening of the International Control Commission in Vietnam. He said: A major task in Paris "will be to devise more effective ways of supervising any agreement and insuring the fair and equitable investigation of complaints." "The nations of Asia—which have a crucial interest in the peace and stability of the region—should be associated with the monitoring of the agreements at which we may arrive."

Harriman reiterated a U.S. offer made at the Manila conference in 1966 to withdraw American forces from South Vietnam "as the other side withdraws its forces to the North, stops the infiltration, and the level of violence thus subsides." North Vietnam also was called on by Harriman to respect the 1962 Geneva accords on Laos. "North Vietnamese troops remain in Laos and are engaged in aggression there," Harriman charged.

Impasses Start

At the meetings of May 15 and 18, the conference reached the first of what were to become a series of impasses. Both parties reiterated the positions they had taken, and it appeared clear that the prime issue in dispute—the control of South Vietnam—was not negotiable. The overt issue being debated at this point in the discussions was the insistence of North Vietnam that the U.S. halt the bombardment of the North as against the refusal of the U.S. to do so unless the military pressure on the Saigon regime were halted

In his opening statement at the May 15 session, Harriman charged that North Vietnam's version of the events leading to the Vietnam war, as outlined in the opening session May 13, was an attempt "to rehash old accusations, to rekindle old controversies, and, above all, to rewrite history." This, Harriman asserted, was an "unfortunate way to begin these conversations."

Harriman defended "the legality of our presence in Vietnam" and, by contrast, cited what he called North Vietnam's persistent violation of the Geneva accords on Vietnam and Laos. He quoted a June 1962 report of the International Control Commission on Vietnam to the Geneva conference that North Vietnam was using the demilitarized zone (DMZ) to infiltrate South Vietnam with men, arms and munitions "with the object of supporting, organizing, and carrying out hostile activities, including armed attacks directed against the armed forces and administration of the zone in the South." Harriman repeated the assertion that the demilitarized character of the DMZ must be reestablished, in accord with the Geneva agreements, that all foreign forces must be withdrawn from the South and that the people of North and South Vietnam must be permitted to decide peacefully on the reunification of their country.

Harriman pointed out 5 "similarities" in the American and North Vietnamese positions in which, he said, "it seems reasonable to hope to find agreement": (1) ". . . We both speak of an independent, democratic, peaceful and prosperous South Vietnam. You also speak of a neutral South Vietnam." (2) ". . . We both speak of peace on the basis of respect of the Geneva accords of 1954—to which we add the 1962 agreements on Laos." (3) ". . . We both speak of letting internal affairs of South Vietnam be settled by the South Vietnamese themselves—which we would clarify adding, 'without outside interference or coercion'." (4) ". . . We both speak of the reunification of Vietnam by peaceful means. . . . This must not only be peaceful but also through the free choice of the people of South Vietnam and North Vietnam." (5) ". . . We both speak of the need for strict respect of the military provisions of the 1954 Geneva accords."

Harriman urged Hanoi to approve 4 "specific and urgent steps which are vital to peace": (1) Restoration of the DMZ to "its original and proper status" as a buffer zone; (2) renewed compliance with the 1962 Geneva accord on Laos, particularly the provision for the withdrawal of North Vietnamese soldiers; (3) full respect for the territorial neutrality and integrity of Cambodia and strengthening of the International Control Commission to carry this out; (4) freedom of the South Vietnamese people "from coercion," particularly in Saigon, "where vicious attacks are being directed against a civilian population." "The continuation of such attacks . . . does not contribute to the atmosphere for successful talks," he declared.

Xuan Thuy, chief North Vietnamese representative, replied by reviewing the background of the Vietnam conflict and accusing the U.S. of violating the 1954 Geneva agreements by carrying "out a policy of intervention and aggression in South Vietnam." The U.S., he asserted, had "invaded South Vietnam and waged a war of destruction against North Vietnam, thus expanding its aggression to the whole of Vietnam." Thuy stressed the American air strikes against North Vietnam, which, he claimed, had caused widespread death and destruction of non-military targets.

Thuy scoffed at the U.S.' restrictive bombing policy instituted Mar. 31. The areas still subject to American raids had "a population of nearly 4.5 million, comprising provinces which are among the biggest and the most populated in North Vietnam, such as Thanhhoa and Nghean," he said. Thuy charged that since Mar. 31 U.S. planes "have concentrated their attacks on the above mentioned area with a much greater intensity than before."

The North Vietnamese demand for an unconditional halt in the American bombings and other acts of war against the North were put in these "specific terms" by Thuy: (1) The U.S. "must stop immediately sending planes and warships for bombing and shelling the part [of North Vietnam] extending from Thanhhoa to Vinhlinh." (2) "The other acts of war" directed at North Vietnam that the U.S. must stop were: "sending planes for reconnaissance flights, dropping of leaflets and 'psychological warfare' gifts, smuggling of commandos by air, sea and by land from Laos, artillery shelling from the southern part of the demilitarized zone, intrusion into the territorial waters [of North Vietnam] by warships and motorboats, provoking and kidnaping North Vietnamese citizens." (3) The U.S. "must definitively stop the bombing raids and all other acts of war on the whole territory" of North Vietnam "without putting any conditions whatsoever" to North Vietnam.

At a press briefing following the May 15 talks, North Vietnamese spokesman Nguyen Thanh Le elaborated further on the U.S. bombing of the North. He produced maps purporting to show schools, dikes and other non-military targets that had been hit by American jets. He assailed Harriman's statements accusing North Vietnam of aggression. Harriman, he charged, was attempting to justify "14 years of aggression against both parts of our country." At the French defeat of Dienbienphu in 1954, Le said, "the U.S. general staff" had "recommended the use of tactical nuclear weapons" to assist the French defenders against the Communist Vietminh.

Summing up the atmosphere of the May 15 session, Le said the U.S. delegation had "refused obstinately to respond to our legitimate and urgent requests, and the requests of the entire world for the unconditional cessation of bombing and all other acts of war."

U.S. press spokesman William J. Jorden, commenting on the talks, said at a separate briefing: "We're not encouraged, in the sense that we got no response to these [U.S.] proposals." But "progress is always possible as long as official conversations are going on."

Harriman's assertion that there were possible areas of agreement in the talks was dismissed at a news briefing May 16 by Nguyen Van Sao, a North Vietnamese spokesman. Sao said: "In fact, our positions are very far apart"; Harriman "is only putting up a smokescreen to camouflage the reality"; Harriman had brought out only "apparent similarities, nothing real."

In a statement to a newsman May 16, Harriman said, "We are now involved in a major propaganda campaign, but one day they [the Communists] will get tired and get down to constructive discussions." Harriman said there were "indications" that if the talks reached a point at which the South Vietnamese government would participate, its delegation would include members of the National Assembly, many of whose deputies had views that differed from those of Nguyen Van Thieu's regime.

During the May 18 session, Harriman denied Thuy's charges of "deliberate destruction [by the U.S.] of non-military targets in North Vietnam." These allegations, Harriman said, "should receive an impartial investigation," and he recalled that several times in the past the U.S. had proposed an investigation by the International Committee of the Red Cross "or another impartial international agency." Harriman rejected Thuy's charges of American violation of the demilitarized zone and again said that it was North Vietnam that "first violated" the DMZ.

The remainder of Harriman's prepared statement was confined to American charges of the presence of North Vietnamese troops in South Vietnam and the presentation of evidence of this presence. Harriman said North Vietnam had been sending armed men into South Vietnam since the late 1950s in violation of the Geneva accords. North Vietnam currently had 85,000 men in South Vietnam, and more than 72,000 of them were in "wholly North Vietnamese army units," he said. Addressing himself to Thuy, Harriman said he was "particularly astounded that you should seem to evade acknowledgment of a simple and verified fact"—the presence of North Vietnamese troops in the South. The establishment of this fact, Harriman pointed out, was necessary so "that we can properly consider your demand for cessation of our bombing of North Vietnam" and later take up "such questions as the withdrawal or regrouping of forces other than those of South Vietnam, from the territory of South Vietnam."

North Vietnamese spokesman Nguyen Thanh Le said at a press briefing later May 18 that in an oral exchange after the prepared statements, Thuy had called for an end to the American bombing of South Vietnam and had denounced what he referred to as the terrorizing of the Saigon population. Le took issue with Harriman's reply to Thuy's allegation that the U.S.' deliberate plan to intervene in Vietnam for colonial purposes was evidenced by statements made in 1953 by Pres. Dwight D. Eisenhower and in 1954 by State Secy. John Foster Dulles. Eisenhower had said that Indochina's tin and tungsten would be lost if the area came under Communist control. Dulles had described South Vietnam as within the U.S.' strategic interest in Asia. Le said Harriman had explained that the statements by Eisenhower and Dulles were just the views of 2 individuals as expressed in a country of free speech.

Commenting on the appointment that day of Tran Van Huong as premier of the South Vietnamese government, Le said the change "reveals once again that the puppet regime is completely corrupt and falling apart."

Thuy, in his May 18 statement, charged that in the 2 previous meetings the U.S. had "sought by all means to elude" "the agreed object of these official conversations": "to determine with the American side the unconditional cessation of the bombings and all other American acts of war" against North Vietnam. In addition to carrying out aggression against South Vietnam, the U.S. "has implemented sinister plans of intervention in Laos and Cambodia," Thuy said. "The very fact that they [the U.S.] have on their own placed Laos, Cambodia and South Vietnam in the protection zone of the Southeast Asian bloc is in itself an illegal and impudent intervention." Thuy said "the 5 points and 3 proposals"

relating to the neutrality of Laos and Cambodia and the inviolability of the DMZ as advanced by Harriman at the May 15 meeting were thus as "diametrically opposed as black and white to
the positions" of North Vietnam. The conference was adjourned
May 18 until May 22.

Pressures on Negotiating Parties

Both parties to the discussion were under continuous and
conflicting international pressures. The U.S. was under steady
pressure from the government of South Vietnam and its Asian
allies neither to yield to the claims of Hanoi nor to reach any
unilateral agreement with North Vietnam.

Just before the conference opened, Pres. Johnson was pressed
to give assurances to this effect to the government of Thailand.
According to reports then published, the American position in
the Paris talks was a major topic of conversation at a meeting of
Johnson in Washington May 8-9 with visiting Thai Premier Thanom Kittikachorn.

In a joint communiqué issued at the conclusion of the U.S.-
Thai discussions May 9, Johnson stated that the South Vietnamese
government must be "a full participant in any negotiations for a
settlement of the conflict in South Vietnam." Johnson reaffirmed
U.S. intentions to consult Thailand and its other Southeast Asian
allies "concerning negotiations, positions and developments" in the
U.S.-North Vietnamese parley. Johnson and Kittikachorn agreed
that the allied position in negotiations would be based on the principles of the allies' Manila communiqué of Oct. 25, 1966. The
Manila statement had called for an end to internal and external
aggression against South Vietnam, the withdrawal of all foreign
troops from South Vietnam and the right of the people of North
and South Vietnam to determine freely the terms for reunification. Johnson and Kittikachorn stated "their determination that
the South Vietnamese people shall not be conquered by aggression
and shall enjoy the inherent right to decide their own way of life
and form of government."

At a dinner for Kittikachorn May 8, Johnson had warned
North Vietnam against continued infiltration of the South despite
the U.S.' decision to limit the air strikes against the North: "I
hope that . . . our adversaries . . . will realize that increased infiltration, sending new MiGs to new airfields south of the 20th Paral-

lel, will not go unnoticed." (A U.S. military spokesman in Saigon reported May 10 that North Vietnamese MiGs had been sighted below the 19th Parallel for the first time. The Communist jets were said to have been observed operating May 8 north of the coastal city of Vinh; one of them had shot down a Navy F-4 Phantom jet in that vicinity May 7. Heretofore, North Vietnamese MiGs were known to fly mainly in the Hanoi-Haiphong area and north toward the Chinese Communist border.)

South Vietnamese Pres. Nguyen Van Thieu had said May 9 that he would never agree to a total end to the raids while North Vietnam "can continue to infiltrate men and weapons into South Vietnam." Thieu reiterated his government's refusal to accept a coalition with the National Liberation Front. He said: "We will never recognize them as an equal political entity." And in a statement issued May 14, the South Vietnamese government's observers at the Paris talks had said that the U.S. should not accede to Hanoi's demand for a halt in the bombing "unless North Vietnam pledges itself and actually proceeds with a de-escalation subject to real and effective means of control." The statement was issued by Bui Diem, head of the South Vietnamese delegation, following a meeting with Harriman. It asserted that it was "out of the question that these talks would involve the substance of the Vietnamese problem without the participation of the Republic of Vietnam [South Vietnam], which will be called to assume a principal role as soon as the conversations concerning its future begins."

North Vietnam confronted its own pressures, which have been less visible in the public record. The National Liberation Front insisted on a voice in the negotiations that were to settle the political fate of the South, and throughout this period the NLF asserted its presence through its role in the massive offensives launched in South Vietnam.

And China pressed Hanoi to stand firm against the U.S. Thus, a *N.Y. Times* report from Washington June 28 quoted U.S. officials as saying that China in recent days had barred the use of its rail lines to ship war supplies to North Vietnam. The last train carrying military equipment to Hanoi through China, largely from the Soviet Union, was said to have entered North Vietnam June 14. U.S. officials were said to have speculated that the interruption of North Vietnam-bound supplies was the result of clashes between Red Guard factions in the 3 provinces bordering North Vietnam or represented a deliberate move by Peking to penalize Hanoi for its participation in peace talks with the U.S. The Soviet Union had protested to China Mar. 31 and Apr. 3 over the detention of a Soviet tanker carrying supplies to North Vietnam. The Soviet news agency Tass reported Apr. 3 that Moscow had assailed "the unlawful detention starting Mar. 27 in Port Whampoa, near . . . Canton, of the Soviet tanker *Komsomolets Ukrainy* carrying a cargo for embattled Vietnam."

(In a speech delivered May 12 and reported in the Western press July 9, Communist Chinese Premier Chou En-lai had confirmed reports that the turmoil associated with the Maoist cultural revolution had severely curtailed rail traffic from China to North Vietnam. Chou, addressing rail transport workers, testified that traffic was at a "standstill" at the Liuchow railway junction in Kwangsi Province, on North Vietnam's northern border. As a consequence, he said, "material cannot be transported to Hankow or to Vietnam." Moscow radio had charged July 5 that rail traffic from Kwangsi into North Vietnam had been held up for several weeks because of armed strife in the province.)

It was reported that China's celebration of its 19th National Day Oct. 1 gave evidence that Peking's ties with North Vietnam had further deteriorated. The Vietnam war had been a major focus of previous National Day celebrations, but the 1968 Peking ceremonies contained only perfunctory references to the war. In contrast with his 1967 National Day speech, in which Communist Party Vice Chairman Lin Piao pledged "resolute support to the Vietnamese people," in 1968 Lin did not even mention the conflict. In his address at the celebration, Foreign Min. Chou En-lai spoke of the war but primarily in terms of what he called the U.S.-Soviet "plot to divide the world." At the 1967 celebrations Chou had emphasized China's willingness to make "maximum national sacrifices" to give "all-out support and aid" to the North Vietnamese; at the 1968 festivities he only pledged China's support for the "heroic Vietnamese people."

The North Vietnamese delegation was not in its usually favored position on the list of guests on the rostrum at the Peking rally. In 1967 North Vietnamese and NLF representatives had been listed directly after the Albanians; in 1968 they followed the delegations of Albania, Pakistan, Burma, Indonesia and New Zealand.

In an earlier speech honoring the North Vietnamese National

Day Sept. 2, Chou En-lai had devoted most of his remarks to an attack on the Soviet Union and referred only perfunctorily to North Vietnam. He predicted that the USSR would betray North Vietnam by recognizing the Middle East and Southeast Asia as a U.S. sphere of influence in return for U.S. recognition of Eastern Europe as a Soviet sphere of influence. He cited the invasion of Czechoslovakia as an example of the U.S.-Soviet division of the world. "It is definite and without any shadow of doubt," he said, "that Soviet revisionism will continue to betray the Arab people and the Vietnamese people."

The Soviet Union, on the other hand, continued its support of North Vietnam. Soviet Foreign Min. Andrei A. Gromyko had advised the U.S. May 12 to "make use of the possibilities given to it" in the Paris talks by taking "such further steps that would actually result in the cessation of the aggressive war against the Vietnamese people and a political settlement." In an interview in the Italian Communist newspaper *L'Unita*, Gromyko pledged that the USSR would continue to give Hanoi military equipment as long as it was needed.

The Soviet Communist Party newspaper *Pravda* warned May 12 that the success of the Paris talks was threatened by U.S. plans to increase its military force in South Vietnam and by the U.S.' reaffirmation of the Manila communiqué of Oct. 1966. *Pravda* claimed that U.S. Defense Secy. Clark Clifford had disclosed that American troop strength in Vietnam would be raised to 750,000 in 1969. The aim of this increase, *Pravda* held, was to enable the U.S. to bargain in Paris "from a position of strength."

North Vietnam continued to receive material support from the Soviet sphere. The North Vietnamese press agency reported June 18 that under an agreement signed in Prague the previous day Czechoslovakia would provide North Vietnam with more economic and military aid. The accord had been signed by North Vietnamese Deputy Premier Le Thanh Nghi and Czech Deputy Premier Frantisek Homouz. A Tass report from Prague said Czechoslovakia would supply machine tools, tractors, medical supplies and "means necessary for strengthening the defense capacity" of North Vietnam.

A North Vietnamese delegation headed by Deputy Premier Le Thanh Nghi visited Moscow, Pyongyang (North Korea) and Peking June 24-July 23 to negotiate new aid agreements.

Nghi arrived in Moscow June 24 and conferred with Soviet

Premier Aleksei N. Kosygin and Deputy Premier Vladimir N. Novikov during the following week and a half. A communiqué issued at the end of the talks July 4 said that a new economic and military aid agreement had been concluded, but it did not disclose the terms. The communiqué affirmed that the Soviet Union would continue to "promote the further strengthening of the defense potential" of North Vietnam and "render support and assistance to the Vietnamese people." (Figures released in Moscow July 5 indicated that Soviet commercial trade with North Vietnam had more than doubled during 1967. The figures showed that Soviet exports to Hanoi had totaled $148 million in 1967, compared with $68.2 million in 1966, but North Vietnamese exports to the Soviet Union had dropped from $25.3 million in 1966 to $20.9 million in 1967.)

Nghi arrived in Pyongyang July 5 and announced there July 7 that he had met with "good success" in talks with North Korean officials on North Korean aid to Hanoi.

Following the arrival of the North Vietnamese in Peking July 9, Hanoi radio announced July 11 that Nghi and Chinese Deputy Premier Li Hsien-nien had discussed China's 1969 aid program to North Vietnam "in an atmosphere of warm militant solidarity and fraternal friendship." According to the broadcast, Li had pledged that China would "extend more effective support to the revolutionary struggle of the fraternal Vietnamese people." He asserted that "any attempt to alienate China and Vietnam will definitely fail." Hsinhua, the Chinese press agency, announced July 24 that the 2 sides had concluded a new economic and technical aid agreement July 23.

Under a 1969 aid agreement signed in Moscow Nov. 25, the USSR promised North Vietnam large supplies of military equipment and civilian goods. The agreement, announced in a joint communiqué Nov. 27, said the Soviet exports would include food, oil products, transport equipment, metals, fertilizers, armaments, munitions and other materiel "needed for building up the defense and strengthening the economy" of North Vietnam. (The exact cost of the 1969 aid pact was not announced in the communiqué. Soviet figures released earlier in 1968 on USSR-North Vietnamese trade in 1967 indicated that Moscow had exported $150 million worth of goods to Hanoi and had imported $20 million worth from North Vietnam.)

Britain, on the U.S.' behalf, sought to reactivate the machinery set up by the Geneva Conference of 1954 to bring peace to Vietnam. British Foreign Secy. Michael Stewart and Soviet Foreign Min. Andrei A. Gromyko conferred in Moscow May 23 on the possibility that their 2 countries might play a joint role in helping end the war. But the positions of Britain and the Soviet Union, co-chairmen of the 1954 Geneva Conference, remained unreconciled. Gromyko reportedly insisted on an unconditional U.S. halt in the bombing of North Vietnam. Stewart, supporting the American stand, asserted that Hanoi must display some sign of military reciprocation before the U.S. raids could stop. Stewart was said to have urged Gromyko to persuade the North Vietnamese negotiators in Paris that their repeated raising of the point of who had started the war served only to impede the discussions.

On his return to London, Stewart said May 24 that the Russians had "not yet in my judgment realized some of the things needed to end it [the war], such as a willingness by North Vietnam to make some response to a stopping of the bombing by the Americans."

The Swiss Foreign Ministry Feb. 21 had announced the appointment of Swiss Amb-to China Oscar Rossetti to the additional post of representative to North Vietnam. The Foreign Ministry had announced Feb. 15 that Rossetti, who had returned to Peking from a Feb. 18-20 visit to Hanoi, had been sent to North Vietnam to point up Switzerland's long-standing offer to use its good offices to help end the war. The ministry said Feb. 21 that Rossetti's trip to Hanoi did not mean Swiss recognition of North Vietnam but was aimed at maintaining a channel of contact with the Communist regime. His Feb. 18-20 mission to Hanoi, the ministry explained, was to check on the $58,000 worth of medicines Switzerland had donated to North Vietnam in 1967 and to make a survey of future needs. Switzerland made similar contributions to South Vietnam.

(North Vietnamese Amb.-to-USSR Nguyen Tho Chanh conferred in Stockholm Feb. 20-25 with Swedish Foreign Min. Torsten Nilsson. After the Feb. 20 meeting, Nilsson said that Sweden was prepared to bring both sides in the war together if they agreed. Chanh Feb. 21 read a 4-page statement assailing the U.S.' "military and political action" in Vietnam. Chanh affirmed that North Vietnam's conditions for ending the war remained acceptance of Hanoi's 4-point peace formula.)

Both the pope and the UN Secretary General sought to use

their influence to bring the parties to a peace agreement.

Pope Paul VI Apr. 14 and June 24 appealed again to both sides in Vietnam to agree to a truce as a first step toward a settlement. In his June 24 remarks the pope expressed the belief that a "satisfactory solution" was "relatively near and easy" if both sides "loyally give signs of a reciprocal arms truce and thus make available a period of serene and fraternal relations between the 2 regions in conflict so that they can then freely decide their own destinies." In his annual Easter message Apr. 14, the pope had called for a "military truce and honorable and fair negotiations" in order to bring the war to an end. He added: "May the show of strength be transformed into a competition of generosity. May victory go not to a presumptive justice of arms but to a justice which recognizes reciprocal rights to freedom and the common needs of work and of peace. . . ."

Archbishop Agostino Casaroli, the pope's chief negotiator with Communist countries, disclosed June 28 that the pope had sought for months to arrange Vietnam peace talks following Pres. Johnson's visit to the Vatican Dec. 23, 1967. Casaroli said the pope had "had recourse" to various governments represented at the Vatican and to friends of both the U.S. and North Vietnam in order "to prepare the beginning of the true and proper direct dialogue." He also disclosed that he and other Vatican diplomats had been sent to several world capitals in support of this mission. Casaroli said that U.S. officials had been "very open" but that "it was not easy to establish contacts with the other side."

In the midst of the impasse in Paris, UN Secy. Gen. U Thant said May 13 that an "unconditional cessation of the [American] bombing of North Vietnam" was "the first and most important step" toward successful peace talks. Speaking at the University of Alberta (Edmonton, Canada), Thant asserted that "the continuation of the bombing has only hardened the determination of the North to prosecute the war and not to negotiate under duress." The bombing, Thant said, was of "questionable morality and doubtful legality." Thant said that if the Paris talks produced an agreement on ending the U.S. air strikes, the negotiations should "lead without interruption to substantial talks involving all interested parties." A permanent political solution to the Vietnam conflict, Thant stressed, should be based on a neutralization of North and South Vietnam, Laos and Cambodia "guaranteed by all big powers." Thant implied that China should participate in the Vietnam peace talks at some future date.

A spokesman for Saigon's UN observer May 14 took issue with Thant's plea for a halt in the bombing of the North. He said "a unilateral cessation of the bombing without any reciprocal restraint on the part of the other side would not help improve the atmosphere surrounding peace talks but would rather result in prolonging the war." "Only a genuine desire for peace and a mutual restraint could lead to meaningful talks," the spokesman said.

Paris Impasse Persists

The impasse in Paris persisted. The U.S. sought to break it through an intensification of the bombing of North Vietnam, followed by a proposal that the talks move into secret session. From May 15 to May 19, U.S. planes carried out widespread raids over North Vietnam. They concentrated on the area south of the 19th Parallel. Among the targets struck were missile sites, bridges, trucks, supply depots and coastal shipping. 3 planes were downed during the 6-day period. (In the May 16 air strike, U.S. pilots reported destroying a MiG-17 on the ground a mile north of Vinh. Heretofore, U.S. military authorities had reported that the Vinh airfield could not handle jets because of its short runway and because the field had been bombed almost daily during the past 2 months.)

At the May 22 session, Xuan Thuy, chief North Vietnamese delegate, rejected a suggestion by U.S. Amb.-at-Large W. Averell Harriman that both sides withhold from the press the prepared statements they had delivered at the meetings and instead give out short and general information. Harriman said his proposal to keep the U.S.-North Vietnamese exchanges secret would reduce the public polemics and help pave the way for the start of more meaningful talks. A North Vietnamese press spokesman reported that Thuy had rejected Harriman's plan because "the whole world is following us with attention" while the U.S. continued to bomb North Vietnam. According to the spokesman, Thuy had asserted that the subject of secret talks would be taken up when conditions required.

The remainder of Thuy's remarks dealt largely with Hanoi's call for unconditional cessation of the U.S. raids on the North. Pres. Johnson's announcement Mar. 31 that the bombing would be restricted to the southern part of North Vietnam was followed by an acceleration of the American air strikes, Thuy said. "What Pres. Johnson calls limited bombing does not represent any limitation in reality." Thuy warned that if the talks collapsed, "the American side would bear the full and entire responsibility."

The U.S. delegation denied Thuy's charges on the American bombing raids and cited the increase of North Vietnamese infiltration of the South. In the past year, the American officials claimed, the infiltration rate had increased from 2,000 men a month to 6,000.

Harriman's reply to Thuy linked a halt in the U.S. bombing with a North Vietnamese agreement on a mutual troop withdrawal along the DMZ. Harriman explained: "We are prepared to discuss the cessation of the bombing, as we have said repeatedly. We are ready to try to establish same basis from which we could properly consider your demand for cessation and, at the appropriate time, such questions as the withdrawal for regroupment of forces other than those of South Vietnam from . . . South Vietnam. I ask you whether you are ready to end your violations of the demilitarized zone. If you agree, we can take immediate action which would be a major step forward."

Thuy's response was a reiteration of Hanoi's charge that it was the U.S., not North Vietnam, that had violated the DMZ. Charging that the U.S. had intensified the war, Thuy said it was up to the U.S. to "proceed to de-escalate." Thuy introduced into the proceedings a statement, made by North Vietnamese Foreign Min. Nguyen Duy Trinh, protesting U.S. attempts to raise the question of Cambodian neutrality at the May 13 session in the absence of Cambodian representatives. The only purpose of the current talks, Thuy insisted, was to discuss a bombing halt.

A statement made by Thuy at the May 27 session was regarded by U.S. officials as coming close to admission of the presence of North Vietnamese troops in South Vietnam. Thuy said: "Vietnam is one country, the Vietnamese are one. . . . When the United States commits aggression against Vietnam, any Vietnamese has the right to fight them, and . . . on any portion of his dear country's territory. This is a sacred and inalienable right."

A prepared statement submitted by Harriman took up details of North Vietnamese military operations in the South. Harriman asserted that "well over 200,000 North Vietnamese have been dispatched into South Vietnam since autumn 1964." He later said that casualties had reduced the current North Vietnamese force there to 85,000 men.

Thuy and Harriman exchanged conflicting views over the intent of the current preliminary discussions. Thuy charged that in violation of the original agreement setting up the conference, the U.S. delegation continued to avoid discussion of Hanoi's demand for a halt in the bombing. He said the U.S.' reply May 4 to North Vietnam's agreement the previous day to enter discussions represented acceptance of "the proposition formulated" by Hanoi: "to determine with the American side the unconditional cessation of bombing and all other acts of war against North Vietnam and, after that, to have conversations on other subjects of interest to the 2 parties."

Harriman replied that "we reject the suggestion now urged by you that the only reason for our meetings is to give the hour and date for the cessation of bombing."

The talks were adjourned May 27 until May 31.

At a press briefing after the May 27 session, Nguyen Thanh Le, North Vietnamese spokesman, cited 3 points to define Hanoi's meaning that the talks were being held to "determine" the cessation of the bombing: "First, the United States must end the bombing and all other acts of war against North Vietnam"; "2d, the United States must end them immediately"; "3d, if the United States sincerely wants it [a bomb halt], the United States can determine it in many ways. . . . As for the details, the American side must take the initiative."

During the recess periods between meetings, U.S. and North Vietnamese officials issued statements on the prospects for the success of the Paris talks.

In an interview with U.S. news media May 20, Harriman and his deputy, Cyrus R. Vance, denied that the talks were deadlocked. Harriman conceded that "there has been a degree of time spent by North Vietnamese on abuse . . ., polemics, using the meetings for propaganda purposes. But there has been no deadlock." The North Vietnamese, Harriman said, would not have entered the negotiations "unless they had expected more than propaganda out of this exercise."

Vance, noting a rocket-and-mortar attack on Saigon May 19, said the onslaught was evidence that "Hanoi is conducting its operations on the ground with an eye to what is going on here in Paris." But Vance said he would not regard what he called Xuan Thuy's negative attitude at the conference or the military action of the other side as a "definitive reply" to the American plea for restraint.

Harriman conceded May 23 that there was "always a possibility . . . that these talks would break down. The talks can just break down on the United States side if they think the North Vietnamese are taking advantage of the [American] restraint in bombing." But Harriman said his remark should not be interpreted as predicting failure: "My own judgment is that we're here for a long time, that the other side feels they want to have talks, and certainly Pres. Johnson has shown every indication of wanting to come to an agreement."

Nguyen Thanh Le reiterated May 24 that the U.S. representatives had "accepted our [Hanoi's] propositions" that the first subject of the peace negotiations would be to determine "the unconditional cessation of the bombing and all other acts of war against North Vietnam." But he charged that "the American side has refused to discuss the subject and has sought several ways to avoid it," while its military forces were escalating the war.

In a separate briefing May 24, attended for the first time by North Vietnamese newsmen, William J. Jorden, the American spokesman, denied that the U.S. had been intensifying the war or avoiding discussion of the bombing question. He said the Communists had recently stepped up attacks around Saigon and Danang.

Consultations

By the end of May, the deadlock in the conference led the parties to consultations.

Cyrus Vance flew to Washington May 28 to report to Pres. Johnson on the progress of the talks in Paris.

After the meeting, Johnson, at a news conference, gave an assessment of the situation based on his talks with Vance. The President said the North Vietnamese negotiators "sought to use these talks for 2 purposes: first, to see if we could be pressured to stop the bombing completely in the southern panhandle of North Vietnam, without compensatory action on their part; 2d," to use the conference "for obviously wide-ranging propaganda. They have been unwilling to enter serious, quiet discussion of the conditions for ending the bombing or any matters of substance." While the talks were in progress, Johnson pointed out, North

Vietnam was "pouring men and supplies" through its southern panhandle and into South Vietnam "at an unprecedented rate." But allied forces, he said, were "destroying something over 20% of what is coming through to the South."

Johnson noted that the Communists had intensified their attacks in the South since the start of the Paris conference, while "we have stopped the bombing of most of the territory and population in North Vietnam." But, he said, the U.S. position at the Paris talks remained unchanged: "If North Vietnam would show some similar restraint, we were prepared to make futher decisions to try to reduce the violence." "While our men deal with the Communist forces in the field, we shall continue patiently to see whether the Paris talks shall yield anything in the way of constructive results," the President pledged.

(Johnson's position in the Paris talks and U.S. military policy in Vietnam were supported by Australian Prime Min. John G. Gorton in a joint Australian-American communiqué issued May 28. The statement was based on talks Gorton had held in Washington with Johnson May 26-28.)

Vance visited the White House May 29 for his 2d day of briefings on the Paris talks with Congressional leaders, cabinet members and other Administration officials. Vance said later that the American negotiators "are not discouraged" at the progress of the discussions. He said he assumed the North Vietnamese "also have as their ultimate objective the finding of a just and honorable peace."

Johnson had said May 23 that the U.S. was determined to "pursue negotiations toward an honorable and peaceful settlement of the war." But, he asserted: "We shall not be defeated on the battlefield while the talks go on. We shall not permit the enemy's mortars and rockets to go unanswered and to permit him to achieve a victory that would make a mockery of the negotiations." "There has been no visible lessening of Hanoi's aggressive efforts. In fact, Hanoi is today telling its forces in the South that they must continue their offensive to support their negotiators in Paris." (Johnson made these remarks in presenting a Presidential Unit Citation to the 26th Marine Regiment and its reinforcing units for actions in defense of the Marine base at Khesanh during its siege by North Vietnamese troops.)

Appearing before the Senate Appropriations Committee May 23, Defense Secy. Clark Clifford said North Vietnam was pursuing a policy of "fight and negotiate" and the U.S. must be prepared to do the same, "both physically and psychologically."

Le Duc Tho, a member of the North Vietnamese Communist Party's Politburo, arrived in Paris June 3 to join the North Vietnamese delegation as a special counselor. Tho asserted that the U.S. side was "jeopardizing the progress of the talks" by refusing, "by dilatory means, to cease unconditionally the bombing and all other acts of war" against North Vietnam. Tho expressed the view that if the American side "renounces its obstinate attitude, talks on other problems interesting to the 2 parties could begin without delay."

Nguyen Thanh Le May 21 had been more specific about the next phase of the Paris talks once the bombing question was settled. He said the conferees would then take up "questions relating to a political settlement of the Vietnamese problem within the framework of the 1954 Geneva accords on Vietnam." Heretofore, the North Vietnamese negotiators had said the following step would deal with "questions of mutual interest."

Xuan Thuy, mocking U.S. demands, suggested May 31 a joint statement in which Hanoi would pledge to "refrain from bombing and [carrying out] all other acts of war on the entire territory of the United States" while the U.S. "commits itself to cease definitively the bombardments and all other acts of war" on North Vietnam.

W. Averell Harriman asked the North Vietnamese negotiators May 31 whether they were "prepared to . . . deal with real issues" by promising to cease the "bombardment and acts of war and subversion" against South Vietnam. Thuy spurned Harriman's suggestion and assailed his charges of aggression by Hanoi as "a calumny."

Thuy's suggestion that North Vietnam pledge not to bomb the U.S. was in response to a call by Harriman for a joint agreement on "the restoration of the DMZ" as a truly neutral buffer area. Harriman had said: "For to take your claims at face value" that only U.S. forces, and not North Vietnamese, were violating the zone, "your side would be giving up nothing" by joining the U.S. in the neutrality pledge "since you are not violating the DMZ while our side would be committing the violations which you allege." Harriman, however, charged that the North Vietnamese 320th Division had crossed the DMZ May 26 to attack allied positions at Dongha.

Thuy refused to discuss the DMZ. He charged that the U.S. was using the issue as a "smokescreen to camouflage its war of aggression" and "to perpetuate the division of Vietnam."

Harriman took issue with Thuy's May 27 statement that "Vietnam is one country" and any "Vietnamese has the right to fight them [the Americans] . . . on any portion of his dear country's territory." Harriman asserted that "there is no basis for your contention that North Vietnamese have a right to invade and use force in the South."

The North Vietnamese government had "the right to speak of the entire Vietnamese problem," Nguyen Tranh Le responded at a news briefing after the talks. Le chided Harriman for questioning Hanoi's right to speak for all Vietnamese. He said: "Is Harriman a Vietnamese? Is he a South Vietnamese? . . . In fact, Harriman acts like nothing more nor less than the governor general of South Vietnam."

Pres. Johnson's charge May 28 that North Vietnam was obstructing the Paris talks had been assailed by Le at a news conference May 29. Accusing the President of "hypocritical, false, lying words," Le asserted that it was "the obstinacy and perfidy" of the American side that was impeding progress in Paris. Le insisted that the U.S., not North Vietnam, was escalating the war while the peace talks were being held. He cited a May 6 U.S. command directive calling for an "all-out" drive and "victory at any price in the next 3 months in order to give more weight to the words of American representatives in Paris." (The U.S. command in Saigon had denied that the May 6 order had related to the Paris talks or had called for victory in 3 months.) Noting other examples of allied plans to intensify the war, Le mentioned Johnson's supplemental budget requests for the war, increased mobilization in South Vietnam and Thai preparations to send 2,500 more combat troops to South Vietnam. (Thai Premier Thanom Kittikachorn had said May 27 that his country would send 5,000 combat troops to Vietnam in July to reinforce the 2,400 already there. Kittikachorn said Johnson had requested the additional Thai troops in his meeting with the President in Washington in April.)

The U.S. apparently sought a way out of the impasse through an understanding with the Soviet Union. In a commencement address at Glassboro (N.J.) State College June 4, Pres. Johnson appealed to the Soviet Union to join the U.S. and other nations "in the spirit of Glassboro" to help achieve world peace. (It was at Glassboro that Johnson had held a summit conference with Soviet Premier Aleksei N. Kosygin June 23-25, 1967.) Despite continuing "disagreements" and the strains in U.S.-Soviet relations caused by the war, the 2 nations had shown a high degree of bilateral cooperation in other areas, Johnson pointed out. The President deplored the fact that despite American initiatives in de-escalating the air war against North Vietnam and in bringing the conflict to the conference table, North Vietnam "had nothing of substance to say to those of us who seek peace in Asia." Hanoi had "offered only propaganda." He conceded that peacemaking was difficult and that "we will face reverses and setbacks." But he expressed hope that Americans would "try in the days ahead to display the fortitude, forbearance and understanding that has symbolized the Glassboro I know. . . ."

The Soviet news agency Tass, commenting on Johnson's speech, said June 4 that it presaged a continued "tough" American position at the Paris peace talks. The Soviet government newspaper *Izvestia* June 12 spurned Johnson's invitation to joint participation in international peace efforts and programs. Soviet-American relations, *Izvestia* said, were "frozen" and would remain so because of "the armed intervention of the United States in Vietnam." The Soviet Union was prepared to resume "normal and business-like relations" with the U.S. when Washington abandoned the policy of intervening militarily in the affairs of other countries, it said.

First Signs of Progress at Talks

As June opened, the results of the consultations of late May were not at first visible. The North Vietnamese continued to insist that the U.S. halt the bombardment as a precondition to negotiations, and the U.S. continued to insist that Hanoi reduce its military pressure on South Vietnam, particularly in the area of the DMZ.

At the June 5 meeting, North Vietnamese representative Xuan Thuy asked: "When will the United States cease the bombing and all other acts of war against the Democratic Republic of Vietnam so that other questions can be discussed?" W. Averell Harriman replied: "I ask you . . . whether you are prepared to discuss forthwith the matters related to the bombing question?" Previously,

Harriman had said that the questions to be discussed included North Vietnam's "massive infiltration" of South Vietnam, its attacks in the demilitarized zone and its shelling of targets across the DMZ.

Thuy again rejected U.S. demands for military reciprocity by Hanoi. Other North Vietnamese representatives held that Hanoi's agreement to attend the Paris talks was itself sufficient response to Pres. Johnson's restriction of air attacks on the North. The U.S. demands for reciprocity, Thuy argued, was "preventing progress" in the talks. Harriman said the U.S. was prepared to halt the bombing "at the appropriate time and under appropriate circumstances."

Harriman's prepared statement was restricted to the fighting in Laos, which he called the "forgotten war." Charging that 40,000 North Vietnamese troops were in Laos in violation of the 1962 Geneva agreements for neutralization of that country, Harriman asserted that "to deny North Vietnamese aggression in Laos is to insult the intelligence of the world public."

An official North Vietnamese weekly, *The Vietnam Courier*, had said in an article published June 6 that the U.S. should set a date for a halt to the bombing of the North. "It is on this sole condition that conversations [in Paris] will be able to progress." In response to U.S. charges of a North Vietnamese military presence in South Vietnam, the weekly stated: "If the U.S. aggression against South Vietnam provoked the indignation of all peoples and raised powerful movements of support and aid for the southern patriots fighting against U.S. imperialism, can one then imagine that the Vietnamese of the North should remain with crossed arms in the face of this massacre of their blood brothers?"

The scope of North Vietnam's military role in the South had been indicated June 6 by Gen. Vo Nguyen Giap, Hanoi's commander in chief. "Our people," Giap said, "are fighting on all battlefields" from the Southern tip of South Vietnam to the demilitarized zone. "In response to the call of Pres. Ho Chi Minh, our people, our nation, our army, from the north to the south, firmly fight them, the Americans." The North Vietnamese Communist Party newspaper, *Nhan Dan*, in an article June 10 said: "Wherever the enemy is, every Vietnamese has the right to go there to fight him." There was no such thing as 2 Vietnams, *Nhan Dan* held. "Any place, any area, any region in Vietnam is Vietnamese territory. He who intrudes into any place, any area, any region of Vietnam, encroaches thereby upon Vietnam and therefore must be resisted by the entire Vietnamese people throughout the country."

Cleveland industrialist Cyrus Eaton June 13 expressed confidence that "we are on the threshold of peace in Vietnam." Eaton's view was based on talks he had held with Harriman and Thuy in Paris June 10-11, with Soviet Premier Aleksei N. Kosygin in Moscow June 1-6 and with Rumanian Communist Party Gen. Secy. Nicolae Ceausescu in Bucharest. Interviewed at his home in Cleveland, Eaton said: "The Russian and North Vietnamese diplomats still have suspicions about United States sincerity, but there is clear room for compromise and this is being worked out." Eaton said Kosygin had told him that the continued American bombing of North Vietnam "is not helping anything, so why not stop it."

The U.S.' concern, however, had shifted from North Vietnamese pressures in the DMZ area to the mortar and rocket attacks against the cities of South Vietnam. At the June 12 session, Harriman accused the North Vietnamese military of having planned the current "terrorist attacks on Saigon," "which could have the most serious consequences for these talks." The Saigon mortar and rocket attacks, Harriman later told newsmen, had "no military objective at all"; they were "just an attempt to terrorize the people."

Thuy stated that the fighting would continue around Saigon as long as American forces remained there. "If the United States pulls out of Saigon, the combat will cease around Saigon." he said.

The June 19th session, however, was marked, for the first time, by a refusal to comment on the matters discussed by the 2 sides during the day's "tea break." Heretofore, these recesses had been devoted to informal talks among the delegates. But Communist sources said June 21 that one of the subjects that had been raised was the shelling of Saigon. The formal meeting June 19 was devoted largely to an exchange of accusations that each side was intensifying the war. In his statement, Xuan Thuy said that Pres. Johnson's Mar. 31 decision to limit the bombing of North Vietnam was a sham and that the U.S. actually was increasing its air strikes. The North had been subjected to 3,500 raids in April and 4,700 in May, Thuy claimed. The U.S., he further charged, had launched helicopter gas-bomb attacks in the Saigon area June 3 for the purpose of "massacring the population."

In his rebuttal, Harriman assailed the shelling of Saigon as "calculated barbarism." More than 600 Vietnamese civilians had suffered casualties in the Saigon attacks, while only one American had been killed, according to Harriman.

Thuy contended that the Saigon attacks were aimed at U.S. and Vietnamese government installations.

William J. Jorden, spokesman for the American delegation, acknowledged after the meeting that U.S. air strikes on the North had increased, but he asserted that they were less intensive than the raids under way a year ago, in May 1967.

The meeting produced a procedural agreement to hold conferences every Wednesday and special sessions at the request of either side.

The imminence of a turn in the discussions was indicated by a flurry of public statements. U.S. Vice Pres. Hubert H. Humphrey urged North Vietnam June 21 to join in an immediate cease-fire to provide an atmosphere more conducive to successful peace talks. He said that the U.S. was prepared to suspend hostilities immediately. Humphrey's proposal was made in an interview with editors of the *N.Y. Times*. Urging an end to "what the enemy calls fight and talk," Humphrey said: "I suggest that we talk." The U.S. was "prepared for a cease-fire any hour of the day. However, Hanoi has shown no such interest. But it may. I think we ought to keep pounding away at it."

Humphrey expressed agreement with Defense Secy. Clark Clifford, who had made an assessment of the Paris talks June 20 that "gave some indication that whatever little movement there has been has been positive." "There is some indication," Humphrey said, "that there is a more responsible dialogue in Paris . . . than there was a week ago, 2 weeks ago, 3 weeks ago." Clifford had said at a news conference in the Pentagon June 20 that there were "bits and straws that indicate that there is some movement" in the negotiations.

But State Secy. Dean Rusk, speaking June 21 at his first formal news conference in nearly 6 months, was less optimistic. Referring to Clifford's remarks, Rusk said: "I won't quarrel with 'bits and straws' in the wind, but we have not yet, I think, taken giant strides."

Before leaving Paris for Washington June 21, Harriman told newsmen that he didn't "want to exaggerate the importance of what has been accomplished so far," but he had been impressed by the presence at the talks of Le Duc Tho, a member of the Politburo of the North Vietnamese Communist Party. "I don't believe they would have sent him unless they were serious about the talks," Harriman said.

Humphrey's cease-fire proposal was discounted June 24 by Xuan Thuy. Speaking to the Anglo-American Press Association in Paris, Thuy said: "The first and most important thing is for the United States to cease immediately and unconditionally the bombing and all other acts of war over the entire territory" of North Vietnam. The peace talks thus far "have not produced any results."

The South Vietnamese government's uneasiness over the peace talks was reflected in a statement made by Premier Tran Tan Huong June 22. He warned that his regime would spurn any attempt to "force us to accept a solution" to end the war. Alluding to the U.S., Huong said "no nation, no matter how friendly it is, can force us to accept a solution that we repudiate."

A demand for a Saigon government role in the Paris peace talks was voiced by members of the South Vietnamese House of Representatives June 26. Duong Van Ba, first deputy secretary general of the house, declared that "we should tell the United States government and the United States people that we suspect that there is now a plot to sell out South Vietnam to the Communists."

At the June 26 session in Paris, the U.S. presented considerably reduced conditions for halting the bombardment of North Vietnam. Cyrus R. Vance, deputy U.S. delegate, called on North Vietnam for "some response which we have not yet seen on the ground in the direction of de-escalation of the violence. This could be done de facto, it could be done by some indication, either directly or indirectly, that such a step is being taken." (Vance was temporarily replacing Harriman, who had returned to the U.S.) This was the first time the American negotiators had urged North Vietnamese military reciprocity in broad, general terms. Previously, U.S. negotiators had called on the Communists specifically to halt infiltration or artillery and infantry attacks around the DMZ.

Thuy replied by again rejecting demands for military reciprocity and repeating the call for cessation of the U.S. raids on the North. He declared that the U.S. had been escalating the air war against the North while making deceitful statements about its peaceful intentions. Thuy read into the conference's record the National Liberation Front's political program of Sept. 1, 1967. It called for replacement of the Saigon government with a coalition regime dedicated to a neutral foreign policy and eventual reunification of North and South Vietnam.

Ground Warfare Declines

An apparent response to the U.S.' reduction of its terms for a *"de facto"* de-escalation of the violence in South Vietnam was the cessation of the mortar and rocket attacks on Saigon and other cities and a reduction in the scale of hostilities. In press accounts from July 1 to July 16, only the following isolated encounters were reported:

• In the action below the DMZ, the U.S. command reported the killing of 49 North Vietnamese in 3 engagements July 2. 2 Americans were killed and 4 were wounded.

• In a series of sharp battles near Giolinh July 5-7, U.S. Marines reported slaying 201 North Vietnamese. 10 Marines were killed and 81 wounded in the clashes. The Marines killed 78 of the enemy in a day-long battle July 5.

• U.S. Marines killed 22 of the enemy and captured an arms supply dump July 9 just north of Conthien. 33 more North Vietnamese were killed July 11.

• The U.S. had announced July 5 that the withdrawal from the combat base at Khesanh had been completed that day. The Marines leveled the bunkers and destroyed other facilities before leaving.

• The U.S. command reported July 9 that 89 North Vietnamese had been killed July 7 in 2 battles with U.S. Marines near Khesanh. U.S. casualties tolaled 13 dead and 38 wounded.

• In action around Saigon, U.S. infantrymen July 4 threw back a combined North Vietnamese/Viet Cong attack on the 25th Division base at Dautieng, about 40 miles northwest of the capital. 10 of the enemy were killed in the 2½-hour battle, while 5 Americans were killed and 56 wounded.

• A U.S. Navy spokesman disclosed July 7 that allied forces had intensified their patrolling on the Saigon River and its tributaries in an effort to block enemy infiltration into Saigon.

• U.S. forces on patrol near Saigon fought 3 sharp engagements July 8-9 and reported killing 38 of the enemy. American casualties were 4 killed and 13 wounded. 19 miles southwest of Saigon, U.S. forces killed 10 of the enemy July 10. South Vietnamese troops July 10 threw back about 200 Viet Cong attempting to penetrate the outer defenses of Saigon about 5 miles west of the capital.

• U.S. and South Vietnamese infantrymen July 16 repulsed an attack in Vinbinh Province 50 miles southwest of Saigon. The infantrymen, supported by artillery and air strikes, reported killing 104 of the enemy. Saigon's forces suffered 2 wounded; U.S. casualties were not disclosed.

• U.S. troops on a sweep near Saigon captured 56 Soviet and Chinese rockets July 3. 3 more enemy caches, containing 60 rockets and more than 1,100 rocket grenades, were discovered July 5 west and northwest of Saigon. South Vietnamese July 14 discovered another arms cache 14 miles northwest of the capital. It included 116 rounds of heavy-weapons ammunition, such as rockets and recoilless rifle shells, 1,125 half-pound blocks of TNT and 2 heavy machine guns.

• A senior U.S. military source disclosed in Saigon July 16 that enemy units of regiment and larger size had withdrawn from Saigon toward the west. (A Viet Cong regiment was believed to average around 1,500 men.) The source said that the Communist pullback indicated that an anticipated attack on Saigon would not occur until late July or early August. Previously, intelligence data had indicated that the Communists would attack in the period July 15-20.

While there was a reduction in ground combat, U.S. B-52 bombers resumed their missions north of the demilitarized zone July 1. The raids were the first since May 9 in which B-52s had been sent over North Vietnam. More B-52 missions were flown July 2-6 and July 14-15.

The U.S. reported July 4 that 2 surface-to-air missiles had been fired that day at B-52s attacking artillery sites and bunkers in the southern panhandle of North Vietnam. The loss of 5 U.S. planes over North Vietnam was reported in the period July 2-8. An F-105 Thunderchief and an A-1 Skyraider were lost July 2; one of the pilots was rescued and the other was listed as missing. 2 F-4 Phantom jets were shot down July 5 and 2 more were lost July 8; 4 of the 6 crewmen were listed as missing. U.S. pilots reported downing a MiG-17 July 9 and a MiG-21 July 10 in dogfights over North Vietnam.

In commenting on the lull in the ground fighting in South Vietnam, Amb. Harriman said in an interview July 12 that the decline in hostilities did not represent the "sort of restraint" the U.S. had in mind in return for a halt in the bombing of North Vietnam. But he said the cessation of rocket attacks on Saigon was a "good sign." Harriman reaffirmed that "one of the [U.S.] conditions for future discussion of political matters" was to have the South Vietnamese government "represented" at the talks once the current phase was over.

Hanoi's Thuy, interviewed July 16 by an American Broadcasting Co. reporter, was quoted July 17 as having said: "Although there have been no rocket attacks on Saigon for several weeks, the Americans maintain their offensives and send out their bombers on ever more devastating missions in the Saigon region. Furthermore, Americans have greatly increased tonnage and sorties of destructive air raids on North Vietnam ever since the [Paris] talks began." Thus, "things have gotten worse" rather than better since the talks began.

This was the first time Hanoi had publicly described the cessation of rocket attacks on Saigon in such a way as to suggest that it represented a scaling down of the war by North Vietnam.

Asked by reporters for comment, Harriman said that the halt in rocket attacks "may have some significance" but that he had not "thought of it as 'reciprocity' because they started their outrageous shellings after the President's [Johnson's] message of Mar. 31 [restricting American bombing of the North], and it is hardly reciprocity to stop an escalation which they took since the President's act of material deescalation of the fighting."

North Vietnamese spokesman Nguyen Thanh Le asserted July 17 that Thuy's remarks had "differed in no way from what he had said before." Le said it was up to the National Liberation Front, not Hanoi, to decide "what takes place in the south of our country—where to hit, when to hit, how to hit."

The July 3 session in Paris was marked by what appeared to be a further conciliatory gesture by Hanoi. The North Vietnamese confirmed that Hanoi intended to release 3 captured American pilots. Radio Hanoi had made the announcement earlier July 3, and Xuan Thuy confirmed the report during a break in the session. Thuy said Hanoi was releasing the pilots because of his government's "humanitarian and lenient policy." Harriman thanked Hanoi and said he hoped the gesture "indicated a willingness to move toward a peaceful setlement."

(North Vietnam July 18 freed the 3 U.S. airmen, all of whom had been captured after being shot down over North Vietnam. The Americans remained in Hanoi until Aug. 2 and were then flown to Vientiane, Laos in an International Control Commission plane. They returned to the U.S. in a commercial airliner, landing in New York Aug. 4. The released men were Maj. James Frederick Low, 43, of Sausalito, Calif., Maj. Fred Neal Thompson, 32, of Taylors, S.C. and Capt. Joe Victor Carpenter, 37, of Victorville, Calif. Low had been downed Dec. 16, 1967, Carpenter Feb. 15 and Thompson Mar. 10. They had been turned over in Hanoi July 18 to 3 Americans opposed to U.S. policy in Vietnam: Mrs. Robert Scheer, of Berkeley, Calif., wife of an editor of *Ramparts* magazine; Vernon Grizzard, of Cambridge, Mass., an anti-draft organizer; Stewart Meacham of Philadelphia, peace secretary of the American Friends [Quakers] Service Committee.)

In his statement delivered at the July 3 session, Thuy asserted that U.S. involvement in Vietnam went "counter to the spirit of the famous Declaration of Independence of the United States." He devoted much of his speech to reading quotations from U.S. critics of the war, including Black Power advocate Stokely Carmichael, the late Sen. Robert F. Kennedy, the late Dr. Martin Luther King Jr. and Sens. J.W. Fulbright (D., Ark.), Wayne Morse (D., Ore.) and Joseph Clark (D., Pa.). Thuy repeated Hanoi's assertion that progress could be made in the talks only after the U.S. "stopped all bombing and other acts of war unconditionally." He rejected U.S. demands for military reciprocity in exchange for a bombing halt since the U.S. was the "aggressor."

In reply, Harriman accused Thuy of "distorting American history" by his reference to the Declaration of Independence. He cited remarks delivered in the Senate June 18 by Sen. Edward W. Brooke (R., Mass.) to the effect that Hanoi should not construe American dissent over the war or U.S. willingness to enter into peace talks as signs of weakness. Noting that Hanoi had called for a withdrawal of foreign forces from South Vietnam, Harriman said: "We agree. I remind you that in the eyes of the vast majority of the people of South Vietnam, it is your forces, too, that are foreign, that came from the outside and that should return where they came from."

At the July 10 session, Thuy accused the U.S. of "spread[ing] rumors on the existence of 'similar points in the positions of both sides,' 'some signs of progress,' of 'new movements,' of 'new ideas on the American side' in the official conversations." In reality, Thuy asserted, there had been no progress and such U.S. statements were "only designed to appease American public opinion, which is demanding a revision of American policy in Vietnam." Nguyen Thanh Le, North Vietnamese spokeman at the talks, added later July 10 that "absolutely nothing has occurred" outside the talks as well.

At a press conference after the July 10 session, Harriman commented: "I can't say any immediate results have been achieved [in the talks], but I still maintain there are straws in the wind, regardless of what he [Thuy] says." Harriman noted in an interview July 12 [made public July 13] that the informal "tea breaks" had "touch[ed] on serious matters." North Vietnamese spokesman Le conceded July 15 that the informal recess talks had dealt with "serious questions" on "rare occasions." But he asserted that the talks had produced "no ray of hope" for resolving the issues.

In his remarks at the July 10 session, Harriman renewed Pres. Johnson's Apr. 1965 offer to provide $1 billion of economic aid to Southeast Asia once peace had come to Vietnam. He said that the U.S. was prepared to stop bombing North Vietnam but that Hanoi was expected "to take steps in the direction of peace." Thuy rejected the offer of economic aid as simply a device by which the U.S. hoped to skirt the main issue of a bombing halt. He referred to the U.S.' claim of having "limited" the bombing of the North as "impudent" since the bombing had actually intensified. (The North Vietnamese Communist Party newspaper *Nhan Dan* asserted July 15 that Johnson's offer of economic aid was merely "bait" with which the U.S. intended to maintain its presence in Southeast Asia. The paper said the Communists would "build a life of plenty" for both North and South Vietnam after the U.S. had been defeated. It added: "The stick-and-carrot policy of the United States is going bankrupt. The stick is broken, and the carrot is rotten.")

The 13th session July 17 lasted $4^1/_2$ hours and was the longest so far, but no progress was reported. Col. Ha Van Lau, sitting in for Thuy, who was reported ill with a cold, repeated Hanoi's 4-point peace plan and demanded again an "unconditional" halt in the U.S.' bombing and "other acts of war" against the North. Harriman referred to the demand as "absurd" and "propaganda." "What would North Vietnam do if the remainder of the bombing of the North ends?" Harriman asked. Would it "slow the pace of the war or continue to heighten the level of aggression?" To that "central question," Harriman declared, the North Vietnamese had "given . . . no answer whatsoever."

NEGOTIATIONS II

The first phase in the negotiations had produced little result. The depth of the differences between the parties was reflected in a report on soundings by the UN Secretary General.

U Thant had conferred with U.S. and North Vietnamese officials in Paris July 6 on what he described as a "mission of exploration" into the talks. Thant emphasized that he was not attempting to mediate the conflict since he saw no "possibility of a 3d-party involvement at this stage." On his return to New York July 13, Thant told reporters he was confident that Hanoi would make a "definite move towards peace" if the U.S. halted all its bombing of North Vietnam. He added that he thought the Paris talks would be a "long process."

In the course of the 2d phase, however, the underlying issue separating the parties—the roles of the National Liberation Front and the Saigon government in a negotiated settlement of the conflict—manifested itself.

Issue of Political Settlement for South Vietnam

The problem of the political settlement for South Vietnam emerged when a North Vietnamese Foreign Ministry statement distributed in Paris July 18 seemed to indicate that Hanoi had modified its insistence that the program of the National Liberation Front (NLF) be accepted as part of a peace settlement. A statement issued in Hanoi July 19 by the NLF appeared to support this view.

The Foreign Ministry statement, among other things, summarized Hanoi's long-standing 4-point program for a settlement of the war. The 3d point of that program had heretofore read: "The internal affairs of South Vietnam must be settled by the South Vietnamese people themselves, in accordance with the program of the South Vietnam National Front for Liberation, without any foreign interference." The July 18 statement, however, rephrased this point to read: "Point 3 affirms the right of self-determination for the South Vietnamese people in the settlement of their internal affairs."

The statement issued by the NLF July 19 said that it was necessary "to let the South Vietnam population settle its own affairs without interference from any foreign country." (The NLF had asserted as recently as June 10 that "the South Vietnamese population must settle its own problems in accordance with the NLF's political program.")

The Foreign Ministry document was distributed by Nguyen Thanh Le, North Vietnamese spokesman at the Paris talks. When asked about the new phraseology, he noted that another passage in the document affirmed that "this position is in conformity with the ardent aspiration of the people of South Vietnam, expressed by the political program of the NLF." The passage Le refered to said that Hanoi's 4-point program provided the "base" for "a correct political solution" in Vietnam since it conformed to (1) the principles of the Geneva accords, (2) the "spirit of the political program" of the NLF and (3) the "realities of the actual situation in Vietnam."

At the July 17 session of the Paris talks, North Vietnamese negotiator Ha Van Lau had reiterated the 4 points and had used the words "in accordance with the NLF program" in reference to the 3d point.

Xuan Thuy, chief North Vietnamese negotiator at the Paris talks, appeared vague when questioned about the rephrasing July 19. After noting that "the memorandum mentions many times the 4-point position of the Democratic Republic of [North] Vietnam as well as the political program of the National Liberation Front," he said: "If, in the passage you express interest in, the National Liberation Front is not expressly mentioned, it is simply a résumé. No interpretation is called for." At his July 19 news conference, (Thuy also brushed aside, but did not reject outright, Vietnam peace proposals that Gov. Nelson A. Rockefeller [R., N.Y.] had made public July 13.* Thuy asserted that "any plan which does not conform with the programs of North Vietnam and the National Liberation Front of South Vietnam would be unrealistic.")

In commenting on the Foreign Ministry statement July 18, U.S. observers noted that the document's use of the word "self-determination" was "virtually U.S. language." They also noted that the appearance of the new phraseology coincided with an increasing North Vietnamese emphasis on the Alliance of National, Democratic & Peace Forces of Vietnam (ANDPF), which had been formed in South Vietnam in April by Communists and non-Communist opponents of the Saigon regime. 2 American jurists—

---

*Rockefeller's proposal envisaged a restoration of peace in Vietnam in 4 phases: (1) A troop pullback by both sides and interposition between them of a neutral, international, "Asian, if possible," peace-keeping force. At the outset of this first phase, the U.S. would withdraw 75,000 of its troops as "token of its good faith." (2) The withdrawal of North Vietnamese and most allied troops from South Vietnam. Some U.S. units would remain but in fixed bases or enclaves. The Viet Cong would stop guerrilla operations and start participating "in the political life of the country." The 2d phase would be monitored by an enlarged buffer force. (3) Free elections under international supervision. All U.S. troops would be withdrawn. (4) Direct negotiations between North and South Vietnam on reunification, which, if decided on, would signal the withdrawal of the peace-keeping force.

Richard A. Falk of Princeton University and Malcome S. Burnstein of Oakland, Calif.—noted in an interview in Grenoble, France July 8 that North Vietnamese leaders had begun placing special emphasis on the alliance as a 3d force in South Vietnamese politics and as a possible bridge between the NLF and the Saigon government. Falk and Burnstein had left Hanoi June 28 after a week's visit during which they had interviewed Premier Pham Van Dong and other high officials. It was reported July 18 that Xuan Thuy had singled out the ANDPF for special comment at a meeting in Paris with American playwright Arthur Miller and other opponents of U.S. policy in Vietnam. In an address broadcast by Hanoi Radio July 19 on the eve of the 14th anniversary of the signing of the Geneva accords, North Vietnamese Pres. Ho Chi Minh praised the alliance as "a great success of the policy of national union against American aggression." Ho also commended the NLF for having spearheaded the struggle in the South.

(U.S. officials in Saigon May 8 had expressed the belief that the Viet Cong were aided in their Saigon offensive by the ANDPF. A U.S. study of the ANDPF found these 2 reasons to link the alliance to the Saigon offensive: [1] a recent editorial in the North Vietnamese army organ *Quan Doi Nhan Dan* had stated that ANDPF units were cooperating with NLF political and military forces in the "struggle against the U.S.-Thieu-Ky clique"; [2] Hanoi newspapers during the previous 2 days had referred repeatedly to the "patriotic armed forces" rather than to the Viet Cong, which had been described by Hanoi journals as the "People's Liberation Army." A U.S. official said that what the North Vietnamese were "clearly implying in all this is that the troops are not under the National Liberation Front. They are saying something new exists— the alliance—and they are building its image as a parallel organization to the front." According to the U.S. study, in 1966 the Viet Cong had proposed the establishment of a "front in the city" that would "broaden the appeal of the National Liberation Front among various classes in Saigon who found it difficult to cooperate clandestinely with the Viet Cong.")

The NLF had expressed views on a settlement for South Vietnam that left little room for the Saigon government. Le Quang Chanh, a member of the NLF Central Committee, said in Grenoble, France July 9 that "as long as there are U.S. troops and troops of the U. S. satellites on Vietnamese territory, there cannot be free elections to elect a national assembly in South Vietnam." Chanh, in Grenoble to attend a meeting on Vietnam being conducted by the World Conference of Jurists, asserted that "reunification cannot be realized in a very near future" because of the need "to heal the wounds of war and rebuild the country." "The time for reunification will be set up according to the aspirations of the peoples of the 2 zones and after consultations between the 2 zones," Chanh said.

Pham Van Chung, press attaché of the NLF's diplomatic mission in Prague, was quoted July 16 as asserting that international supervision of post-war elections in South Vietnam would be considered "international interference" by the NLF. Chung was also quoted as saying that it would "obviously take longer than 2 years" to reunify North and South Vietnam after the war ended. Chung's remarks were reported in Paris by Sanford Gottlieb, executive director of the National Committee for a Sane Nuclear Policy, and by the Rev. Rodney Shaw, program director of the World Peace Division of the Methodist Church. The 2 Americans had conferred with Chung for 8 hours July 13.

Concern on the part of the Saigon government that an agreement might be reached in Paris prejudicial to its interests had resulted in the reiteration of its terms for settling the war. Premier Tran Van Huong warned July 6 that South Vietnam would not accept an unconditional cease-fire and that Saigon needed "a certain amount of time" before serious peace talks could begin. "The essential thing is that South Vietnam and her allies obtain some successes, notably in the military domain," Huong said. "With this, we can accept or impose modifications of current positions." Huong emphasized that a precondition for a cease-fire was the withdrawal of all Communist forces, both northerners and southerners, from South Vietnam.

Bui Diem, South Vietnam's ambassador to the U.S. and chief observer at the Paris peace talks, renewed Saigon's call for direct negotiations between North and South Vietnam. Diem said July 9: "There are 2 protagonists in the war, North and South Vietnam. If a solution is really wanted, the 2 must be together." Diem asserted that "the Paris conversations have only the mandate of determining the circumstances of the cessation of the bombing [of North Vietnam] and have no competence over the future of Vietnam—which is a matter for the Vietnamese people to decide." He maintained that one set of talks need not "exclude the other."

Diem denounced the new Alliance of National, Democratic & Peace Forces of Vietnam as "only another puppet organization, more so than the so-called Front of National Liberation itself."

Pres. Nguyen Van Thieu reaffirmed July 10 that South Vietnam would not negotiate directly with the NLF since it was "simply a tool of Hanoi." But he added that "any [NLF] member . . . could be a member of the Hanoi delegation." Thieu said the expected Communist summer offensive against Saigon and other major cities might come in 2 weeks and could be the "last battle, the last all-out effort by the Communists." He asserted that the offensive "may help to shorten the way to peace" since Hanoi would only seek peace after it had learned that it "cannot win, politically or militarily."

In remarks delivered July 20 on the 14th anniversary of the signing of the Geneva accords, South Vietnamese Premier Tran Van Huong renewed the call for direct talks between North and South Vietnam. In a separate speech, Vice Pres. Nguyen Cao Ky declared: "The only way to win over the Communists is by military strength. We cannot have any coalition with them."

U.S.-Saigon Consultations

South Vietnam's concern over the Paris talks led to consultations with Washington. U.S. Defense Secy. Clark Clifford had visited South Vietnam July 14-18 to confer with American and South Vietnamese officials. This was Clifford's first visit to South Vietnam as Defense Secretary.

Prior to his departure from Washington, Clifford had said at a news conference July 11 that intelligence information indicated "a great deal of enemy activity" despite a lull in the ground fighting. Citing the Communist build-up in the I Corps area below the demilitarized zone (DMZ) and in the III Corps area around Saigon, Clifford said he had to "face the realities" of the "possibility of a new [enemy] offensive this month or possibly in August." According to intelligence data, he said, 8 or more enemy divisions were concentrated in the 5 provinces comprising the I Corps area. Asked when U.S. forces could begin withdrawing from South Vietnam, Clifford said he "would be unwilling to predict withdrawal of any American troops in 1969" unless there were favorable developments in the Paris talks. "I believe we must proceed on the assumption that if the enemy chooses to fight, that we must remain there," Clifford said. (In an interview July 10, South Vietnamese Pres. Nguyen Van Thieu had asserted that the U.S. could "perhaps begin to withdraw major American units in 1969" because the South Vietnamese had "done very well" in improving their armed forces.)

Among those accompanying Clifford were Gen. Earle G. Wheeler, chairman of the Joint Chiefs of Staff; William P. Bundy, Assistant State Secretary for Far Eastern affairs; Paul C. Warnke, Assistant Defense Secretary for international security affairs; and Phil Goulding, Assistant Defense Secretary for public affairs. Clifford and his aides arrived in Saigon July 14. Clifford conferred with U.S. officials July 15, met with South Vietnamese government leaders July 16 and visited the U.S. bases at Danang and Phubai in the I Corps area July 17. The officials flew to Honolulu July 18 for a conference between Pres. Johnson and South Vietnamese Pres. Thieu; they returned to Washington July 20. (Clifford July 18 denied a report that he had persuaded Thieu to agree to a complete halt in the bombing of North Vietnam and to meet with NLF representatives as a preliminary to the inclusion of the NLF in expanded peace talks.) On his arrival at Tansonnhut Air Base July 14, Clifford affirmed that the U.S. was "interested in doing all we can" to develop the fighting capacity of the South Vietnamese army. He noted in particular that American factories would be producing the M-16 automatic rifle at a "substantially more rapid rate" toward the end of the year and that the U.S. intended to distribute the .223-caliber M-16s to all South Vietnamese units, "even at the expense of our forces." (Brig. Gen. Winant Sidle, chief information officer for the U.S. command, said July 14 that South Vietnamese fighting units would be given preference over American logistical troops in distribution of M-16s. Currently all U.S. combat troops were equipped with the M-16.) Clifford reiterated that he could not give a timetable for the start of U.S. troop withdrawal, as this depended on certain "imponderables," such as the rate of development of the South Vietnamese army, the intentions of the Communist forces and the progress of the Paris talks.

Clifford told reporters at Danang July 17 that he expected the enemy to launch a major new assault throughout South Vietnam within 2 months. He described the current fall-off in ground fighting as the "lull before the storm" and added: "We proceed on the assumption that enemy combat plans at this time are coupled with the desire to make an impression on the conferees in Paris, that if they might be able to bring off some spectacular accomplishment that this could affect the negotiations"; U.S. field commanders intended "to see that no such spectacular result is obtained by the enemy." Clifford said some North Vietnamese troops had pulled back from the northern provinces of South Vietnam into the DMZ "where they apparently are being refitted and refurbished."

Clifford's visit to Saigon was followed by a conference at the presidential level. Pres. Johnson conferred with South Vietnamese Pres. Thieu in Honolulu July 19-20 and then denied rumors that they had met "to discuss stopping the bombing." The meeting was held at Thieu's request after he had announced July 8 that the possibility of a new Communist offensive made it imperative that he postpone a state visit to the U.S. scheduled for late July and early August. Thieu accordingly suggested that Johnson meet him "for a few days" somewhere in the Pacific.

Among those accompanying the President were State Secy. Dean Rusk, CIA Dir. Richard Helms and White House aide Walt Rostow. Defense Secy. Clark Clifford, Assistant State Secy. William Bundy, Amb.-to-South Vietnam Ellsworth Bunker and Gen. Earle G. Wheeler flew to Honolulu from Saigon for the conference.

Among the officials accompanying Thieu were Defense Min. Nguyen Van Vy, Foreign Min. Tran Chanh Thanh, Economy Min. Au Ngoc Ho, Amb.-to-U.S. Bui Diem and Gen. Cao Van Vien, chief of the South Vietnamese Joint General Staff.

On his departure from Saigon July 18, Thieu told reporters that he was not going to Hawaii "to surrender to Communists, to sell out the nation, to concede territory or to accept a solution involving coalition with Communists imposed by the United States, such as Communists and a number of unscrupulous politicians have charged." Thieu vowed that "as long as Communist aggression continues, we will continue to fight with even greater effort, because we are determined never to accept surrender to Communists or peace involving coalition with them."

Johnson and Thieu arrived in Honolulu July 18, conferred for some 10 hours July 19 and concluded the meeting with a joint communiqué July 20. (Johnson returned to his Texas ranch later July 20, and Thieu arrived back in Saigon July 22.)

In welcoming remarks July 18, Johnson told Thieu that "our

pledge to help your people defeat aggression stands firm against all obstacles and against any deception." He referred to the Paris talks and expressed hope that they would mark "the first step on the difficult path to peace, an honorable peace under which the people of your country will determine their own future." Johnson placed special emphasis on Saigon's "policy of reconciliation and peace."

Following the conference July 19, Johnson told reporters July 20 that "the big rumors about meeting here to discuss stopping the bombing or to pull out or to do these things are just pure, absolute tommyrot and fiction." He affirmed that his Administration was "determined to defend South Vietnam" while continuing to explore "every avenue that might lead to peace." Johnson described his meeting with Thieu as a "good conference" that had produced "no great differences."

Thieu declared that he had "no apprehensions at all and no doubt on the commitment of the United States government and people" to South Vietnam. He said the most important result of the conference had been to reaffirm the commitment of both countries to "work closely together to defend South Vietnam's independence" and to assure that "aggression" did not succeed.

The communiqué issued July 20 said:

... Pres. Thieu stated his government's determination to continue to assume all the responsibility that the scale of the forces of South Vietnam and their equipment will permit, while preparing the Vietnamese nation and armed forces for the important and decisive role that will be theirs in the coming stages of the struggle. ...

[The Presidents] noted that the last 6 months have revealed a major and continuing change in North Vietnamese strategy. With greatly stepped-up infiltration of men and modern equipment from the North, Hanoi has sought and continues to seek military and psychological successes that would shift the balance of the conflict in its favor in a relatively short period. ... As a result, it now appears that North Vietnamese comprise over 70% of the main force battalions on the other side, as compared to 26% in late 1965. ...

[The Presidents] agreed that the pattern of military activity on the other side continues to indicate renewed offensive action at some time in the next 2 months. Military factors—enemy regrouping and effective allied spoiling actions—appear to account for the drop in the level of fighting over the last 2 to 3 weeks, including the lull in indiscriminate attacks on the civilian population in Saigon.

The 2 Presidents noted the negative position of North Vietnamese negotiators at Paris ... and concluded there had been no response to the major limitation of bombing put into effect on Mar. 31. ... Hanoi appeared to be continuing to follow the policy of 'fighting while negotiating,' long foreshadowed in North Vietnamese strategic documents. The 2 Presidents called on the authorities in Hanoi to respond to the substantial de-escalation initiated on Mar. 31 and open the door to serious peace negotiations. . . .

Pres. Thieu reported that the increase in [South Vietnamese] volunteers, the extension of the draft to 18- and 19-year-olds, and the calling back to service of veterans and reserve officers have brought the armed forces of South Vietnam to a level of 765,000 men in June—some 48,000 more than the original goal for this date. With the mobilization law enacted at the end of May, it is expected that the total will exceed 800,000 men by the end of 1968. . . . It is also anticipated that an additional 200,000 men will be made available at the end of 1968 in auxiliary and paramilitary forces, such as the police and self-defense forces. Pres. Johnson . . . [noted that] M-16 automatic rifles have already been provided to all regular Vietnamese infantry, airborne, marine and ranger battalions. . . . Increased production of the M-16 should make it possible to get the weapon into the hands of all South Vietnamese forces during 1969. . . .

The 2 Presidents deplored the use of the [Paris] discussions for propaganda purposes on the North Vietnamese side. . . . They agreed that the basic objective in the Paris talks is to open the way to a stable and honorable peace. In the face of continued high infiltration and other military actions directed from Hanoi; however, they saw no alternative but to continue to press for realistic discussions on the appropriate actions by both sides.

The 2 Presidents again affirmed that the Republic of Vietnam should be a full participant playing a leading role in discussions concerning the substance of a final settlement and that their 2 governments would act in full consultation with each other and with their allies, both in the present phase and throughout. . . .

Pres. Thieu reaffirmed the policy of his government to resolve the internal problems of all the South Vietnamese people in an amicable, just and peaceful way in accordance with the principle of one man, one vote. . . . He offered full participation in political activities to all individuals and members of groups who agree to renounce force and to abide by the Constitution of Vietnam.

Pres. Thieu further stated that, when peace was restored, it would be the policy of his government to explore all the avenues which may lead to the reunification of Vietnam by peaceful means, through the free and democratic choice of all Vietnamese in the North and in the South. To that end he would consider favorably the gradual development of relations beneficial to both South Vietnam and North Vietnam, subject only to essential safeguards against renewed subversion. . . .

Pres. Johnson . . . [affirmed that] U.S. forces are fighting to repel external aggression. The United States has no other ambitions in Vietnam. It desires no bases, no continued military presence and no political role in Vietnamese affairs. As North Vietnam takes its men home and ends its aggression against South Vietnam, U.S. forces will be withdrawn, in accordance with the Manila Communique.

The United States will not support the imposition of a 'coalition government,' or any other form of government, on the people of South Vietnam. The people of South Vietnam—and only the people of South Vietnam—have the right to choose the form of their government. . . .

The 2 Presidents stated that a complete cessation of hostilities must be part of a final peaceful settlement. . . . They concluded that such a cessation would be possible whenever the government of North Vietnam is prepared earnestly to examine the arrangements required. Effective controls and guarantees would be necessary. The 2 Presidents thus solemnly called on the authorities of North Vietnam to forsake the path of violence and to take the road toward peace now open to them through the Paris talks, which should lead to negotiations involving directly North Vietnam and South Vietnam. Until these hopes are realized, the 2 Presidents confirmed their determination to halt aggression and to defend the Republic of Vietnam. . . .

On his return to Saigon July 22, Thieu told the South Vietnamese that the Honolulu conference had produced no significant changes in relations between Washington and Saigon. The "rumors" that the U.S. wanted to halt the bombing of North Vietnam, withdraw part of its forces and impose a coalition government on South Vietnam were purely "imaginary," Thieu said. In an allusion to the 1968 Presidential race in the U.S., Thieu asserted: "Any President of the United States should not consider only his personal position on Vietnam" but "should consider what the Americans are doing here in Vietnam and the responsibility of the United States in the world." "You are in Vietnam to fight for yourself and to fight for the freedom of all humanity," Thieu told Americans.

The North Vietnamese Communist Party newspaper *Nhan Dan* asserted July 22 that the Honolulu conference had "failed to produce any novelty." "The aim of the Honolulu conference was to patch up the ruined cardboard castle of the U.S. puppets," the paper declared. "But the wand did not work, and the U.S. puppets have only revealed their bellicosity and obduracy."

Nguyen Thanh Le, North Vietnamese spokesman at the Paris talks, told reporters July 22: "The Honolulu meeting revealed that the position of the United States remains infinitely obstinate. It is more clear that the United States still refuses to stop its bombing against the Democratic Republic of Vietnam and that it refuses to withdraw its troops from South Vietnam." The U.S. was still determined to support "the puppet government" of South Vietnam "as an instrument of a neo-colonial policy in South Vietnam."

Following the U.S. consultations with Saigon, W. Averell Harriman asked the Hanoi representatives at the July 24 meeting in Paris whether a statement issued by the North Vietnamese Foreign Ministry July 17 constituted a softening of their government's position. Noting that the ministry, in restating its peace terms, had not made the usual stipulation that acceptance of the program of the NLF was a prerequisite to peace, Harriman said the North Vietnamese statement thus "affirmed the South Vietnamese people's right of self-determination in the settlement of their internal affairs. This wording is consistent with the positions taken by the United States. Does [it] correctly state the views of your government? If so, then the way lies open to making progress toward a peaceful settlement."

In reply, Col. Ha Van Lau, a North Vietnamese delegate, reaffirmed his government's "full support" for the NLF program as "the just political line which fully responds to the aspirations of the South Vietnamese people."

In his prepared statement, Harriman also called on North Vietnam to accept "realities" by recognizing the role the South Vietnamese government must play in a peace settlement and by dealing with the Saigon regime in this matter.

At a news conference later July 24, Nguyen Thanh Le denied reports that South Vietnamese Pres. Thieu and Vice Pres. Nguyen Cao Ky had sent unofficial representatives to Paris in May and June to sound out North Vietnamese officials about the political future of South Vietnamese leaders. "We have not met anyone . . . representing the puppet government," Le said.

Col. Lau, at the July 31 session, rejected, as an "extremely absurd demand," State Secy. Rusk's call for North Vietnamese military restraint in exchange for a halt in the U.S. bombing of the North. Asserting that Rusk's "warlike and aggressive stand" was contrary to "the peaceful aspirations of the American people," Lau reiterated that "we completely reject" the U.S. demand for reciprocity. Lau repeated his denial that the North Vietnamese Foreign Ministry's July 17 statement on peace aims was an easing of Hanoi's terms.

Harriman, in his prepared statement, renewed the U.S. charge that 40,000 North Vietnamese troops were in Laos in violation of the 1962 Geneva agreements. He suggested that Lau accompany him to Laos to inspect the "damning evidence" of North Vietnamese "aggression" against Laos. Lau dismissed Harriman's charges as "a diversion" from the bombing issue.

At his news conference July 30, Rusk discounted arguments that an apparent battlefield lull in South Vietnam constituted a North Vietnamese de-escalation and that the U.S., therefore, should halt the bombing of the North. He said: "We need to have . . . something better than just committing ourselves to a course of action on our side leaving the other side with complete freedom of action to move men from North Vietnam into South Vietnam in whatever way they wish." Rusk argued that if Hanoi had truly slowed its operations in the South in response to the U.S. bombing limitation, which was instituted Mar. 31, then "we must know what would happen from some responsible, authoritative source, direct or indirect," "if we stop the bombing" of the North. "If the present lull in the fighting . . . indicated that a political decision has been taken" by Hanoi, Rusk said, "I see no reason why . . . they cannot find ways to let us know what these political decisions are." Reasserting that North Vietnam had not responded to Pres. Johnson's "major act of de-escalation" Mar. 31, Rusk said it was unfair to have the U.S. carry out "another major act of de-escalation, whether or not Honoi does anything." "We can't make peace in Southeast Asia on that basis." Rusk denied that his demand that Hanoi give a direct response as to its intentions amounted to a hardening of the American position. This had always been the view of the Johnson Administration, he said.

White House press secretary George Christian said later July 30 that Rusk's remarks were not a hardening of the U.S. stand at the Paris talks. "In our judgment, there has been no change on either side since the President's Mar. 31 proposal and acceptance of the talks." Christian said.

Fighting Intensified

During the days of consultations, evidence began to accumulate that the belligerents were preparing for an increase in hostilities. Pres. Johnson asserted July 31 that Communist forces in South Vietnam were "preparing a massive attack on our forces and those of our allies." Speaking at his news conference, Johnson said intelligence information from allied commanders in Saigon indicated that the relative lull in the fighting did not mean the Communists were practicing restraint but were preparing for a major onslaught. He quoted an official military report that "North Vietnam's efforts to expand and diversify its military logistic capabilities continues unabated." Johnson, therefore, ruled out any new act of unilateral U.S. de-escalation and warned that "there is always a chance we will have to act promptly on additional measures if the enemy puts our men in danger." The President stressed that the U.S. had "exercised great restraint" in bombing the North and that "we are not invading North Vietnam." Johnson quoted these points in the intelligence report to support the claim that the North Vietnamese were accelerating their military preparations:

● "Water traffic activity" in North Vietnam was at a record level. In one recent week 1,200 small cargo crafts were observed south of the 19th Parallel, "4 times the weekly average observed" since Apr. 1968.

● Truck traffic moving south was 25% "above the weekly average since Apr. 1," but U.S. pilots had destroyed 40% of the total. Total truck traffic "will probably be 3 times greater" in July than in March.

● The total amount of ammunition and other supplies shipped from southern North Vietnam toward South Vietnam had increased from an average of 107 tons a day in March to a current level of 320 tons a day.

Johnson expressed hope that his decision to limit the bombing of the North would evoke "some similar acts of restraint" by North Vietnam: "I want to give them all the time necessary to consider it and talk to their allies about it."

Johnson's statement was assailed Aug. 2 by Nguyen Thanh Le, spokesman for the North Vietnamese delegation at the Paris talks, as "threats to intensify" the war. Because of "threats to intensify the war of aggression, the American side must bear the entire responsibility for the consequences it will have caused," Le said. Le denounced U.S. leaders as "shameless liars" for calling on Hanoi to exercise restraint while more American troops were arriving in South Vietnam.

The lull in fighting was shattered by an intensification of combat in August. Savage conflict raged from the Mekong delta to the area around the demilitarized zone (DMZ). Operations included (a) an allied sweep of the Ashau Valley Aug. 4-8, (b) a brief South Vietnamese incursion into the DMZ Aug. 15 in pursuit of a North Vietnamese battalion and (c) an attempted seizure by North Vietnamese soldiers Aug. 18 of Tayninh (capital of Tayninh Province), northwest of Saigon and 10 miles from the Cambodian border. *Among the major actions:*

● The U.S. command reported Aug. 7 that U.S. and South Vietnamese amphibious troops had killed 252 Viet Cong in the Mekong delta Aug. 1-7. Allied casualties totaled only 3 Americans and 4 South Vietnamese wounded. The fighting was centered 110 miles southwest of Saigon on the northern edge of the U Minh Forest, a Viet Cong stronghold. Many of the enemy were slain by helicopter gunships firing rockets and machineguns.

● Heavy fighting erupted again in the delta Aug. 12-13. Allied soldiers killed 181 Viet Cong 16-21 miles south of Saigon. U.S. losses were put at 15 dead and 32 wounded; South Vietnamese casualties were 5 killed and 22 wounded.

The allied troops were part of a force of 75 battalions guarding enemy infiltration routes into Saigon.

● South Vietnamese troops made another incursion into the delta Aug. 14 and discovered 3 enemy munitions factories 54 miles south of Saigon. They seized 4,800 hand grenades and thousands of fuses and grenade springs. The government troops, airlifted to the area in U.S. helicopters, encountered no opposition.

● About 3,000 U.S. and South Vietnamese troops were helicoptered Aug. 4 into the Ashau Valley, 27 miles southwest of Hue, for the 2d time in 1968. As in the previous move into the valley in April, the allied soldiers sought to block the massing of North Vietnamese troops in the I Corps area for a possible new offensive. As of Aug. 8, the allied sweep was reported to have made only light contact with the enemy: 15 North Vietnamese troops were killed in 4 days of sporadic fighting; 2 U.S. soldiers and 8 Vietnamese were killed and 40 allied soldiers wounded. South Vietnamese soldiers turned up what was described as an abandoned enemy base camp of 50 barracks a mile southeast of Tabat, an abandoned outpost. Other allied soldiers found 1,567 weapons and assorted military equipment. The area was hit by 15 B-52 bomber strikes during the operation.

● South Vietnamese and U.S. troops took a heavy toll of North Vietnamese troops in fighting Aug. 15 inside and near the DMZ. In the aftermath of a battle just north of Giolinh, government forces moved well into the buffer strip in pursuit of a North Vietnamese battalion. Saigon claimed its forces had killed 165 Communist troops in the $7^1/_2$-hour engagement. Meanwhile, U.S. Marines killed at least 56 other North Vietnamese at 3 other strategic positions below the DMZ. Allied casualties in both actions were reported to be extremely light.

● In the battle for Tayninh, an estimated 600 Viet Cong and elements of 2 North Vietnamese divisions slipped into the provincial capital during the night of Aug. 17 following attacks around the city. They began attacking government offices and installations Aug. 18. Later Aug. 18, U.S. reinforcements, spearheaded by an armored column of the 25th Infantry Division, moved into Tayninh and engaged the infiltrators. House-to-house fighting raged throughout the day, but during darkness early Aug. 19, the Viet Cong/North Vietnamese force withdrew from Tayninh. About 3 blocks of houses were destroyed by fires set by the Viet Cong and by rocket, mortar and machinegun fire, leaving more than 200 families homeless. According to incomplete casualty reports, 15-20 Americans and 86 Viet Cong were slain.

● Widespread assaults on allied positions took place throughout South Vietnam Aug. 18. In the heaviest fighting in 3 months, Viet Cong and North Vietnamese forces carried out 19 separate attacks, 15 of them in Tayninh and Binhlong Provinces, northwest of Saigon near the Cambodian border. The other assaults were aimed at an allied outpost at Dakseang in the Central Highlands and at another allied installation in northern Thuathein Province south of Phubai. A battalion of the North Vietnamese 352C Division attacked the Dakseang outpost but was repulsed. The strike in the Thuathein area resulted in the killing of 12 U.S. Marines and 4 government soldiers. Allied losses during the day's attacks totaled about 30 killed, while at least 300 Viet Cong and North Vietnamese were reported slain.

Vietnamese civilians and U.S. soldiers suffered heavy casualties in accidental ground and air attacks Aug. 8, 9 and 10:

• In the Aug. 8 incident, a U.S. unit killed 72 civilians and wounded 240 in the Mekong delta town of Cairang while repelling 3 Viet Cong ambushes. More than 450 homes were destroyed or damaged. In the first of the 3 ambushes, a water-borne U.S. river force, returning from a 10-day operation in the delta's U Minh Forest to the south, was fired on by about 100 Viet Cong on the banks of the Xano Canal, which leads into the Cantho River. The other 2 ambushes, involving troops of the same U.S. 9th Infantry Division units, took place near Mykanh and Cairang on the Cantho River. In counterattacking, the U.S. troops, using guns and several flame-throwers, accidentally fired over the Viet Cong ambush positions and hit Cairang, a government-controlled town 83 miles southwest of Saigon. In the confused fighting, South Vietnamese troops on shore mistakenly fired on the American river convoy. 10 U.S. soldiers were wounded and one boat was damaged in the engagement.

• A U.S. F-100 Super Sabet jet accidentally strafed American troops in the Ashau Valley Aug. 10, killing 8 men and wounding 5. The U.S. command said the plane, providing air support to 101st Air Cavalry Division troops seeking out North Vietnamese troop concentrations, fired "in the vicinity of a U.S. unit" near Tabat.

• The U.S. command reported Aug. 11 that 4 Marines had been wounded Aug. 9 when they were fired on by 5th Infantry Division artillery at a base 2 miles southwest of Dongha. The base suffered minor damage.

The intensity of the conflict was indicated in the combat statistics released by the belligerents. The flow of American troops to Vietnam continued. The U.S. command announced Aug. 1 that 4,500 men of the First Brigade of the 5th Infantry Division had arrived in South Vietnam. The number of American troops in the country was thus increased to 541,000. The reinforcements were assigned to Quangtri and Thuathien Provinces.

The Viet Cong claimed Aug. 5 that it had inflicted heavy losses on allied troops between Jan. 1 and June 30. The Viet Cong communiqué, published in North Vietnamese newspapers Aug. 9, said: "A total of 380,000 enemy, including 133,000 Americans and satellite troops, were killed, wounded or captured"; 4,440 allied planes had been downed or destroyed on the ground; 8,730 allied military vehicles had been destroyed, including 4,560 tanks and armored troop carriers, and more than 700 big guns. The Viet Cong had "pushed the war right into the camps of the enemy. We have hit the various nerve centers and key positions of the enemy and posed an instant threat to them . . . , especially in Saigon's Cholon district."

Hanoi Radio said Aug. 17 that U.S. planes had dropped 84,-600 bombs on the North in July, compared with 42,600 in June.

The increasing force of the raids was coupled with the unabated "massacre of the people of South Vietnam," the broadcast charged. And the U.S. Defense Department reported Aug. 17 that American planes had flown 107,000 attack missions against North Vietnam between Feb. 1965, when the raids started, and July 1968. The department said the planes had dropped 2,581,876 tons of bombs and rockets on North Vietnam during the $3^1/_2$-year period.

In Paris, the U.S. reciprocated Hanoi's release of prisoners. At the Aug. 7 session, W. Averell Harriman announced that the U.S. would soon release 14 North Vietnamese captive seamen who had been seized by the U.S. in July 1966. The men had been taken when their torpedo boat attacked U.S. warships in the Gulf of Tonkin. 5 others in the group had been returned to North Vietnam previously. Harriman gave the North Vietnamese negotiator, Col. Ha Van Lau, the names of the men to be freed, and he expressed hope that their release would lead to wider exchanges of U.S. and Communist prisoners. U.S. military authorities released the 14 North Vietnamese Oct. 21. The men were taken by a U.S. naval vessel to the vicinity of Vinh, North Vietnam, where they boarded a small boat and made their way ashore. Under terms of a U.S.-North Vietnamese agreement worked out in Vientiane, Laos, a 36-hour truce was arranged to cover a 228-square-mile land and sea area in the vicinity of Vinh to permit the release of the North Vietnamese. Of the 19 captured in the 1966 naval engagement, 2 had been freed in 1967 because of illness and 3 others had been released in March after North Vietnam had repatriated 3 American pilots.

(Hanoi acknowledged the American action Oct. 22 but assailed the U.S. for holding other North Vietnamese in "illegal custody" and demanded that all be set free. The statement, broadcast by Hanoi Radio, said that "the Americans have illegally captured and detained civilians and military personnel aboard Vietnamese cargo ships and fishing boats within DRV [North Vietnamese] territorial waters" in violation of the 1954 Geneva agreements.)

(The U.S. Navy Dec. 16 released 7 North Vietnamese civilian seamen seized by U.S. naval forces in international waters in the Gulf of Tonkin Oct. 22, 1967. Their capture had never previously been reported. The men, held in custody in South Vietnam, were set free by being placed aboard a motorized junk 24 miles east of

Vinh. The release of the seamen had been negotiated by U.S. and North Vietnamese representatives in Vientiane.)

Harriman asserted at the Aug. 14 meeting in Paris that North Vietnam's "rigid and unyielding demand" for an unconditional halt in the bombing was being voiced "for propaganda purposes." "You have proposed nothing, you have offered nothing" to advance a settlement, Harriman said. Xuan Thuy, chief North Vietnamese delegate, insisted that Hanoi's demand was "legitimate, realistic and reasonable" and that "it lies with the Americans to make the move" to break the deadlock in the 3-month-old talks.

William J. Jorden, spokesman for the American delegation, said after the talks that the U.S. still awaited word from North Vietnam on whether a relative lull on the battlefield was intended as the restraint Pres. Johnson had requested as a condition for halting the bombing of the North. Thus far Hanoi had "given us no indication whatsoever that this is what they are interested in or that they are trying to convey that kind of notion," Jorden said. In view of Hanoi's silence on this matter, "the totality of our information suggests that they are using the present period of time to prepare for major military action."

(Le Duc Tho, a member of the North Vietnamese Communist Party's Politburo, had rejoined his government's delegation in Paris Aug. 13 after a 6-week trip to Hanoi. Cyrus R. Vance, the 2d-ranking member of the U.S. delegation, had returned to Paris Aug. 12 after conferring with Pres. Johnson in Washington.)

Defense Secy. Clark M. Clifford said Aug. 15 that the substantive phase of the Paris negotiations could start if North Vietnam informed "us that they have reduced the level of combat and that they will continue to reduce the level of combat, and that that constitutes a de-escalatory step." For the U.S. to halt the bombing of the North without such assurances from Hanoi, Clifford said, would place American troops near the DMZ in "greater jeopardy. "In view of North Vietnam's refusal to indicate that the lull represented de-escalation, the U.S. must assume that the Communists were preparing for another offensive, Clifford said. He reported that North Vietnamese infiltration into South Vietnam was continuing at a rate of 30,000 men a month.

South Vietnamese Pres. Nguyen Van Thieu assailed the Paris negotiations Aug. 15 as a "trick" by Hanoi "to take us in the wrong direction." "Peace will came," he said, "because our armed forces can achieve an absolute victory in the future."

Johnson States Position

The U.S. position was spelled out in a major address by Pres. Johnson Aug. 19. He asserted in a speech at the Veterans of Foreign Wars convention in Detroit that the U.S. would make no further moves to de-escalate until North Vietnam made it clear that it would make a serious move toward peace.

"The next move must be theirs," Johnson said. Referring to his Mar. 31 curtailment of bombing and offer to halt bombing in response to the enemy's "prompt de-escalation," the President said: "We have made a reasonable offer and we have taken first a major step. That offer has not been accepted. This Administration does not intend to move further until it has good reason to believe that the other side intends seriously to join us in de-escalating the war and moving seriously toward peace. We are willing to take chances for peace, but we cannot make foolhardy gestures for which your fighting men will pay the price by giving their lives."

Johnson specifically rejected a halt in the bombing of North Vietnam or an end of the search-and-destroy missions by U.S. forces in the South. He said: A bombing halt would permit the enemy to "pour" men and supplies "against the DMZ, against our men and our allies, without obstruction." If the search-and-destroy missions were abandoned, the enemy could "assemble without interference around Saigon, Danang, Hué and other cities and deliver their attacks at times and places of their choice." Johnson appealed "to all well-intentioned citizens who are demanding that Americans stop the bombing" to tell him "what they are demanding of Hanoi" and to ask themselves, "why, oh why, do we hear nothing of any demands on Hanoi?"

Johnson stressed his desire for peace and emphasized his insistence that it be on "honorable terms." He reiterated these terms: reinstatement of the DMZ at the 17th Parallel, with the matter of the unity of Vietnam to be decided in the future by the people of the North and the South; removal of all foreign forces from Laos; withdrawal of U.S. forces from Vietnam 6 months after the fighting ended; a one-man one-vote, free election, with the candidates pledged to forsake violence and live by the constitution.

After listing his terms for an honorable peace, Johnson added:

"I doubt that any American President will take a substantially different view when he bears the burdens of office and he has available to him all the information that flows to the commander-in-chief, and he is responsible to our people for all of the consequences of all the alternatives that are open to him." He expressed "faith" that "when the political campaign is all over, and the man takes up the responsibility of the Presidency—whoever he may be—he will take a similar view" and "will stand up and insist on an honorable peace."

Johnson asserted that "there are some among us who appear to be searching for a formula which would get us out of Vietnam and Asia on any terms, leaving the people of South Vietnam and Laos and Thailand and all the others to an uncertain fate." He warned that "this course would be disastrous" to the interests of the U.S. and to the world, "now and in the years to come." He said that "there is no serious and responsible leader in Asia who does not know that the struggle now taking place in Vietnam is the hinge on which the fate of Asia will swing—one way or the other—for many years, far into the future."

(Republican Presidential nominee Richard M. Nixon, in an address to the VFW convention earlier Aug. 19, also stressed the goal of an honorable settlement in Vietnam and opposed a bombing halt without reciprocity by the enemy. Johnson's remarks about Vietnam, Nixon said Aug. 20, were "realistic." "We all want to see the bombing halted and the war ended," he said, "but we cannot halt the bombing unless there is some move on behalf of the enemy.")

The Aug. 21, 28 and Sept. 4 sessions of the Paris talks were dominated by the North Vietnamese delegation's concentration on the American opposition to the war in Vietnam and on its criticism of the Vietnam planks of the Democratic and Republican Party platforms. At the Aug. 21 session, Xuan Thuy, head of the North Vietnamese delegation, assailed Johnson's Aug. 19 assertion that the U.S. would make no further moves to de-escalate the war until Hanoi made a serious move toward peace. Thuy asserted that Johnson's stand was counter to that of many U.S. political figures and publications favoring an unconditional halt to the bombing. In reply, Averell Harriman cited a recent Harris poll reporting that Americans opposed a unilateral halt in the raids by 61%–24% margin.

(William J. Jorden, spokesman for the U.S. delegation, disclosed after the Aug. 21 meeting that prior to and since the opening of the talks "a number of 3d parties have been deeply concerned and interested in helping" to end the U.S.-North Vietnamese deadlock.)

The State Department said Aug. 27 that Harriman had been "instructed to tell the Hanoi delegation to stop miscalculating or trying to interfere in internal American affairs and get down to the serious business of making peace in Southeast Asia." The statement was in direct reference to a news conference remark Aug. 26 by Nguyen Thanh Le, spokesman for the Hanoi delegation, urging Americans to press for a change in Washington's Vietnam policy. Referring to the current Democratic Party platform hearings in Washington, Le had said: "It is certain that the American people will give a new thrust to the movement of struggle against the war and to demand that the present and future leadership of the United States change its Vietnam policy—that is, to demand an end of the war of aggression, unconditional cessation of the bombing of North Vietnam and withdrawal of American troops."

Thuy, speaking at the Aug. 28 session, said that the instructions to Harriman to inform him to cease "trying to interfere in internal American affairs" were "truly comic" because "it is the United States that has intervened in Vietnam." Ridiculing the elaborate security precautions taken in Chicago, site of the Democratic Party convention, Thuy said "in the present electoral campaign, in order to cope with the indignation of the people, the U.S. authorities have had to use barbed wire and tens of thousands of their troops and police agents."

Thuy charged at the Sept. 4 session that the stand of Richard M. Nixon, the Republican Presidential nominee, "has always consisted in urging escalation of the war to the highest levels" but that Nixon was now "compelled to talk about 'peace' . . . simply to mislead public opinion." Thuy said that Vice Pres. Hubert H. Humphrey, the Democratic candidate, "has for the last 4 years closely adhered to Pres. Johnson's war policy" and was an "apologist" for the conflict. Thuy said that the 2 parties' platforms proved both parties "still refuse to draw practical lessons" from the "recent defeats" of the U.S. in Vietnam. He characterized clashes between Chicago police and demonstrators during the Democratic national convention as "savage repression" of antiwar sentiment.

Harriman defended the Democratic and Republican platform stands on Vietnam, saying "they both demonstrate the indisputable fact that the people of the United States are dedicated to peace, but they both emphasize that the United States is determined there will be a just and honorable peace in Vietnam."

Communist Forces Step Up Fighting

There was a renewal of Viet Cong rocket attacks on Saigon and a series of Viet Cong/North Vietnamese attacks throughout South Vietnam during the 2d half of August. U.S. and Communist forces suffered heavy casualties in the intensified fighting. U.S. losses for the period Aug. 18-24 totaled 308 killed and 1,134 wounded; 4,755 Communists were listed as slain that week. U.S. combat deaths Aug. 25-31 were put at 408, the highest weekly total since June 1, and 2,513 Americans were wounded. Viet Cong/North Vietnamese fatalities in the same period: 4,476. The 2-week losses raised total American casualties reported since 1961 to 27,508 killed and 171,809 wounded.

The high casualties reflected savage fighting in the Mekong delta, the Saigon area and the northern provinces. Saigon came under rocket attack Aug. 22 for the first time in 2 months. A U.S. spokesman said 22 rockets had smashed into the city's downtown section, killing 18 persons and wounding 59 others. 2 rockets struck the National Assembly building, one of them ripping off a section of the roof.

(U.S. State Department officials Aug. 22 denounced the Saigon shelling as a deliberate rejection of Pres. Johnson's appeal for de-escalation and restraint by North Vietnamese and Viet Cong forces. The number of Vietnamese civilians killed in the attack, the department said, "again clearly illustrates the callous disregard with which the enemy regards the lives of innocent noncombatants in this war.")

The Saigon shelling was one of several operations that started Aug. 18 with an outbreak of mortar and ground attacks throughout the country. More than 700 Viet Cong troops were said to have been slain in the 4 days of fighting. In one action, Aug. 21, U.S. troops killed 182 Viet Cong in a rubber plantation 44 miles northeast of Saigon. 2 Americans were killed and 23 wounded. The fighting started when Viet Cong troops opened fire on a column of armored personnel carriers of the U.S. 25th Infantry Division.

Viet Cong forces Aug. 23 carried out heavy rocket and mortar attacks on cities, provincial capitals and military installations. The heaviest attacks centered on the U.S. airfield at Danang, the cities of Hué and Quangtri, and a U.S. Special Forces camp at Duclap, near the Cambodian border 130 miles northeast of Saigon. The shelling of the Duclap camp was followed by a ground assault by an estimated 1,200-1,500 North Vietnamese troops. About $\frac{1}{3}$ of the stronghold, defended by 300 *montagnard* tribesmen and 13 American advisers, was overrun. The North Vietnamese also seized several strategic hills overlooking the camp and fought their way into the town of Duclap. Savage fighting continued through Aug. 24. An allied relief column led by U.S. Special Forces men fought its way into the besieged camp Aug. 25, raising the number of defenders to about 600 men. The North Vietnamese were forced to retreat from the camp and surrounding points the following day. U.S. authorities estimated that 643 North Vietnamese had been killed in the 3 days of fighting. More than 200 North Vietnamese weapons were captured. At least 58 government troops and 2 American advisers were killed; 91 government soldiers and 9 Americans were wounded. (Another 47 North Vietnamese were killed Sept. 8 in an unsuccessful attack on the camp.)

Allied commanders reported Aug. 26 that more then 6,000 Communist soldiers had been killed since Aug. 18; more than 1,000 of them were said to have died Aug. 25-26 in the smashing of attacks in the Central Highlands and coastal lowlands.

U.S. troops killed 103 Viet Cong troops Aug. 28-29 on infiltration routes near Saigon. The fighting started when soldiers of the U.S. 101st Air Cavalry Division spotted a company-sized unit 32 miles northwest of the capital. 16 Americans were killed and 25 were wounded.

Government national police reported Aug. 29 that terrorist attacks had killed 120 civilians Aug. 18-24 compared with 62 the previous week. Among those slain were hamlet chiefs, village officials and pacification workers. The U.S. mission reported that the number of civilians killed in terrorist attacks since Jan. 1 totaled 3,000. The Viet Cong also had abducted 4,850, many of whom were local government officials.

A U.S. Special Forces Camp at Hathanh, 14 miles west of Quangngai, was overrun Aug. 30 but was recaptured Sept. 2. At least 12 enemy soldiers were killed as the Americans fought their way into the camp. U.S. casualties were 4 killed and 5 wounded.

A U.S. spokesman reported Aug. 30 that U.S. paratroopers, acting on information provided by a defector, had captured a North Vietnamese regimental headquarters 12 miles south of Hué the previous week, killing 176 North Vietnamese. 7 Americans were killed. 7 anti-aircraft guns and 435 other weapons were captured.

The Viet Cong's National Liberation Front Aug. 30 announced "a new general offensive now underway." Hanoi Radio broadcast an "official appeal" of the NLF's Command for Central Vietnam, urging the Viet Cong and their supporters in central South Vietnam to "hit, destroy, annihilate the enemy." It said: "Violent attacks have started against the U.S. and puppet enemy everywhere in central Vietnam, and the situation for great victories is very favorable."

Using women and children as shields, a Viet Cong force Sept. 6 attacked a company of U.S. 101st Airborne Division troops guarding the village of Aptrangdau, 26 miles northwest of Saigon. 33 Americans and 48 Viet Cong were killed. 6 enemy soldiers were captured and 118 civilians were held for questioning.

A South Vietnamese general and a U.S. general were killed in helicopter crashes Sept. 8 and 13:

● Brig. Gen. Truong Quang An, 36, commander of the South Vietnamese 23d Division, an American colonel and 4 other persons were killed Sept. 8 when North Vietnamese gunners shot down their 'copter near Duclap, 130 miles northeast of Saigon. The other dead included the American pilot and co-pilot. The only survivors were 2 U.S. gunners.

● Maj. Gen. Keith L. Ware, 52, commander of the U.S. First Infantry Division, and 7 other Americans were killed Sept. 13 when his command helicopter crashed in flames near the Cambodian border, 60 miles north of Saigon. U.S. headquarters in Saigon said the cause of the crash was not determined, but a Hanoi broadcast Sept. 14 claimed Viet Cong gunfire had brought down the helicopter.

Ware was the 4th Amerrican general killed in the war. An was the first South Vietnamese general to die in combat.

The fighting of mid-September was marked by a savage battle Sept. 11-16 in and around Tayninh, on a major invasion route to Saigon, and by a major allied thrust Sept. 13 into the southern half of the demilitarized zone:

● Tayninh, 50 miles northwest of Saigon, became a major target of North Vietnamese/Viet Cong forces in an assault launched Sept. 11. The attack cost Communist forces at least 500 men killed by Sept. 16. More than 200 allied troops, mostly government soldiers, were killed or wounded. It was the 2d attack on Tayninh in less than a month; a similar attack had been repulsed by allied forces Aug. 20.

The assault began with rocket and mortar attacks on U.S. and South Vietnamese military bases around Tayninh. The shelling was followed by a ground thrust into the city by 2 columns of about 1,500 men. Some penetrated the center of Tayninh while others seized positions on the northeastern and northwestern outskirts. About 2,000 government forces were rushed in and by the following day the Viet Cong were cleared from most of the city. Fighting, however, raged for 4 more days in the vicinity. In an engagement Sept. 13, Viet Cong attackers attempted to storm a U.S. artillery base just north of the city in the wake of a 200-round mortar and rocket barrage. The raiders were driven back with a loss of 58 men by American ground and helicopter fire. Government troops reported killing 90 guerrillas in the city's outskirts Sept. 14, and U.S. troops searching for the remnants of the enemy force claimed the slaying of 31 more Sept. 14. The last outburst of enemy activity in the area took place Sept. 16 when a U.S. 25th Division convoy came under heavy fire 9 miles to the southeast. The attack was repelled with a loss of 7 American lives. Viet Cong losses were listed as 26 killed.

• The drive into the southeastern part of the demilitarized zone was carried out Sept. 13 by U.S. and South Vietnamese infantry and armored troops supported by planes, artillery and U.S. Navy ships. Penetrating 2 miles into the buffer area in the 4th such allied assault since May 1967, the joint force killed 158 North Vietnamese troops. 22 U.S. soldiers were wounded. More than 250 North Vietnamese were reported killed the same day in other clashes with allied troops just below the DMZ. 8 Americans were killed and 93 wounded in these operations.

The thrust into the DMZ was aimed at preventing an expected drive south by 2 North Vietnamese divisions and at neutralizing enemy pressure on allied outposts along the 40-mile stretch of South Vietnam's northern frontier. Augmenting the ground assault, U.S. B-52s bombed targets in and around the DMZ Sept. 17-18. Striking for the first time since Aug. 17, the B-52s dropped bombs on 13 targets on both sides of the Benhai River, part of the demarcation line between North and South.

In another DMZ area clash Sept. 17, a U.S. Marine artillery base 4 miles south of the buffer zone, the Rockpile, was swept by

Communist small-arms and mortar fire. 25 Marines were killed and 126 wounded.

A force of 2,000 U.S. Marines was airlifted Sept. 17 into the southern section of the DMZ to cut the supply lines of an estimated 7,000 troops of the North Vietnamese 320B Division, who posed a threat to U.S. military bases just below the buffer area. 4,000 more Marines swept into the DMZ Sept. 27 in a coordinated pincers action aimed at trapping the North Vietnamese. The operation, the longest sustained U.S. drive inside the DMZ, claimed the lives of 742 North Vietnamese through Oct. 1, according to American spokesmen. U.S. casualties during that period were listed as 65 killed and 77 wounded.

The Sept. 17 offensive, first reported Sept. 20, had been preceded by U.S. B-52 saturation raids on North Vietnamese targets inside the zone. The ground operation started with the landing by helicopter of troops of the 3d Marine Division on the southern banks of the Benhai River. In the first 4 days of fighting, the Marines, sweeping south, were reported to have killed 110 North Vietnamese and to have captured nearly 500 rifles. This was the first time that a U.S. force had been brought to the border of North Vietnam before beginning an assault.

A North Vietnamese force, apparently trying to escape from the buffer zone, was engaged by South Vietnamese troops near Giolinh Sept. 22-23. A government spokesman reported that 98 of the enemy had been killed.

The U.S. Marines had discovered an abandoned and destroyed North Vietnamese regimental camp in the DMZ $1^1/_2$ miles south of the Benhai River Sept. 21. The Marines said they had also found 120 North Vietnamese bodies in recently dug graves.

Targets in the DMZ were shelled Sept. 30 by the battleship *New Jersey*, which had arrived from the U.S. the previous day. The warship, recently brought out of the mothball fleet, had last seen action in the Korean war. It was the world's only active battleship.

Among other developments in the ground fighting:

● A Viet Cong force Sept. 22 attacked a South Vietnamese prisoner-of-war camp at Binhson (18 miles north of Quangngai) and shot to death 20 Viet Cong captives who had refused to leave the camp with the attackers, a government military command spokesman said. According to the spokesman, the government guards were driven away by a heavy mortar assault, and 70 civilians in a nearby town were wounded by the shelling. 10 of the camp's defenders were killed and 9 wounded.

• A North Vietnamese force laid siege Sept. 28 to a U.S. Special Forces camp at Anduc and to the nearby provincial district headquarters of Thuongduc, 30 miles southwest of Danang. The 2 outposts were heavily shelled by rockets and mortars Sept. 28 and 29. 3 ground attacks on the bases in the 2 days were repulsed and 191 North Vietnamese killed. The defenders' casualties totaled 16 killed and 12 wounded. Continued North Vietnamese shelling through Oct. 2 raised civilian losses at the 2 bases to 46 killed and 103 wounded. Hundreds of U.S. and South Vietnamese soldiers were sent to the area Oct. 6 to relieve enemy pressure on the 2 outposts. A government battalion was helicoptered into a valley $2^1/_2$ miles northwest of the camps while a U.S. Marine battalion was reported advancing toward the area from the southwest. U.S. B-52 bombers pounded enemy targets in the area Oct. 5-6.

• The former U.S. Marine base at Khesanh, abandoned July 6, was reoccupied by Marines without opposition Oct. 4. A Marine unit was brought by helicopters to the base just blow the DMZ to secure a hill for 2 artillery batteries supporting a U.S./South Vietnamese sweep of the sector.

(A U.S. Army Chinook helicopter collided Oct. 3 with a 2-engine American C-7 Caribou cargo plane that had just taken off from the Camp Evans airstrip 11 miles north of Hué. All 24 Americans aboard the 2 aircraft were killed.)

At the Sept. 11 session of the Paris Conference, the shortest since the start of the talks, both sides aired conflicting battlefield claims. U.S. Amb. W. Averell Harriman reported that more than 12,000 North Vietnamese soldiers had been killed since Aug. 18. Despite "these crushing defeats, your government seems prepared to go on expending its most precious national treasure—its youth —in a senseless and callous manner," Harriman said. Xuan Thuy, head of the North Vietnamese delegation, said that 62,000 allied troops had been killed in August. More U.S. soldiers were rebelling against the war and refusing to obey their officers' orders, he claimed. Thuy warned that "many more U.S. troops will have to find a useless death" unless the U.S. began "seriously moving toward peace."

Defoliation Defended & Attacked

U.S. officials asserted at a news conference in Saigon Sept. 20 that the American defoliation of selected areas of South Vietnam was "a complete success," had caused no harmful effect on human or animal life and had yielded no evidence of significant alteration to the country's ecology. In another report made public at the news conference, a U.S. Agriculture Department official, Dr. Fred H. Tschirley, said, however, defoliants had resulted in "undeniable ecologic change," that the change was not irreversible but that "recovery may take a long time."

According to the U.S. officials: The spraying of chemicals to destroy the forest and jungle cover used by Communist forces and to expose their supply routes to aerial observation had "unquestionably saved allied lives." About 3,500 square miles, or 5% of South Vietnam, had been defoliated during the war. The U.S. had spent $34 million on defoliation in 1967, and the 1968 campaign was being maintained on a similar level.

Tschirley's report was based on a study he had made in the spring of 1968; only part of it was released, the rest remained classified. He said his one-month survey "can in no sense be considered a complete, authoritative assessment on the ecological effects" of the defoliation. *Among Tschirley's findings:*

● Defoliation "has no measurable effect on atmospheric moisture and thus would have no effect on precipitation."
● The "possibility of flooding or changes in the water table as a result of defoliation are subjects that need careful consideration." "The relative susceptibility of specific species in the . . . forests of Vietnam is not known."
● "The greatest danger resulting from defoliation" of forests "is that such areas will be invaded by bamboo," which spreads quickly and deters the growth of other plants.
● "The effect of defoliation on animals does not appear to have been extreme." But "I know far less about animals than about plants."

2 American scientists Sept. 20 criticized the U.S. officials in Saigon for ignoring what they called the harmful results of defoliation:

● Harvard biologist George Wald took issue with the statement that chemical sprays did not cause long-term damage to rice crops. "I can think of one immediate long-term effect," he said. "That is, that old people and children are probably dying of starvation."
● Washington University biologist Barry Commoner, a board member of the American Association for the Advancement of Science, praised Tschirley's report, particularly the phase dealing with damage to timberlands. How the U.S. officials in Saigon "can ignore that I do not understand," he said.

NEGOTIATIONS III

A complicated set of behind-the-scene discussions and conflicting political developments unfolded in September. They resulted, by the end of October, in an agreement by the U.S. to end the bombardment of North Vietnam in return for assurances of restraint on the part of the Viet Cong and North Vietnam far less binding than those that had so far been insisted on. In a background story published Nov. 1, the *N.Y. Times* printed an account of the turning point in the Paris talks. It said:

● The U.S.' latest formula for ending the bombing, which was accepted by Hanoi, had been drawn up in Washington after Pres. Johnson had conferred with his top advisers in a series of meetings ended Sept. 17. The basis of the formula was an understanding that Johnson required not "a humiliating public act of reciprocity" from Hanoi but some assurance that a complete bombing halt would not mean "additional punishment" to allied troops. The U.S. sought "not restraint before a bombing halt but after." Amb. W. Averell Harriman, head of the American delegation at the Paris talks, had been instructed to present the formula to Hanoi's representatives.

● The formula stated: "The President simply could not maintain a cessation of the bombing of North Vietnam unless it was very promptly evident to him, to the American people, and to our allies that it was indeed a step toward peace. If there were abuses of the demilitarized zone, Viet Cong or North Vietnamese attacks on the cities or other populated areas, such as provincial capitals, in South Vietnam, or a refusal by Hanoi authorities to enter promptly into serious political discussions that included the elected government of South Vietnam, a bombing cessation simply could not be sustained."

● At the Oct. 9 session in Paris, the North Vietnamese representative had asked Harriman whether the U.S. would "stop the bombing if we give you an affirmative clear answer to the question of Saigon government participation" in the talks. Gen. Creighton Abrams and U.S. Amb. Ellsworth Bunker, asked by Pres. Johnson to assess Harriman's report and the effect of positive response to Hanoi's query, said in a joint statement: "We interpret the exchange as meaning that Hanoi is ready for a shift in tactics from the battlefield to the conference table. Hanoi would move forward" on receiving an affirmative answer. Johnson then instructed Bunker to discuss the matter with South Vietnamese Pres. Nguyen Van Thieu. Thieu approved the American bombing halt, but he said allied military pressure in South Vietnam should continue. Johnson held a White House meeting with his advisers Oct. 14, and it was agreed that Hanoi should be given an affirmative reply.

2d Battlefield Lull

The new turn first manifested itself in a 2d lull on the battlefields of South Vietnam. A steady decline in combat fatalities of both sides was reported for the 4 successive weeks between Sept. 15 and Oct. 12. The decrease in the tempo of fighting was coupled with reports of a withdrawal of Viet Cong and North Vietnamese troops from positions around South Vietnamese cities and of the pullback from South Vietnam of 40,000 to 60,000 North Vietnamese and Viet Cong troops.

U.S. air strikes against North Vietnam, however, continued unabated. The U.S. lost its 900th plane over North Vietnam Sept. 30. The aircraft was downed during a 116-mission raid against supply lines and military storage depots. U.S. planes Oct. 3 carried out the heaviest raid on the North since July 2. Pilots returning from the 143-mission strike said they had destroyed 45 supply craft and 31 trucks and had severed roads in more than 20 places, causing at least 2 landslides. A U.S. TA-4 Skyhawk, spotting targets for the battleship *New Jersey*, had been shot down by North Vietnamese groundfire Oct. 1. The pilot and observer bailed out over the South China Sea and were later rescued. Hanoi charged Oct. 5 that the U.S. was intensifying air strikes against North Vietnamese dikes and dams. A statement issued by the North Vietnamese Water Conservation Ministry reported more than 30 air attacks on dikes, locks and dams in the southern provinces of Nghean, Hatinh and Quangbinh since September.

American deaths for the period Oct. 6-12 totaled 167, the lowest U.S. weekly death toll recorded since July 14-20, when 157 GIs had been listed as slain. A government report Oct. 8 said 1,654 enemy soldiers had been killed Sept. 29—Oct. 5, the lowest weekly Communist death toll in 2 months. 2,866 Viet Cong and North Vietnamese had been killed Sept. 22-28 and 3,380 Sept. 15-21, the U.S. claimed.

The slackening of ground action was confirmed by the South Vietnamese armed forces' official weekly war bulletin issued Oct. 17. It said: "Enemy activity continued decreasing during the week. A total of 175 enemy-initiated incidents continued during the period, compared to 282 for the previous week."

The report that 40,000 to 60,000 Communist troops might have pulled out of South Vietnam was based on U.S. intelligence speculation quoted by the Associated Press Oct. 18. It was believed

202 SOUTH VIETNAM 1968

the North Vietnamese/Viet Cong force had moved into North Vietnam, Laos and Cambodia to reequip and reorganize for further combat. U.S. military sources, however, did not discount the possibility that the pullback was connected with the Paris negotiations.

U.S. officials in Saigon had reported Oct. 15 that most, if not all, North Vietnamese regulars apparently had moved out of range of South Vietnam's heavily populated areas. Communist infiltration into South Vietnam also was said to have declined; the September total was believed to be well below the 20,000 men said to have moved into the South in August. A U.S. general said the enemy had been "fading away all over the place."

Among military actions reported during the battlefield lull:

• U.S. forces were reported Oct. 6 to have launched a drive to relieve North Vietnamese pressure around the 2 small allied outposts of Anduc and Thuongduc, 30 miles south of Danang. 30 North Vietnamese were said to have been killed through Oct. 7. Another 31 were slain in an unsuccessful North Vietnamese attack on a U.S. Marine bivouac position in the area Oct. 12.

• U.S. troops engaged 300 enemy soldiers along the northeast invasion corridor to Saigon Oct. 11, but most of the Communist force escaped. The action took place near Trangbang, 27 miles northwest of the capital. 26 enemy bodies were found. American casualties totaled 6 killed and 16 wounded.

• At least 3 government outposts near Hieuthien (northwest of Saigon) came under Communist mortar attacks from bases inside Cambodia Oct. 13.

• Communist mortar and rocket shells Oct. 14 struck the provincial capital of Quangngai and a nearby government regimental headquarters. 4 civilians were killed and 8 were wounded in the city. Military casualties at the base were termed light.

• The battleship *New Jersey* Oct. 14 shelled the North Vietnamese island of Hon Matt, 14 miles south of the 19th Parallel. The *New Jersey* earlier that day had pounded a cave storage area 18 miles to the southwest, near Vinh.

• South Vietnamese troops killed 75 Communist soldiers Oct. 16 on the southeastern edge of the DMZ, 2 miles east of the allied outpost at Giolinh.

• A U.S. Navy and Coast Guard task force, assisted by helicopter gunships, attacked Communist positions in the Mekong delta province of An Xuyen (155 miles southwest of Saigon) Oct. 18 and damaged or destroyed 125 structures and 40 water craft. In another action, a U.S. Navy patrol boat Oct. 19 sank a Communist junk near Vungtau (40 miles southwest of Saigon) after the junk had fired on Vungtau. At least 15 Communist crewmen were killed. 5 civilians had been killed and 19 wounded in the Vungtau shelling.

• A U.S. C-47 transport, en route from Tansonnhut airfield near Saigon to Danang, crashed Oct. 21 in the Central Highlands, about 175 miles northeast of Saigon. All 24 American passengers and crewmen were killed.

The U.S. Marine base near Dongha, close to the demilitarized zone (DMZ), came under Communist shelling Oct. 22 for the first time in 56 days. 3 Marines and 3 civilians in the town of

Dongha were killed.

At least 178 Communist troops were killed Oct. 23 by U.S. artillery shelling about 35 miles southwest of the American base at Danang. The force reportedly was heading for Danang when it was spotted in the open by U.S. Marines.

More than 500 enemy soldiers were reported killed Oct. 25 in a series of allied-initiated attacks. 232 had been slain in a battle in the southern edge of the DMZ. The fighting had started when an American unit, on a routine search mission, came on a force of 400 to 500 North Vietnamese troops. The battleship *New Jersey*, supporting U.S. troops in combat for the first time, shelled the enemy in bunkers and trenches. The shelling accounted for more than half the North Vietnamese fatalities. U.S. losses totaled 6 killed and 29 wounded.

Communist troops Oct. 26 launched their first major ground assault in South Vietnam in a month. A force of 500 to 600 men attacked a U.S. First Division base in Tayninh Province 59 miles north of Saigon, near the Cambodian border. The enemy was repulsed with a loss of about 100 men killed. American casualties totaled 8 killed and 33 wounded.

U.S. B-52s bombed the Tayninh area 22 times Oct. 26-29 in an effort to break up the reported massing of North Vietnamese soldiers. Most of the aerial strikes were centered in the northeast corner of the province, about 50 miles north of Saigon and about 10 miles from the Cambodian border. The build-up of North Vietnamese soldiers in the area had started 3 months previously and, according to a U.S. spokesman, had "been going on off and on ever since."

B-52s Oct. 29 bombed North Vietnamese positions in the DMZ and targets just inside North Vietnam. The targets hit included artillery bases, storage areas and truck parks, all within a 12-mile radius of Conthien, the U.S. base 2 miles south of the DMZ.

In Paris, at the Sept. 18 session, Xuan Thuy reworded North Vietnam's position on the U.S. bombing of the North, but U.S. authorities did not regard the changed wording as a basic in Hanoi's stand. Thuy said: An unconditional halt in the American raids would "open the way for a movement toward a peaceful solution to the Vietnam problem." It would be "a first step opening the way to move toward a peaceful solution on the basis of respect for the fundamental rights of the Vietnamese people."

204 SOUTH VIETNAM 1968

Cyrus R. Vance, deputy head of the American delegation, paraphrased a key sentence in a speech made by Pres. Johnson in Detroit Aug. 19. "As for ending the remaining bombing of North Vietnam, we ask that you give us reason to believe that you intend seriously to join us in de-escalating the fighting and moving seriously toward peace," Vance said.

The Sept. 25 session was marked by a U.S.-North Vietnamese exchange on the strength and legitimacy of the U.S.-supported South Vietnamese government. Replying to Harriman's call for acceptance of the Saigon regime as a reality, Thuy asserted, "Yes, indeed, it is an extremely vicious and dirty reality." Thuy argued that the South Vietnamese presidential elections in Sept. 1967 were fraudulent because they had been conducted "at the gunpoint of more than a million United States, satellite and puppet troops."

Scoffing at Thuy's claims of "the weakness of the government of South Vietnam and its armies," Harriman said Saigon's forces had "inflicted heavy losses on the North Vietnamese army and the Viet Cong forces in the field."

U Thant on UN Action

UN Secy. Gen. U Thant speculated Sept. 23 that a majority of the UN General Assembly's 124 members would support a halt in the U.S. bombing of North Vietnam if a resolution to that effect were submitted at the Assembly's 23d session (which opened Sept. 24). Speaking at a news conference, Thant suggested this draft resolution:

The General Assembly, deeply concerned at the war in Vietnam, convinced that essential first steps should be taken to move the conflict from the battlefield to the conference table, so as to lead to meaningful and positive steps towards a peaceful settlement of the problem,
Requests that the bombing of North Vietnam should cease.

Thant said that his recent discussions with world leaders and government representatives had reflected "a general feeling among the international community" that an ending of the bombing was a prerequisite to peace. Perhaps this sentiment should be tested by putting the matter to a General Assembly vote, Thant said. Without a bombing halt "I don't see how the stalemate can be broken," Thant declared. "I don't see the light at the end of the tunnel for another year or so."

Thant's statement drew a sharp rebuke form U.S. Amb.-to-

UN George W. Ball Sept. 23. After calling on Thant to protest his remarks, Ball told newsmen that the U.S. did not regard Thant's discussion of Vietnam at his news conference "as in any way helpful in furthering the serious and sensitive negotiations now in progress in Paris." Thant's statement, Ball said, "was made with no advance information or consultation with us. I don't know whether there was any with North Vietnam."

Thant's remarks were also sharply criticized by Nguyen Huu Chi, South Vietnamese observer at the UN. Chi asked: "Which should revolt the conscience of the international community, the bombardment of certain military targets in a small portion of North Vietnam . . . to slow down Communist aggression against the South, or the systematic holocaust of human targets in South Vietnam by means of the most sophisticated weapons supplied by the entire Communist block." "The answer to that question," Chi said, "would raise serious reservations as to whether U Thant's convictions faithfully reflect the opinion and conscience of the world."

Thant denied Sept. 24 that he had said he planned to encourage any member state to place the Vietnam question on the Assembly's agenda. A statement released on his behalf said Thant had "made clear that this was not a realistic idea in the present circumstances" and that he still believed it would "not be useful" for the UN to take up the Vietnam question. Thant also explained that in his Sept. 23 statement he had meant that any Assembly resolution on the bombing of the North would be approved by a simple majority, not by a $^2/_3$ majority as required on important questions.

In spurning any suggestion of a UN General Assembly vote on the bombing, Nguyen Thanh Le, spokesman for the North Vietnamese delegation at the Paris peace talks, reiterated Hanoi's view Sept. 25 that the "Vietnamese problem is not within the jurisdiction" of the UN. Le, however, expressed satisfaction in seeing "more and more countries and delegations of countries at the United Nations publish declarations to support the people in the struggle and to condemn the [U.S.] aggression . . . against Vietnam."

Thant had called Sept. 16 for "a complete and unconditional cessation of the bombing of North Vietnam." Speaking at a Paris news conference after meeting with French Foreign Min. Michel Debré, Thant said: "Without this I don't see how the problem can be moved from the battlefield to the conference table." Debré said Pres. Charles de Gaulle supported Thant's view because "it conforms to reality if one wishes to assure a solution of the Vietnamese problem."

Thant's comment had been prompted by a statement earlier Sept. 16 by Nguyen Thanh Le. Le had said that North Vietnamese diplomats in Paris had no plans to meet with Thant. Le added: "As a statesman of Asia, we hope he uses his influence with the United States government to struggle for an unconditional halt to the bombing and all other acts of war" against North Vietnam.

In the introduction to his annual report to the UN General Assembly, Thant said that the Vietnamese conflict was, basically, a nationalist struggle and should be isolated from "adverse international influences" "to let the Vietnamese themselves deal with their own problems." As a first step, Thant reiterated his plea for a halt in the U.S.' "bombing and all other acts of war against North Vietnam." "In my view, it is for the side which is militarily more powerful to take the initiative," he said. Thant declared that the parties to the talks in Paris should aim for the reunification of North and South Vietnam and for the "neutralization of the entire Indochinese peninsula, including all of Vietnam."

Progress Toward Bombing Halt

A shift in American policy on the bombing issue was signalled in a series of reports in the early weeks of October. Vice Pres. Hubert H. Humphrey, in a major election campaign speech Sept. 30, urged a bombing halt in terms more conciliatory than those the Johnson Administration had so far used. Humphrey pledged that if elected President, he would end the bombing if there was "evidence, direct or indirect, by deed or word, of Communist willingness to restore the demilitarized zone between North and South Vietnam."

At the Oct. 2 meeting in Paris, however, Thuy denounced Humphrey's proposal for ending the bombing. Thuy said: "This means that Mr. Humphrey, like Mr. Johnson, still demands reciprocity. Moreover, he even threatened to resume the bombing of North Vietnam. As regards Mr. Nixon, the warlike Presidential candidate of the Republican Party, he is clearly not satisfied with the deceitful words of Mr. Humphrey. We repeat once more that we do not accept any kind of reciprocity."

A lack of progress in the Paris talks was conceded by Truong Chinh, the 3d-ranking member of the North Vietnamese Communist Party's Politburo, it was reported in Washington Oct. 6. Chinh's assessment of the negotiations was made in a report delivered at a Hanoi meeting, believed held in August or early September, in honor of the 150th anniversary of the birth of Karl Marx. Chinh said: "Due to the perfidious and obdurate attitude of the United States, the aggressors are purposely trying to confuse black and white and to deny the truth." The American negotiators, Chinh added, "deliberately evade the pivotal question: namely, that the United States must unconditionally cease the bombing and all other acts of war over the entire territory of North Vietnam." Chinh called on the North Vietnamese people to "overcome pacifist ideas and grasp the motto of 'long-drawn-out fighting and relying mainly on oneself'."

South Vietnamese Pres. Nguyen Van Thieu had warned Sept. 17 that "we cannot accept peace proposals from any individual or any group other than the just formula for peace which the government is pursuing." Thieu's statement reportedly was aimed at South Vietnamese groups, including militant Buddhists, advocating a softer position on peace.

South Vietnamese Foreign Min. Tran Chanh Thanh declared Sept. 30 that his government would not consider itself "bound by any [peace] agreement between powers excluding South Vietnam unless South Vietnam gives its full consent." The statement was made in a White Paper setting out Saigon's peace conditions. The paper also affirmed Saigon's refusal to cede any territory to North Vietnam as part of a peace settlement.

Ford Foundation Pres. McGeorge Bundy proposed Oct. 12 an unconditional halt in the bombing of North Vietnam and a substantial withdrawal of American forces from South Vietnam starting in 1969. Bundy, who had advocated escalation of the war during his service as a foreign policy aide to Presidents Kennedy and Johnson, made the suggestion in an address to a symposium at DePauw University (Greencastle, Ind.). Asserting that "we must lift this burden from our lives," Bundy said that "continuation on our present course is unacceptable" because the American people "simply will not support the current level of cost and sacrifice for another period of years." Bundy foresaw "no solution to the war in Vietnam through United States military escalation" nor "military victory against North Vietnam by a level of United States military force which is acceptable or desireable, either in our own interest or in the interest of world peace."

Bundy recalled that the original purpose of the bombing of North Vietnam was to give "a prompt and resolute demonstration of American will and purpose" when a Communist military victory appeared imminent. But that purpose was "far out of date," and "the particular values which the bombing of the North still has for the limitation of infiltration and resupply are far outweighed by its political costs," he said. Furthermore, the stopping of the bombing "would shift the burden of response from Washington to Hanoi." Bundy called for a halt to the air strikes "early in 1969" if they had not been stopped before. He said the gradual pullout of the bulk of American forces could be carried out without resulting in the defeat of South Vietnam. He proposed that at least 100,000 U.S. troops should be stationed in Saigon for years if the Communists resisted a "decent settlement" of the war.

Defense Secy. Clark Clifford confirmed Oct. 31 that he had "strongly recommended" stopping the bombing as a "further move toward peace in Vietnam." He said the Joint Chiefs of Staff, as well as Gen. Creighton Abrams, had advised Pres. Johnson "that under the present circumstances they consider a cessation of the bombing to be a perfectly acceptable risk."

At the Oct. 9 session of the Paris talks, Xuan Thuy, Hanoi's chief representative, called on Pres. Johnson to order an unconditional halt to the bombing of North Vietnam in order to facilitate progress in the negotiations. "If Pres. Johnson really wants to solve the Vietnam problem peacefully, he still has enough time and power now to do so," Thuy said. He charged that recent shelling by American "commando ships" of Homme Island north of the 20th Parallel was "an extremely serious new step of escalation." The 20th Parallel was above the northern limit of U.S. air and naval bombardment set by Johnson Mar. 31.

W. Averell Harriman reiterated Johnson's previous demands that North Vietnam give some "reason to believe that you intend seriously to join with us in de-escalating the war and moving seriously toward peace."

At the Oct. 16 session, Harriman, concentrating on the economic aspects of the Southeast Asian problem, urged North Vietnam "to work with us in finding the way to peace and in moving to the goal of cooperation among nations." Harriman suggested that once peace was achieved "both North and South Vietnam could establish economic, cultural and family ties." Urging Hanoi to take part in regional economic cooperation, Harriman said: "There is no reason why North Vietnam could not participate in the economic and other benefits now being brought to the area by many cooperative efforts, such as the Asian Development Bank, the Mekong Coordination Committee and the UN Economic Commission for Asia and the Far East."

Thuy asserted that the U.S. could prove its interest in a peace settlement if it would recognize the National Liberation Front and "discuss with it questions concerning the 2 sides in Vietnam."

The North Vietnamese Communist Party newspaper *Nhan Dan* Oct. 17 again ruled out Hanoi's compliance with the American demand for military de-escalation in exchange for a U.S. stop to the bombing.

A new American offer to Hanoi to halt the bombing of North Vietnam in exchange for a de-escalation of war activities by Hanoi was reported Oct. 16. The report raised speculation that the deadlocked talks in Paris could begin moving toward a start of substantive U.S.-North Vietnamese negotiations. A spokesman for the American delegation in Paris, William Jorden, said after the Oct. 16 session that there had been "movement" in the talks but that it was too early to report progress. The departure to Hanoi Oct. 14 of Le Duc Tho, senior adviser to the North Vietnamese delegation, had indicated that a major review of the Communist position was under way.

Peking radio Oct. 19 confirmed Western accounts of a possible breakthrough by reporting that the discussions had "entered a delicate stage." This was the first time that Chinese Communist authorities had informed their people that negotiations to end the war were in progress. An official dispatch said: "The Vietnam-U.S. 'Paris talks' started officially on May 13. By now [North] Vietnam and the United States had held 26 official meetings."

A White House statement Oct. 16 had denied that there had been a basic shift in the American position on Vietnam. It said that the U.S.-North Vietnamese impasse had not been broken. Pres. Johnson expressed similar thoughts in phone conversations later Oct. 16 with the 3 candidates for the U.S. Presidency.

Details of the reputed new American offer to Hanoi were reported by the *N.Y. Times* in a dispatch from Washington Oct. 17. Quoting authoritative sources, the dispatch said the U.S. had offered to accept North Vietnamese demands for an unconditional halt to the aerial strikes in exchange for Hanoi's assurance that such a move would lead to peace. The latest proposal was said to have omitted the demand for military "reciprocity," repeatedly rejected by Hanoi. According to the *Times*, the North Vietnamese assurances sought by Washington included pledges to: (a) restore the neutrality of the demilitarized zone; (b) refrain from using the bombing pause to increase the infiltration of men and matériel into South Vietnam; (c) decrease attacks on South Vietnamese cities and populated areas.

The possibility of a cessation of the bombing of the North was said to have been the topic of discussion of several meetings U.S. Amb. Ellsworth Bunker held with South Vietnameses Pres. Nguyen Van Thieu in Saigon Oct. 16-22. At the Oct. 16 and 17 discussions, Thieu was said to have urged the U.S. to insist that North Vietnam agree to these 3 conditions in exchange for halting the bombing of the North: (1) A guarantee that the neutrality of the demilitarized zone would be respected; (2) a halt to the shelling of South Vietnamese cities and towns; (3) an agreement to South Vietnam's participation in the Paris peace talks.

In a TV report Oct. 19, Thieu declared that North Vietnam had continued to refuse to make any concessions that would lead to a bombing halt and that the current lull in the fighting did not constitute a military de-escalation on the part of Hanoi. Thieu charged that North Vietnam had "been obstinately demanding a total bombing halt without proving that they are willing to reciprocate for our goodwill for peace. They are still posing obstacles on the path toward peace." Thieu attributed the decrease in the fighting to the heavy casualties suffered by the Communists and their consequent inability to muster "enough strengh to attack us." Thieu asserted that "we will only recognize a de-escalation on the side of the enemy if Hanoi makes an announcement in which they make clear when and how they would de-escalate." In the event that North Vietnam agreed to de-escalate, Saigon would insist on being included in the Paris peace talks, Thieu said. Thieu asserted that South Vietnam remained opposed to the National Liberation Front's participation in the talks. "We will never recognize the Liberation Front, and so we will never negotiate with them as an entity, much less as a government."

Thieu declared Oct. 22 that he was "willing and ready to take any action which can hasten the establishment of a just and honorable peace." His statement was in reply to a call by Vice Pres. Humphrey Oct. 20 for his (Thieu's) cooperation with Pres. Johnson in seeking peace. Humphrey had also stated that South Vietnam should not have the final say as to whether and when the U.S. should halt the bombing of North Vietnam. In response to this, Thieu said he "does not oppose the cessation of the bombing . . . when we have good reason to believe that North Vietnam seriously intends to join us in de-escalating the war and enter into prompt and direct talks" with South Vietnam.

Pres. Johnson said Oct. 24 that the U.S. was still awaiting a reply from Hanoi to the latest American offer to halt the bombing of North Vietnam in exchange for North Vietnamese de-escalation. Asserting that there had been "no basic change, no breakthrough," Johnson said at a news conference that the U.S. was continuing its efforts "to bring about some kind of an understanding which would result in substantive discussions" between U.S. and North Vietnamese peace negotiators in Paris and "ultimate settlement of the Southeast Asia problem."

The President was asked whether he believed the relatively low number of battle fatalities incurred Oct. 13–19 (U.S. 100, South Vietnamese less than 200 and Communists 1,243) reflected "some kind of a lull on the part of the enemy" or his "inability . . . to inflict heavier casualties." The President said he was "very pleased that the casualties are no higher than they are." But he said he hesitated "to use this much overworked word 'lull' when 1,500 people give their lives in one week. In some places it is not a lull. The last thing I would do is to lull anyone into a false sense of security."

A Hanoi broadcast Oct. 25 declared that Johnson's statement had shown that he was "still unwilling to unconditionally end the bombing." Commenting on the widespread reports of a possible peace breakthrough, the broadcast said: The U.S. "propaganda machine spreads fabricated news, saying that Hanoi has accepted a number of United States conditions in exchange for an end to the United States bombing"; "this constitutes an absolutely deceitful argument of a psychological-warfare nature."

Defense Secy. Clark Clifford said Oct. 25 that Johnson had

ordered that "there be no reduction in the level of military pressure that we put on the enemy in South Vietnam" while the Paris talks were in progress. Clifford said he could not provide details of the current American peace effort because Johnson "has directed his Cabinet members to refrain from commenting on developments in Paris." Clifford confirmed a report that 30,000 to 40,000 North Vietnamese troops had been withdrawn from South Vietnam. But he said he did not know whether "this is a sign" of North Vietnamese military de-escalation.

North Vietnam had failed to clarify its position on the American peace offer at the latest Paris negotiating session, held Oct. 23. William J. Jorden, spokesman for the U.S. delegation, said at a briefing after the meeting that he had found the results "a little discouraging." At the meeting, Xuan Thuy, chief North Vietnamese representative, had denounced the South Vietnamese government "desperately clamoring for the fight against the South Vietnam National Liberation Front" while others were seeking a peaceful solution of the war. Averell Harriman accused Thuy of "extravagant and extraordinary" claims on behalf of the NLF. Harriman asserted that the NLF "was born in Hanoi in 1960" and was controlled by the North Vietnamese Communist Party.

New Zealand Premier Keith J. Holyoake said in Saigon Oct. 28 that the U.S. peace proposal "should be enough to persuade North Vietnam to go to the conference table for a peaceful settlement at the earliest possible date." Holyoake, who had begun a state visit to South Vietnam Oct. 26, said in a joint statement with Pres. Nguyen Van Thieu that he supported the South Vietnamese government's demand for a major role in the Paris peace talks if and when they entered a substantive phase.

(Holyoake had visited South Korean Pres. Chung Hee Park Oct. 17-24. A joint communiqué issued in Seoul Oct. 24 said "the 2 leaders had reaffirmed their agreement that all the allies [fighting in South Vietnam] should play a part in determining the nature of any settlement of the conflict.")

(A joint communiqué issued at the conclusion of talks Holyoake had held with Pres. Johnson in Washington Oct. 9–10 said that the situation in Vietnam had shown improvement but that Hanoi "still shows no disposition to scale down the fighting." Holyoake and Johnson called for "both a strong military posture and intensive diplomatic pressure" to achieve a just peace.)

It was reported Oct. 23 that the U.S. was keeping the Soviet

Union informed of its diplomatic moves to break the stalemate with North Vietnam. The State Department confirmed that State Secy. Dean Rusk had discussed the matter with Soviet Amb. Anatoly F. Dobrynin Oct. 18 and 21.

U.S. Ends the Bombing

U.S. planes ended all raids over North Vietnam Nov. 1 as ordered by Pres. Johnson.

3 hours and 45 minutes before the bombing halt went into effect, a Marine Corps F-4 Phantom jet was shot down by anti-aircraft fire during a 144-mission attack on North Vietnamese installations in the Donghoi area 19 miles north of the Mugia Pass. The 2 crewmen were rescued by an Australian destroyer after their plane crashed into the South China Sea. The downed jet was the 915th U.S. aircraft lost since the start of the American air strikes over the North in Feb. 1965. During that period about 100,000 missions had been flown and 2.8 million tons of bombs dropped.

Warships of the U.S. 7th Fleet, including the aircraft carrier *Constellation* and the battleship *New Jersey*, were reported to have left the Gulf of Tonkin off the North Vietnamese coast to take up new positions off South Vietnam.

U.S. officials in Washington made clear Nov. 1 that the planes used in the attacks on the North would be diverted for intensified raids on targets in South Vietnam and to increase by 3-fold the air strikes on the Ho Chi Minh Trail in Laos. The trail, originating in North Vietnam, was used to infiltrate men and supplies into South Vietnam.

Laotian Premier Souvanna Phouma Nov. 1 lauded the U.S. decision to halt the bombing of North Vietnam as a step toward peace. He expressed hope that the U.S. would also stop the raids on Laos. But a source at the U.S. embassy in Vientiane said U.S. policy toward Laos remained unchanged. He said that "armed reconnaissance" flights over Laos (meaning the air strikes) would continue.

The halt in the bombing was followed by a general lull in the ground fighting in South Vietnam, but scattered actions were reported.

Prior to the lull, Saigon came under Communist rocket attack Oct. 31-Nov. 1. At least 21 Vietnamese civilians were killed and

more than 70 wounded in the 20-rocket bombardment. The most
damaging attack was carried out Nov. 1 against a Roman Catholic
church where congregants had gathered for a morning mass. 19
persons were killed and 64 wounded.

Among other actions:

● A U.S. Navy LST anchored on the Maytho River in the Mekong delta,
about 34 miles southwest of Saigon, was blasted by a Communist mine Nov.
1. 19 Americans and one South Vietnamese were killed. 4 Americans and one
South Vietnamese were reported missing.

● A U.S. jet plane accidentally bombed a Marine Corps unit Nov. 3. 6
Marines were killed and 8 wounded. The plane had been called in to sup-
port a Marine attack on a suspected Communist position 7 miles southwest of
Danang.

The decision to stop the bombing was made by Pres. Johnson
and publicly announced by him in a TV-radio address the evening of Oct. 31. In his TV address, Johnson said he had reached the
decision to halt the bombing of North Vietnam "on the basis of
the developments in the Paris talks, and I have reached it in the
belief that this action can lead to progress toward a peaceful settlement of the war." The U.S. could "now expect . . . prompt,
productive, serious and intensive negotiations in an atmosphere
that is conducive to progress," he said.

The President said that in exchange for a bombing halt, Hanoi
had agreed to the participation of the South Vietnamese government at the Paris talks, while the U.S. had approved a role for
the NLF. But the U.S. informed Hanoi that this "in no way involves recognition of the National Liberation Front in any form,
yet it conforms to the statements that we made many times over
the years that the NLF would have no difficulty in making its
views known."

Although Johnson did not announce any specific North Vietnamese act of de-escalation of the war, repeatedly demanded by
the U.S. as a condition for a halt in the bombing of the North,
he referred to 2 U.S. prerequisites that were part of the latest
American peace formula. The President said that Washington had
made clear to Hanoi that "we cannot have productive talks in an
atmosphere where the [South Vietnamese] cities are being shelled
and where the demilitarized zone is being abused." It was also
made clear to Hanoi, Johnson added, "that a total bombing halt
must not risk the lives of our men."

Johnson cautioned that "arrangements of this kind are never
foolproof. For that matter, even formal treaties are never fool-

proof, as we have learned from our experience. But in the light of progress that's been made in recent weeks, and after carefully weighing the unanimous military and diplomatic advice and judgment rendered to the commander-in-chief, I have finally decided to take this step now and to really determine the good faith of those who have assured us that progress will result when the bombing ceases and to try to ascertain if an early peace is possible."

Earlier in his statement, Johnson had reviewed the events immediately leading to his decision to halt the bombing. He disclosed that: "A few weeks ago" the Paris talks had "entered a new and a very much more hopeful phase" after months of deadlock. "As we moved ahead, I conducted a series of intensive discussions with our allies and with senior and military and diplomatic officers of the U.S. government on the prospects for peace." Congressional leaders and all Presidential candidates also were briefed by the President. "Last Sunday [Oct. 27] evening and throughout Monday we began to get confirmation of the essential understanding that we had been seeking with the North Vietnamese on the critical issues between us for some time." In talks with Gen. Creighton W. Abrams, U.S. commander in South Vietnam, recalled to Washington Oct. 29 for briefing, the President and Cabinet members weighed his "judgment" and "recommendations at some length. Now, as a result of all these developments, I have now ordered that all air, naval and artillery bombardment of North Vietnam cease as of 8 a.m., Washington time, Friday morning. . . . This decision very closely conforms to the statements that I have made in the past concerning a bombing cessation. . . . The Joint Chiefs of Staff, all military men, have assured me, and Gen. Abrams very firmly asserted to me [at the Oct. 29 meeting], that in their military judgment this action would not result in any increase in American casualties."

State Secy. Dean Rusk said Nov. 1 that the U.S. believed that its decision to stop the bombing was "a constructive step, will open the way to serious talks and will not endanger our own and allied forces in the field." But he urged "some government and leading personalities [who] have over many months undertaken to tell us that something good would happen if we stopped the bombing" "to make a maximum effort to assure that their advice has substance in it." He asserted that the U.S. would "be interested in what others may do to insist upon actions by Hanoi that will move us toward peace."

Johnson's decision to halt the bombing of North Vietnam was supported by the U. S.' 3 major Presidential candidates: Vice Pres. Humphrey Oct. 31 called the bombing cessation "very wise and prudent" and said "I've been hoping for months that it would happen." Richard M. Nixon Oct. 31 expressed hope that the bombing halt would "bring some progress" in the Paris talks on the war. On the NBC "Meet the Press" program Nov. 3, Nixon pledged to "cooperate in any way Pres. Johnson determines will be helpful" in seeking peace in Vietnam. He said he would be willing, as President-elect, to go to Saigon or Paris to help "get the negotiations off dead center." He said he felt that the period between the election and the inauguration of the new President "could be very critical" and that "if the United States right then could present a united front with Pres. Johnson—if he could knock down the idea that Hanoi is going to gain by political division in the United States what they cannot gain on the battlefield—this might get these talks off dead center." He said he would not "sit out . . . and wait and let . . . [Pres. Johnson] stew in his juice and then hope" to achieve success in the negotiations "after January." 3d party candidate George C. Wallace said Oct. 31: "I hope and pray" Johnson's decision to stop the bombing would bring "an honorable peace." "I couldn't care less who gets credit for it. . . . I only want the President to be successful."

NEGOTIATIONS IV

The new phase of the discussions had been scheduled to begin Nov. 6 and was to be expanded to include the representatives of the South Vietnamese government and the National Liberation Front (NLF), the political arm of the Viet Cong. The expanded talks, however, were postponed Nov. 5, on the U.S.' initiative, after South Vietnamese Pres. Nguyen Van Thieu had announced Nov. 2 that his government would not attend unless North Vietnam agreed to negotiate without the NLF participating as a separate delegation. The U.S., confident that Thieu would eventually end his boycott, rejected an NLF suggestion for 3-party meetings of NLF and North Vietnamese representatives with a U.S. delegation representing the "American government and the government of Saigon." A U.S. official said: "There can be no conference on the future of South Vietnam without the presence of the government of South Vietnam." The North Vietnamese rejected a U.S. suggestion that their delegations hold a token meeting Nov. 6 to maintain diplomatic contact across the conference table.

Acceptance of the expanded Vietnamese peace talks in Paris had been announced in separate statements issued by Hanoi Nov. 1 and by the NLF Nov. 3. Hanoi's approval, made public in a communiqué released on behalf of Xuan Thuy, chief North Vietnamese delegate at the Paris talks, acknowledged that W. Averell Harriman had informed him Oct. 30 of Pres. Johnson's plan to halt the bombing of North Vietnam Nov. 1. Thuy did not say the raid stoppage was "unconditional," as Hanoi had repeatedly demanded. Thuy said that "in order to find a peaceful settlement of the Vietnam problem," a meeting including representatives of North and South Vietnam, the NLF and the U.S. "will be held in Paris, not earlier than Nov. 6."

A North Vietnamese government statement Nov. 2 hailed the halt in the bombing as "a great victory for the entire Vietnamese people of both the North and the South." The U.S. had stopped the raids, the statement said, because it was facing "great defeats in Vietnam and increasing condemnation and pressure from peoples throughout the world." Hanoi affirmed its willingness to participate in 4-party talks in Paris. But it said this did not imply North Vietnamese recognition of the "puppet regime" of South Vietanam. Charging that the South Vietnamese government was a "tool of the U.S. aggressors" and represented "nobody," the statement restated the North Vietnamese position that the NLF was the only "authentic representative of the South Vietnamese people."

At a news conference Nov. 2, Thuy interpreted the U.S.-North Vietnamese agreement on the composition of the expanded talks to mean that 4 separate delegations would participate—"independent delegations with the right to speak." This position apparently contradicted the view of the U.S., which had envisioned 2 delegations—the U.S. and South Vietnam on one side, North Vietnam and the NLF on the other. Thuy asserted that if South Vietnam refused to join the talks, "that will mean that they do not desire peace, and the American side will have to bear the full responsibility." Thuy agreed to one of the 3 conditions for Saigon's presence at the Paris negotiations. He characterized the forthcoming talks as a new phase and not a continuation of the

discussions that the U.S. and North Vietnam had been conducting
since May. The latter meetings had dealt only with "unconditional cessation of bombing and all other acts of war by the
United States" against North Vietnam, Thuy recalled, while the
new talks would have "4 delegations, and the objective will be to
discuss a solution to the problem of peace in Vietnam."

North Vietnamese Pres. Ho Chi Minh exhorted the Vietnamese people Nov. 3 to press their "determination to fight and to
win" the conflict against the U.S. He said the U.S. had been
"compelled to unconditionally stop the bombardments of North
Vietnam."

The Nov. 3 statement announcing the NLF's agreement to
take part in the Paris talks said this did "not signify in any way"
NLF recognition of the "puppet administration of Saigon." The
statement, issued by the NLF's Paris information bureau (established in October), said the front remained the "authentic representative of the South Vietnamese people." The communiqué said
a 6-member NLF delegation would be headed by Mrs. Nguyen
Thi Binh, 41, a member of the front's Central Committee.

Mrs. Binh and her staff arrived in Paris Nov. 4. The other
members were identified as Duong Dinh Thai, interim chief of
the front's mission in East Berlin and director of the Liberation
Press Agency bureau there; Tran Van Tu, the NLF representative
in Warsaw; Lam Van Khai and Tran Thanh Cau, officials of the
front's foreign relations commission; Mrs. Pham Thanh Van,
interpreter. (Although France did not recognize the NLF diplomatically, its delegation was treated by France as though it had
diplomatic status. Official cars were provided for the delegation,
and Mrs. Binh was given the use of Post & Telecommunications
Ministry facilities Nov. 5 for a press conference at which she
claimed that the NLF had liberated 4/5 of South Vietnam and
"fulfills the role of a government in the liberated regions.")

Saigon Boycotts Negotiations

Pres. Thieu's decision Nov. 2 to boycott the Paris talks was
announced in an address at a joint session of the South Vietnamese National Assembly.

The inclusion of the NLF in the talks as a separate delegation,
Thieu charged, "would just be another trick toward a coalition
government with the Communists in South Vietnam." Thieu in-

sisted that "at the negotiating table, we will only know of one delegation—the North Vietnamese delegation. We will only talk to them." Thieu said Hanoi must also meet 2 other conditions before Saigon would participate in the talks: North Vietnam must publicly acknowledge that it advocated serious peace talks; such discussions must be an "entirely new phase of the talks, not just a continuation of the present exploratory talks" between the U.S. and North Vietnam.

Thieu's position received wide support in Saigon. After his speech, more than 100 persons, including at least 50 Assembly members, marched to the U.S. embassy in Saigon to express their approval of Thieu's refusal to join the Paris talks.

Vice Pres. Nguyen Cao Ky was said to have voiced opposition to the U.S. decision to halt the bombing. A Vietnamese Assembly representative quoted Ky as having told a group of legislators Nov. 2 that "we can trust the Americans no longer—they are just a band of crooks"; the U.S. was "unmasking itself as a true and dirty colonialist power."

In his first response to Pres. Johnson's decision to halt the bombing, Thieu had asserted in a commuiqué Nov. 1 that the U.S. had acted unilaterally. But "since we have a peace-loving tradition, the government of Vietnam is not against the cessation of the bombing," Theiu said. Thieu expressed doubt that North Vietnam would de-escalate the war in response to the bombing halt. As a result, Saigon "has not found enough good reasons to have a common agreement with the United States goverment on this matter," Thieu said.

It was reported Nov. 5 that Thieu and other South Vietnamese officials at first had agreed to accept Johnson's formula for ending the bombing. After Hanoi's agreement to the terms Oct. 27, U.S. Amb. Ellsworth Bunker was said to have called on Thieu Nov. 1 to agree to a joint U.S.-South Vietnamese communiqué of concurrence. It was then that Thieu raised his objections and advanced his prerequisites for South Vietnamese participation in the talks. Bunker was said to have informed Thieu, Ky and Foreign Min. Tran Chanh Thanh that the U.S. could not raise the conditions since Hanoi had already approved Johnson's proposals.

Bunker issued another appeal to Thieu Nov. 5 to end his boycott of the Paris talks. Speaking over the U.S.' armed forces radio and TV stations in South Vietnam, Bunker said a peace settle-

ment "requires the free and active participation of the representatives of the South Vietnamese government." Thieu's refusal to
enter the talks, Bunker said, was a "sincere and honest" expression "of a president to his people who have suffered aggression,
have been subject to a brutal and ruthless invasion and have made
great sacrifices in life and treasure." Bunker assured South Vietnam that the U.S. supported its view that NLF participation in
the Paris meetings would not imply recognition of the front. He
said the U.S. also was determined that the talks would not result
in the imposition of a coalition government on Saigon.

Thieu reaffirmed Nov. 5 that "we will never attend the Paris
talks if we have to talk to the NLF as an independent delegation."

As a condition for ending his boycott of the expanded Paris
talks, Thieu Nov. 8 proposed a 2-sided conference headed by
South Vietnam and the U.S. on one side, with Saigon in the dominant role, and a combined North Vietnamese/National Liberation Front (NLF) delegation on the other. The plan was rejected
later Nov. 8 by Xuan Thuy, Chief North Vietnamese delegate.

Explaining his formula in a speech, Thieu said: "Each side
is to consist of a single delegation headed by the principal party.
Our side—the victims of aggression—will be headed by South Vietnam. Our delegation will include the United States and, if necessary, our other allies. The other side is the side of the Communist aggressors, to be headed by North Vietnam, which directs the
aggression against the Republic of [South] Vietnam. Their delegation can include members of Hanoi's auxiliary forces, labeled as
the National Liberation Front."

Thuy opposed the merger of the North Vietnamese and NLF
representatives as a single delegation on the ground that Hanoi
had agreed with the U.S. that "it was to be a 4-party conference
of independent delegations." "If the United States and Saigon
want to be one delegation, that leaves 3 delegations," and North
Vietnam would not object to this formula, Thuy said.

The South Vietnamese government Nov. 9 closed the newspaper *Than Dan* for allegedly implying in an editorial that Thieu
was thwarting the Paris peace talks and advocated continuing the
war. (The Saigon regime suspended 2 other newspapers Nov. 9;
this brought to 10 the number silenced in 2 weeks for alleged
anti-government views.)

South Vietnamese militant Buddhist leader Thich Tri Quang

Nov. 9 denied Thieu's claim that the people were united behind his [Thieu's] stand on peace talks. Tri Quang charged that the people's "fight for the right of self-determination, freedom and democracy" had been rejected by the government.

Thuy Nov. 11 reiterated the view that the U.S. and North Vietnam had agreed only to a 4-party conference composed of the U.S., South Vietnam, North Vietnam and the NLF. Saigon's refusal to attend, Thuy charged, was being used by the U.S. as a pretext to delay the start of the expanded meetings. If South Vietnam refused to join the talks, the discussions should start as a 3-sided conference, Thuy said. He made this suggestion before 1,500 people in Paris at a rally sponsored and attended largely by Vietnamese living in the French capital.

South Vietnamese Information Min. Ton That Thien said Nov. 12 that his government wanted written assurances from North Vietnam on an agenda as well as the composition of the participants as a condition for joining the talks. "We want Hanoi to put things on paper and sign them so there are no misunderstandings," Thien said.

(The North Vietnamese army newspaper *Quan Doi Nhan Dan* denied Nov. 12 that Hanoi had reached a tacit agreement with the U.S. to let American planes continue reconnaissance flights over North Vietnam during the bombing halt. The newspaper said U.S. press reports of North Vietnamese "tacit acceptance of spy flights" were not true.)

Defense Secy. Clark M. Clifford warned South Vietnam Nov. 12 that if it persisted in boycotting the talks, the U.S. might proceed without Saigon and conduct negotiations with North Vietnam on its own. Speaking at a news conference in Washington, Clifford said: "There are a great many subjects that can be covered between the United States and Hanoi of a military nature. ...We could work out steps that could lead to a diminution in the level of the combat" in South Vietnam. Since the U.S.' objective in South Vietnam was to provide "a military shield," the question of a "political settlement in South Vietnam" was "up to South Vietnam and Hanoi."

Clifford refused to speculate as to why South Vietnam had refused to join the expanded conference after it had apparently agreed with the U.S. to do so. Clifford recalled that Pres. Thieu, apprised of the progress being made in the U.S.-North Vietnamese negotiations in Paris, had approved Oct. 29 the signing of a joint

U.S.-South Vietnamese communiqué that would have affirmed the agreement to halt the bombing of North Vietnam and to proceed with the expanded conference. Thieu later Oct. 29 said he could not accept the arrangement because he had no time to send a delegation to Paris by Nov. 2, Clifford said. Clifford continued: "Then the next day . . . that one reason, which had been time only, had expanded into some 4 or 5 reasons [for not attending], every one of which [would] consume a substantial amount of time."

Clifford complained that after Pres. Johnson had made a decision that "could be a major step toward peace," "then in the last out of the 9th inning, . . . suddenly they [South Vietnam] say, 'No, we can't go along.'" Clifford added: "After all that we have done in that country, . . . with the knowledge that we had gotten to the point where we had the sort of agreement that we had been working toward, I believe the President was absolutely right in not giving Saigon a veto on the plan." Clifford said the U.S. would continue its efforts "to iron out the problems that have come up" with the South Vietnamese government in the hope "that they will join in talks very soon."

Clifford conceded that the North Vietnamese artillery attacks from the demilitarized zone (DMZ) on U.S. positions Nov. 10 and the shelling of 30 provincial and district capitals in South Vietnam since the Nov. 1 bombing halt constituted a violation of the U.S.-North Vietnamese agreement that had paved the way for the expanded peace talks. But, he said, he was "willing to proceed with these efforts to get the talks started, and not conclude that these violations are sufficient to warrant stopping all that has gone on, until a pattern emerges." In the meantime, the U.S. would watch the situation carefully, Clifford said. "If it should prove to be an isolated instance, that is one facet. If it should prove to be the beginning of a pattern, that would something entirely different."

Walt W. Rostow, Pres. Johnson's special assistant, had said Nov. 10 that since the start of the bombing halt the DMZ had been "exceedingly quiet" and "there is no abnormal" movement of men and supplies from North Vietnam through Laos into South Vietnam. Rostow expressed regret at the shellings of South Vietnamese cities, particularly Mytho and Cantho, but he said it did not pose a danger to "the appropriate, necessary environment for the sustaining of the bombing halt and for productive talks."

South Vietnamese Information Min. Ton That Thien Nov.

13 criticized Clark Clifford's warning that the U.S. might proceed without Saigon and negotiate alone with North Vietnam. Thien said: "The U.S. can do what it likes. It is clear we cannot win the war without the U.S. But the U.S. cannot win the war without us. That also applies to making peace." The South Vietnamese government was shocked at Clifford's remarks because the U.S. "is our ally." "They can go ahead and talk, but their conclusions certainly will be of no validity at all."

Denying what he said was Clifford's allegation that South Vietnam had agreed to a 4-sided conference and then reneged, Thien said: "At no stage, at no time, with no one had Pres. Thieu agreed to the so-called 2-side 4-delegation formula." Saigon insisted that the NLF not be considered a "separate entity" from the North Vietnamese delegation. The NLF "can sit at the back or the head, but not as a separate delegation. And if Hanoi calls them the NLF, then we walk out."

(The South Vietnamese government Nov. 14 suspended the English-language *Saigon Daily News* for 3 months for printing the details of Clifford's criticisms of the Saigon regime. A government official complained that the newspaper had carried an account of Clifford's statement under a 3-column headline but had given the government's rebuttal a "tiny" one-column headline.)

U.S. Presidential assistant Walt Rostow said Nov. 14 that South Vietnam was boycotting the talks because it feared that "the Paris arrangements were so structured as to force them into a coalition government" with the NLF. Rostow assured Saigon that the Johnson Administration "has always been opposed to a coalition government in South Vietnam. We are never going to use our leverage, and I dare say the next Administration will take the same view."

U.S. officials in Washington said Nov. 17 that Amb. Ellsworth Bunker was working out final details with the South Vietnamese on arrangements for Saigon to send a delegation to the suspended talks.

Saigon Yields, Agrees to Attend Talks

The South Vietnamese government announced Nov. 26 that it had decided to abandon its boycott of the expanded Paris talks. The Saigon statement said that "it is prepared to participate in the new talks . . . with the Hanoi delegation to show the goodwill of the Republic of Vietnam and to test the good faith of Hanoi." U.S. and North Vietnamese delegates then started discussions in Paris Dec. 2 on the procedures for holding the enlarged conference of U.S., North Vietnamese, South Vietnamese and National Liberation Front (NLF) representatives.

Saigon's Nov. 26 statement, issued by Foreign Min. Tran Chanh Thanh, was the culmination of several weeks of U.S.-South Vietnamese negotiations. Thanh said: "As a result of these discussions, the United States government has submitted to the government of the Republic of South Vietnam a statement" which supported "in their essential aspects" Thieu's position of Nov. 2 and "the 2-sided formula" for the expanded talks as proposed by him Nov. 8. "The sovereignty of the Republic of South Vietnam has been respected. The governments of the other allied nations have been consulted and wholeheartedly support the agreement achieved through the close cooperation" of the U.S. and South Vietnam.

The announcement was accompanied by a U.S. statement reassuring South Vietnam that its sovereignty would be respected and that the U.S. would oppose the imposition of "any coalition government" on South Vietnam. The statement reviewed Washington's position on the understanding it had reached with North Vietnam about the composition of the expanded conference. The statement recalled that North Vietnam had accepted the U.S. view that South Vietnam would participate in the enlarged talks "as a separate delegation, forming with the United States delegation one side of the meeting. United States negotiators made clear to Hanoi that it might bring on its side of the table any persons it wished. The North Vietnamese . . . accepted this proposal and indicated that they would bring to the meeting members of the so-called National Liberation Front. In the light of these facts, the arrangements agreed in Paris provide in essence for a 2-sided meeting. . . . Whatever others may claim, and however they may organize their side, the U.S. has not agreed and will not agree that the meeting is, or can correctly be described as a 4-sided or 4-party conference."

The U.S. insisted that "the North Vietnamese delegation must talk directly and seriously" with the South Vietnamese representatives in Paris. It said that in the talks South Vietnam would "take the lead on all matters which are of principal concern to South Vietnam." This was a tacit rejection of Saigon's demand for a dominant role in a U.S.-South Vietnamese delegation as outlined in the "2-sided formula" advanced by Thieu Nov. 8.

In further comment on the U.S.-South Vietnamese accord, Foreign Min. Thanh said Nov. 27 that all of his government's original demands and conditions for ending its boycott of the Paris talks "have been met. This has been a big victory for the South Vietnamese government and people."

Pres. Thieu announced Nov. 27 the appointment of Vice Pres. Nguyen Cao Ky to "oversee and control" the South Vietnamese delegation to the Paris talks. In a radio-TV address, Thieu said Ky's task would be to "consult with the government in Saigon, receive instructions from Saigon and direct negotiating efforts in Paris, as well as other activities in Paris." Thieu said a Saigon delegation would participate in the Paris conference "within the next 10 days at the latest."

Pres. Johnson Nov. 26 welcomed South Vietnam's decision to join the talks. He said: "This step opens a new and hopeful phase in the negotiations; but, as I have said before, we must expect both hard bargaining and hard fighting in the days ahead."

Hanoi Radio asserted Nov. 28 that the North Vietnamese delegation in Paris would not talk to Saigon's representatives. "In settling the Vietnam problem, we will talk only with the United States," the statement said. Hanoi suggested that the war be ended by a 3-sided agreement of the U.S., North Vietnam and the NLF.

At the Dec. 2 procedural talks in Paris, Cyrus R. Vance, acting head of the U.S. delegation, and Ha Van Lau, 2d-ranking member of the North Vietnamese delegation, also exchanged protests over alleged military activities in North Vietnam and in the demilitarized zone. The 2 men had met Nov. 24 to discuss U.S. reconnaissance flights over North Vietnam. Vance had called for the meeting to protest North Vietnam's firing on U.S. surveillance craft. Lau filed a counterprotest against continuation of the flights. In disclosing the North Vietnamese protests, Nguyen Thanh Le, chief spokesman for Hanoi's negotiating team, said Nov. 26 that U.S. reconnaissance planes over North Vietnam "have been punished and will continue to be punished." Le charged that the U.S. observation flights over the North were "continuing and multiplying" and were carrying out attacks "under the deceitful pretext of protecting its pilots." Le said these activities violated the U.S. bombing halt and posed a threat to peace.

Impasse Over Shape of Conference Table(s)

In the final meetings of 1968, the conference deadlocked. The principal stumbling block was the table (or tables) at which the 4 delegations were to be seated. Col. Ha Van Lau, 2d-ranking member of the North Vietnamese delegation, insisted on a square table with a delegation at each side. This would support Hanoi's view of the understanding it had reached with the U.S. on the expanded talks that 4 separate delegations would attend. The U.S. position, as outlined by Cyrus Vance in talks with Lau, called for a rectangular table with North Vietnam and the NLF on one side and the U.S. and South Vietnam on the other, or 2 tables, one for the allies and one for the Communists. The North Vietnamese announced Dec. 10 that they had further proposed 4 tables—one for each delegation; they would be set in a rectangle or circle with equal spaces between the tables.

Other procedural points still unsettled were the order in which the delegations were to speak and their visual designations. The Communists insisted on national flags, the allies advocated nameplates. The procedural points already agreed to included the number of participants—10 to 12 for each of the 2 sides— allied and Communist—and the use of English and Vietnamese as the official languages, with French used for informal exchanges and documents.

Vice Pres. Nguyen Cao Ky, head of the South Vietnamese delegation, arrived with his staff in Paris Dec. 8 to participate in the talks. Ky said his delegation would "not demand any advantages or privileges. We will not demand that those on the other side surrender. We ask only that justice and reason prevail." Ky asserted that the only reason he was participating in the talks was to demand an end to Communist aggression against South Vietnam. "I will not ask for anything more, but I will accept nothing less." The expanded peace talks "must not be regarded as a meeting resulting from Soviet Russian, Red Chinese or American pressure," Ky declared. Ky said he was not completely satisfied with the way the U.S. and North Vietnamese delegations had been conducting their talks since May, but he did not elaborate. Ky met later with W. Averell Harriman, head of the U.S. delegation. Harriman later called his discussion with Ky "constructive."

Ky's official title was "adviser and coordinator" of Saigon's delegation. The actual negotiations were to be handled by ex-Foreign Min. Pham Dang Lam, who had served as South Vietnam's official observer at the preliminary U.S.-North Vietnamese talks between May and November. The other members of Saigon's delegation were Nguyen Xuan Phong, a former minister in charge of the government's Viet Cong defection program, Vuong Van Bac, a member of the defunct People-Army Conference, an advisory body created by the previous Saigon government, Mrs. Nguyen Thi Vui, also a former member of the People-Army Conference, and Prof. Nguyen Ngoc Huy.

The Saigon government's decision to participate in the talks had been indorsed Dec. 7 by a joint session of the South Vietnamese Senate and House of Representatives. 80 legislators favored participation, 21 opposed and 40 present did not vote. The vote had been preceded by a debate on another resolution that said the Assembly "reaffirmed its position that it is strongly against all attempts to partition the country, or to establish a government of coalition with the Communists in any form." This resolution, however, never came to a vote. The Senate Dec. 5 had voted, 44-5, in favor of participating in the conference following Pres. Nguyen Van Thieu's request for parliamentary indorsement. But the Assembly, refusing to ballot separately, insisted that Thieu's request should be considered at a "special joint session" of the legislature. Upholding the Assembly's view, the South Vietnamese Supreme Court ruled Dec. 6 that the combined houses must vote on the matter because the constitution empowered the National Assembly "to declare war and open peace talks." The court held that the National Assembly meant a joint session of both houses.

Harriman returned to the U.S. Dec. 2 to brief Pres. Johnson and Pres.-elect Richard M. Nixon on the Paris peace talks. Harriman met with Johnson and the cabinet in the White House Dec. 4. After the meeting, Harriman told newsmen that he planned to seek a formal truce in the demilitarized zone (DMZ) to replace the informal U.S.-North Vietnamese agreement to respect the neutrality of the buffer strip. Harriman said that some North Vietnamese troops had withdrawn from the DMZ but that Hanoi's failure to take out all its forces was "most annoying" to the U.S. Harriman conferred with Nixon in New York Dec. 5 and urged Nixon, who had been elected President Nov. 5, to send an observer to the Paris talks before he assumed office Jan. 20, 1969.

The U.S. and South Vietnamese delegations held their first working session Dec. 9 to coordinate their positions. Another meeting, held Dec. 12, was attended by Harriman, chief U.S. negotiator, and South Vietnamese Vice Pres. Ky. Ky expressed objections to any seating plan that would place the NLF on an equal footing with Saigon.

A new seating plan, in the form of 4 separate suggestions, was advanced by Cyrus R. Vance, deputy head of the U.S. delegation, in discussions with North Vietnam's Ha Van Lau. The suggestions: (1) 2 half-oval tables placed against each other to form a broken oval; (2) 2 half-circle tables, placed to form a broken circle; (3) 2 half-circle tables, slightly spaced, with 2 rectangular tables between them for secretaries and tape recorders; (4) 2 half-circle tables pushed together to adjoin the secretarial tables. Vance's 4th suggestion was made after Lau, objecting to the U.S.' "concept of 2 sides," called for a table formed in a complete, unbroken circle. This was aimed at emphasizing Hanoi's view that the talks should be 4-sided, with the NLF sitting as a separate delegation.

The U.S. and South Vietnamese representatives held further talks Dec. 15, 16 and 17. Implying disagreement with the U.S. approach to the seating arrangements, Ky said after meeting with Harriman Dec. 17 that "we are faced with many pressures, and we are prepared to face them."

U.S.-South Vietnamese differences had broken into the open Dec. 16 when Ky publicly assailed Defense Secy. Clifford for having again "shown a gift for saying the wrong thing at the wrong time." Ky was referring to a statement in which Clifford Dec. 15 blamed South Vietnam for delaying the procedural talks in Paris. Speaking on the CBS-TV program "Face the Nation," Clifford had said: "I have not heard that the Americans have raised any objection about any of the [procedural] details—we are ready to agree to anything. Amb. Harriman and Amb. Vance . . . have said, 'We are ready to sit down at any kind of table.' It is Hanoi and Saigon that have raised the question about these details, and it seems to me that there ought to be sufficient pressure of world opinion on them to get them going to the talks." Clifford suggested that when the expanded talks start, the U.S. and North Vietnam should agree to a quick de-escalation of the fighting while Saigon, Hanoi and the NLF work out a political settlement. The U.S., Clifford said, had no "obligation" to keep 540,000 troops in South Vietnam until there was a political settlement of the war.

Denying that Saigon was impeding the talks, Ky said his team was working closely with the U.S. on drawing up a joint strategy and that there were "no divergencies" between the 2 sides. Pham Dang Lam, Saigon's chief negotiator, said Dec. 16: "We don't understand what Mr. Clifford is talking about. It isn't we who raised procedural questions." Ky said Dec. 18 that "my problem is, I have to fight not only my enemies but also my so-called friends. . . . I think we on our side have many irresponsible people who ought to keep their mouths shut."

Ky left Paris for Saigon Dec. 22 to report to Pres. Nguyen Van Thieu. In a taped CBS-TV interview Dec. 21 (the transcript was made public by CBS Dec. 22) Ky had said that his talks with Thieu would include "the possibility to have a direct contact with all opposition groups in South Vietnam," including the NLF. Ky said: "We never accept and we will never accept the Front as an entity, but [we will recognize] its reality." On his return to Saigon Dec. 23, Ky said the South Vietnamese government would hold direct talks with the NLF, but only after North Vietnamese troops withdrew from South Vietnam and the war ended. Previously, Saigon had insisted that it would deal with members of the NLF only as individuals, not as a group.

In a meeting with Lau Dec. 19, Vance was reported to have warned that a Communist attack on Saigon could result in an indefinite delay in the peace talks and lead to a resumption of U.S. air attacks on North Vietnam. The alleged threat by Vance was reported later by the North Vietnamese but was denied by William J. Jorden, spokesman for the American delegation. The North Vietnamese announcement quoted Lau as having replied to Vance that "the menaces brandished by the United States have never shaken the Vietnamese people's determination to fight for independence and liberty."

NLF representative Tran Buu Kiem Dec. 23 rejected any direct contacts between the NLF and Saigon. He said that "if one wants to settle a conflict, one settles it between the direct adversaries," who, he claimed, were the Viet Cong and the U.S. Kiem said the U.S.' refusal to enter into direct talks with the NLF was "neither realistic nor conducive to peace in South Vietnam."

A joint statement issued by the North Vietnamese and NLF

delegations Dec. 26 insisted that the U.S. and South Vietnam accept the Communist proposal for a round table if they wanted an "honorable peace" in Vietnam. The statement, issued by NLF spokesman Tran Hoi Nam, said that if the allies accepted the Communist suggestion, "all other procedural questions will be settled rapidly and easily." Accusing Saigon of sabotaging the talks, Nam said that as long as the current South Vietnamese government remained in power, "it will be difficult for the conference to begin; and even if it can be held, it will be difficult to reach results."

NLF delegation head Tran Buu Kiem paid a courtesy call on French Foreign Min. Michel Debré Dec. 26. South Vietnam's chief negotiator, Pham Dang Lam, said that in receiving Kiem, Debré "somehow has prejudged the nature of the talks that are about to open, and even the final settlement." A French official said that there was "nothing unusual" in Debré's meeting with Kiem because the foreign minister also had received Lam.

Duputy U.S. delegate Vance briefed Pres. Johnson and Pres.-elect Nixon on the progress of the Paris talks during a visit to the U.S. Dec. 21-27. Johnson said at his news conference Dec. 27 that Vance had told him "he believes that we can get going in substantive talks after his retutn" to Paris.

Pres. Nguyen Van Thieu was disclosed Dec. 27 to have dismissed about 30 members of South Vietnam's 80-man peace delegation. All had been handpicked by Vice Pres. Ky. A government statement said the aides had been relieved for a "violation of national discipline" by leaving Saigon for Paris without written permission from Thieu or their immediate superiors in Saigon. A Saigon delegation official in Paris Dec. 29 described the dismissals as a "minor administrative matter." The personnel involved, he said, were "purely auxiliary members . . . and the dismissals will not affect the delegation itself."

FIGHTING CONTINUES

Despite the agreement to end the bombing of North Vietnam and to reduce the military pressures on South Vietnam, fighting continued in Vietnam. Most of the encounters took place either in the area of the DMZ (demilitarized zone) or the western borders of South Vietnam.

North Vietnamese guns inside the DMZ shelled U.S. Marine positions just south of the DMZ Nov. 10 for the first times since the U.S. had halted the bombing of North Vietnam Nov. 1. A U.S. military spokesman said a Marine air and artillery counter-attack had hit a North Vietnamese rocket-firing position inside the DMZ and destroyed 10 bunkers. 4 Marines were killed and 41 wounded in the shelling. A U.S. spokesman reported Nov. 10 that in the previous 24 hours North Vietnamese mortar fire, apparent-ly from within South Vietnam just below the DMZ, had hit the town of Camlo, a U.S. Marine base to the northeast, and 2 South Vietnamese bases in the Giolinh area.

The South Vietnamese government was reported Nov. 9 to have filed with the International Control Commission a protest charging that since the start of the bombing halt the Communists had shelled populated areas in 14 South Vietnamese provinces; the shelling killed 53 civilians and wounded 183. The Saigon pro-test cited 2 specific incidents, both of which had occurred at the start of the bombing halt—the bombardment of a Roman Catho-lic church in Saigon and the shelling of the city of Dongha. A previous South Vietnamese protest filed with the ICC (reported Nov. 7) had called attention to a Viet Cong shelling of the Mekong delta city of Mytho (35 miles west of Saigon) in which 5 persons had been killed.

Other Mekong delta cities were reported heavily shelled. The district town of Thiobinh (140 miles southwest of Saigon) was struck Nov. 10 for the 3d time in 4 days. One Vietnamese soldier was killed and 17 persons, including 11 civilians, were wounded. Another delta city, Cantho, came under Viet Cong attack Nov. 9 and 10. Cantho was the headquarters of the South Vietnamese IV Corp tactical zone. The South Vietnamese military command had reported Nov. 7 that 107 Communist troops had been killed near the delta city of Caolanh, 64 miles southwest of the capital. Government forces, comprising rangers, infantry and national militia, suffered 9 killed and 30 wounded.

The U.S. command reported Nov. 7 that 150 U.S. soldiers had been killed Oct. 27-Nov. 2, compared with 109 slain the pre-vious week, which had one of the lowest weekly fatality figures of the war. This raised the U.S. combat death toll since 1961 to 29,-184. 1,393 Communist soldiers were reported killed Oct. 27-Nov. 2.

U.S. B-52 bombers carried out heavy raids Nov. 8-9 against a suspected force of 60,000 men reportedly massing for a major offensive in the Communist War Zone C stronghold about 5 miles from the Cambodian border in Tayninh Province. The bombers dropped 1,500 tons of explosives on suspected bases, infiltration routes and supply dumps. The estimate of 60,000 Viet Cong/North Vietnamese troops in the area had been given by Lt. Gen. Cao Tri, South Vietnamese commander of the III Corps area. Tri said that according to captured enemy documents, the Communists were planning a "total attack" in contrast to their unsuccessful attempt in September to occupy some of the provinces along the Cambodian border. U.S. intelligence reports had placed the number of enemy troops in the III Corps area at 35,000.

The U.S. command reported Nov. 12 that the U.S. had lost its first plane since the halt to the bombing of the North. The aircraft, a Marine Corps A-4 Skyhawk jet, was downed by enemy fire about 25 miles south of the DMZ; the pilot was killed. The plane was the 316th fixed wing aircraft lost in South Vietnam.

U.S. Warns Against DMZ Violations

The U.S. government charged Nov. 13 that North Vietnamese military operations in the demilitarized zone violated the U.S.-Hanoi agreement that had ended the bombing of the North. The U.S. warned that attacks from the DMZ threatened the talks in Paris. The statement, authorized by Acting State Secy. Nicholas deB. Katzenbach, disputed Hanoi's claim that Washington had agreed to a 4-sided conference with the U.S., North Vietnam, South Vietnam and the National Liberation Front (NLF) sitting as separate delegations.

The statement said the U.S. took "a serious view" "of the verified instances since Nov. 9 in which North Vietnamese forces fired on allied forces south of the DMZ from positions within the DMZ." The U.S. held to the view that "serious talks could not be conducted if the DMZ were abused." As for the composition of the talks, the statement said: "Pres. Johnson had made absolutely clear ... the presence of the National Liberation Front in no way involves recognition of the Front in any form. We do not consider the NLF to be an independent entity. ... The NLF will be present only as Hanoi's choice. We made it clear from the outset that we viewed this arrangement as 2-sided and we continue to regard it that way." Washington "refutes" Hanoi's "claims that we have agreed to a 4-sided or 4-party conference." Katzenbach denied Hanoi's charges that the continued U.S. reconnaissance flights over North Vietnam since the Nov. 1 bombing halt violated the U.S.-North Vietnamese agreement. North Vietnam, he said, had agreed and had repeatedly stated that "the activities that we undertook to stop were all bombardments and all other acts involving the use of force. . . . Reconnaisance is not an act involving the use of force."

A North Vietnamese official in Paris, who refused to be identified or quoted directly, said Nov. 16 that Hanoi would honor the DMZ' neutrality if the U.S. did not start bombing the North again. Denying U.S. charges of North Vietnamese military activity in the buffer zone, the official asserted that the U.S. had violated the DMZ with naval and ground fire. The North Vietnamese official insisted that the U.S. reconnaissance flights over the North violated the U.S.-North Vietnamese agreement on the bombing halt. But he said the flights did not completely invalidate that agreement because the U.S. had kept its pledge not to bomb the North.

Nguyen Thanh Le, spokesman of Hanoi's delegation in Paris, had accused the U.S. Nov. 15 of increasing its "aggression" in South Vietnam and of continuing reconnaissance flights over the North behind a "smokescreen" of false charges that Hanoi was violating the DMZ. Le chided the U.S. for refusing to enter the Paris talks until South Vietnam ended its boycott. This refusal to negotiate without Saigon proved that the U.S. was "stubborn, treacherous, doubledealing and bellicose," Le said.

Allied officials Nov. 14 had reported at least 12 North Vietnamese violations of the DMZ since Nov. 1 and at least 72 Viet Cong shellings of South Vietnamese cities and towns; 24 civilians were killed and 180 wounded by the shelling. The U.S. command said that North Vietnamese troops had used the DMZ on 5 occasions Nov. 11 and 12 as a safe area through which to move troops and vehicles and from which to fire at U.S. reconnaissance planes.

Reports by U.S. reconnaissance pilots made public Nov. 15 said that troop and supply movements in North Vietnam had quadrupled since the bombing stopped. More than 400 vehicles were said to have been spotted between the 17th and 19th Parallels, compared with about 100 before the bombing ended.

Some of the trucks were said to have moved into Laos at the 18th Parallel and at a point just south, while a great many others had arrived at staging areas a few miles north of the DMZ. According to the aerial observations, all bombed-out bridges between the 17th and 19th Parallels had been made usable.

U.S. artillery and planes were reported Nov. 16 to have destroyed 3 bunker complexes and a 5-truck convoy in the southern (South Vietnam's) part of the DMZ, 2 to 5 miles northwest of an allied base at Giolinh. 35 North Vietnamese were reported killed.

In the following weeks, the fighting intensified. The upsurge was marked by the loss of 3 U.S. planes over the North, increased military activity inside the DMZ, a Viet Cong command order for the launching of a new offensive, and sharp clashes along the Cambodian border and in the Saigon area and the Mekong delta.

The first of the 3 planes to be downed, an unarmed Phantom RF-4C reconnaissance aircraft, was lost over North Vietnam's southern panhandle Nov. 23. A Hanoi broadcast said that antiaircraft fire had brought down the jet (the first lost over the North since the bombing halt) over Quangbinh, 40 miles north of the DMZ. The broadcast said the pilot had parachuted and was captured. The 2 other planes—an unarmed reconnaissance aircraft and an armed escort plane—were lost in 2 separate incidents over North Vietnam Nov. 25. A U.S. spokesman said other U.S. planes attempting to rescue the downed pilots had come under surface-to-air missile fire and had engaged in dogfights with North Vietnamese MiGs.

(Hanoi claimed Nov. 28 that 8 U.S. planes had been shot down over North Vietnam since bombing halt.)

The U.S. command said Nov. 23 that 210 "indications of enemy activity or presence" in the DMZ had been recorded between Nov. 1 and Nov. 22. The "indications" ranged from sightings of enemy vehicles to Communist artillery attacks in the DMZ. The South Vietnamese Foreign Affairs Ministry said Nov. 30 that it had filed a complaint with the International Control Commission about Communist activity in the DMZ.

U.S. and South Vietnamese forces engaged North Vietnamese in the DMZ 29 times between Nov. 1 and Dec. 1, mostly by air attack. The first U.S. artillery strike inside the DMZ since the bombing halt occurred Nov. 21. The shelling was in response to attacks by North Vietnamese gunners on 2 U.S. reconnaissance planes flying over the southern half of the buffer strip. The planes were not hit, but the North Vietnamese gun emplacements were said to have been silenced. The North Vietnamese Foreign Ministry charged Nov. 21 that U.S. artillery in the southern half of the DMZ had shelled 3 North Vietnamese villages in the northern section of the zone. U.S. ships stationed off Cua Viet, just south of the zone, had supported the artillery, the ministry said.

U.S. and South Vietnamese troops entered the DMZ Nov. 26 for the first time since the bombing halt. They fought 2 engagements against North Vietnamese soldiers regarded as posing a threat to allied positions just below the DMZ. In the first engagement, a squad of government troops killed 3 enemy soldiers and captured one. In the other engagement, a U.S. 3d Marine Division patrol entered the zone and shortly afterward called for reinforcements and air support. The enemy was said to have withdrawn after several hours of fighting. The U.S. force had moved into the zone following intelligence reports that enemy troops 500 yards inside the DMZ threatened the Marine base at Conthien. The U.S. and South Vietnamese units withdrew from the DMZ later Nov. 26. Washington sources reported Nov. 28 that Gen. Creighton W. Abrams, commander of U.S. forces in Vietnam, had personally ordered the U.S. raiding party into the zone. But Abrams was said to have cleared the operation first with the National Military Command Center in the Pentagon in order not to jeopardize the current peace efforts in Paris.

Hanoi Radio Nov. 29 broadcast a Viet Cong order calling for a new offensive to "utterly destroy" U.S. and South Vietnamese forces and pacification teams. The broadcast said the operation was directed against allied search-and-destroy units that were "destroying our villages and occupying our areas." This was in reference to "Operation Phoenix," an allied counter-intelligence and counter-terrorist drive launched earlier in 1968 to recoup positions lost during the Communists' Tet offensive in January. The Viet Cong statement charged that the allies had established "spy cells, called 'Phoenix Organization,' composed of hooligans and diehard cruel agents ... dispatched to villages and hamlets to work as informants to assassinate, abduct and intimidate our compatriots."

The increased intensity of the fighting was reflected by a sharp upward turn of allied casualties Nov. 17-23, government officials reported Nov. 29. 246 government soldiers were killed, compared with 128 the previous week. The U.S. weekly death toll was 160, 33 higher than the previous week. Communist fatalities for the Nov. 17-23 period were listed as 2,175. This was the highest figure claimed since Sept. 22-28, when 2,866 enemy had been reported slain. A government summary accompanying the casualty list said: "During the week [ended Nov. 23], the enemy continued increasing his activity, especially his initiated attacks and shelling."

The U.S. command reported Nov. 28 that U.S. troops had killed 58 Communist troops Nov. 27 about 40 miles north of Saigon near the Cambodian border. U.S. casualties totaled 8 wounded. The clash erupted when a U.S. force, conducting a sweep 4 miles north of Locninh, came under attack by a unit using small arms, automatic weapons and rocket grenades. It was estimated that U.S. and South Vietnamese forces had killed nearly 1,500 North Vietnamese and Viet Cong in November in War Zone C along the Cambodian border. About $2/3$ of the enemy casualties had been inflicted by troops of the U.S. First Cavalry Division (Airmobile), positioned astride several major attack routes to Saigon, 60 miles to the southeast.

U.S. helicopter gunships Nov. 30 spotted an enemy force 4 miles north of Caibe, in the Mekong delta, about 50 miles southwest of Saigon. U.S. troops were flown in by other helicopters and killed 70 of the enemy.

The Danang area had been the scene of a major allied operation launched Nov. 21 against an estimated 1,000 North Vietnamese troops and 150 Viet Cong political agents. In fighting through Dec. 9 (when the operation was officially ended), 1,019 enemy troops were reported killed and 71, identified as Viet Cong agents, were captured. U.S. Marine losses totaled 107 killed and 523 wounded. The enemy force had been encircled in a 15-mile perimeter by 5,000 Marines and 2,000 South Vietnamese and South Korean soldiers. The Marines were reported to have killed another 24 North Vietnamese in mopping-up operations through Dec. 11. The offensive was aimed primarily at weeding out the Viet Cong agents, who were said to be mingling with the 3,000 Vietnamese civilians in the area, about 15 miles south of Danang.

2 U.S. companies of about 250 men, guarding an approach to Saigon 28 miles northwest of the capital, had come under attack Dec. 1 by a North Vietnamese force of 200 to 300 men. The attacking North Vietnamese were repulsed with 48 men killed. U.S. casualties: one killed and 36 wounded.

U.S. and South Vietnamese forces in Saigon were placed on alert Dec. 14-16 in anticipation of a possible attack on the capital. For the first time in several months, American soldiers in Saigon were restricted to their quarters (from 7 p.m. to 7 a.m.) during the 2-day period. In an apparent attempt to disrupt a possible onslaught on Saigon, U.S. B-52 bombers had carried out heavy raids Dec. 12-13 against targets on the northern approaches to the capital. The air strike closest to Saigon was 26 miles to the northeast. According to U.S. intelligence accounts (reported Dec. 12), North Vietnamese and Viet Cong battalions were shifting from border regions closer to populated areas north and northwest of Saigon, west of Danang and along the central coast west of Quinhon.

The U.S. command Dec. 15 reported 3 more allied-Communist clashes in the DMZ. This brought to 41 the number of such incidents described as "significant" since the start of the bombing halt Nov. 1. In one of the DMZ engagements, U.S. fighter-bombers and artillery attacked about 50 enemy soldiers observed in 3 positions about 13 miles from the coast. Pilots reported damage to about 35 bunkers. In a previous DMZ clash Dec. 11, a U.S. Marine company of 150 men, patrolling the southern half of the buffer strip, come on a North Vietnamese force in bunkers about 25 miles from the coast. 12 Marines were killed and 30 wounded. 8 North Vietnamese were slain. The American unit was reinforced by another 150-man company, while U.S. planes and artillery bombarded the enemy positions.

An unarmed U.S. RF-4C reconnaissance plane was shot down over North Vietnam Dec. 9. It was the 4th American aircraft lost over the North since the Nov. 1 bombing halt. The 2 crewmen were reported to have been rescued by helicopter after they parachuted into the Gulf of Tonkin, 10 miles north of Donghoi, North Vietnam. 2 U.S. F-4 Phantom jets Dec. 19 attacked a North Vietnamese antiaircraft position west of Donghoi after being fired on, the U.S. command reported Dec. 21. The jets were accompanying a reconnaissance aircraft at the time. It was the 4th time that American planes had fired on a target in North Vietnam since the bombing halt.

The U.S. command reported Dec. 19 that American combat deaths in Vietnam had risen to more than 30,000. The 222 U.S. soldiers slain Dec. 8-14 (30 more than the previous week) brought to 30,279 the number of Americans killed since Jan. 1, 1961. Viet

Cong/North Vietnamese combat fatalities in the 7-year period totaled 425,329, the command said. About 198 South Vietnamese and 2,059 Viet Cong-North Vietnamese had been killed Dec. 8-14. South Vietnamese forces had captured 521 Communists in the same period. The Viet Cong announced Dec. 29 "the abolition of the South Vietnamese government puppet regime" in the northern province of Quangngai and the establishment of a People's Revolutionary Council to rule the province. A Viet Cong statement broadcast by Hanoi radio threatened "the most severe punishment for any puppet who illegally tries to rule, control or oppress the people of Quangngai."

Pressures on Cambodia

U.S. officials in Washington quoted Cambodian leaders Oct. 4 as publicly admitting for the first time that Viet Cong and North Vietnamese forces were using Cambodian territory for attacks on South Vietnam. The wider employment of Cambodia as a sanctuary and staging area—with alleged Cambodian complicity—also had been indicated in intelligence reports made public in Saigon Sept. 28.

The U.S. officials said that Cambodian Chief of State Norodom Sihanouk had conceded in a recent speech that "though having accepted recognition of our frontiers, the Vietnamese Reds have sent their troops to [the provinces of] Ratanakiri and Mondulkiri," bordering South Vietnam. "Many of them," Sihanouk disclosed, "have come to live on our territory." U.S. military officials had said that the 2 provinces were used as supply routes into South Vietnam. A report broadcast Oct. 3 by Cambodian State Secy. for National Security Sosthene Fernandez (monitored by U.S. sources) had complained that "despite efforts of [Svayrieng] provincical authorities to repel them, armed Vietnamese [Viet Cong and North Vietnamese] are continuing to install themselves on Khmer [Cambodian] territory near the frontier." "The Vietnamese are becoming increasingly hostile to the local people and authorities," he said. Svayrieng Province jutted into South Vietnamese territory close to Saigon.

Heretofore, Cambodian officials had denied U.S. charges that Viet Cong and North Vietnamese forces operated on Cambodian soil. Sihanouk had acknowledged several times that Viet Cong forces might have intruded briefly but had insisted that they had left when Cambodian authorities asked them to leave.

According to intelligence reports disclosed to newsmen in Saigon Sept. 28: Viet Cong/North Vietnamese military activity "in the area of Cambodia closest to Saigon" had "increased 3-fold" since Nov. 1967. "They now have munitions, workshops, hospital huts, prisoner-of-war camps, supply depots and training centers in the area." New weapons and ammunition for Communist troops were being transported over Cambodian highways in trucks sometimes driven by Cambodian military personnel. *The intelligence sources also reported:*

• One of the major base camps in Cambodia was located at Ba Thu, 35 miles west of Saigon. It served as a center for outfitting and retraining Viet Cong/North Vietnamese units. The 30th Viet Cong Battalion had crossed the Cambodian border into the Ba Thu area in May. Several hundred houses, cafes, and refreshment stands had been built there by Viet Cong sympathizers recruited from Haunghia Province in South Vietnam. The battalion had reassembled around Ba Thu May 9 and had marched to another area to exchange old weapons for Soviet-made AK-47 rifles, mortars and rockets shipped from the Cambodian villages of Ph Senta and Ph Trapeang Run.

• A Viet Cong administrative headquarters had been established in Cambodia. Its function was to coordinate political activities in several provinces near Saigon and along the Cambodian border.

• A Cambodian major commanding a 40-man Combodian unit operating from an outpost north of Ba Thu had been paid in money and ammunition for trucking military supplies twice a month to the Ba Thu area.

A Communist military presence in Cambodia was further evidenced by a Saigon report of a clash across the border Sept. 20. Lt. Gen. Do Cao Tri, commander of South Vietnam's III Corps, reported Sept. 24 that government howitzers had fired on Viet Cong mortars inside Cambodia after the enemy guns had shelled South Vietnamese troops in covering the retreat of a fleeing Viet Cong force. The enemy unit had sought to overrun a government outpost at Phuoctan, 2 miles from the Cambodian border.

Cambodian Chief of State Prince Norodom Sihanouk asserted Nov. 11 that as a result of allied attacks on his country's border in the previous 5 days, he was forced to reconsider his position on the status of 11 U.S. servicemen captured by Cambodian forces July 17. The men had been seized after their landing craft strayed into Cambodian waters on the Mekong River. Rejecting a conciliatory note in which State Secy. Dean Rusk had requested the release of the Americans, Sihanouk told newsmen: "I cannot examine any possibility of liberating the prisoners for the moment."

"If I get something from Pres. Johnson directly, I will re-examine the situation."

Sihanouk had said Nov. 7 that he would free the U.S. captives if Johnson "sends me a cablegram, promising that the military will do their best to refrain from bombing our villages along the Cambodian border." He had said previously that he would not release the Americans until the U.S. accepted Cambodia's claims in its border disputes with South Vietnam and Thailand. (According to Sihanouk, more than 200 Cambodians had been killed by U.S. planes bombing and strafing Viet Cong supply lines along the (Cambodian border.)

But Sihanouk Dec. 19 announced the release of the 11 U.S. soldiers and one South Vietnamese. At another news conference held later Dec. 19, Sihanouk also announced the release of a U.S. helicopter gunner, who had been taken when he fell or jumped into Cambodia from his aircraft Nov. 27. The crewman remained hospitalized in Pnompenh with a leg injury suffered in the fall. Sihanouk, who had previously demanded compensation in exchange for the release of the 11 U.S. captives, said the men (who left Pnompenh Dec. 20) were set free "without any condition" as "a gift to the United States." But Cambodia would keep the landing craft "as a small indemnity to Cambodia," he said. Sihanouk said a letter sent to him in November by the U.S. prisoners had "deplored" the shooting incidents along the Cambodian-South Vietnamese frontier and the U.S. attacks on Cambodian territory in pursuit of Viet Cong and North Vietnamese forces. At a news conference in Bangkok, Thailand (enroute to the U.S.), the released men Dec. 20 confirmed sending the letter to Sihanouk. They said they had expressed regret over civilian Cambodian deaths resulting from accidental U.S. bombings on the border.

The U.S. State Department confirmed Dec. 19 that there had "not been any exchange of any material of goods for persons involved in the matter."

The Cambodian government had charged Nov. 17 that U.S. and South Vietnamese patrol boats had shelled the Cambodian village of Prekkoeus in Kampot Province Nov. 16. It reported 12 civilians (9 women and 3 children) killed and 12 wounded. Pnompenh said the allied boats had fired from the South Vietnamese side of the Gianthanh River above the village. In a previously reported border incident, Cambodia had charged that U.S. helicopter gunships Nov. 6 had fired on the Cambodian village of

Preytoul, killing one person and wounding 23 others.

Holiday Truces

Allied and Communist forces observed separate Christmas truces on the Vietnamese battlefield. The Viet Cong also observed a 3-day New Year's truce starting Dec. 30, but U.S. and South Vietnamese forces refused to acknowledge it.

South Vietnamese Pres. Nguyen Van Thieu had announced Dec. 2 that government forces would observe a 24-hour Christmas battle truce starting at 6 p.m. Dec. 24 for humanitarian reasons. The U.S. command said Dec. 3 that American forces also would observe the cease-fire. The Communist Christmas truce, announced by the Viet Cong Dec. 5, extended from 1 a.m. Dec. 24 to 1 a.m. Dec. 27. The U.S. command reported Dec. 27 that the allies' Christmas truce had been violated by 140 Communist-initiated engagements, 47 of which were considered significant because casualties were inflicted.

Allied refusal to participate in a New Year's truce was disclosed Dec. 28 by South Vietnamese Premier Tran Van Huong. He said the decision was based on the number of Communist violations of the Christmas truce.

U.S. POLITICAL DEVELOPMENTS

Debate in Washington

Vietnam continued to be a major and divisive factor in American politics throughout 1968.

Pres. Johnson gave prominence to his Vietnam policies in his State-of-the-Union message, delivered in a televised address before a joint session of Congress Jan. 17. He said that although the U.S. was making progress at home, abroad and in Vietnam, great efforts were still needed in all areas to meet the challenges the nation faced and to achieve the goals that "the fighting and our alliances are really meant to protect." He said that the war in Vietnam was costing the U.S. about $25 billion a year.

The President declared in his message that the nation was "challenged at home and abroad" but that it was "our will that is being tried, and not our strength." He expressed belief that the nation had the physical and moral strength and the will "to meet the trials that these times impose."

Johnson reiterated that in Vietnam "our goal is peace, and peace at the earliest possible moment." The U.S. position on a bombing halt (which at that time had not yet taken place) remained as stated in his San Antonio speech in Sept. 1967, he said: "The bombing would stop immediately if talks would take place promptly and with reasonable hopes that they would be productive. And the other side must not take advantage of our restraint as they have in the past. This nation simply cannot accept anything less without jeopardizing the lives of our men and our allies. If a basis for peace talks can be established on the San Antonio foundations, . . . we would consult with our allies and with the other side to see if a complete cessation of hostilities—a really true ceasefire—could be made the first order of business."

A rebuttal to the President's message was presented by 17 Republican members of Congress in a one-hour telecast Jan. 23. They called for a step-up in the Vietnam war as well as for domestic changes. The keynote was delivered in a filmed introduction by ex-Pres. Dwight D. Eisenhower, who said: "It is essential that members of the party in power become convinced that new measures and new directions are required to preserve and strengthen our free system."

Among the comments touching on Vietnam:

Sen. John G. Tower (Tex.)—The Administration "for too long" had followed a "policy of gradualism" in Vietnam that "prolonged the fighting." "This war could be over today if the Johnson Administration had acted with determination instead of with vacillation." "We stand for the effective utilization of America's vast air and sea superiority. We stand for quarantine of the enemy supply lines so that he can no longer fight. We stand for firm resistance to naked communism in Vietnam as we did in Greece, Berlin, Korea and Cuba. We also stand for the complete protection of American ships in international waters."

Sen. Thomas H. Kuchel (Calif.)—"The Administration has failed to make clear our goals [in Vietnam] to friend and foe alike. It has not been candid with the American people in facing up to the complex and difficult road which lies ahead."

A "confrontation" with the Saigon government on the question of "corruption" and inefficiency was urged Jan. 25 by Sen. Edward M. Kennedy (D., Mass.) after his return from a visit to Vietnam as chairman of the Senate Judiciary Subcommittee on Refugees. Addressing the World Affairs Council of Boston, Kennedy said: The Saigon government was "infested . . . with corruption"; half of the $30 million a year in U.S. refugee aid for South Vietnam was pocketed by government officials and province chiefs. "I believe the peeple we are fighting for do not fully have their hearts in the struggle, and . . . the government that rules them does not have its heart in the cause of the people." The Saigon government "should be told . . . that if they find it impossible to attract the people of Vietnam to their own constitutional government, the American people will rightfully demand serious alterations in the nature of United States involvement."

Appearing on the CBS-TV "Face the Nation" program Jan. 28, Kennedy said "I do not see how we can possibly tolerate the increased losses of American troops . . . and still see this cancer of corruption in all aspects of the Vietnamese government." Asked if he was suggesting that the Saigon government be told to "shape up or we're going to ship out," Kennedy replied, "Well, I think that perhaps is what we should do." Kennedy also said: Apart from the issue of corruption, the U.S. should consider "moderating our whole effort" in Vietnam and, if negotiations were not initiated soon, "modify" its goal to "much more of a clear-and-hold operation."

In a speech before the American Advertising Federation in Washington Feb. 5, Kennedy again urged a "confrontation" with Saigon leaders to tell them "that unless they have sufficient interest in the survival of their own country to mobilize that country for war, to draft their young men at 18 and 19 years of age, to stop the sale of deferments, to place themselves on a 7-day week as do the members of the American mission and to eliminate the system of buying positions of military and political power—unless they have this kind of interest, they cannot long expect us to maintain ours."

(In the Senate Mar. 7 Kennedy denounced Administration policies in Vietnam as "immoral and intolerable." "Are we God?" he asked. "Are we empowered to decide which cities, villages and hamlets will be destroyed? Do we have the authority to kill thousands and thousands of people . . . because we say we have a commitment?")

Senate Democratic leader Mike Mansfield (Mont.) said in a speech at the University of Maine in Orono Feb. 11: "Even if we could, we should not seek to synthesize a government or system for South Veitnam." It was not the U.S. purpose to "insure that any political structure shall be enshrined over the smoldering ruins of a devastated Vietnam."

Chairman Richard B. Russell (D., Ga.,) of the Senate Armed Services Committee was quoted in the *Atlanta Journal-Constitution* magazine Feb. 4 as having opposed the U.S.' involvement in the Vietnamese war from the very beginning. "But, frankly," he said, "I don't see how we could come out of there now and abandon the field to Communist forces."

Speaking at the University of Idaho in Moscow Feb. 17, Sen. Albert Gore (D., Tenn.) said: The U.S.' national security was involved in Vietnam because of its large military effort and because of the effects of the involvement on the U.S.' "real national interests." It was incumbent on the Administration to extricate the U.S. from the "morass" by negotiating a disengagement of U.S. forces "on condition that Vietnam be neutralized."

Sen. Birch Bayh (D., Ind.) Jan. 27 advocated U.S. withdrawal if the South Vietnamese did not demonstrate within a year a capacity for self-government. He said the U.S. must "take the role of a mother robin and push the South Vietnamese out of the nest."

In a Senate speech Feb. 5, Sen. Jacob K. Javits (R., N.Y.) urged working through the Soviet Union for "a political and diplomatic compromise" on Vietnam based on the "recognition that there is a fundamental stalemate in Vietnam."

Sen. Frank Church (D., Ida.), on the Senate floor Feb. 21, denounced Administration policy in Vietnam. He said: "The notion that we can restore stability to that half of the world which has just thrown off colonial rule, or worse still, that it has fallen to us to act as rear guard for the shrinking empires of a bygone day, is not even worthy of being called a policy. It is a grandiose dream of men who suffer from the dangerous delusion of American omnipotence." Church called for "an agonizing reappraisal" of U.S. foreign policy to "seek out the rational middle ground where the limits of our intervention are drawn to correspond with the limits of our resources."

Speaking in the Senate Feb. 26, Democratic leader Mansfield indorsed UN Secy. Gen. U Thant's Feb. 24 call for a bombing halt. Mansfield urged a trial suspension of air attacks against North Vietnam "as a step toward peace." "Escalating our peace efforts," he said, would be "preferable" to responding to "the insatiable calls for more men as the war spreads and intensifies." Mansfield exempted from his proposal air support for U.S. forces south of the DMZ, particularly at Khesanh.

Mansfield's remarks led to a minor Senate debate. Assistant Democratic leader Russell B. Long (La.) said "the American people are getting disgusted of this talk of a pause, or pulling your punches when the enemy is slugging you. I for one hope Gen. Westmoreland will be provided with all the troops he requests." Chairman J.W. Fulbright (D., Ark.) of the Senate Foreign Relations Committee said the Administration should consult Congress before making any decision to commit more troops to Vietnam, whereas Sen. George Murphy (R., Calif.) said "the time has not only come, but passed, that the military decisions should be left to the military." Sen. Jack R. Miller (R., Ia.) called for the removal of restraints on air and sea attacks before increasing U.S. troop strength. In a statement issued later Feb. 26, Sen. John Sherman Cooper (R., Ky.) said an increase in U.S. troop strength in Vietnam "would undoubtedly lead to a further involvement by North Vietnam, Communist China and the Soviet Union."

A statement advocating "more imaginative and intensive efforts" toward negotiations was issued Mar. 4 by 18 House Democrats. They asserted that the war "cannot be ended in near future by military means." They said the Administration should let it be known that it would accept a role for the Viet Cong in the formation of a new government for South Vietnam.

Pres. Johnson said during a White House ceremony Mar. 11 that the nation had the resources to "deal with any foe anywhere in the world except within our own boundaries." "Our weaknesses are caused by pitting our strength against each other and chewing on ourselves," he declared. In presenting 2 Medals of Honor Mar. 12, he said: "I think if we are steady, if we are patient, if we do not become the willing victims of our own despair, if we do not abandon what we know is right when it comes under mounting challenge—we shall never fail." "Responsibility never comes easy. Neither does freedom come free." Speaking before the Veterans of Foreign Wars in Washington Mar. 13, Mr. Johnson said: America took up arms only to "help the nation-builders," to "shield the weak," to "bar aggression" and to "build the lasting peace that is our country's single purpose today. We sent our young men abroad because peace is threatened —in other lands tonight, and ultimately in our own. . . . We seek to intimidate no man. But neither shall we be intimidated. And from American responsibilities—God willing—we shall never retreat. There is no safety in such a course. Neither reason nor honor nor good faith commends such a course."

Opposition to further increases in U.S. forces in Vietnam was expressed Mar. 10 by ex-Presidential aide McGeorge Bundy in a talk at Harvard University. "I do not believe a basic case has been made for a significant reinvestment of troops from our side," he said.

2 resolutions indicating opposition to further U.S. troop increases in Vietnam were introduced in the House Mar. 12. One, sponsored by a bipartisan group of 22 members led by Rep. William S. Moorhead (D., Pa.), would declare it was the sense of Congress that the U.S. "should not increase its military involvement in Vietnam." The 2d resolution, with 17 sponsors, opposed a further troop increase "without the explicit consent of the Congress" and until Pres. Johnson presented "clear justification" for the increase.

Support for the Administration side came Mar. 15 from ex-Pres. Dwight D. Eisenhower in Indio, Calif. He said that he thought the U.S. was "on the right track" and not "stalemate[d]" but that "if you're just going to make it a matter of attrition only, that's bad. . . .I'm in favor of doing something with more strength. I don't know just what."

Senate Hearings

The Administration and the Senate Foreign Relations Committee engaged Feb. 20-26 in a "credibility gap" dispute over the purported Aug. 1964 North Vietnamese attacks on 2 U.S. destroyers in the Gulf of Tonkin. The incidents had led to the first U.S. air strikes against North Vietnam and to Congress' adoption of the so-called "Tonkin resolution," which was cited by the Administration later as authorization for escalation in Vietnam. The resolution approved "all necessary measures" to "prevent further aggression."

The dispute involved questions as to whether (a) there was provocation on the part of the destroyers, (b) there was sufficient proof of attack to warrant retaliation and (c) the Administration had given Congress enough or truthful data about the Tonkin incidents prior to the approval of the resolution.

The dispute began Feb. 20 when the committee held a hearing to re-examine the events. Defense Secy. Robert S. McNamara testified in closed session. Afterwards, without the approval of the committee and against the specific advice of its chairman, Sen. J.W. Fulbright (D., Ark.), McNamara released a statement on his testimony. His statement said: The fact that the 2d Tonkin attack (Aug. 4) had actually taken place was established by intelligence reports of a "highly classified and unimpeachable nature" (Pentagon officials later indicated that the reports were obtained by monitoring radio communications between the North Vietnamese patrol boats and their shore commands). One report received prior to the attack revealed an intention to attack; another, received during the attack, reported the attack was under way; another reported a loss of 2 North Vietnamese boats.

In a statement Feb. 21 Fulbright berated McNamara for giving "only one side of the story" and suppressing information raising questions about the 2d attack. "This . . . deceives the American public," Fulbright said. Sen. Albert Gore (D., Tenn.) joined Fulbright in asking whether the intelligence reports gave "unimpeachable" proof of an attack. Gore said that on 3 different points the reports provided information that "was completely in error." He said McNamara had reported a Joint Staff confirmation of the attack, based on incoming messages, without mentioning that the confirmation was made Aug. 6, 2 days after the decision to retaliate.

The McNamara testimony was attacked on the Senate floor Feb. 21 and 28 by Sen. Wayne Morse (D., Ore.), who said he considered the destroyers' mission a "decoy operation," "a hostile action," an attempt "to get the North Vietnamese to involve themselves in a dispute with us." The *Maddox*, one of the destroyers, "was a spy ship under instruction to stimulate the electronic instruments of North Vietnam," he said. He charged that its mission was to distract North Vietnamese vessels while South Vietnamese vessels were attacking North Vietnamese radar installations.

In a UPI interview Feb. 23, Capt. John J. Herrick, 47, who had been aboard the *Maddox* and in command of the *Maddox* and the other destroyer, the *Turner Joy*, said he had "no doubt" that the ships were attacked. He denied that the attacks were provoked. "I don't know how you would stimulate an electronic reaction," he said, since his ship carried only "passive" radio equipment capable only of listening. He said that the 2d attack occurred during a cloudy night when observations were made with radar and sonar and that while he had doubts "as to number," he had no doubts that torpedoes were detected in the attack.

A transcript of the McNamara testimony, released by the committee Feb. 24, disclosed that Herrick had informed higher command 15 hours before the 2d attack that North Vietnam considered his ships "as enemies." The question of South Vietnamese boats attacking North Vietnamese positions along the Tonkin coast one and 2 days before also was broached. McNamara said the U.S. destroyers were "not aware of the details" of the South Vietnamese attacks and were not trying to divert the enemy's attention. Fulbright then produced Herrick's message that the North Vietnamese considered his patrol "directly involved" with the South Vietnamese operations and, because of this, considered his ships as enemies. McNamara said the U.S. had supplied the boats and training for the South Vietnamese operation. He said the operations were under the command of the South Vietnamese, but later he said a U.S. Military Assistance Command liaison officer was probably in charge.

The transcript also revealed that after the engagement Herrick had sent to Washington a message urging "complete evaluation before any further action." He based this advice on his "review of action," which "makes many recorded contacts and torpedoes fired appear doubtful." He reported: "Freak weather effects and over-eager sonarman may have accounted for many reports. No actual visual sightings by *Maddox*." McNamara said that after receiving this message he had called Adm. U.S. Grant Sharp, commander-in-chief, Pacific, to say: "We obviously don't want to carry out the retaliatory strike unless we are damned sure what happened." He said that after 5 more hours of evaluating admittedly "ambiguous" and "conflicting" reports from the destroyers about the engagement, the decision to retaliate was given.

Appearing on the ABC "Issues and Answers" program Feb. 25, Fulbright charged that the response" of the U.S. to the Tonkin incidents "was not commensurate with the provocation" and that the "decision to go to war and then to bring the resolution to Congress was based on inadequate evidence and conflicting reports. The Tonkin resolution, he said, was introduced "under a completely false idea of what had happened," and his own support of the resolution was "based upon information which was not true."

The Administration side was presented Feb. 25 by Asst. State Secy. William P. Bundy on the NBC "Meet the Press" program. Bundy maintained that the U.S. had not provoked the attack on the destroyers, that the mission of the ships had been "fully disclosed" to Congress and that the Congressional resolution had been "worked out in consultation" between the White House and Congress. A White House statement from Austin, Tex. Feb. 26 said the President felt that Congress had been given the full facts before it approved the resolution and that there was no doubt that the attacks on the destroyers were unprovoked.

Morse on the Senate floor Feb. 28 reiterated his contention that the destroyers had operated in a "provocative" manner. "We were out to bloody their nose," he said. Morse revealed a previously secret Navy message from Herrick to the 2 destroyers between the 2 attacks. The message warned that "U.S. ships in the Gulf of Tonkin can no longer assume that they will be considered neutrals exercising the right of free transit. They will be treated as belligerents from first detection and must consider themselves as such."

State Secy. Dean Rusk testified on Vietnam policy for 10 hours, 41 minutes before the largely hostile Senate Foreign Relations Committee in a nationally televised hearing Mar. 11-12. Because Rusk had resisted a public appearance before the committee—this was his first in almost 2 years—and because the committee refused to hold executive sessions for the customary briefings by the State Secretary on world situations, contact between Rusk and the committee had been reduced to a minimum. His only previous appearance before it in 1968 was a briefing on the *Pueblo* incident.

During the course of the hearing it became evident that about $3/4$ of the committee members were critical of, if not hostile to, the Administration's policy in Vietnam. Rusk defended the policy as vital in opposing "militant communism" and in upholding U.S. commitments. But he disclosed that the Administration was conducting an "A to Z" review of its Vietnam policy.

A major goal of the hearing, it developed, was to get an Administration pledge to consult with the committee prior to any future policy decisions on Vietnam. This proposal was pressed by Fulbright. Specifically, the committee sought prior consultation on a pending request—reportedly made by Gen. William C. Westmoreland, U.S. commander in Vietnam—for 206,000 more U.S.

troops for Vietnam. "I think the Senate should share in this decision," Fulbright told Rusk Mar. 11. What the committee wanted, he said, was "consultation . . . before the conclusion is announced." Fulbright opened the 2d day's hearing with the same demand. But the extent of Rusk's commitment was: "If more troops are needed, we will, as we have done in the past, consult with appropriate members of Congress." Asked at the end of the hearings if he was satisfied with this response, Fulbright said: "No, he never . . . [said] that he would consult before the decision is made."

The hearing ostensibly was on the foreign aid bill, but, after Rusk presented his statement on the aid program, Fulbright broached the Vietnam issue with a denunciation of Adminitration policy as "wrong and nothing short of disastrous." Rusk's position was that the U.S. was "organizing the peace" by delimiting aggression, which, if not resisted, would "change the world balance of power against us."

Rusk testified Mar. 11: "Both sides suffered some severe setbacks" in the Tet offensive, the situation was "serious" but "not hopeless." "The alternative of abandoning this effort is catastrophic—not just for Southeast Asia but for the United States." Pres. Johnson's peace proposals were met with "a battery of no's" from Hanoi, and, "unhappily, there is no indication that they are prepared to move away from what they call their fight-and-negotiate strategy—that is, some kind of discussion that might give them protection against the bombing of the North while they go ahead full-blast with their own military operations directed against the South." Concerning the 1964 Tonkin Gulf attack on the 2 U.S. vessels, "my own conclusion is that 2 attacks were delivered on our vessels which were operating where they had a right to be—they were not engaged in offensive operations against North Vietnam—that obviously any vessel on patrol is going to look and listen, but looking and listening on the high seas, cannot be interpreted as warranting an attack."

Among remarks made by committee members Mar. 11:

Fulbright—The information the Administration gave Congress on the 1964 Tonkin incidents "was not true" and was one the "striking discrepancies" between "events and the description of them by the Administration" that had damaged the U.S. position in the world.

Sen. Karl E. Mundt (R., S.D.) (to Rusk)—"You are as aware as we are that the shift of opinion in this country is in the wrong direction [away from support of Vietnam policy]." "Something more convincing has to come from the Administration as to what this is all about" to justify "the sacrifices we are making." Failure to set priorities on whether the war in Vietnam was more important than the war on poverty at home was contributing to "the divisiveness which I hate to see developing in the country." Was the Vietnam conflict "a war or a WPA project?"

Sen. Mike Mansfield (**D.**, Mont.)—"A feeling of unrest, frustration and uneasiness, to put it mildly," was growing in the Senate and the country at large over Vietnam. "I certainly hope that there is some way we can get out of this difficulty."

Sen. Wayne Morse (**D.**, Ore.)—"We cannot sit here in our security and our safety while American boys are dying . . . in a war we don't dare declare. . . . There is incipient uprising in this country in opposition to this war, and it's going to get worse. . . . Give the United Nations 6 months, send up some feasible resolutions, stop the bombing, stop the killing by escalating, fall back [to defensible enclaves] and then say [to the UN] if you don't move in within 6 months we're going to start an orderly withdrawal. We'll have to evacuate thousands of Vietnamese because they'll be massacred as soon as we take our bayonets out, but that's the proposal . . . to make to the world."

Sen. Clifford P. Case (**R.**, N.J.)—If "our success in South Vietnam can only be accomplished by the destruction of South Vietnam," must the U.S. "inexorably . . . pursue this course?" (Rusk's answer was that "the purpose is not to destroy Vietnam and "it is very difficult to go down a hypothetic alley of that sort.") There was "a line to be drawn between honorable meeting of commitments and pig-headed pushing in the direction of a course which has become more and more sterile."

Sen. Stuart Symington (**D.**, Mo.)—He too had "increasing doubts" about the policy in Vietnam. The U.S. had consistently "underrated" the ability of the Vietnamese Communists and "over-rated" the ability of South Vietnamese allies.

Sen. John Sherman Cooper (**R.**, Ky.)—"I have felt that your emphasis has been upon a military solution." "I think the Administration has a duty to go much further than it has in the past" in making overtures for negotiation.

Sen. Frank J. Lausche (**D.**, O.)—It was time for talk to "come to an end." The Senate should vote on whether to "pull out" of Vietnam, pull back allied forces into "enclaves" or "repeal the Tonkin resolution."

Sen. Frank Church (**D.**, Ida.)—The U.S. was being forced into a position of supporting a South Vietnamese government where there was a "general pattern of corruption and draft-dodging."

Rusk testified Mar. 12, in reply to Mundt's query as to whether a U.S. pullout from Vietnam might possibly "encourage . . . Communist aggression in some other area of the world, some place even more difficult to defend against or much closer to home: "Senator, this is one of the most fundamental questions before our nation and before the world, and each one ought to draw off and think soberly and quietly what he thinks about it. . . . I have tried to emphasize the overwhelming importance of the fidelity of the United States, and the necessity for people to understand that at the end of the day we will meet our commitments. We will stretch out our hands in every possible way to make peace. We will try to resolve every problem by peaceful means. But if there is ever any doubt on that subject, there is a catastrophic war ahead. . . . These are things that one should approach on one's knees, but this is very much at the heart of the matter."

In reply to Sen. Claiborne Pell's (D., R.I.) query as to whether Rusk saw "a point at which we can arrive when we will say the amount of suffering . . . to the South Vietnamese, will have more than justified what we would lose by not continuing," Rusk said: While "it is for Providence to make moral judgments . . . , I am concerned about the moral myopia of some of the discussion that I have heard." There were moral questions involved—in the North Vietnamese aggression against South Vietnam and their "contempt" for the 1962 Geneva agreement, in Peking's or Hanoi's "interference" in Cambodia and in "our making a pledge and how we respond to it. But I think deeply that the chief moral question is to be faced by those who are not prepared to sit down and make peace."

Presidential Defenses

Pres. Johnson Mar. 16-25 delivered a series of speeches defending his Administration's Vietnam and domestic policies.

In a major address before the National Farmers Union (NFU) convention in Minneapolis, Minn. Mar. 18, the President appealed for a "total national effort" to win the war and peace in Vietnam. "We love nothing more than peace," he said, "but we hate nothing worse than surrender and cowardice." In Vietnam, Johnson said, he sought to uphold the middle course between the extreme views of (a) those who advocated that the U.S. "go in quickly with all flags flying and get it over with quickly regardless of the dangers involved" and (b) those who thought "that you can just have peace by talking for it, by wishing for it, by saying you want it, and that all you need do is pull back to the cities." In the first instance, he said, "we do not seek a wider war." In the 2d, the enemy's Tet offensive showed that lives could not be saved "by moving the battlefield in from the mountains to the cities."

Addressing the National Alliance of Businessmen in Washington Mar. 16, the President had said: "We are going to win [in Vietnam]. . . . We shall do whatever is required. . . . The Communists have made it clear that . . . they are unwilling to negotiate or to work out a settlement except on the battlefield. If that is what they choose, then we shall win a settlement on the battlefield. If their position changes—as we fervently hope it will—then we . . . and our allies are prepared to immediately meet them anywhere, any time, in a spirit of flexibility and understanding and generosity. But make no mistake about it, . . . we are going to win."

During a ceremony in the Rose Garden in the White House for the first 16 graduates of the Foreign Service Institute's training center for specialists in the Vietnam pacification program, the President said Mar. 21: "Peace will come to Vietnam. The terror of an invading enemy will be turned back. The work of reconstruction will go on." "And a nation will rise strong and free." During the Tet offensive, South Vietnamese farmers, students and workers had resisted the attackers and protected allied personel. "Stories like these were repeated up and down this ravaged land. We did not read about them. The enemy attack is what got the headlines."

Johnson received encouragement from former Presidents Harry S. Truman and Dwight D. Eisenhower. Truman Mar. 20 expressed general support for Mr. Johnson's foreign and domestic policies. In a copyrighted article in the April issue of *Reader's Digest*, Eisenhower declared: "I will not personally support any peace-at-any-price candidate who advocates capitulation and the abandonment of South Vietnam." While he had no objection to "honorable dissent," some people, believing "we have no business being in Vietnam," were "terribly and dangerously wrong." "In my opinion it would be grossly immoral not to resist a tyranny whose openly avowed purpose is to subjugate the earth—and particularly the United States of America."

Strong support for Johnson within the Democratic Party had been found in surveys reported Mar. 16-28. A *N.Y. Times* survey published Mar. 24 said the President could win more than 65% of the votes at the Democratic National Convention, more than enough to win renomination. Most Democratic state chairmen supported Johnson, according to a Mar. 15 AP survey.

But public approval of Johnson's performance as President and his handling of the war were at their lowest points in Gallup Polls released Mar. 30.

At San Fernando Valley State College in Northridge, Calif. Mar. 25, State Secy. Rusk was reported to have told reporters at an off-the-record briefing that Vietnam policy criticism had reached the point that it raised the question "Whose side are you on?" "I am on the side of those who are not afraid to recognize past error, who refuse to blindly pursue bankrupt policies which will rend us from our friends and drain us of our treasure, in the fruitless pursuit of illusions long since shattered," Rusk declared. "I'm on the side of those who do not shout down others; but who listen, challenge and then propose a better policy for America." As for whether he approved of refusal to answer a military draft call: "I think he [the man called] would have to face the consequences. If I were to be called up, I would go. Each person has to examine his own conscience and do what he thinks is right."

Administration policies were also defended by Vice Pres. Hubert H. Humphrey. In a speech in Richmond, Va. Mar. 30, he contrasted the President's goal in Vietnam of "real peace for our children and ourselves" with "the promise of peace as an election-year gimmick." "Others feel that more could somehow be done to bring peace today," he said, "yet I must admit that their concern has yet to be matched by their specifics." In a statement Mar. 18, Humphrey had commented on the Presidential campaigns of Sens. Robert F. Kennedy and Eugene J. McCarthy. The latter's campaign, he said, "has been decent, honest and gentlemanly." But Kennedy, he said, had switched his stand on Vietnam. When he was a member of his brother's Administration, Kennedy was for "sticking it out" in Vietnam, Humphrey said. "Now he finds our effort 'immoral.'" (In a speech at Manhattan, Kan. Mar. 18, Kennedy conceded his share of responsibility for setting U.S. policy in Vietnam in the beginning, but he said: "Past error is no excuse for its own perpetuation.")

Humphrey had defended the Johnson policy Jan. 13 in a speech in Fresno, Calif. before the Democratic State Committee. Rebutting the contention of "some people" that "we are in an immoral war," Humphrey told the group the U.S. was "in Vietnam not to conquer but to save." "The bible says, 'Blessed are the peacemakers,'" he said, adding that it did not refer to "the talkers, the walkers and the paraders, but the peacemakers." He said: "It would be hazardous, foolhardy and indecent to turn our backs on 10 free countries and 250 million free people in Southeast Asia. ... I believe that the national security of the United States and the peace of the world are at stake when there is talk of that commitment being broken—especially when the reasons for it are as strong as ever."

Republican Presidential Nomination Campaign

Gov. George Romney of Michigan had entered the race for the Republican nomination for President in 1967, and he made a month-long "background" tour of 12 countries Dec. 7, 1967-Jan. 3, 1968. Before leaving on the tour, which included South Vietnam, Romney told reporters Dec. 5 that "nobody's going to brainwash me." This remark was a reference to his statement Sept. 4, 1967 that during a 1965 visit to Vietnam he had received "the greatest brainwashing that anyone can get." Romney said on his departure from New York Dec. 7 that he would make it clear abroad that the 1968 Presidential election "will not lead to any United States withdrawal from Vietnam."

Romney asserted in Saigon Dec. 27 that "military victories are being won" in Vietnam but that "corresponding victories in the political, economic and social fields" also would have to be won. "There remains the problem of the United States tending to do far too much of the job themselves," he said. On his return to the U.S. Jan. 3, Romney said: He had found that the war in Vietnam was "the single most consuming issue throughout the world." The image of America abroad "is still a plus but is declining." What "we need" was "a global foreign policy which is more cohesive and less dominated by expediency." "We must beware of the short-term, unilateral or military approach and pursue long-term, multilateral and political solutions. And we need to state honestly and openly what our intentions and our involvements are."

In a major speech, Romney said Jan. 15 that the U.S. should make its goal a "guaranteed neutralization" of South Vietnam and Southeast Asia through a settlement between the Saigon government and the Viet Cong. He said the major powers should agree to the neutralization and arrange for international supervision of the area. His plan encompassed removal of all foreign troops and bases, a ban against alliances by the Southeast Asian nations with "outside blocs," national self-determination and economic development of the area. "A key point in setting forth any viable concept for a Vietnam settlement is that the United States not dictate its terms," Romney said. "The conditions must be worked out by the principal protagonists, ourselves included, with help from the international community. One of my general concerns with U.S. foreign policy is that it has been too quick to impose our own views on others, that it has tended to reduce the confidence and responsibility of others by playing a takeover role."

Romney criticized current Administration policy for too much reliance on military solutions "where there can be none" and for making "no true progress" toward pacification of the countryside. He charged that "we have appeared to shift our terms for talks which could lead to a settlement; and we have missed, whether by design or mishandling, possible opportunities to get negotiations started." Romney made these remarks in a speech at the Keene State College in New Hampshire.

At a Concord, N.H. news conference Jan. 16, Romney said the "internal solution" he was advocating for Vietnam did not mean that he favored a coalition government between the current Saigon regime and the National Liberation Front, the political arm of the Viet Cong. This, he said, was "not a valid approach at this time." Romney had told newsmen in Washington Jan. 8 that he opposed a bombing halt "unless we have some basis for a settlement on a satisfactory basis."

Romney warned in Manchester, N.H. Feb. 6 that "we are going right down the road to World War III, and we'd better decide whether we want to do it there [in Vietnam] at that particular place at this particular time." Romney asserted in Concord, N. H. Feb. 15 that Richard Nixon was "a me-too candidate on Vietnam" who offered "no more than a blurred carbon copy of the discredited Johnson policies." Romney said in Superior, Wis. Feb. 19 that "when you want to win the hearts and minds of people you don't kill them and destroy their property. You don't use bombers and tanks and napalm to save them."

Nixon Feb. 1 had officially declared himself a candidate for the Republican Presidential nomination. The Nixon announcement was made in an open letter to the voters of New Hampshire, where Nixon's name was formally entered in the Presidential primary just before the deadline Jan. 31. After visits to Wisconsin, Oklahoma and Colorado, Nixon returned to New Hampshire Feb. 11 and told a Concord audience that "peace in the Pacific is the issue." He criticized the Administration for failing to "explain the war" to the public and to the U.S.' allies. In Green Bay, Wis. Feb. 5, Nixon had told reporters that the war should be "prosecute[d] ... more effectively" and that Johnson would be "much

better advised to tell truth" instead of claiming that the "war is
going better" and "peace is around the corner." He said the President should not have suspended the bombing of Hanoi and
Haiphong before the recent Communist offensive.

In a major statement of the campaign, Nixon pledged Mar.
5 that "new leadership" to be elected in November "will end the
war" in Vietnam. Speaking in Hampton, N.H., Nixon said that
if the war were not over in November, "the American people will
be justified to elect new leadership, and I pledge to you the new
leadership will end the war and win the peace in the Pacific."
Nixon said he did not mean "withdrawal from Vietnam" or
the use of a "push-button technique" to end the war. But the
war "can be ended," he declared, if "we mobilize our economic
and political and diplomatic leadership." Nixon said in Washington that night that he would "keep the pressure on" militarily
but apply more diplomatic, economic and political pressure, especially in reference to the Soviet Union, and this might be the
"key to peace." Nixon had made a similar assertion Feb. 28 when
he said: Pres. Johnson could end the war by November. If he
failed to do so, "a new administration will be elected. We will end
the war and we will win the peace."

In a statement that later was to become controversial, Nixon
told newsmen Mar. 9-10 that he would resist pressure to detail
his war-ending plans because "no one with this responsibility who
is seeking office should give away any of his bargaining positions
in advance." "I'm not going to take any positions that I would
be bound by at a later point," he said. "One of the advantages of
a new President is that he can start fresh without being imprison-
ed by the formulas of the past."

Campaigning in Wisconsin Mar. 14, Nixon called for "Eisenhower diplomacy"—the Eisenhower Administration "ended . . .
[the Korean] war and kept the nation out of other wars for 8
years"—and for a greater role for South Vietnamese soldiers to
bring the war to an end. The U.S. should help the South Vietnamese fight the war, "not fight it for them," he said.

In Littleton, N.H. Mar. 6, Nixon proposed a post-war plan
to end the draft and create a volunteer professional armed service
with higher pay.

Among other Nixon statements:

At Concordia College (before an audience of 4,000), Fort Wayne, Ind.
May 3—Nixon reaffirmed his pledge for a "moratorium" on Vietnam discus-

sion. "Let's not destroy the chances for peace with a mouthful of words from some irresponsible candidate."

In an NBC radio address Mar. 28—"America must reappraise . . . its role and its responsibilities in the world and the resources which we and . . . other nations can bring to the meeting of those responsibilities. Economically, diplomatically, militarily, the time has come to insist that others must assume the responsibilities which are rightly theirs. We must do our full share, both in maintaining order and in helping the have-not nations onto their feet. . . . Vietnam must be the last agony of the old order, because there is question whether the old order could sustain another."

In Washington (at an American Society of Newspaper Editors luncheon) Apr. 19—Nixon would remain silent on the Vietnam issue "as long as there is hope for successful negotiation."

In an interview published in the July issue of *Good Housekeeping* magazine—There was "no alternative to the war going on." "We have to stop it with victory or it will start all over again in a few years."

Gov. Nelson A. Rockefeller of New York opened his campaign for the Republican Presidential nomination May 1 in Philadelphia with a speech critical of Administration foreign policy. Speaking at a World Affairs Council luncheon, Rockefeller said: "The war in Vietnam is the most painful and dramatic proof" of "the need to review and reassess past and present policies." There could be "no purely military solution" in Vietnam. The war there should be "de-Americanized." Rockefeller praised Pres. Johnson's "courageous" initiative "in seeking a just peace," and he condoned the participation in South Vietnam's political life of "any group that seeks its objectives through the political process rather than by wrecking it by force or subversion."

Answering questions before an audience of about 15,000 at the University of Kansas in Lawrence May 9, Rockefeller called for better defense of South Vietnam's villages and hamlets by U.S. and South Vietnamese forces during the Paris talks so that the Saigon government could increase its strength in the countryside. He warned that otherwise, the Communists could win at the negotiating table "the things" that "20,000 wonderful young Americans" had sacrificed their lives for. But he agreed that the South Vietnamese "have got to have the right to choose what kind of government they want"—even if the choice turned out to be a Communist government.

Rockefeller July 13 proposed a Vietnam peace plan that, he said, could end the war within 6 months if it were accepted by North Vietnam. Issuing his plan at a news conference in New York, Rockefeller blamed the slow pace of the Paris peace talks on "a lack of mutual trust about ultimate aims" and Hanoi's anticipation that the fall Presidential election might soften the U.S. terms for a settlement. "These obstacles can be reduced if America affirms now a concrete plan for peace," he asserted. Rockefeller's proposal envisaged a restoration of peace in Vietnam in 4 phases: (1) A troop pullback by both sides and interposition between them of a neutral, international, "Asian, if possible," peace-keeping force. At the outset of this first phase, the U.S. would withdraw 75,000 of its troops as "token of its good faith." (2) The withdrawal of North Vietnamese and most allied troops from South Vietnam. Some U.S. units would remain but in fixed bases or enclaves. The Viet Cong would stop guerrilla operations and start participating "in the political life of the country." The 2d phase would be monitored by an enlarged buffer force. (3) Free elections under international supervision. All U.S. troops would be withdrawn. (4) Direct negotiations between North and South Vietnam on reunification, which, if decided upon, would signal withdrawal of the peace-keeping force.

Rockefeller also proposed immediate steps the U.S. could take to increase South Vietnam's share of the war burden. He suggested that the U.S. reduce and possibly abandon its troops' "search and destroy" missions; cut back by as much as one-half "the swollen American civilian staffs engaged in the pacification program"; re-equip the South Vietnamese Army and begin a U.S. troop withdrawal as the Saigon forces' strength increased (he asserted that 10,000 U.S. troops could be withdrawn each month "provided North Vietnam does not increase its rate of infiltration"). The "tragedy of Vietnam," Rockefeller said, was that the war had been "conducted without a coherent plan for peace," "manned by a draft that holds millions in needless doubt as to their future" and "financed by a headlong inflation that imperils our whole economic life."

Democratic Presidential Nomination Campaign

Sen. Eugene McCarthy (D., Minn.) had entered the race for the Democratic Presidential nomination in 1967, principally as a peace candidate and in opposition to Pres. Johnson's Vietnam policies. McCarthy announced Jan. 3 that he would enter the New Hampshire primary in order to present Johnson with "a more direct confrontation" on the war issue. In Washington Jan. 1, McCarthy had expressed a New Year's wish for a "reasonable

—not perfect—negotiated settlement" of the war, which, he said, was "draining off our material . . . and our manpower resources," was "creating great anxiety in the minds of many Americans and . . . [was] weakening . . . our moral energy to deal" with domestic and other world problems. In Washington Jan. 4 McCarthy said he was in favor of "stopping the bombing now and seeking to negotiate." He criticized the Administration for "passing over . . . 2 or 3 chances for negotiations" and said he believed there were "real opportunities for negotiations now."

In a speech Jan. 12 before about 6,000 students and faculty members of the University of California at Los Angeles, McCarthy evoked long applause by suggesting "that this Administration is afraid to negotiate." He drew applause also with his declaration that the war "is not morally defensible because the objectives are not credible." "What comes with victory?" he asked. "No one gives us a hint. I suggest there can be no victory because we are following a policy that is not an American policy. It has never been our policy to use our power against a backward and primitive people." McCarthy had told newsmen Jan. 5 that it "would be" helpful to have a word of support from either Sen. Robert F. (D., N. Y.) or Sen. Edward M. (D., Mass.) Kennedy. Neither had publicly indorsed the McCarthy candidacy. Robert Kennedy, also a critic of U.S. policy in Vietnam, had originally welcomed McCarthy's challenge as "a healthy influence on the Democratic Party." But Kennedy told a questioner Jan. 8 that he did not think backing McCarthy would "further the cause" of antiwar protests. Kennedy Jan. 4 renewed his previously expressed belief that he would support Pres. Johnson for reelection.

McCarthy told a college audience in Portland, Ore. Feb. 2 that the Administration's Vietnam course was "not supported by historical study or by the recommendations of scholars." He said it was "ignoring the moral judgment of the theologians and religious leaders and . . . ridiculing and opposing students and young people . . . upon whom the principal burden of the war, both in fighting it and making moral judgments about our involvement, does in fact fall." In Washington Feb. 3 he issued a statement charging that "the Administration's reports of progress [in the war] are the products of their own self-deception." Referring to an Administration assessment that the Viet Cong and North Vietnamese had suffered "a complete failure" in their Tet offensive, McCarthy said: "If taking over a section of the American embassy, a good part of Hué, Dalat and major cities of the 4th Corps area constitutes complete failure, I suppose by this logic that if the Viet Cong captured the entire country, the Administration would be claiming their total collapse."

N.H. Primary a McCarthy 'Victory'

Pres. Johnson and ex-Vice Pres. Nixon polled the most votes in New Hampshire's Democratic and Republican Presidential preference primary elections Mar. 12. But Sen. McCarthy, the only major Democratic on the ballot, was conceded to have scored a moral "victory" in the contest.

McCarthy won 28,721 votes (5,511 of them Republican write-ins) in the primary in a surprising show of strength against the President, who polled 29,021 votes (1,778 GOP write-ins). An organized write-in campaign for Johnson had been supported by the Democratic State Committee and led by the state's major Democratic office-holders. McCarthy had campaigned actively in the state as a critic of Johnson's Vietnam policy. He won 20 Democratic National Convention delegate votes; Johnson won only 4.

In the Republican primary, Nixon received 79% of the vote while a write-in drive gave Nelson A. Rockefeller 11%. All 18 GOP National Convention delegates went to Nixon.

(A Louis Harris survey published in the Mar. 25 edition of *Newsweek* indicated that McCarthy's strong showing in the New Hampshire primary was due more to an anti-Johnson vote than to an anti-war vote. According to the survey, if the war had been the major issue, McCarthy would have received only 22% of the vote instead of 42%.)

Kennedy Enters Race

Following McCarthy's apparent display of strength against Johnson, Sen. Robert F. Kennedy Mar. 16 announced his own candidacy for the Democratic Presidential nomination. "I am convinced that this country is on a perilous course," Kennedy said. "I run to seek new policies—policies to end the bloodshed in Vietnam and in our cities. . . . I run because it is now unmistakably clear that we can change these disastrous, divisive policies only by changing the men who are now making them." "The reality of recent events in Vietnam has been glossed over with illusions,"

Kennedy declared.

Kennedy said he was in favor of (a) de-escalation in Vietnam, (b) a greater role in the war for the South Vietnamese and a lesser one for the U.S., (c) pressure on the South Vietnamese to end corruption and to draft 18- and 19-year-olds, (d) negotiating with the National Liberation Front (it should be made clear, he said, that the NLF "is going to play a role in the future political process of South Vietnam"), (e) a halt to the bombing of North Vietnam pending useful negotiations.

The announcement of Kennedy's candidacy was made at a televised news conference in the caucus room of the Senate Office Building, the room in which his late brother, John F. Kennedy, had announced for the Presidency in 1960. Kennedy said the results of the New Hampshire primary had removed a major barrier to his candidacy—the possibility of a charge that "a personal struggle" between himself and Johnson would be divisive. He said the primary had demonstrated that the division in the country and the Democratic Party was caused by Johnson's policies.

Kennedy had told newsmen Mar. 13, the day after the primary, that he was "reassessing the possibility of whether I will run against Pres. Johnson." He said Mar. 14 that he could not support Johnson for renomination, and he said Mar. 17 that he would have "great reservations" about supporting Johnson if the Democrats renominated him and the Republicans nominated a candidate favoring de-escalation in Vietnam. Johnson's policies "could be catastrophic," he warned.

In a Chicago speech Feb. 8, Kennedy had delivered a sharp attack on U.S. policy in Vietnam. Asserting that it was time "to take a new look at the war in Vietnam" and that "our nation must be told the truth," Kennedy said:

"A total military victory is not within sight" and "probably beyond our grasp." It was an "illusion" to believe that "unswerving pursuit of military victory . . . is in the interest of either ourselves or the people of Vietnam." Neither could the war remove the threat of communism in Asia. "We must actively seek a peaceful settlement" in Vietnam and "can no longer harden our terms every time Hanoi indicates it may be prepared to negotiate, and we must be willing to foresee a settlement which will give the Viet Cong a chance to participate in the political life of the country." "A political compromise is not just the best path to peace but the only path, and we must show as much willingness to risk some of our prestige for peace as to risk the lives of young men in war." "We have misconceived the nature of the war" and "sought to resolve by military might a conflict whose issue depends upon the will and conviction of the South Vietnamese people." It was an "illusion that we can win a war which the South Vietnamese cannot win for themselves." It was an "illusion" to think that "the American national interest is identical with—or should be subordinated to—the selfish interest of an incompetent military regime." The current Saigon government was "unwilling or incapable of being an effective ally in the war against the Communists." The enemy offensive against the cities, "savagely striking at will across all of South Vietnam, has finally shattered the mask of official illusion with which we have concealed our true circumstances" and "demonstrated that no part or person of South Vietnam is secure from . . . attacks." A belief that the war could "be settled in our own way and in our own time on our own terms" was a still further "illusion." "Such a settlement is the privilege of . . . those who crush their enemies . . . or wear away their will to fight. We have not done this, nor is there any prospect we will." "The central battle in this war cannot be measured by body counts or bomb damage but by the extent to which the people of South Vietnam act on a sense of common purpose and hope with those that govern them." "The best way to save our most precious stake in Vietnam—the lives of our soldiers—is to stop the enlargement of the war, and . . . the best way to end casualties is to end the war."

Discussing Kennedy's announcement of his candidacy Sen. McCarthy said in a TV interview in Green Bay, Wis. Mar. 16 that he had made "no deals" with Kennedy and was "not prepared to deal" but would continue to seek the nomination through the California primary. He had made his move, he said, when "a lot of other politicians were afraid to come down into the playing field. . . ." McCarthy said that Kennedy, in a talk with him Mar. 13, had hinted that Kennedy could "win more easily" and "make a better President" but, McCarthy said, "I think I'm still the best potential President in the field." McCarthy said he and Kennedy could "make a consistent case against the Johnson policies and the Nixon policies" because they were in essential agreement on the issues.

McCarthy had said Mar. 14 that indications had begun to appear that Pres. Johnson's poor showing in New Hampshire was encouraging Kennedy to run. McCarthy said Mar. 19 that he would support Kennedy if his own attempt was defeated at the convention.

The Johnson Administration and Kennedy engaged in dispute over reports Mar. 17 that Kennedy had offered to stay out of the Presidential race if Pres. Johnson appointed a commission to study a revision of U.S. policy in Vietnam. Initial reports of the story were broadcast by Roger Mudd of CBS and published Mar. 19 by *Time* and *Newsweek* magazines.

According to the Newsweek version (Mar. 25 issue): Kennedy adviser Theodore Sorensen met secretly with Johnson at the White

House Mar. 11. Sorensen promised that Kennedy would agree not to run if the President appointed a commission "to re-elvaluate" the U.S. involvement in Vietnam. Johnson "expressed interest." Kennedy, his brother, Sen. Edward M. Kennedy (D., Mass.), and Sorensen "pursued the proposal" at a secret meeting Mar. 14 with Defense Secy. Clark Clifford. Robert Kennedy suggested to Clifford a Presidential statement that the war "required re-evaluation" and a Presidential commission to do the study. He suggested as members himself and 9 others, persons "whose well-established views left no doubt that their recommendation would change the course of the war." Clifford took the proposal to Johnson, who objected because "it was a political deal," "provided encouragement for Hanoi" and "amounted to an abdication of Presidential authority." Clifford informed Sorensen later Mar. 14 of the rejection. Kennedy announced his candidacy Mar. 16.

Kennedy Mar. 17 called reports of the incident an "incredible distortion" and suggested that the Administration had leaked the allegedly distorted reports contrary to "the traditional rules of confidence governing White House conversations." The affair was illustrative of why "the American people no longer believe the President," Kennedy declared. Kennedy said that he and Clifford had discussed the commission plan "not as a proposal by either of us" and that he had stressed that if the commission "were more than a public relations gimmick" and its creation and membership "signaled a clear-cut willingness to seek a wider path to peace in Vietnam," he would consider his candidacy unnecessary.

According to the Kennedy version: Sorensen's meeting with the President Mar. 11 was at Johnson's invitation. Sorensen broached the idea of a commission that could recommend a new Vietnam policy. But both Johnson and Kennedy had first heard the proposal from a Midwestern Democratic leader. The President liked the idea, and the White House Mar. 13 asked for recommendations on membership from Sorensen, who had discussed the idea with Kennedy. An appointment was set up by Edward Kennedy. Robert Kennedy and Sorensen met Mar. 14 with Clifford, who knew of the idea, and it was discussed as that more than as a proposal by anyone. Robert Kennedy said his "declaration of candidacy would no longer be necessary" if the plan were adopted; he would serve on the commission but did not insist on it and felt he should not be chairman. He and Sorensen suggested members for the commission. Clifford later informed Sorensen of the President's rejection of the proposal because (a) it would displease Senate committee chairmen if Kennedy were on the commission, (b) the President already knew of the views of its proposed members and could consult them, (c) the idea was close to being a "political deal." Later, a White House aide, unaware of the plan's rejection, called Sorensen for his recommendations on names. Later "that night" Kennedy "decided to run for President."

Kennedy opened his campaign for the Presidential nomination Mar. 18 with a strong attack on Johnson's Vietnam policy. He made his opening address before a wildly cheering audience at Kansas State University in Manhattan, Kan. Kennedy denounced the Johnson policy as "bankrupt." He assailed corruption in South Vietnam and the South Vietnamese practice of buying deferments from military service "while American Marines die at Khesanh." Kennedy also assailed the "brutal" Viet Cong. "They have shown their willingness to sacrifice innocent civilians, to engage in torture and murder and despicable terror to achieve their ends," he declared. Kennedy said there can be "no easy moral answer to this war, no one-sided condemnation of American actions. What we must ask ourselves is whether we have a right to bring so much destruction to another land."

Johnson Out of Election Contest

Pres. Johnson Mar. 31 made a nationally televised speech in which he announced the revision of his policies in Vietnam. In a surprise passage at the end of the speech, Johnson said he would not accept nomination for another term as President. He said in the address:

Tonight I want to speak to you of peace in Vietnam and Southeast Asia. No other question so preoccupies our people. No other dream so absorbs the 250 million human beings who live in that part of the world. No other goal motivates American policy in Southeast Asia.

For years, representatives of our government and others have traveled the world seeking to find a basis for peace talks. Since last September they have carried the offer that I made public at San Antonio. And that offer was this: That the United States would stop its bombardment of North Vietnam when that would lead promptly to productive discussions—and that we would assume that North Vietnam would not take military advantage of our restraint.

Hanoi denounced this offer. . . . Even while the search for peace was going on, North Vietnam rushed their preparations for a savage assault on the people, the government and the allies of South Vietnam. Their attack—during the Tet holidays—failed to achieve its principal objectives. . . .

The Communists may renew their attack any day. . . . This much is clear: If they do mount another round of heavy attacks, they will not succeed in destroying the fighting power of South Vietnam and its allies. But tragically, this is also clear: Many men—on both sides of the struggle—will be lost. . . .

There is no need for this to be so. There is no need to delay the talks that could bring an end to this long and this bloody war. Tonight, I renew the offer I made last August: to stop the bombardment of North Vietnam. We ask that talks begin promptly, that they be serious talks on the substance of peace. . . .

We are prepared to move immediately toward peace through negotiations. So tonight, in the hope that this action will lead to early talks, I am taking the first step to de-escalate the conflict. We are reducing—substantially reducing—the present level of hostilities, and we are doing so unilaterally and at once.

Tonight I have ordered our aircraft and our naval vessels to make no attacks on North Vietnam except in the area north of the demilitarized zone where the continuing enemy build-up directly threatens allied forward positions and where the movement of their troops and supplies are clearly related to that threat.

The area in which we are stopping our attacks includes almost 90% of North Vietnam's population, and most of its territory. Thus there will be no attacks around the principal populated areas, or in the food-producing areas of North Vietnam.

Even this very limited bombing of the North could come to an early end—if our restraint is matched by restraint in Hanoi. But I cannot in good conscience stop all bombing so long as to do so would immediately and directly endanger the lives of our men and our allies. Whether a complete bombing halt becomes possible in the future will be determined by events.

Our purpose in this action is to bring about a reduction in the level of violence that now exists. It is to save the lives of brave men—and to save the lives of innocent women and children. It is to permit the contending forces to move closer to a political settlement. . . .

Now, as in the past, the United States is ready to send its representatives to any forum, at any time, to discuss the means of bringing this ugly war to an end, I am designating one of our most distinguished Americans, Amb. Averell Harriman, as my personal representative for such talks. In addition, I have asked Amb. Llewellyn Thompson, who returned from Moscow for consultation, to be available to join Amb. Harriman at Geneva or any other suitable place—just as soon as Hanoi agrees to a conference.

I call upon Pres. Ho Chi Minh to respond positively, and favorably, to this new step toward peace.

But if peace does not come now through negotiations, it will come when Hanoi understands that our common resolve is unshakable, and our common strength is invincible. Tonight, we and the other allied nations are contributing 600,000 fighting men to assist 700,000 South Vietnamese troops in defending their little country.

Our presence there has always rested on this basic belief: The main burden of preserving their freedom must be carried out by them—by the South Vietnamese themselves. We and our allies can only help to provide a shield behind which the people of South Vietnam can survive and can grow and develop. On their efforts—on their determinations and resourcefulness—the outcome will ultimately depend. ...

Last week Pres. [Nguyen Van] Thieu ordered the mobilization of 135,000 additional South Vietnamese. He plans to reach as soon as possible a total military strength of more than 800,000 men. To achieve this, the government of South Vietnam started the drafting of 19-year-olds on Mar. 1. On May 1, the government will begin the drafting of 18-year-olds. Last month, 10,000 men volunteered for military service. That was $2^1/_2$ times the number of volunteers during the same month last year. Since the middle of January more than 48,000 South Vietnamese have joined the armed forces, and nearly half of them volunteered to do so. All men in the South Vietnamese armed forces have had their tours of duty extended for the duration of the war, and reserves are now being called up for immediate active duty. ...

... We shall accelerate the re-equipment of South Vietnam's armed forces in order to meet the enemy's increased firepower. And this will enable them progressively to undertake a larger share of combat operations against the Communist invaders.

On many occasions I have told the American people that we would send to Vietnam those forces that are required to accomplish our mission there. ... We have previously authorized a force level of approximately 525,000. Some weeks ago, to help meet the enemy's new offensive, we sent to Vietnam about 11,000 additional Marine and airborne troops. ... But the artillery and the tank and the aircraft and medical and other units that were needed to work with and support these infantry troops in combat could not then accompany them by air on that short notice. In order that these forces may reach maximum combat effectiveness, the Joint Chiefs of Staff have recommended to me that we should prepare to send during the next 5 months the support troops totaling approximately 13,500 men. A portion of these men will be made available from our active forces. The balance will come from reserve component units, which will be called up for service. ...

Now let me give you my estimate of the chances for peace. ... I cannot promise that the initiative that I have announced tonight will be completely successful in achieving peace any more than the 30 others that we have undertaken and agreed to in recent years. But it is our fervent hope that North Vietnam, after years of fighting that has left the issue unresolved, will now cease its efforts to achieve a military victory and will join with us in moving toward the peace table. ...

As Hanoi considers its course, it should be in no doubt of our intentions. It must not miscalculate the pressures within our democracy in this election year. We have no intention of widening this war. But the United States will never accept a fake solution to this long and arduous struggle and call it peace. ...

Our objective in South Vietnam has never been the annihilation of the enemy. It has been to bring about a recognition in Hanoi that its objective—taking over the South by force—could not be achieved. We think that peace can be based on the Geneva accords of 1954, under political conditions that permit the South Vietnamese—all the South Vietnamese—to chart their course free of any outside domination or interferences, from us or from anyone else.

So tonight I reaffirm the pledge that we made at Manila: that we are prepared to withdraw our forces from South Vietnam as the other side withdraws its forces to the North, stops the infiltration, and the level of violence thus subsides.

Our goal of peace and self-determination in Vietnam is directly related to the future of all of Southeast Asia, where much has happened to inspire confidence during the past 10 years. . . .

At Johns Hopkins University about 3 years ago, I announced that the United States would take part in the great work of developing Southeast Asia, including the Mekong valley, for all the people of that region. . . . I repeat on behalf of the United States again tonight what I said at Johns Hopkins— that North Vietnam could take its place in this common effort just as soon as peace comes. . . .

During the past 4½ years, it has been my fate and my responsibility to be Commander in Chief. I have lived daily and nightly with the cost of this war. I know the pain that it has inflicted. I know perhaps better than anyone the misgivings it has aroused. And throughout this entire long period I have been sustained by a single principle: that what we are doing now in Vietnam is vital not only to the security of Southeast Asia but it is vital to the security of every American.

Surely, we have treaties which we must respect. Surely, we have commitments that we are going to keep. Resolutions of the Congress testify to the need to resist aggression in the world and in Southeast Asia. But the heart of our involvement in South Vietnam under 3 different Presidents, 3 separate Administrations, has always been American's own security. And the larger purpose of our involvement has always been to help the nations of Southeast Asia become independent, and stand alone self-sustaining as members of a great world community, at peace with themselves, at peace with all others. And with such a nation our country—and the world—will be far more secure than it is tonight.

I believe that a peaceful Asia is far nearer to reality because of what America has done in Vietnam. I believe that the men who endure the dangers of battle there, fighting there for us tonight, are helping the entire world avoid far greater conflicts, far wider wars, far more destruction, than this one.

The peace that will bring them home someday will come. Tonight, I have offered the first in what I hope will be a series of mutual moves toward peace. . . .

Finally, my fellow Americans, let me say this: "Of those to whom much is given much is asked. I cannot say—and no man could say—that no more will be asked of us. Yet I believe that now, no less than when the decade began, this generation of Americans is willing to pay the price, bear any burden, meet any hardship, support any friend, oppose any foe, to assure the survival, and the success of liberty."

Since those words were spoken by John F. Kennedy, the people of America have kept that compact with mankind's noblest cause. And we shall continue to keep it.

. . . Throughout my entire public career I have followed the personal philosophy that I am a free man, an American, a public servant and a member of my party—in that order—always and only. For 37 years in the service of our nation . . . I have put the unity of the people first. I have put it ahead of any divisive partisanship. And in these times, as in times before, it is true that a house divided against itself by the spirit of faction, of party, of region, of religion, of race, is a house that cannot stand.

There is division in the American house now. There is divisiveness among us all tonight. . . . I cannot disregard the peril of the progress of the American people and the hope and the prospect of peace for all peoples, so I would ask all Americans whatever their personal interest or concern to guard against divisiveness and all of its ugly consequences.

52 months and 10 days ago . . . the duties of this office fell upon me. I asked then for your help and God's, that we might continue America on its course binding up our wounds, healing our history, moving forward in new unity to clear the American agenda and to keep the American commitment for all of our people. United we have kept that commitment. And united we have enlarged that commitment. . . .

What we won when all of our people united just must not now be lost in suspicion and distrust and selfishness and politics among any of our people. And believing this as I do I have concluded that I should not permit the Presidency to become involved in the partisan divisions that are developing in this political year.

With American sons in the fields far away, with America's future under challenge right here at home, with our hopes and the world's hopes for peace in the balance every day, I do not believe that I should devote an hour or a day of my time to any personal partisan causes or to any duties other than the awesome duties of this office—the Presidency of your country.

Accordingly, I shall not seek, and I will not accept, the nomination of my party for another term as your President. But let men everywhere know, however, that a strong and a confident and a vigilant America stands ready tonight to seek an honorable peace; and stands ready tonight to defend an honored cause, whatever the price, whatever the burden, whatever the sacrifice that duty may require.

Sen. Robert F. Kennedy Apr. 1 called Johnson's decision not to run "truly magnanimous." At a news conference in New York, Kennedy praised the President's decision and his curtailment of U.S. attacks on North Vietnam. Kennedy said he had sent Johnson a telegram "respectfully and earnestly" requesting a personal meeting and expressing his "fervent . . . hope that your new efforts toward peace in Vietnam will succeed."

Johnson's speech was hailed by Sen. Eugene McCarthy Apr. 1 as deserving "the approval and the honor and respect of every citizen of the United States." By combining his renunciation of renomination with the de-escalation in North Vietnam, McCarthy said, the President "left no doubt as to what his commitment was, his commitment to peace and to an end of the war."

Republican Presidential candidate Richard M. Nixon said Apr. 1 that he was delaying the issuance of a "comprehensive statement on Vietnam which I had planned this week" to "avoid anything that might, even inadvertently, cause difficulty for our negotiators" following Johnson's order for a bombing curtailment. Nixon said that while "a bombing halt by itself would not be a step toward peace," if the U.S. "has finally gotten assurances that it would be reciprocated, then further steps toward peace may become possible." "I assume," he said, "that the President would not have announced a bombing halt under present conditions unless his action was based on private diplomatic information available only to the government" and "that intensive and delicate diplomatic moves are now under way, possibly involving the Soviet Union. . . . As I have often said, I believe that the key to peace in Vietnam probably lies in Moscow." Nixon noted that the U.S. had suffered its greatest casualties in the Korean War "after peace talks began" and that the war in Vietnam was being fought for "larger purposes"—"to make possible the conditions of a wider and a durable peace." He said this was "a time for both hope and realism—a time to explore every avenue toward settlement, but at the same time, to keep up our guard against the tempations of a camouflaged surrender."

Humphrey Becomes a Candidate

Vice Pres. Hubert H. Humphrey announced his candidacy for the Democratic Presidential nomination Apr. 27, nearly a month after the withdrawal of Pres. Johnson from the race. (A Humphrey-for-President campaign office had already been opened in Washington Apr. 11 by Sen. Walter F. Mondale [D., Minn.], and ex-Pres. Harry S. Truman was honorary chairman of the Humphrey committee.)

In his campaign, Humphrey stressed general peace themes. He had said in New York Apr. 22 that the U.S.' world role was "to concentrate on the arts of peace" as well as to "do our part to protect world security by maintaining whatever strength is necessary to meet our commitments to the UN charter and the regional treaties to which we are signatory." He hinted at possible future efforts toward a rapprochement with Communist China. "Through affirmative action to meet human needs," he said, "we can build security and peace." Humphrey said there was a need to replace the "iron curtains" in the world with "open doors."

"America's role" in the world was "a demanding one" because the world was "so intricately interdependent that the possibility of withdrawal or isolation simply does not exist," Humphrey contined. While it was "fashionable" to discuss foreign policy "in terms of American power," and this was "useful," he said, there was a danger that in the discussion the "alleged abuses" of national power would be emphasized and its "positive uses" denied. "We must choose our policies and priorities carefully, yes," Humphrey asserted. "But let us not delude ourselves into believing that we are not influencing developments in the world by not exercising our power, And I mean national power of all kinds—economic, military, diplomatic, moral. An American failure to participate would itself have enormous and . . . very dangerous consequences in the world. . . . We have not shrunk from the bitter necessity of helping to repel armed aggression with our armed might. But the basic use of American strength has been in the peaceful and constructive pursuits of mankind. This is our unique contribution."

Humphrey asserted in Huntington, W. Va. Apr. 24 that there was "nothing more important to the American people and to the world than to bring this sad and painful and costly [Vietnam] war to a conclusion without humiliation or defeat."

On NBC's "Meet the Press" program Apr. 28, Humphrey said he could not promise, if elected President, not to send U.S. troops into troubled areas abroad because such a policy could invite Communist expansions. He supported current U.S. policy of sending troops "where required by our own national security." He rejected, as "not an accurate statement," a charge of Sen. Robert F. Kennedy that the Johnson Administration was responsible for the "indiscriminate introduction of American troops" in the internal struggles of other nations. Humphrey said he would run on the Administration's record, but he emphasized that "I am my own man" and would "speak out on what I think is necessary."

On NBC's "Today" program Apr. 29, Humphrey said: The Administration "might have overstated" its repeated pledges to go "any place any time" to engage in peace talks with North Vietnam. Everybody had understood that Pres. Johnson had meant that the U.S. would go to a meeting site "that would be conducive to an honorable discussion, a reasonable place." "Whatever the overstatement might have been—and sometimes I think it's just as well to recognize we might have overstated—we must find a sutiable place to begin the talks." The Administration was "searching directly and honorably for the path for peace." He expressed hope that the peace effort would not be "an issue of conflict" during the campaign, that the candidates would cooperate to allow the President free diplomatic rein to conduct the peace negotiations.

Humphrey May 11 assailed Democratic critics of the Administration with the admonition that "you do yourself, your party and your President and your country a disservice by constantly downgrading your President, your party and your country." In New York May 23, Humphrey called for less emphasis on "containment" of communism and more on "peaceful engagement" with the Soviet Union and its East European allies, who appeared to be gradually "tearing down" the Iron Curtain. At a Hamline University (St. Paul, Minn.) convocation May 27, Humphrey said that "anybody" could get the nation into a bigger war but that the job of statesmanship and of the next President was to continue the current U.S. policy to "de-escalate" and to "limit" the Vietnam war. The major tasks before the statesmen were to " get this war wound up," gain from the Paris negotiations "something with which both sides can live" and focus on peace.

Humphrey May 17 made a statement on the Paris talks that drew denials from Paris and Washington. Humphrey, visiting the University of Maine in Orono, had been asked by a student: "Will we negotiate with the NLF [National Liberation Front, political arm of the Viet Cong]?" Humphrey replied: "It has now been agreed at the Paris meetings that the North Vietnamese can have whomever they want on their side and that we can have whomever we want on our side." Within an hour a Humphrey aide issued a clarifying statement saying that Humphrey was only restating the U.S. position and had not meant to say there was a new development in Paris. The matter of representation "has not come up *per se* in Paris," the aide said. A State Department statement and other sources quoted by the press in Paris also stressed later May 17 that the matter had not come up in Paris talks. The State Department said the U.S. delegation in Paris had "publicly and privately made clear the necessity and the importance of participation by the South Vietnamese government at the appropriate time," but "the matter has not been discussed further, nor have specific proposals been made or considered on either side, in Paris or at any prior time."

Among Humphrey's other campaign statements:

July 12—The U.S. should redefine its national interest. "That interest surely does not run to maintaining the *status quo* wherever it is challenged. We are not the world's policemen. How peoples wish to govern themselves, and how they wish to change their governments—that's their business." American foreign policy should shift from confrontation and containment of communism to "reconciliation and peaceful engagement." "The most important area of reconciliation—and the top priority for American foreign policy in the next decade—is that of East-West relations. This particularly includes relations among the United States and the Soviet Union, Western Europe and Eastern Europe. Adherence to this priority will minimize the possibility of direct conflict. It will minimize the possibility that conflict among the developing nations may involve the major powers. Finally, it will permit a reallocation of the world's resources away from massive military budgets to constructive human development."

Aug. 1—The South Vietnamese government was wrong to imprison former peace candidate Truong Dinh Dzu, who had advocated a coalition government and talks with the Viet Cong. "This action represents a definite step backward in the effort to strengthen the political institutions of South Vietnam." Free elections should take place in South Vietnam and should include the National Liberation Front. "I would permit individuals regardless of their political persuasion to take part in an election in South Vietnam just as they do here."

McCarthy's Campaign

Continuing his campaign for the Democratic Presidential nomination, Sen. Eugene McCarthy said at Morris Harvey College in Charleston, W. Va. Apr. 16: The Vietnam war "has drawn off our material, intellectual and moral strength." "This is the people's year to pass judgment on a President and his foreign policy." "The people want an end to the war in Vietnam, and they want it very quickly. This is the burden that now rests on the present Administration and will rest on any succeeding Administration."

McCarthy said in Pittsburgh Apr. 17: State Secy. Dean Rusk should be replaced as "an encouraging sign of the Administration's willingness to change its course" in Vietnam. The question was "not so much our willingness to seek a settlement but rather our readiness to accept the full implication of what settlement will require of us." This called for "a basic change of diplomatic approach in which we must view negotiations not as the continuation of war by other means but rather as a process of joint conciliation designed to end the human suffering on both sides."

McCarthy, campaigning in California May 11, asserted that his candidacy had been instrumental in Pres. Johnson's withdrawal from the campaign, in moving the U.S. into the Paris talks on Vietnam and in setting "America free."

Among statements McCarthy made May 11:

● In Sacramento—"It is clear now that the great majority of the people in this country have concluded that the war in Vietnam must be brought to the quick end. . . . We have by this effort written the plank of the Democratic Party even before we get to the convention, and I think we have gone a long way also toward writing the platform of the Republican Party."

● In Fresno—"Think of what our position would be today if we had not raised the challenge to Pres. Johnson, if we had backed off and gone along quietly. I think it will be fair to say that we would not be entering negotiations in Paris today, and we would not have reached a judgment in this country that the war be ended quickly. We will not go off on military adventures again until we have done something about the ghettos in our cities."

At a New York rally in Madison Square Garden May 19, McCarthy told an enthusiastic crowd of more than 19,000 persons that his campaign had evoked a "public judgment" that the Vietnam war should be ended. He pledged to continue until it was ended.

McCarthy criticized Vice Pres. Humphrey and Sen. Robert F. Kennedy during a KGW-TV interview in Portland, Ore. May 22. McCarthy attacked them for misguided views on the Vietnam war. Humphrey, he said, presented the Administration's case, "sometimes even more forcefully" than Pres. Johnson himself. Kennedy, he said, had come "very slowly to a position of opposition." Kennedy's record on Vietnam, McCarthy declared, "has been, until very recently, one of approving the involvement." McCarthy said the Administration had developed "a kind of mind-set" focusing on counter-insurgency and military-aid groupings in developing nations. He said if Kennedy "were to proceed as he evidently has proceeded, on what he has supported in the past, we might have further involvements like Vietnam. I don't think you would if I were President."

Speaking to 6,000 persons in the San Francisco Cow Palace May 22, McCarthy called Humphrey the war's "most ardent apologist" and said he was not convinced that Kennedy had as yet "entirely renounced the misconception" concerning the world role of the U.S. that had led to the increasing involvement in Vietnam.

Robert Kennedy's Campaign & Assassination

Sen. Robert F. Kennedy, 42, was shot by a Jerusalem-born Arab in Los Angeles June 5 as he was leaving a celebration of a victory he had won in California's Democratic Presidential primary. Kennedy died June 6. The assassin, Sirhan Bishara Sirhan, apparently acted in the belief that Kennedy's sympathies and actions were pro-Israeli and anti-Arab.

In the California primary June 4, Kennedy had won the state's 172 Democratic National Convention delegates and 46% of the Democratic vote. Sen. Eugene McCarthy, his principal opponent, received 42% of the vote.

Among Kennedy campaign remarks prior to the California test:

In Philadelphia Apr. 2—"I think we have to reexamine our whole position in Vietnam." A bombing halt was only a part of what should be "a coordinated plan" to attain a negotiated peace. It should also be recognized that "we will have to negotiate with the National Liberation Front."

In Portland, Ore. Apr. 17—"American foreign policy has become identified with power, and in that obsession we have forgotten our purposes. . . . The authority with which we speak, the respect in which we are held diminishes." The U.S. must "reassure the world of our judgment and our purposes," and "there is no more important task . . . than to end the war in Vietnam . . . honorably, without surrender of our limited interests."

At Oregon State University, Corvallis Apr. 18—"We made our position clear 2 years ago that we'd go anytime, any place" to discuss ending the Vietnam war. "I don't think that we should be responsible for continuing to raise other terms and other conditions in connection with the [current] negotiations [on a site for preliminary talks]. . . . We said we wanted to talk about peace. I think we should go and talk about peace."

At Purdue University, Lafayette, Ind. May 1—The U.S., "the strongest nation in the world," should not be concerned over whether it would "lose face" by agreeing to a site for talks on Vietnam. "The important thing—our responsibility to our own men and our own people—is to get the talks started, and try to reach an honorable settlement to this costly and divisive war."

In Portland Ore. May 17—The U.S. economic crisis involved various Administration failures. But "the underlying problem is the war in Vietnam," which "has twisted our economy completely out of shape." As long as the war spending existed, "we will have to pay for the mistakes of the past."

At the University of Oregan, Eugene May 18—"Perhaps it would be better for all concerned—as it would have been for the last 2 years—if the government of South Vietnam were to commence its own talks with the National Liberation Front."

Ted Kennedy States Views

Sen. Edward M. (Ted) Kennedy (Mass.) seemed a possible contender for the nomination as the Democratic Convention approached. Clarifying his position on Vietnam, Kennedy Aug. 12 proposed a 4-point plan the end the war, which he termed "the tragedy of our generation." Kennedy presented his proposals in a speech before the Chamber of Commerce in Worcester, Mass.

To bring an end to the conflict, Kennedy declared, the U.S., "as soon as possible," should: (1) "end unconditionally all bombing of North Vietnam"; (2) "negotiate with Hanoi the mutual withdrawal from South Vietnam of all foreign forces, both allied and North Vietnamese"; (3) "accompany this withdrawal with whatever help we can give to the South Vietnamese in the building of a viable, political, economic and legal structure that will not promptly collapse upon our departure"; (4) "demonstrate to both Hanoi and Saigon the sincerity of our intentions by significantly decreasing this year the level of our military activity and military personnel in the South."

Under his plan, Kennedy said, the U.S. could end its involvement in the war "with honor," and the Paris talks would not founder on the problems of a coalition government, election procedures or the make-up of future cabinets in South Vietnam.

Kennedy defended the call for a bombing halt by saying that the bombing had not reduced the movement of enemy men and material and that "an end to the killing in Vietnam can never be negotiated as long as the bombing of North Vietnam continues." "Halting the bombing would thus save many more American lives than it would ever endanger," he declared.

Kennedy said the U.S. could help build a Vietnamese society but must make clear to the South Vietnamese government "our intention to withdraw from the South as Hanoi withdraws" and "our complete unwillingness thereafter to bear the burden of their responsibility and pick up the pieces of their failure." Saigon, he said, "must not be given a veto over our course in Paris, our cessation of the bombing, or our mutual withdrawal of troops." "They must be given clear notice," he said, "that their chief prop will be taken away as soon as we can conclude such negotiations with Hanoi."

Kennedy asserted that the hopes of the U.S. in its effort to help South Vietnam "build a nation" had "foundered in miscalculation and self-deception," had been "stymied by the stubbornness of the foe, but, above all, . . . [had] been buried by the incompetence and corruption of our South Vietnamese allies."

McCarthy After the Assassination

Less than a week after Kennedy's death, Sen. McCarthy met

June 11 with Pres. Johnson at the White House for a briefing, and he announced the resumption of his campaign at a news conference in Washington June 12. "The issues," he said, "remain essentially the same" as before the Kennedy murder—the need (1) to reexamine military policy in Vietnam and, more importantly, "the militaristic thrust of American foreign policy," (2) to bring before the people "the pressing domestic needs and particularly the problems of poverty and racism," and (3) to continue "the test of the American political process." McCarthy asserted that he would find it difficult to support Humphrey as the Presidential nominee because Humphrey had given "rather wholehearted" support to the Administration's policy in Vietnam.

McCarthy concentrated his attacks on Humphrey's identification with the Administration's Vietnam and other policies. "Where does he stand on Vietnam?" McCarthy asked in a Chicago speech June 30. "He favors negotiation, and so do we all. But how does he feel about escalation? Is he against it? When did his opposition begin—1965, 1966, 1967, Mar. 31, Apr. 21, last week? Does he agree with the basic assumption of American foreign policy, which I have questioned in this campaign? Does he favor increasing of the military—or does he oppose it, as I do? Does he favor the present draft laws? I suggest he state his position instead of misrepresenting mine. So far, we have been led to believe that the Vice President has always supported, and still supports, our policy in Vietnam, the underlying issue of the day." McCarthy urged Humphrey to join him in public debate "on the crucial issues facing America." If Humphrey felt that he was not free to discuss the issues, McCarthy said, "let him be set free." "Let the President release him to speak his full mind and to defend or reject the policies of this Administration."

On the NBC "Meet the Press" program July 7, McCarthy said he would give up a planned trip to Paris if he thought it would interfere with the talks.

At a press conference in Louisville, Ky. July 19, McCarthy said that differences between himself and Humphrey over Vietnam had narrowed, and there might no longer be any differences. McCarthy said: Humphrey recently had taken more "progressive approaches to a solution to the war . . . than I think the Administration has been recommending." As for Humphrey's advocacy of accommodations short of "immediate unilateral withdrawal" from Vietnam, "I [McCarthy] haven't advocated unilateral

withdrawal either." It was possible that Humphrey had "come
at least as far as my position." The 2 rivals should have a public
meeting in which "we can clarify our differences, if there are
any differences, and, if we find ourselves in agreement, . . . some
conflicts and some confusion within the party can be straightened
out. . . ."

McCarthy said in a statement issued in Baltimore July 23:
The Johnson Administration remained "inflexible" on Vietnam,
and the war therefore "must continue to be a crucial issue" in
the campaign. "The Administration is as yet unwilling to do what
is necessary to end the war by political settlement." "At a time
when the United States should be working for a broadened or
more representative South Vietnam government, the Administration has chosen to strengthen its ties to the present Saigon
regime."

McCarthy finally said in Sacramento, Calif. Aug. 10 (in answer to questions of California delegates to the Democratic
National Convention) that if Humphrey's views on Vietnam
came "reasonably close" to his own (McCarthy's) views, he could
support him as the Democratic Presidential nominee.

In remarks prepared for an Aug. 15 rally at Madison Square
Garden in New York and carried on closed-circuit TV to 48 other
rallies across the country, McCarthy demanded that the Democratic platform "affirm that there must be a new government in
Saigon open to the participation of the National Liberation Front."
He said that should Saigon refuse to accept such a new government, U.S. forces and assistance should be phased out.

McGovern Enters Race

Sen. George S. McGovern (S.D.) announced in the Caucus
Room of the Old Senate Office Building Aug. 10 that he was a
serious and active candidate for the Democratic Presidential nomination. He committed himself to the "twin goals for which Robert
Kennedy gave his life—an end to the war in Vietnam and a passionate commitment to heal the divisions in our lives here at
home." McGovern, 46, a former history professor, described the
assassinated Senator as "the most talented and passionate political
leader of this generation." He emphasized that he made no claim
"to wear the Kennedy mantle" but said he "might serve as a
rallying point for his [Kennedy's] supporters."

McGovern praised Sen. Eugene McCarthy for his opposition to the Vietnamese war and Vice Pres. Humphrey for his stand on social justice. He declared that he could support either one if one of them were nominated by the Democratic National Convention. But he implied that neither Humphrey nor McCarthy was strong enough in foreign and domestic affairs. McGovern, urging a strong antiwar plank in the Democratic platform, declared that his candidacy "may strengthen both the platform and our leadership in those inseparable aspirations of peace abroad and social justice in our own troubled country."

McGovern called for an immediate halt in the bombing of North Vietnam. He said: The U.S. involvement in Vietnam was "the most disastrous political, moral, diplomatic blunder in our national history." "The senseless search-and-destroy operations . . . on the ground, which kill the innocent along with the combatant, should also cease now. The loss of American youth and the slaughter of the Vietnamese should stop now." McGovern advocated "a systematic reduction of our overgrown military-industrial complex" and the diversion of the resulting resources to the reconstruction of cities and rural America. He proposed ending the draft and replacing it with a "voluntary program."

(McGovern had been named previously to head the Committee for a Democratic Convention, a group formed the weekend of Aug. 3 to rally strength against the nomination of Humphrey and against the Administration's Vietnam policy.)

Following his entrance into the Presidential race, McGovern began a campaign that included TV appearances, speeches, interviews and delegate-raising meetings. Among his statements:

Aug. 12—(At an airport news conference in New York) He considered "racism at least as great a threat to the nation as the war in Vietnam." This belief separated him from McCarthy, who "has chosen to concentrate his campaign almost entirely on ending the war in Vietnam."

Aug. 14—(In Cherry Hill, N.J.) He would oppose a platform indorsing the Administration's Vietnam policy. Democrats should insist that the bombing of North Vietnam be stopped and that the political base of the South Vietnamese government be widened.

Aug. 19—(At a news conference in Washington) There must be massive de-escalation in Vietnam, and the U.S. should withdraw about 250,000 American troops. U.S. troops in Vietnam should "avoid firing unless to defend themselves."

In the campaign for the California primary, just before Kennedy's assassination, similarities between his views and those of Sen. McCarthy were reported. Both opposed further military escalation in Vietnam and both opposed U.S. bombing of the North. McCarthy favored the formation of a new government in the South and the acknowledgment that the government would include the National Liberation Front, the political arm of the Viet Cong. He said the Administration should publicize its acceptance of such a coalition government in the South. Kennedy rejected McCarthy's proposal to form a coalition government "even before we begin the negotiations." McCarthy denied that he had said he "was going to force a coalition government. . . . I said we should make sure we are willing to accept that if the South Vietnamese want to continue the fighting." (In a panel discussion on KRON-TV in San Francisco June 2, McCarthy said: "He [Kennedy] said he wouldn't force a coalition. I feel that, directly or indirectly, that's what we have to do.")

Republican Convention & Vietnam

The Republican National Convention opened in Miami, Fla. Aug. 5, and the delegates chose Richard M. Nixton Aug. 8 as their Presidential candidate. Spiro T. Agnew won the Vice Presidential nomination.

The keynote address, delivered by Gov. Daniel J. Evans of Washington Aug. 5, dealt at length with Vietnam. Evans, considered a political moderate and a dove on the Vietnam issue, sharply criticized the Democratic Administration for the war. His address reflected the moderate tone of the proposed Republican platform.

Evans spoke of the frustrations posed by the Vietnam war, a war "in which we spend a million dollars every 20 minutes; a war which has cost us nearly 150,000 casualties and nearly 20,000 American lives; a war which . . . we have not won in Saigon, cannot negotiate in Paris and will not explain to the American people." He argued, however, that despite these frustrations, America still had an obligation and responsibility to the people of South Vietnam; America's entry into the war "by the path of error" could not justify its exit "through the door of default." Nevertheless, Evans insisted, first priority must be given to resolving America's internal conflicts. He warned that "if we can't unite our own nation, then we can't preserve the hope of others."

Evans had been introduced to the convention by New York Mayor John Lindsay, who asserted that the Vietnam war had

"paralyzed progress at home in pursuit of deadly folly abroad"
and ranked "among the most disastrous foreign policy blunders
in our history."

Ex-Pres. Dwight D. Eisenhower, in an address to the convention by closed-circuit TV from Walter Reed Army Medical Center in Washington, D.C., emphasized the dangers of communism.
He denounced Americans who were disposed "to ignore these aggressive moves, to discount the blatant threats, to seek, in effect,
for surface accommodations rather than to insist upon mutual acceptance in practice of principle." He described communism as
"a formidable foe—an expansionist tyranny which respects only
toughness and strength and still displays little interest in travel-
ing the pathways to peace, with honor and justice." Referring to
Vietnam, he said: "It is one thing to call for a peaceful settlement of this struggle. It is quite another to call for retreat by
America. The latter is the best way I know to stockpile tragedy
for our children."

The 1968 Republican platform was adopted by the delegates
without controversy. The differences that existed, most notably
over the Vietnam plank. were resolved during the formulation of
the platform by a 102-man committee headed by Senate Republican
leader Everett McKinley Dirksen (Ill.). On Vietnam, the differences were over whether to stress peace or to uphold the U.S.
commitment. Cooperation between the Nixon and Rockefeller
forces on this issue resulted in the final compromise, which contained wording acceptable to both sides. Both were content with
the call for a new strategy to permit "de-Americanization" of the
war.

Nixon had presented his views on the party's proposed Vietnam policy in a statement to Dirksen's committee Aug. 1. His
position paper, his first on the subject since the Paris talks began,
declared that "the war must be ended," but "a negotiated settlement" and the conference table must be made "wide enough, and
the issues placed upon it broad enough, to accommodate as many
as possible of the powers and interests involved." Until this happened, he said, the war "must be waged more effectively"—not
by further military escalation but by "a dramatic escalation of
our efforts on the economic, political, diplomatic and psychological fronts." He called for "a new strategy" with increased reliance
on "small-unit action, on routing out the Viet Cong infrastructure,
on police and patrol activities, on intelligence-gathering, on the

strengthening of local forces." He said "far greater and more urgent attention" should be paid to training and equipping the South Vietnamese to fight the war. "As they are phased in, American troops can—and should—be phased out," he said.

The Vietnam plank stressed the need for an honorable negotiated peace and "progressive de-Americanization" of the war. It pledged the party to "a program for peace in Vietnam—neither peace at any price nor a camouflaged surrender of legitimate United States or allied interests—but a positive program that will offer a fair and equitable settlement to all, based on the principle of self-determination, our national interests and the cause of long-range world peace." The platform urged "de-Americanization" of the war in conjunction with a new policy focused less on territorial control and more on "the political framework on which a successful outcome ultimately depends." This framework involved "the security of the population, . . . developing a greater sense of nationhood and . . . strengthening the local forces." The plank indicted the Johnson Administration for a "breach of faith with the American people." Specifically, it censured the "heavy involvement" of U.S. troops in Vietnam and a "piecemeal commitment of men and material" that had "wasted our massive military superiority and frittered away our options." "The result," it said, "has been a prolonged war of attrition." The platform expressed the party's intention to avoid foreign policy actions that would tend "to make the United States a world policeman" and to undertake "an exhaustive reassessment of America's worldwide commitments and military preparedness." It stressed, however, that the "best hope for enduring peace lies in comprehensive international cooperation."

In his speech accepting the Presidential nomination, Nixon Aug. 8 promised "action" on "a new policy for peace abroad, a new policy for peace and progress and justice at home." The "first priority foreign policy objective" of his administration, Nixon said, would be "to bring an honorable end to the war in Vietnam." He said "a policy to prevent more Vietnams" was needed, and "all America's foreign commitments must be reappraised." Nixon called for "a new internationalism" with respect to America's allies and said it was time for "an era of negotiations" with leaders of the Communist world. He pledged to "restore the strength of America so that we shall always negotiate from strength and never from weakness." Nixon urged that

America's goals "be made clear" in such negotiations. He held that the Communists should be told that the U.S. did "not seek domination over any other country" and would "never be belligerent" but would be "as firm in defending our system as they are in expanding theirs." Nixon said he would "extend the hand of friendship to all people," and specifically the Russian and Chinese peoples. He promised to restore the international prestige of the U.S.

Democratic Convention Split on Vietnam

Vice Pres. Hubert H. Humphrey won his party's Presidential nomination Aug. 28 at a Democratic Convention that was beset by violence on the Chicago streets outside and by bitter dissension inside the convention hall. Sen. Edmund S. Muskie, 54, of Maine was nominated Aug. 29 as Vice Presidential candidate.

The 35th Democratic National Convention, one of the wildest ever witnessed in the U.S., was held Aug. 26-29. It served as a display case for the party's deep division on Vietnam. The convention rejected a dovish peace plank on Vietnam in favor of a plank indorsing the Johnson Administration's policy. The antiwar plank had been fashioned by followers of the 2 major losing candidates for the Presidential nomination—Sens. Eugene J. McCarthy and George S. McGovern. The rejection of their plank alienated McCarthy and many of his backers, especially younger people brought into the campaign by McCarthy's antiwar stand during the primaries. Humphrey, McCarthy and McGovern had debated before the California delegation the morning of Aug. 27. Humphrey defended Pres. Johnson's Vietnam policies. McGovern attacked both the war and its costs in diminishing domestic programs. McCarthy repeated his earlier statement that "I could not support a Democratic candidate whose views [on Vietnam] did not come close to what mine are." McCarthy said after the convention that he could not support Humphrey. McGovern said he would back Humphrey.

Chicago Mayor Richard J. Daley assumed responsibility for maintaining order both inside Chicago's International Ampitheater, and outside, where brutal clashes took place between policemen and young antiwar demonstrators. In the convention hall, his strict security force was bitterly resented by many delegates. Outside, his police force used clubs and tear gas against demonstrators.

Thousands of antiwar, anti-Humphrey, pro-McCarthy, hippie, Yippie (Youth International Party) and other protesters converged on the city and called for mass demonstrations, marches and sleep-ins in city parks. (Demonstrators originally estimated that 100,000 protesters would come to Chicago, but it was reported that only about 10,000 to 15,000 actually arrived.) The major coordinating group for the demonstrations was the National Mobilization Committee to End the War in Vietnam, a coalition of about 100 antiwar groups ranging in outlook from leftwing militance to center moderation. Almost all of the protesters were in their teens or 20s, and almost all were white.

Sen. Daniel K. Inouye (Hawaii) delivered the keynote address. Inouye cited the problems of student revolt, crime, riots and war. "Why," he asked, "when we have at last had the courage to open an attack on the age-old curses of ignorance and disease and poverty and prejudice—why are the flags of anarchism being hoisted by leaders of the next generation?" Some, he said, blamed all problems on the Vietnam war and advocated the end of the war as a solution. Inouye agreed that the war must be ended, but, he emphasized, it must be ended responsibly. "Just as we shun irresponsible calls for total and devastating military victory," he declared, "so must we guard against the illusion of an instant peace that has no chance of permanence."

The platform plank indorsing the Johnson Administration policy in the Vietnamese war was adopted Aug. 28 by a vote of $1,567^3/_4$ to $1,041^1/_4$ after a 3-hour debate punctuated by chants of "Stop the war!" The plank, presented as the majority choice of the platform committee, advocated: (a) A halt in the bombing of North Vietnam "when this action would not endanger the lives of our troops in the field" and would "take into account the response from Hanoi"; (b) withdrawal of all foreign forces from South Vietnam only after negotiating "with Hanoi an immediate end or limitation of hostilities"; (c) establishment of a postwar government by free elections with international supervision and participation open to all who "accept peaceful political processes." The plank "applaud[ed] the initiative of Pres. Johnson which brought North Vietnam to the peace table" and called on Hanoi to "respond positively to this act of statemanship."

The antiwar plank supported by backers of McCarthy, McGovern and Sen. Edward Kennedy was presented as a minority report of the platform committee. It called for: (a) An unconditional cessation of all bombing of North Vietnam; (b) negotiation of a phased, mutual withdrawal of U.S. and North Vietnamese troops from South Vietnam; (c) encouragement of South Vietnam "to negotiate a political reconciliation with the National Liberation Front looking toward a . . . broadly representative" government for South Vietnam; (d) reduction of U.S. offensive operations in South Vietnam, "thus enabling an early withdrawal of a significant number of our troops."

The debate, without precedent in convention history, took place the afternoon of Aug. 28. The argument for the majority Administration plank was presented by Sens. Edmund S. Muskie (Me.) and Gale McGee (Wyo.), Gov. Warren Hearnes (Mo.), Mrs. Gerri Joseph of Minnesota, Reps. Ed Edmondson (Okla.), David Pryor (Ark.) and Hale Boggs (La.). The minority position was presented by Rep. Phillip Burton (Calif.), Senatorial nominee Paul O'Dwyer of New York, Kennedy Administration aide Kenneth O'Donnell of Massachusetts, Sen. Albert Gore (Tenn.), Sen. Wayne Morse (Ore.), Kennedy Administration aide Theodore C. Sorensen of New York and Pierre Salinger, White House press secretary in the Kennedy Administration and adviser to the McGovern campaign.

Muskie began the debate with the assertion that the 2 planks differed not in the objective of a negotiated settlement of the war but only in the means of achieving that objective. While there were "real differences," he said, "the dividing line is not the desire for peace or war; the dividing line is limited to means, not ends." A prolonged demonstration erupted after Salinger's claim that the late Sen. Robert F. Kennedy would have supported the dovish plank. A chant of "Stop the war!" spread from the New York and California delegations to other delegates and into the galleries. The convention was brought to order with difficulty. As the vote was announced and it was revealed that the Humphrey plank had passed by a 60-40 margin, a protest rendition of We Shall Overcome arose from New York delegates wearing black armbands.

The debate ended with a message from Gen. Creighton W. Abrams, the U.S. commander in Vietnam. Boggs, chairman of the platform committee, read it as Abrams' reply to his question at a White House briefing on the estimated additional casualties that would result from an unconditional bombing halt. Boggs

said Abrams' answer was that within 2 weeks of such a halt the
enemy could be able to increase its military capacity in the South
5-fold.

The McCarthy view on the Vietnam plank, released Aug. 17,
called for "a 2-stage process toward a final peace." In the first
stage a new government would be established in South Vietnam
through negotiations by the U.S., North Vietnam, South Vietnam and the NLF. This government would include "all major
elements of the population" and have substantial NLF participation. In the 2d stage, there would be elections for a permanent
government after all foreign forces withdrew from the South and
an internationally-supervised cease-fire was in effect. McCarthy
proposed withdrawal of U.S. support and forces if South Vietnamese leaders refused to agree to a broadly-based, interim coalition government.

A compromise dovish plank on Vietnam was offered Aug. 20
by supporters of the late Sen. Robert F. Kennedy. It proposed a
halt in the bombing of North Vietnam, a cease-fire and negotiations between Saigon and the NLF. But it provided that bombing
could be resumed "if that later proves to be necessary." During
the attempt to attain a "cease-fire and standstill in place" on
the battlefield, the U.S. would try to de-escalate hostilities, but
U.S. troops, would be "free to take necessary protective action
at all times." It would make "continued American support" of
Saigon contingent on prompt action by Saigon to undertake "discussions with those South Vietnamese who are in fact fighting
the central government, to seek an early end to the evil war between those 2 groups."

The final dovish plank, which became the minority report of
the platform committee on Vietnam, was negotiated Aug. 23 by
Richard N. Goodwin, representing McCarthy; Pierre Salinger,
representing McGovern; Theodore C. Sorensen, former special
counsel to Pres. Kennedy; John H. Gilligan, Senatorial candidate
in Ohio, and William G. Clark, Senatorial candidate in Illinois.

In his speech accepting the Presidential nomination, Humphrey Aug. 29 emphasized "3 realities that confront this nation"—
"the necessity for peace in Vietnam and in the world, . . . for
peace and justice in our cities and in our nation" and "for unity
in our country." "One cannot help but reflect the deep sadness
that we feel over the troubles and the violence which have erupted,
regrettably and tragically, in the streets of this great city

[Chicago]" he declared. "Surely we have now learned the lesson that violence breeds counterviolence and it cannot be condoned, whatever the source." Humphrey mentioned the differences within the party, and "even within the ranks of all of the Democratic Presidential candidates," over the issue of Vietnam. But "I hope you will also recognize the much larger areas of agreement," he said. "The question is not the yesterdays but the question is what do we do now? . . . If there is any one lesson that we should have learned, it is that the policies of tomorrow need not be limited by the policies of yesterday."

(Humphrey told the Democratic National Committee in Chicago Aug. 30 that "the most foolish thing a man could do would be to be wedded inflexibly to every word" of the party platform. "We will do our best," he said, "to adjust our message and our policies to the realities. Let's not get ourselves into any inflexible position.")

In the streets of Chicago, a week of tensions and sporadic violence had blossomed into full-scale rioting Aug. 28 when police and National Guardsmen battled youths in downtown Chicago. The Aug. 28 violence followed an afternoon rally when protesters tried to leave Grant Park and march towards the Loop area in an attempt to reach the International Amphitheater. To keep the demonstrators from the amphitheater, security forces chased them along downtown streets and attacked them with clubs, rifle butts, tear gas and chemical Mace. Newsmen estimated that 2,000 to 5,000 youths were involved in the disorders Wednesday (Aug. 28) night. Some protesters threw bottles and rocks at the police; many carried the flags of anarchy and of the Viet Cong. The afternoon rally in Grant Park, sponsored by the National Mobilization Committee to End the War in Vietnam, had been attended by about 15,000 people. A series of marches Aug. 29 involved thousands of demonstrators, some of them led by Democratic delegates; each demonstration was an attempt to march on the International Amphitheater, but all were turned back by the police and National Guard. The Aug. 29 marches also followed a Grant Park rally. Tom Hayden, leader of the National Mobilization Committee, said at the rally: "It may be that the era of organized, peaceful and orderly demonstrations is coming to an end and that other methods will be needed." Rennie Davis, another Mobilization Committee coordinator, advocated a U.S. National Liberation Front whose slogan would be: "There can be no peace in the United States until there is peace in Vietnam."

Presidential Campaigns

The Vietnam war actually figured less prominently in the campaigning of the candidates than many observers had anticipated.

Pres. Johnson Sept. 10 defended his Vietnam policy and urged Europe to take a larger share of its defense burden. Speaking before the American Legion convention in New Orleans Sept. 10, he warned that if the bombing of the North Vietnamese panhandle were halted without a de-escalation of Hanoi's war effort, "the military capacity of the enemy to hurt our forces would greatly increase." He rejected 2 alternatives to continued bombing—an invasion of the panhandle or an allied pullback from the region near the demilitarized zone.

In Los Angeles Sept. 10, Humphrey said that Nixon took "a little harder line" than he did on the Vietnam and Communist issue. But he urged Nixon and 3d party candidate George Wallace to join him in a statement informing Hanoi that none of of them would take a softer stand in the peace negotiations if elected. Such a joint statement had first been proposed by Humphrey in a Sept. 1 statement that said: "North Vietnam must understand that a political campaign . . . [in the U.S.] will not result in our granting . . . concessions which it cannot obtain through the legitimate processes of negotiation now under way in Paris. The time to negotiate is now, not later. The time to stop the killing is now, not later." (A Nixon spokesman later rejected the proposal as a political gimmick.) In a question-and-answer session with college students in Philadelphia Sept. 9, Humphrey had expressed the belief that, "negotiations or no negotiations, we could start to remove some of the American forces [from Vietnam] in early 1969 or late 1968." "Substantive negotiations" on a peace pact may very well start before I become President," he said. Encountering some antiwar demonstrators, Humphrey pledged if elected to "literally give my life for the cause of peace in this world and peace for mankind." In another question-and-answer period with young people in Denver later Sept. 9, Humphrey said the minority plank on Vietnam rejected at the Democratic Convention was "so mildly different" from the majority plank that he would have had no difficulty in accepting it and running on it.

During his Los Angeles visit Sept. 10, Humphrey elaborated on his Vietnam statements. He said that his belief that the Paris talks might result in progress toward peace was based on speculation and not on official information. He asserted that, while he had no strong objections to the dovish Vietnam plank and would have accepted its adoption as an expression of the party's will, he would have "felt a right and indeed an obligation to make some interpretation and elaboration on my own." Specifically, he said, the minority plank's talk of an unconditional bombing halt "sort of ... papered over some of the real problems we have."

In a live TV broadcast from Toledo to Europe via the Canary Bird communication satellite Sept. 23, Humphrey pledged to "reassess the entire situation in Vietnam" and to "take the action that that situation requires" if elected. He said he looked forward to a reduction of U.S. forces in Vietnam in 1969 and expressed hope for "a cease-fire as well" unless "unknown things happen or developments that we cannot foresee now take place." Although he said he had "no particular difficulty in supporting our Administration's policies." Humphrey remarked that "men of independent judgment and strong conviction from time to time have different points of view" and that no President desired to have only "yes men around him."

Humphrey pledged Sept. 30 that if he were elected President, he would stop the bombing of North Vietnam—provided Hanoi showed "willingness to restore the demilitarized zone between North and South Vietnam." In a major speech televised nationally from Salt Lake City, Humphrey said: "... I would stop the bombing ... as an acceptable risk for peace because I believe it could lead to success in the negotiations and thereby shorten the war. This would be the best protection for our troops. ... [B]efore taking action—I would place key importance on evidence—direct or indirect—by deed or word—of Communist willingness to restore the demilitarized zone. ... [If Hanoi] were to show bad faith, I would reserve the right to resume the bombing." "The lesson of Vietnam" was that the U.S. should "carefully define" its goals and priorities and within that context "formulate policies which will fit new American guidelines." It would be possible to withdraw some U.S. troops from combat in Vietnam in 1969. He would press for political, economic and social reforms by the

South Vietnamese government.

In a TV interview Oct. 1, Humphrey added that the Ho Chin Minh Trail through Laos would be excluded from the bombing halt.

Members of the North Vietnamese delegation to the Paris talks criticized Humphrey's speech as "nothing new." Le Duc Tho, special counselor to Hanoi's Paris negotiators, said Oct. 1 that Humphrey had made "the same demand for reciprocity, which we reject."

An attack on Humphrey's Vietnam position was launched in the Senate Oct. 3 by Republican Senators. GOP Presidential nominee Nixon Oct. 1 had sent GOP members telegrams suggesting that Humphrey be pressed to specify whether he was breaking away from the Administration position.

In his first formal political speech since the Democratic National Convention, Sen. Eugene J. McCarthy (Minn.) Oct. 8 announced his conditions for supporting Humphrey for President. The conditions were: acceptance of a "new government" in South Vietnam, draft-law reform, including immediate relief for those conscientiously objecting on nonreligious grounds to fighting in Vietnam, and reform of the Democratic Party to prevent "another Chicago." McCarthy made this speech in New York at a fundraising dinner for Democratic Senatorial candidate Paul O'Dwyer. He spoke after Humphrey had phoned him from Washington and requested his support. Humphrey reported Oct. 9 that he was "not prone to start meeting conditions" for support.

Sen. Muskie, Democratic Vice Presidential nominee, opened his campaign in front of the Alamo in San Antonio, Tex. Sept. 8 with an appeal to "get our emotions under control" and to "start using our heads." He said this was not the time "to make votes" by "playing upon the discontent and uneasiness of the voters," by "playing off one group of Americans against another" or by "probing or irritating the sore spots which divide us." In the first few weeks of his campaign Muskie concentrated on the issues of Vietnam and crime.

Muskie had discussed Vietnam even before the official opening of his campaign. At a news conference in Chicago Aug. 29, a few hours after being nominated, Muskie said that while he "instinctively reacts in similar ways" to Humphrey on the issue of Vietnam, he might differ on the matter of a unilateral cessation of the bombing of North Vietnam. As he had done on NBC's

"Meet the Press" program Aug. 25, Muskie indicated support for halting the bombing without conditioning it on a reciprocal military scale-down by Hanoi. In a speech to the American Political Science Association in Washington Sept. 5, Muskie said that he favored a negotiated settlement of the war and that "calculated risks" should be taken to achieve the settlement. In Washington Sept. 6, Muskie said he thought the candidates should present "the thrust" of their thinking about the course of U.S. policy in Vietnam without delineating specific positions or decisions lest it "destroy the posture of our government [at the Paris negotiations] or the possibility of getting a settlement."

Campaigning in Indiana Sept, 11, Muskie told University of Notre Dame students in South Bend that most Americans agreed that the war should not be settled by military victory but by negotiations. The terms of the settlement, he said, should be "the product of all disagreement and controversy; this is the American way." In Indianapolis, he said a bombing halt could be "a valuable potential step to substantive negotiations" but warned that "we could throw it away if it is used prematurely or when the enemy is not receptive to it." Asked whether a bombing halt would "play into the hands of the Communists," Muskie said: "We must have a meaningful movement toward peace before the bombing halt."

Nixon made his first suggestion about a Vietnam peace settlement in a question-and-answer session at a conference of UPI editors and publishers in Washington Oct. 7. Asked about his plans for achieving peace, Nixon referred to the 1952 Presidential campaign, when Gen. Dwight D. Eisenhower "did not indicate exactly . . . how he would end the [Korean] war," but, after his election, agreed to a settlement some observers held Pres. Harry S. Truman would have been unable to accept because of his susceptibility to "sell-out" charges from the opposition. "We might be able to agree to much more . . . [in January] than we can do now," Nixon said. He said the possibility would exist particularly if, by January, the military situation were improved and the South Vietnamese were doing more of the fighting.

In the course of a series of nightly radio talks, Nixon said Oct. 27: He would "do nothing that might interfere" with the Paris negotiations. In contrast, Humphrey "has provided a classic example of what a President must not do" during such negotiations: "He has talked too much and too loosely about Vietnam."

By trying to please every audience and appease every faction, he can only have sown consternation among our friends and confusion among our adversaries. A government cannot afford to negotiate and vacillate at the same time; neither can we restore America's leadership if we simply trade one credibility gap for another one." He (Nixon) was against imposing a coalition government on South Vietnam. "To the Communist side, a coalition government is not an exercise in cooperation but a sanctuary for subversion. Far from ending the war, it would only insure its resumption under conditions that would guarantee Communist victory." Viet Cong participation in a South Vietnamese government would be acceptable "provided they renounce the use of force and accept the verdict of elections."

George C. Wallace, the 3d-party candidate, had entered the Vietnam discussion Oct. 3 when he announced that Gen. Curtis E. LeMay, 61, ex-Air Force chief of staff, would run on his American Independent Party ticket as Vice Presidential candidate. Appearing with Wallace at a nationally televised news conference in Pittsburgh, Pa., LeMay said he "would use anything that we could dream up, including nuclear weapons, if it was necessary," to fight the Vietnam war. But he added that "I don't think it's necessary in this case or this war to use" nuclear arms.

Wallace, who had assured audiences during his campaign that he would use only conventional weapons in Vietnam, was questioned by newsmen about LeMay's remark. All LeMay had said was "that if the security of the country depended on the use of any weapon in the future he would use it," Wallace answered. "We can win and defend in Vietnam without the use of nuclear weapons," Wallace asserted.

LeMay said he desired "not to use any weapons," but "once the time comes that you have to fight, I would use any weapon . . . in the arsenal that is necessary." While he did not believe nuclear weapons were "necessary in Vietnam," LeMay said, he was "certainly not going to . . . tell our enemies that I advocate that under all circumstances I'm not going to use nuclear weapons."

Both major party candidates expressed concern about LeMay's remarks. Humphrey said Oct. 3 that "it would be disastrous" if anyone who spoke "so lightly about the use of nuclear weapons" should "come into a position of high responsibility." Nixon said Oct. 3 that he disagreed "completely" with LeMay on nuclear weapons in Vietnam and that it "shows why I think it so important to have in the White House a man who knows we must have civilian control over the military." "I do not believe nuclear bombs or weapons should be used in Vietnam," Nixon said.

During a local TV interview in Buffalo, N.Y. Oct. 4, Wallace defended LeMay's remarks but ruled out any possibility of using nuclear weapons in Vietnam. "If we cannot win with conventional weapons, I would not advocate the use of nuclear weapons," Wallace said. "All Gen. LeMay says is not to tell the enemy what you're going to do." Wallace told newsmen in Jersey City, N.J. Oct. 5 that he would push for "peace through strength" and maintenance of U.S. military superiority, but "we would not use nuclear weapons in Vietnam."

Nixon Elected President

Richard M. Nixon was elected President and Spiro T. Agnew Vice President Nov. 5. Following the election Nixon met with Pres. Johnson Nov. 11. He then said that Johnson and State Secy. Dean Rusk could speak "for the next Administration" as well as for the departing one in major foreign policy matters until the new Nixon Administration assumed office. Nixon said he hoped by this decision that "some very significant action and progress toward peace" could be made during the 60-day interim period.

Nixon made these remarks after a cordial all-afternoon visit to the White House. Nixon aides met simultaneously with White House staff members. While there, Nixon received briefings by State Secy. Rusk, Defense Secy. Clark M. Clifford, Gen. Earle G. Wheeler, chairman of the Joint Chiefs of Staff, CIA director Richard Helms and Special Presidential Asst. Walt W. Rostow.

The President-elect specifically referred to Vietnam, the Middle East and U.S.-Soviet relations as foreign policy areas in which, "if progress is to be made . . . , it can be made only if the parties on the other side realize that the current Administrations is setting forth policies that will be carried forward by the next Administration." "I gave assurance in each instance," he said, "to the Secretary of State and, of course, to the President, that they could speak not just for this Administration but for the nation, and that meant for the next Administration as well." Nixon held that these were matters—"Vietnam . . . at the top of the list—which cannot await decision and cannot afford a gap of 2 months in which no action occurs."

DOMESTIC EVENTS IN SOUTH VIETNAM

Reports from Saigon during 1968 disclosed the efforts of Pres. Nguyen Van Thieu's administration to recover from the Tet offensive, to deal with corruption and to consolidate its position as against its opposition.

Emergency Economic Powers Refused

Addressing a joint session of the National Assembly Feb. 9, Pres. Thieu asked for authority to rule by decree for a year on economic and financial matters. He said that the Communists' Tet offensive had "enabled us to realize even more clearly the urgent problems that must be resolved." His request for emergency economic powers, however, was rejected by 85-10 vote of the House of Representatives Mar. 1 and by 40-3 vote of the Senate Mar. 7. As a result of this rejection, the Thieu government was required to continue to submit each economic and financial measure to the legislature.

In debate prior to the House vote, most deputies had argued that it would be unconstitutional to cede decree powers to the president. The chairman of the finance and economy committee, urging the approval of Thieu's request, had pointed out that about 50% of South Vietnam's industry had been destroyed during the Tet offensive, that the government would lose an estimated $32 million in revenues, and it would cost about $40 million for relief and about $50 million to finance the expansion of the armed forces. A House official disclosed Mar. 12 that a petition calling for a no-confidence vote in the Thieu government for its alleged inefficiency in meeting the Tet offensive had been shelved temporarily. More than 50 petition signatures had been collected the previous week, but reported government pressure on several representatives to withdraw their names left the motion short of the 45 required to bring it to a vote.

As part of his austerity program, Thieu Feb. 28 had announced the permanent closing of all night clubs and dance halls in the country. Such establishments had been ordered closed by Thieu Jan. 31, when he had proclaimed martial law in the wake of the Tet drive.

The government had not hesitated to use forceful action in labor matters. A strike of 1,000 Saigon electrical power plant workers started Jan. 11 but was forcibly broken by police Jan. 13. Under a "mobilization" decree signed by Premier Nguyen Van Loc, 200 workers were rounded up by police and forced at gunpoint to board trucks. They were then driven to 7 power plants in the city. 130 of the strikers had been seized at the headquarters of the General Federation of Trade Unions, where they were staging a sit-down. 6 leaders of the Electrical Workers Union were arrested Jan. 12 after an inconclusive bargaining session with officials of the government-operated power plant (formerly owned by a French firm) and the Labor Ministry. The union demanded a 12% wage increase. Saigon dockworkers walked off their jobs Jan. 12-13 in sympathy with the electrical workers.

Military Mobilization

South Vietnam Feb. 11 began to mobilize an additional 65,000 troops. The build-up, proposed by Pres. Thieu, was designed to be completed by June 30 and to raise the strength of South Vietnam's forces by 10% to 765,000 men. In an address at a joint session of the National Assembly Feb. 9, Thieu had cited the Tet offensive in requesting that extra troops be called up. His proposals included the curtailment of military deferments, the immediate drafting of 18- and 19-year olds, the abolition of military discharges except for medical reasons and the recall of veterans with less than 5 years of service. Thieu said all government officials under age 45 would be given military training and armed. Thieu's mobilization action was, in effect, an implementation and acceleration of a decree he had issued in Oct. 1967 but had not put into effect because of public protest against its restrictions.

Thieu Mar. 21 announced new plans to expand his country's armed forces by 135,000 men. The increase would raise the military force to 900,000 including regular troops and militia and local defense forces. Enlarging the armed forces required a speedup in the drafting of 19-year-olds and the recruitment for the first time, starting in May, of 18-year-olds, Thieu said. He said veterans under 33 years of age with less than 5 years of military experience would be recalled to service.

Premier Nguyen Van Loc Apr. 7 signed a decree raising the draft age, effective June 1. Under the ruling, former enlisted men could be recalled up to age 40; veterans who had served as commissioned or non-commissioned officers could be re-drafted up to age 45.

In an address to a joint session of the Senate and House Apr. 10 Thieu called for passage of legislation authorizing a "general mobilization of the nation's manpower and resources." "We must increase our war potential," he said, "in order to be strong enough to talk peace with the Communists," since they "only agree to peace when they cannot . . . win."

Thieu's request for wide mobilization powers was granted by the National Assembly June 15 despite criticism that it would permit him to draft anyone in South Vietnam. The defense committee of the South Vietnamese House of Representatives had opposed Thieu's proposal on these grounds Apr. 17.

Thieu's general mobilization bill, providing for the induction of about 200,000 persons into the armed forces by the end of 1968, was passed by a joint session of the National Assembly June 15. Thieu signed the measure June 19 in public ceremonies held in Hué. Under the new law: Men between the ages of 18 and 43 would be inducted into the regular armed forces; men between the ages of 44 and 50 and 16- and 17-year-old youths would serve in the civilian part-time People's Self-Defense Organization; veterans with 12 years of service could be recalled; veteran non-commissioned officers in their late 40s or early 50s would be recalled; an estimated 90,000 17-year-olds in the People's Self-Defense Organization would be subject to transfer to the regular forces.

Corruption Attacked, Officials Replaced

The issue of corruption also preoccupied the Saigon government during 1968. Describing corruption as "a shame for the whole nation and the population," Pres. Thieu Mar. 21 vowed a campaign of "eradication," but he warned that this would be "a very difficult task that requires much courage, many efforts and great patience." Thus far, he said, 40 military officers and civilians found guilty of corruption had received death sentences and prison terms and had been subjected to "disciplinary measures."

Maj. Gen. Nguyen Duc Thang had been reported Jan. 26 to have resigned his posts as head of the Revolutionary Development (pacification) program and as deputy chief of staff. His request to leave the army had been rejected. Thang was said to have quit the pacification campaign because of his disillusionment with the government's inability to curb corruption in the army and government and to act against other social ills. Thang reportedly believed that the government's failure to cope with these problems would undermine the pacification program by leading villagers to lose faith in the aims of the Saigon regime. (Maj. Gen. Nguyen Van La replaced Thang as deputy chief of staff. La had served as chief of the national police and as commander of the Saigon military district under Ex-Pres. Ngo Dinh Diem.) 2 army officers who had been dismissed in the fall of 1967 on corruption charges were reported Jan. 29 to have been appointed to new military posts: Lt. Col. Duc Dat, former chief of Phuoctuy Province, made assistant commander of the 18th South Vietnamese Division. Lt. Col. Nhat Quan, former mayor of Vungtau, was appointed artillery commander of the III Corps, which included several provinces around Saigon. Dat had been ousted in 1967 with the announcement that he would be "severely punished" for "having committed mistakes while discharging his duties and having indulged in illegal activities." Quan had been ordered to report to the Defense Ministry for disciplinary action.

Pres. Thieu Mar. 1 replaced 7 provincial chiefs in a move to eliminate corruption and promote efficiency in the provinces. (He also appointed an 8th provincial chief to succeed an official who had been killed in the Tet offensive.) Among those ousted was Lt. Col. Phan Van Khoa, chief of Thuathien Province and mayor of Hué. He had been denounced by Buddhists and other groups. Khoa had been criticized again in February for hiding when Communist troops invaded Hué during the Tet offensive. In addition to Thuathien, the provinces affected by the changes were Darlac, Binhthuan, Vinhlong, Angiang, Baxuyen, Tuyenduc and Quangduc. It was the first time a chief of state personally appointed provincial chiefs; previously they had been named by the corps commanders and were directly responsible to them. Thieu removed 4 more provincial chiefs Mar. 26 and dismissed 2 more Mar. 30. The 4 provinces involved in the Mar. 26 action were in the Mekong delta—Gocong, Kienhoa, Vinhbinh and Phongdinh. The province chiefs replaced Mar. 30 were in Giadinh and Bienhoa, surrounding Saigon.

Thieu undertook a reconstruction of his government in May. Premier Nguyen Van Loc and his 17-member cabinet resigned May 18. Thieu immediately appointed Tran Van Huong, 64, as premier and called on him to form a new cabinet. Opposition to Loc and his ministers had been building up in the National Assembly since the start of the Tet offensive. The premier had been accused of not responding quickly enough to the attack. Deputies also had argued that Loc and his cabinet were technicians, that they had been appointed as a compromise between Thieu and the military and, thus, did not reflect the country's varied political views. Anti-Loc sentiment in the Assembly's lower body—the 135-member House of Representatives—had come to a head Apr. 29 when a special session was called by 45 deputies to consider the ouster of the premier and his cabinet. A motion of no-confidence was submitted but failed to come to a vote after 3 hours of debate. Several deputies denounced Loc as "incompetent" and accused his government of being corrupt. Thieu then announced May 9 that he would soon make major changes in the government.

The new premier, Huong, had run 4th in the presidential elections in Sept. 1967 and had served as premier late in 1964 and early in 1965. His views on ending the war were similar to Thieu's. Huong advocated a negotiated settlement but opposed dealing with the National Liberation Front. Prior to the current talks in Paris, Huong, however, had expressed the view that negotiations should be held between North and South Vietnam rather than between the U.S. and North Vietnam.

Huong announced the formation of a new cabinet May 25, and the cabinet was sworn in the same day. Only one ministry in the new 19-member cabinet—Agriculture & Land Reform—was controlled by a faction supporting Vice Pres. Nguyen Cao Ky. In the previous 17-member cabinet, the Ky faction had held 7 seats. Ky and his followers, however, succeeded in the week-long negotiations in preventing Pres. Thieu from appointing a close associate—Lt. Gen. Tran Thien Khiem, ambassador to Nationalist China—to the critical Defense Ministry post. Khiem instead was appointed interior minister, while the incumbent defense minister, Lt. Gen. Nguyen Van Vy, retained his position. Vy and Khiem were the only military officers in the cabinet; there had been 6 in the previous one. Huong was to hold the additional post of head of pacification. Negotiations to bring members of the Dai Viet and Tan Dai Viet parties into the cabinet had failed. Leaders of the 2 parties had insisted on more powerful posts than had been offered by Thieu and Ky.

The new cabinet: *Premier and Pacification*—Huong. *First Minister of State and General Inspector*—Mai Tho Truyen. *2d Minister of State and Open Arms Minister*—Phan Quang Dan. *3d Minister of State*—Vu Quoc Thuc. *Pacification Secretary*—Col. Hoang Van Lac. *Defense & Veterans Minister*—Lt. Gen. Nguyen Van Vy. *Interior*—Lt. Gen. Tran Thien Khiem. *Foreign*—Tran Chanh Thanh. *Economy*—Au Ngoc Ho. *Public Works, Communications & Transport*—Tran Luy. *Labor*—Dam Si Hiem. *Education & Youth*—Nguyen Van Tho. *Agriculture & Land Reform*—Truong Thai Ton. *Justice*—Le Van Thu. *Information*—Ton That Thien. *Ethnic Minorities*—Paul Nhur. *Secretary to the Premier's Office*—Huynh Van Dao.

Thieu Acts Against Political Opponents

In Feb. 1968, Pres. Thieu launched a campaign against his political opposition. The government arrested more than 20 of its political opponents in Saigon Feb. 20-25. No official reason was given for the arrests, but government sources hinted at the com‑pilation of a government list of people who might be used by the Viet Cong in establishing an eventual coalition government.

4 of those placed in "protective custody" Feb. 20-21 were militant Buddhist leader Thich Tri Quang, Truong Dinh Dzu, the peace candidate who had run 2d in the Sept. 1967 presidential elections, ex-Economy Min. Au Truong Thanh and Ho Thong Minh, defense minister in the government of the late Pres. Ngo Dinh Diem. 2 close aides of Tri Quang's were arrested Feb. 22: Thich Ho Giac and Thich Lieu Minh. A Buddhist spokesman said both were "pressured" into going to National Police headquarters. Among those seized Feb. 23 were Vu Huong Khanh, who had finished 8th in the presidential elections, labor union officials Tran Huu Quyen and Vo Van Tai and several more Buddhist monks.

A government spokesman, confirming the arrests of Tri Quang, Thanh, Minh and Dzu, said Feb. 23 that they had been "invited by the police to a safe area . . . to insure their safety." The names of Dzu and several others arrested were reported to have been found on a captured Viet Cong list of possible participants in a coalition government.

The arrests were carried out in the wake of the formation

Feb. 18 of a new political group aimed at creating national unity. The organization, called the Committee for the Safety of the Nation, was made up of rival Saigon politicians, former generals and representatives of South Vietnam's religious sects. Following the group's 2d meeting Feb. 21, Sen. Tran Van Don, co-chairman of the organization's 34-member standing committee, appealed to Vietnamese to "participate in our effort to ensure the safety of our nation." He said the committee urged the government to "unify its policy" to pave the way for "all elements of the nation to participate in the anti-Communist effort." Don insisted that his plea did not constitute a call for a government of national unity. But he said he hoped the committee would eventually establish provincial branches to promote that type of regime The standing committee members included among critics of the current regime: ex-Chief of State Phan Khac Suu, ex-Premier Tran Van Huong and Dai Viet Party leader Ha Thuc Ky. A special aide to Vice Pres. Nguyen Cao Ky, Dang Duc Khoi, Feb. 21 denied reports that the committee was "pro-Ky." Khoi, who had taken part in the establishment of the committee, later resigned from the committee.

Vice Pres. Ky remained one of the most outspoken opponents of Pres. Thieu. In an interview published Mar. 31 in the West German magazine *Stern*, he assailed American policy in Vietnam and criticized his own government as useless and corrupt. Discussing the U.S. presence in his country, Ky said: "The Americans are here to defend their interests, which do not always correspond with those of Vietnam. They are here because they want to remain in Asia and to stop communism in Asia—and not because they have any particular concern about us. And they understand our need but not our tragedy." Ky took issue with Sen. Robert F. Kennedy, a frequent critic of the Saigon regime. Kennedy's concept of democracy was "simply laughable, as is his concept of freedom," Ky said. "Oh, this Kennedy, who spits at us because we are corrupt and hates me when I reply: 'Yes, we are.' " Chiding the U.S. for attempting to introduce its own brand of democracy to South Vietnam, Ky asked: "But what the devil does that mean when you are dying of hunger? What sense does it make to talk about an executive, legislature or elections if the Vietnamese peasant now needs a bowl of rice to survive?" Ky dismissed South Vietnamese elections as "a loss of time and money. . . . They have served to install a regime that has nothing in common with the people—a useless, corrupt regime." Ky added: "We need a revolution. The laws we have protect the rich. We must make new laws that will give power to the poor."

The government Mar. 15 released Vo Van Tai, an official of the Vietnamese Confederation of Labor, who had been placed under "protective custody" during the Feb. 20-25 sweep. Tai's release followed pressure exerted by the U.S. embassy and the American Federation of Labor & Congress of Industrial Organization (AFL-CIO). The AFL-CIO's international representative, Irving Brown, had said during a visit to Saigon Mar. 13 that Tai's seizure had "caused considerable harm to the cause of the South Vietnamese amongst trade-union people in America and throughout the world." Brown said he had expressed concern in a recent meeting with Pres. Thieu.

3 more of those arrested, peace leader Truong Dinh Dzu, ex-Economy Min. Au Truong Thanh and Judge Tran Thuc Linh, were freed Apr. 14.

But Dzu was rearrested May 1. Dzu was seized at a Saigon hospital, where he was undergoing treatment for a heart ailment and for the effects of a 12-day hunger strike. Dzu's wife said he was arrested "because he said he believed that the solution to the war is a coalition [government]. . . . If Robert Kennedy was here and began talking about peace, he would be arrested too."

The Interior Ministry Apr. 27 had ordered Dzu rearrested for having "indulged in activities under the guise of peace and neutralism in line with the Communists which weakened the nation's anti-Communist spirit and had a damaging effect on the war effort of the people and the armed forces." The ministry's statement quoted Dzu as having said in a London *Times* interview that "only a coalition government with the Communists is a realistic solution to the Vietnam war. The outcome of any peace negotiations must be a coalition government." Pres. Thieu had vowed Apr. 18 that Dzu would be jailed for his alleged remarks to the British newspaper. When informed of Thieu's reaction, Dzu said Apr. 18 that he "did not advocate a coalition with the National Liberation Front as such. But I think we should try to get an accommodation with non-Communist elements of the front."

A court-martial in Saigon July 26 convicted and sentenced Dzu to 5 years in prison on charges of conduct "detrimental to the anti-Communist spirit of the people and the armed forces."

This was the first time a major political figure had been tried under a 1965 government decree that provided for prosecution of persons "who interfere with the government's struggle against communism." The verdict could not be appealed. During the 2-hour trial Dzu told the 5-man court: "I did not commit any acts harmful to the struggle of the people. I have committed no crime. I have only expressed my own thoughts on how to end the war."

(Saigon Radio June 30 announced the release of militant Buddhist leader Thich Tri Quang.)

Maj. Gen. Duong Van Minh, South Vietnamese chief of state 1963-4, returned to Saigon Oct. 5 after more than 4 years of exile in Bangkok, Thailand. Widely known as "Big Minh," he had been sent out of South Vietnam in Jan. 1965 after being deposed in 1964 by Lt. Gen. Nguyen Khanh, who then headed the government. Pres. Thieu had invited Minh Sept. 14 to return to South Vietnam as part of a "continuing policy of national unity and reconciliation." Thieu offered Minh a government post as his personal adviser.

Several new political groupings made their appearance during 1968:

The formation of a new political group opposed to the Saigon government and seeking to participate in peace talks was announced by the Viet Cong press agency Apr. 27. The report said that the new organization, the Alliance of National, Democratic & Peace Forces of Vietnam (ANDPF), had been established at a meeting in Saigon Apr. 20-21. The press agency said ANDPF had pledged to support the Viet Cong, even though many of its members were reported to be non-Communists. Trinh Dinh Thao, a lawyer, was said to have been elected chairman of the organization's Central Committee. The vice chairmen elected were identified as Lam Van Vet and Thich Don Hau, a Buddhist monk. Hanoi dispatches, quoting NLF (National Liberation Front) reports, said ANDPF membership included "Saigon personages, intellectuals, students, writers, newsmen, industrialists, businessmen, officers, public employes, etc., representing different leanings."

Hanoi Radio announced Apr. 28 that a manifesto adopted at ANDPF's inaugural meeting was similar to the program adopted by the NLF in 1967. *The manifesto said:*

● The South Vietnamese government should be overthrown and replaced by a "national union government" of an independent, neutral and democratic

country, whose "territorial integrity ... must be recognized and respected by all governments of the world."
• The reunification of North and South Vietnam "is the eager aspiration and sacred obligation of our entire people." But "unification cannot be achieved overnight" because of the different political systems of the North and South.
• The alliance was "prepared to enter into discussions with the United States government," but the NLF "cannot be absent from the settlement of any problem in South Vietnam."
• The alliance advocated "joint action and discussions" with the NLF "for the purpose of striving together to regain national independence. ..."
• The U.S. must end its "war of imperialist aggression" and withdraw its troops and bases from Vietnam.

The alliance's suggested participation in peace talks with the U.S. was rejected by Washington Apr. 29. A State Department statement said: "It seems obvious to us that this is an artificial organization, a creature of the National Liberation Front and Hanoi. And there is certainly similarity of positions taken and complementary language between the NLF and the alliance."

10 ANDPF leaders were convicted and sentenced to death *in absentia* by a South Vietnamese military court July 12 on charges of "rebellion" and "attempting to operate for the Communists under the false name of peace and neutrality." The ANDPF officials, including ANDPF Pres. Trinh Dinh Thao, had disappeared shortly before the alliance's formation had been announced.

The People's Front for National Salvation, formed Feb. 18, had held its first convention in Saigon Mar. 10. The session was attended by more than 1,600 delegates representing rival political factions, Buddhists, the Hoa Hao and Cao Dai religious sects, student groups and civic organizations. A resolution adopted by the front's 49-member central committee stated: "On the basis of the lessons learned from the recent Communist attacks, we know we must win the support of the masses, mobilize them and get their wholehearted participation in every aspect of the war effort. The fundamental conditions for attaining these goals are the political and leadership appeal of the entire administration ... and all religious and popular groups." Well-known political leaders such as ex-Chief of State Phan Khac Suu and ex-Premier Tran Van Huong were absent from the convention, although they had attended the front's preparatory meeting Feb. 18.

The Liberal Democratic Force was formed in Saigon Mar. 27. At a meeting attended by about 1,000 delegates, the LDF vowed to oppose communism and support democracy. It said the party would become "an active part of the democratic and political sphere, either as the governing party or the opposition." The LDF reportedly was supported by Pres. Thieu. It was said to have been established to counteract the new National Salvation Front, supposedly backed by Vice Pres. Nguyen Cao Ky.

The formation of a pro-government multiparty People's Alliance for Social Revolution was announced July 1. In a formal ceremony inaugurating the new political grouping, Pres. Thieu said July 4: The Alliance was "a major step toward grass-roots political activity. I welcome the Alliance, which is the largest organization so far and includes people from all walks of life." An Alliance manifesto read at the meeting declared that the new organization was "determined to wipe out corruption, do away with social inequalities and root out the entrenched forces of militarists and reactionaries who have always blocked progress." The Alliance said it was composed of 28 different political and religious groups. The 2 major ones were the recently-formed People's Front for National Salvation and the Free Democratic Force.

The formation of another political party—the Vietnam Force —had been announced June 30 by Phan Ba Cam, a militant anti-Communist. Cam said the party, which claimed the support of 6 non-Communist political groups, would seek a peaceful end to the war, the unification of North and South Vietnam and the building of a Socialist economy.

Pres. Thieu Oct. 10 denied reports that his regime had suppressed an attempted *coup d'etat*. In a radio-TV address to the nation, Thieu said these accounts were "rumors" spread by "Communists and their henchmen." A government press office spokesman had said earlier Oct. 10 that "you can say there was an attempted coup but that it failed." But the same office, quoting from the presidential communiqué later that day, said reports of a coup were "false rumors spread by the Communists and uninformed people." An unidentified government spokesman had announced Oct. 9 that several South Vietnamese marine and army officers, described as followers of Vice Pres. Ky, had been arrested in Saigon after the smashing of the alleged uprising. Another government source said that an attempted coup had been planned by "those who have been affected by the anti-corruption program who were trying to get rid of Pres. Thieu and Premier Tran Van Huong." Reports of the coup followed the issuance by Thieu Oct. 8 of an order by Thieu placing government forces on full alert. Government press chief Nguyen Van Noan said Thieu's directive, confining troops to their barracks and canceling their overnight passes, was issued after intelligence sources had warned that "troublemakers" were about to act against the government.

WAR PROTEST MOVEMENT

Protests Take Diverse Forms

Opposition to U.S. policies in Vietnam appeared in a variety of ways during 1968.

When the 2d session of the 90th Congress reconvened Jan. 15, an anti-war demonstration was held at the foot of Capitol Hill by about 5,000 women, led by ex-Rep. Jeanette Rankin, 87, the first woman member of Congress (elected in 1916). The demonstrators were barred from the Capitol grounds under an 1882 law, but a small delegation led by Miss Rankin presented to House Speaker John W. McCormack (D., Mass.) and Senate Democratic leader Mike Mansfield (Mont.) a petition to withdraw U.S. troops from Vietnam. The demonstrators, who called themselves the Jeanette Rankin Brigade, included Mrs. Martin Luther King Jr. and women from throughout the country. In the Senate, Sens. Wayne Morse (D., Ore.) and Ernest Gruening (D., Alaska) tried to put the women's petition into the *Congressional Record* but were blocked by the Senate precedent, upheld by Vice Pres. Hubert H. Humphrey, presiding officer, that no business be transacted the first day of a session.

At the White House Jan. 18, Negro singer Eartha Kitt told Mrs. Lyndon B. Johnson at a gathering of 50 white and black women that the war in Vietnam was the reason for juvenile delinquency. Miss Kitt's statement, described by some observers as a "tirade" or "angry outburst," was made unexpectedly at a meeting of "women doers" called to discuss ways of counteracting crime and rioting. Miss Kitt said: "You send the best of this country off to be shot and maimed. They rebel in the street. They will take pot and they will get high. They don't want to go to school because they're going to be snatched off from their mothers to be shot in Vietnam." Mrs. Johnson, visibly shaken by Miss Kitt's statement, replied: "Because there is a war on—and I pray that there will be a just and honest peace—that still doesn't give us a free ticket not to try to work for better things such as against crime in the streets, better education and better health for our people." The Rev. Dr. Martin Luther King Jr. said in Manhattan, Kan. Jan. 19 that Miss Kitt's statement "described the feelings of many persons" and was a "very proper gesture."

448 writers and editors announced in a full-page advertisement in the Jan. 30 *N.Y. Post* that they would not pay the then proposed 10% U.S. income tax surcharge because they believed "American involvement in Vietnam is morally wrong." $1/_3$ of the signers said they would not pay "that 23% of our current income tax which is being used to finance the war in Vietnam." The advertisement had been rejected by 8 daily newspapers, including the *N.Y. Times*, the *Washington Post* and the *Christian Science Monitor*.

At a news conference in New York Feb. 16, leaders of the National Committee for a Political Settlement in Vietnam—Negotiation Now urged the U.S. and other participants in the 1954 Geneva conference to adopt a new strategy for peace. They urged an end to U.S. bombing of North Vietnam and negotiations with all parties to the conflict. The men making the proposal were Prof. Clark Kerr, of the University of California, Robert W. Gilmore, president of the N.Y. Friends Group, Inc., Prof. Seymour Martin Lipset of Harvard, and the Most Rev. John J. Dougherty, president of Seton Hall University.

The National Mobilization Committee to End the War in Vietnam organized war protest marches and rallies in 17 U.S. cities Apr. 27. The largest demonstration took place in New York, where an estimated 87,000 persons marched to a Central Park rally to hear speakers denounce the war and racism. The speakers included Mrs. Coretta King, widow of Martin Luther King Jr., and Mayor John V. Lindsay. (Rival Loyalty Day parades were held the same day in New York, attracting a combined total of 6,000 marchers.) Antiwar demonstrations had been staged in the U.S. and other countries Apr. 26 under sponsorship of the Students Mobilization Committee in New York. More than 200,000 New York City college and high school students were reported to have boycotted classes as an antiwar gesture. Thousands of students staged rallies and demonstrations in other American, European and Asian cities, among them Prague, Paris and Tokyo.

Protests and student unrest, directly or indirectly connected to the opposition to the war and related problems, swept U.S.

colleges and universities thoroughout the spring and fall of 1968. In a study released Aug. 26, the National Student Association reported that students in at least 101 colleges and universities had staged at least 221 major demonstrations during the period Jan. 1-June 15, 1968, but the Vietnam war was a cause of the protest in only a minority of the cases. 38,911 students (2.6% of the total enrollment at the schools studied) participated in the protests. Professors participated in 18 of the demonstrations. Black power, with 97 cases, led the list of reasons for the demonstrations, followed by student power, in 50 cases, and Vietnam in 26. Other reasons included protests against the Dow Chemical Co., in favor of a particular professor or administrator, against armed campus police and against bad food.

Among developments reported:

• An Ad Hoc Committee on Vietnam announced in Cambridge, Mass. Jan. 16 that 3,077 Harvard University and Radcliffe College undergraduates, 51% of the undergraduate student body, had signed a statement calling on Pres. Johnson to "refrain from further escalation of the war and to make serious and sustained efforts, including de-escalation, to reach a negotiated settlement." The committee said that 338 members (54%) of the Harvard faculty of arts and sciences and 722 "other Harvard students, faculty and staff had signed the statement, which had been telegraphed to Johnson Jan. 15. Among the signers were Prof. Edwin O. Reischauer of Harvard, ex-U.S. ambassador to Japan, Mary Bunting, president of Radcliffe College, and Fred L. Glimp, dean of Harvard College.

• Dean Louis Pollak of the Yale Law School announced Feb. 14 in Washington that more than 500 faculty members representing 50 law schools had signed a statement calling on the legal profession to support candidates opposing the war in Vietnam and to demonstrate that "opposition to the present policy is not limited to a few extremists but comes from many moderate citizens." Paul M. Bator of Harvard told reporters that about 4,000 law students had signed the statement.

• Columbia University in New York became embroiled in a series of complicated incidents when dissident students, led by members of Students for a Democratic Society (SDS), seized several campus buildings in April and were forcibly removed by city policemen. A 2d student invasion of a campus hall occured May 21 following the suspension of 4 radical students for failure to answer a summons to the dean's office; the students had been charged with participating in the April disruptions. Policemen quietly cleared the building early May 22; but as they began to clear the campus, new violence erupted. Several fires were set; students were accused of hurling bricks, kicking, biting and swearing; policemen were accused of drawing guns, unnecessarily using nightsticks and dragging students from buildings and beating them. As the fall session approached, SDS staged several rallies and demonstrations but was not able to mobilize the support it had gained during the spring rebellion. A demonstration by 150 students halted registration briefly Sept. 18, but no arrests were made and no police summoned to the campus. A commission headed by Harvard

Law Prof. Archibald Cox investigated the April disorders. Its report, issued Oct. 5, found that the major conditions that set the stage for the rebellion were the Vietnam war; the university's connection with the Institute for Defense Analyses (IDA); racial strife; the university's relations with the surrounding community, and its insistence on building a gymnasium on public parkland separating Columbia from the black Harlem community.

● Fresh violence broke out in Berkeley, Calif. Aug. 30-31 during demonstrations against U.S. policy in Vietnam and Chicago police tactics during the Democratic National Convention. City Manager William C. Hanley Sept. 2 declared a state of civil disaster resulting from 3 days of continued violence, including "sporadic gunfire, dynamiting of private property, the shooting of an officer and several arson attempts."

● Students had announced plans to burn puppies in napalm at Grossmont College in El Cajon, Calif. Nov. 10 and at the University of Cincinnati Nov. 11, but no puppies were actually burned. Members of the student groups sponsoring the plans said later that they had not really intended to burn a dog but wanted only to dramatize their opposition to the Vietnam war.

● About 100 students occupied the administration building of the University of Connecticut in Storrs Nov. 11. The youths left Nov. 12 when the state police commissioner, called by university Pres. Homer D. Babbidge Jr., threatened to use force to evict them. The demonstrators demanded amnesty for 4 professors and 8 students involved in an Oct. 30 demonstration that prevented Dow Chemical Co. personnel from holding recruiting interviews on campus. Babbidge rejected their demands. The issue of campus recruiting flared again Nov. 26 and Dec. 10 when state troopers were summoned to break up demonstrations. 12 persons were arrested and 4 injured Nov. 26 as about 100 students and professors tried to prevent Olin Mathieson Corp. personnel from holding job interviews. The Dec. 10 demonstration was against recruiting by 3 Defense Department agencies; 67 were arrested in this demonstration, and students jostled policemen in order to get arrested.

● Nguyen Huu Chi, South Vietnam's permanent observer at the UN, and James Reston, executive editor of the *N.Y. Times*, were forced to cancel separate speeches at NYU Dec. 4 when antiwar demonstrators invaded 2 meetings at the university's Loeb Student Center. The demonstrators, led by SDS, stormed into the meetings, chanted slogans, threw an egg and water at Chi and tore up Reston's notes. 2 students were suspended; one person was arrested.

Communist Influence Seen in Dissent

Chairman Richard H. lchord (D., Mo.) of the House Committee on Un-American Activities (HUAC) said Dec. 6 that his committee had found evidence of Communist participation in the Chicago demonstrations during the Democratic National Convention. Ichord said that New Left leaders who testified before HUAC evidently considered communism "quite passé" but that their activity in Chicago "was certainly in [the Communists'] interests."

The HUAC hearings Dec. 2-6 were quiet compared to earlier sessions, which were marked by noisy New Left protests. Thomas E. Hayden, 28, a founder of the militant Students for a Democratic Society (SDS), testified Dec. 3 that no one was picketing the hearings because the committee had lost its authority in the country. The committee also heard testimony from 3 leaders of the antiwar Mobilization Committee, Robert Greenblatt, 30 (who testified Oct. 4), Rennard Davis, 28 (Dec. 3), and David Dellinger (Dec. 4).

Hayden and Dellinger testified that they had met with North Vietnamese and Viet Cong representatives in Paris before the Chicago confrontation but insisted that the demonstrations had not been influenced by those meetings. Greenblatt had said Oct. 4 that he had participated in similar meetings in Paris and Prague in June. Davis, Hayden and Dellinger all testified that the Chicago protesters had no intention of disrupting the convention and had tried to avoid violence. After New Left and antiwar groups had met in Lindenhurst, Ill., Mar. 23-24 to plan the convention demonstrations, spokesmen including Davis and Dellinger had told newsmen Mar. 25 that they planned to use peaceful tactics in Chicago but would not try to impose non-violence on others. Davis had said Mar. 23: "The [Democratic] delegates should be allowed to come to Chicago, so long as they give their support to a policy of ending racism and the war. I favor letting the delegates meet in the International Amphitheater and making our demands and the actions behind these demands escalate in militancy as the convention proceeds."

Former leaders of the Student Mobilization Committee to End the War in Vietnam had walked out of the organization's national convention in New York June 29 after charging that the group had been taken over by Trotskyites who had packed the convention. The 5th Avenue Peace Parade Committee, the student group's parent organization, voted July 11 to evict the student committee from its New York headquarters as a result of the alleged takeover. The leaders of the walkout, who charged that the takeover had been engineered by members of the Young Socialist Alliance, formed a rival group called the Radical Organizing Committee. Trotskyite leader Kipp Dawson was quoted in the *N.Y. Times* July 14 as denying that the convention had been stacked. She said that the former leaders sought to "dilute" the antiwar effort whereas the majority of the group wanted to emphasize this effort by mass demonstration. (The student group, organized in 1966, had sponsored numerous antiwar street demonstrations and student strikes.)

Dissenters Attack Draft & Military Service

Dissent against U.S. policy in Vietnam often took the form of attacks on the draft, on military service, on defense contractors such as the Dow Chemical Co. (manufacturer of napalm), on defense research at colleges and universities and on military training on campus. Draft evasion and desertion from military service became increasingly a form of anti-Vietnam protest. Atty. Gen. Ramsey Clark reported Jan. 12 that 952 men had been convicted in 1967 of violating Selective Service laws. There had been 536 convictions in 1966 and 272 in 1965. 1,648 prosecutions were begun in 1967, compared with 1,015 in 1966 and 506 in 1965. (In fiscal 1944 there were 4,609 draft offense convictions, in 1968 8,422 convictions.) Clark reported that in 1967 the average sentence for draft-law violation was 32.1 months, compared with 25.4 months in 1966.

Among events involving protest against the draft and/or military service:

● A jury in Federal District Court in Boston June 14 convicted Dr. Benjamin Spock, 65, and 3 others of conspiring to aid, abet and counsel draft registrants to violate the Selective Service law. A 5th defendant was acquitted. Found guilty with Spock were the Rev. William Sloane Coffin Jr., Michael Ferber and Mitchell Goodman. Marcus Raskin was found innocent. Judge Francis J. W. Ford July 10 imposed 2-year sentences on the 4 convicted men and $5,000 fines on all but Ferber. Ferber, a Harvard graduate student, was fined $1,000. All were freed on bond pending appeal. In sentencing them, Ford denounced the defendants' anti-draft activities as virtual "rebellion against the law" and as "in the nature of treason."

In a subsidiary finding June 14, the jury had held that none of the defendants were guilty of one of the 4 charges against them: conspiring to counsel men to give up their draft registration and classification cards. In his charge to the jury June 14, Judge Ford had said: The "crucial issue" in the case was conspiracy. "We are not trying the legality, morality or constitutionality of the war in Vietnam or the rights of a citizen to protest. We are not trying the United States of America or Pres. Johnson, nor are we trying the registrants who took part in demonstrations,"

Commenting on the verdict June 14, Spock said: "My main defense was I believed a citizen must work against a war he considers contrary to international law. The court has found differently. I will continue to press my case."

New York Mayor John V. Lindsay had taken the stand as a surprise defense witness June 10. He said he had met with Spock and others prior to the holding of an anti-draft demonstration scheduled for Dec. 5, 1967 at New York's Whitehall Street induction center. Lindsay said Spock "apparently did not know the details" of the planned demonstration but that Spock informed him that "he intended to get arrested." Spock had been taken into custody at the rally.

(The national board of the American Civil Liberties Union [ACLU] had voted 26-20 in New York Mar. 2 to defend persons under indictment for counseling draft-evasion in protest against the Vietnam war. In reversing a Jan. 12 vote, the board Mar. 2 agreed to offer legal and financial aid to Spock and his co-defendants. ACLU Executive Director John de J. Pemberton Jr. said that the union would not take a position on the legality or conduct of the war but would confine itself to the issues of free speech.)

• The Rev. Philip F. Berrigan was found guilty by U.S. District Court juries in Baltimore Apr. 16 and Oct. 16 of destroying draft records.

In the case decided Apr. 16, Berrigan and 3 other antiwar protestors were convicted of destroying government property, mutilating government records and impeding Selective Service procedures. Berrigan and Thomas P. Lewis, an artist, were each sentenced May 24 to 6 years in prison. David Eberhardt received a 3-year prison term. The sentencing of the 4th defendant, the Rev. James Mengel, was postponed pending psychiatric tests. The 4 had been arrested Oct. 27, 1967 after pouring duck blood on records at the Selective Service headquarters in Baltimore.

Shortly after their sentencing May 24, Berrigan and Lewis pleaded not guilty to charges that they and 7 other Roman Catholic antiwar militants had broken into another Selective Service headquarters, at Catonsville, outside Baltimore, May 17. Berrigan, Lewis and 7 other pacifists had taken about 600 individual draft records from the office and had burned them in a parking lot. The others arrested were Berrigan's brother, the Rev. Daniel Berrigan,

47, a Jesuit from Cornell, N.Y.; Brother David Darst, 26, of St. Louis; John Hogan, 33, who had recently resigned from the Maryknoll order; Mrs. Marjorie B. Melville, 38, a former Maryknoll nun; Thomas Melville, 37, her husband, a former Maryknoll priest; George Mische, 30, a Washington peace organizer; Mary Moylan, a nurse.

All 9 were convicted Oct. 16. Judge Roszel C. Thomsen Nov. 8 imposed sentences on the defendants ranging from 2 to $3^1/_2$ years. Philip Berrigan, 44, and Thomas Lewis received $3^1/_2$-year jail terms. 3-year prison terms were given to Daniel Berrigan, Thomas Melville, and Mische. The 4 other defendants received 2-year sentences.

● U.S. District Judge George Hart in Washington Mar. 7 dismissed a suit filed by student groups against Selective Service Dir. Lewis B. Hershey's recommendation that local draft boards reclassify to 1-A status students who participated in illegal antidraft demonstrations. The suit was filed by the National Student Association, Students for a Democratic Society, Campus Americans for Democratic Action and 15 student council presidents. The plaintiffs said that Hershey's recommendation, contained in an Oct. 26, 1967 letter, was an attempt to stifle legitimate dissent. Judge Hart said the letter merely was an expression of Hershey's "personal opinion" and had "no legal effect whatsoever." He said that persons who believed their draft status had been changed because they opposed the war had other administrative and judicial remedies. 12 New Jersey men had filed suit in U.S. District Court in Camden, N.J. Jan. 25 challenging Hershey's recommendation. The draft classifications of the 12 had been changed to 1-A after they had turned in their draft cards to protest the Vietnam war.

The Justice Department said Sept. 6 that Hershey's letter about treatment of antidraft protestors "appeared to have invited local boards to undertake . . . [draft] reclassification in a punitive fashion." In a brief filed with the Supreme Court in a case involving the reclassification of a divinity student, Solicitor Gen. Erwin N. Griswold said Hershey's order might be in violation of the draft law and the Constitution. The divinity student, James J. Oesterich, of Cheyenne, Wyo., who attended the Andover Newton Theological School in Newton, Mass., had turned in his draft card to the Justice Department in Oct. 1967 in protest against the Vietnam war. As a result, Oesterich lost his deferment and was ordered to report for induction.

• The U.S. Supreme Court May 27, in a 7–1 decision, upheld a 1965 amendment to the Selective Service law that made it a criminal offense to burn or otherwise mutilate a draft card. The ruling reversed a decision of the First Circuit Court of Appeals in Boston, which had held that the law was invalid on the ground that Congress' main motive in drafting it was to stifle dissent. Although the appeals court had upset the draft card burning conviction of the appellant in the case, David P. O'Brien, 21, of Cambridge, Mass., it had upheld his sentence on the ground that he had been guilty of not having his draft card in his possession. O'Brien, who had burned his card in Boston in Mar. 1966, had been convicted and given an indeterminate sentence of from 30 days to 4 years, plus 2 years' probation. The Supreme Court decision, written by Chief Justice Warren, contended that "we cannot accept the view that an apparently limitless variety of conduct can be labeled 'speech' whenever the person engaging in the conduct intends thereby to express an idea." (The American Civil Liberties Union had urged the court to consider the public burning of draft cards an act of "symbolic speech" protected by the First Amendment.)

• Capt. Dale E. Noyd, 34, 12-year Air Force veteran and former psychology professor, was convicted in Clovis, N.M. Mar. 8 by a 9-member court-martial of willfully disobeying a lawful order to train pilots to fly in Vietnam. He was sentenced Mar. 9 to a year at hard labor, dismissal from the service and forfeiture of all pay and allowances. Noyd had been charged with disobeying a lawful order Dec. 4, 1967 when, shortly after he completed retraining, he refused to fly with a student pilot in an F-100 jet fighter. He said the fighter pilots would probably be sent to Vietnam to fight in a war he considered immoral. Noyd, a member of the American Humanist Association, said he was a religious humanist, not a pacifist. He contended that he was conscientiously opposed to the war in Vietnam, not to all wars. Noyd's counsel argued that "religious compulsion" rendered Noyd incapable of obeying the order. The defense further contended the Air Force had illegally rejected the petition for conscientious objector status and thus had curtailed Noyd's religious freedom. Noyd's efforts to resign or to win conscientious objector status within the Air Force had been denied since Dec. 1966.

• Decisions handed down by the U.S. Supreme Court and lower tribunals rejected the pleas of Army Reservists to restrain the

Army from sending them to Vietnam on the ground that the action was illegal:

In an 8-1 decision Oct. 7 (Justice William O. Douglas dissenting), the Supreme Court rejected a suit of 256 reservists challenging the 1966 law that empowered Pres. Johnson to call up the reservists without a declaration of war or national emergency. The decision thus cleared the way for their transfer to Vietnam. 113 of the men were from the Cleveland area, stationed at Fort Meade, Md.; the others were from New York, New Jersey and Mississippi, stationed at Fort Lee, Va. The ruling canceled a restraining order, granted by Douglas Sept. 12, which had postponed the shipment of the 113 men to Vietnam pending a full Supreme Court hearing of the case.

Federal District Court in Baltimore Oct. 14 rejected a suit by 91 reservists from Boston (stationed at Fort Meade) requesting that they not be sent to Vietnam because they had not received proper training. Judge Roszel C. Thomsen ruled that the "law does not require, nor indeed permit, this court to review the Army's conclusion whether or not a man is qualified to perform his duties." The Supreme Court Oct. 16 upheld the federal court's decision by rejecting the reservists' appeal.

Federal Judge Robert Mehrige Jr. in Richmond Nov. 26 rejected a suit by 96 New York State reservists requesting release from service on the ground that they had been called up illegally because no state of emergency existed. Mehrige held that "wars may exist without a formal declaration of same. . . . The armed forces of the United States are now, . . . engaged in a state of war in Southeast Asia."

Justice Douglas Dec. 6 rejected a plea of 386 California National Guardsmen for a delay in their transfer to Vietnam. Douglas, however, questioned "whether these men can be sent abroad to fight in a war which has not been declared by Congress."

The Supreme Court Dec. 16 refused to review the federal government's constitutional right to mobilize reservists for the Vietnam war in the absence of an official declaration of war. (Douglas dissented.) The decision related to the appeal of 57 reservists who had argued that they had enlisted in the belief that they would not be activated "in the absence of a war declared by Congress or a national emergency declared by Congress or by the President."

● Some draft evaders or deserters sought asylum in churches or on college campuses:

In Boston, U.S. marshals moved into the Arlington Street Church May 22 to seize convicted draft evader Robert A. Talmanson, 21, who had been granted asylum there May 20 by authorities of the Unitarian-Universalist Church. About 30 to 40 sympathizers attempted to block the church doorway and clashed with police as they were removing Talmanson from the building. Talmanson had been convicted and sentenced to 3 years' imprisonment for failure to report for induction. Another youth who had been granted asylum with Talmanson, Spec. 4 William Chase, 19, of Dennis, Mass., remained in the church. Army authorities sought to remove his name from a company roster in Vietnam to pave the way for his seizure. Chase had returned home on leave after serving a year in Vietnam. Due to report back in April, he had refused to return to the Army.

FBI agents June 3 dragged 2 draft resisters from the Church of the

Mediator in Providence, R.I., where they had taken sanctuary May 31. A crowd of about 50 sympathizers tried to block the arrests. One of the arrested pair, Anthony D. Ramos, 23, of East Providence, R.I., was seized under a Jan. 24 indictment charging him with failure to report for induction Aug. 18, 1967. The other, Ronald Moyer, 23, of White Plains, N.Y., was arrested for violating his bond on a draft-refusal charge in New York.

U.S. marshals June 15 entered the Washington Square Methodist Church in New York and arrested Donald Baty, 22, of Huntington, N.Y., for having refused induction Mar. 4. Arraigned in federal court later June 15, Baty refused to stand and plead and was held in contempt.

9 AWOL servicemen who said they had "resigned" from the armed forces took sanctuary July 15 in St. Andrew's Presbyterian Church in the San Francisco suburb of Marin City and chained themselves to 9 clergymen who supported their anti-war views. The men attended a service of "communion and celebration to acknowledge" their decision to quit "military service for reasons of conscience." The servicemen were arrested by MPs July 17. One of the 9, Pvt. George Dounis, was sentenced to 4 years at hard labor and given a dishonorable discharge at a court-martial in San Francisco. 4 others were given prison sentences ranging from 6 months to 3 years.

U.S. Army Pvt. William S. Brakefield, 19, AWOL from Ft. Devens, Mass. since Oct. 2, was given sanctuary by anti-war students at City College in New York Oct. 31. The sanctuary was ended Nov. 7 by police who moved into the campus and arrested Brakefield and 164 demonstrators, more than $^1\!/_2$ of whom were listed by college authorities as non-students. Brakefield was given a 7-day sentence in Criminal Court Nov. 13 on charges of criminal trespass. Having already served the jail term since his arrest, Brakefield was released and turned over to an Army MP. Brakefield had said at his trial that he had come to City College "to unite students with the soldiers and to give an example that there are soldiers who support them."

Pvt. Jack O'Connor, AWOL from Ft. Bragg, N.C. since Sept. 14, was given sanctuary Oct. 29 at a student center at the Massachusetts Institute of Technology in Cambridge, Mass. O'Connor was arrested Nov. 10 by a military official. His sanctuary was sponsored by MIT Resistance, a student anti-draft group.

• The country's first anti-war demonstration organized and led by soldiers was held in San Francisco Oct. 12. More than 7,000 persons, including 200 soldiers, about 100 reservists and 700 veterans, marched through the city. The parade ended at City Hall where speakers denounced U.S. policy in Vietnam.

The Resistance, an anti-draft group, sponsored a nationwide protest Nov. 14 in observance of "National Turn in Your Draft Card Day." The demonstrations were marked by the mutilation of draft cards (or papers symbolizing them), the mailing back to draft boards of induction papers and other anti-war protests. Students in at least 17 California colleges tore up draft cards.

Deserters in Sweden, U.S. Ties Strained

Increasing numbers of U.S. military deserters sought asylum in Sweden:

Sweden Jan. 9 granted asylum to 4 U.S. Navy men who had deserted in Japan Oct. 24, 1967. The Swedish Aliens Commission, which granted approval, said that it did not consider the Americans "political refugees" but that they were permitted to remain in Sweden on "humanitarian grounds." By Mar. 19 the number receiving asylum in Sweden—most of them after deserting in West Germany—had reached 28. At least twice that number were in Sweden.

3 American deserters in Sweden had returned to West Germany Mar. 11 and 12. 2 of them, Pvts. Robert Beasley, 19, of Casey, Ill., and Michael A. Prewett, 20, of Dell City, Okla., gave themselves up to the U.S. embassy in Stockholm after 24 hours in Sweden and were returned to West Germany Mar. 11. The 3d defector, Pvt. Ray Jones, 20, of Pontiac, Mich., surrendered to U.S. Army authorities in Frankfurt, West Germany Mar. 12. Jones, a Negro and the U.S.' first Europe-based soldier to be granted asylum in Sweden, said he had fled there ,in Jan. 1967 in protest against racial bias in the U.S. and against the Vietnam war. Jones said he had decided to end his self-imposed exile "to protest the way we [American deserters] were being used in Sweden. By going there, I made my point about Vietnam. But I was being used in Sweden by the Swedish."

The presence of American deserters in Sweden and Sweden's opposition to the war in Vietnam strained diplomatic relations between Washington and Stockholm sufficiently so that U.S. Amb. William A. Heath was called back to Washington Mar. 12 for consultations. Prior to leaving, Heath had conferred Mar. 11 with Foreign Min. Torsten L. Nilsson. After the talks, Nilsson said Washington's and Stockholm's views on the war were "irreconcilable at present." Conceding that ties between the 2 coun-' tries were "a little strained," Nilsson expressed hope that they would improve when the war was over.

Among incidents in Sweden that had aroused U.S. protests: the appearance of Swedish Education Min. Olof Palme, 42, as head of an antiwar demonstration in Stockholm Feb. 21 (Palme marched beside visiting North Vietnamese Amb.-to-USSR Nguyen Tho Chan); assassination threats against Amb. Heath; attacks on

U.S. officials; the smashing of U.S. embassy windows. Premier Tage Erlander declared Mar. 12 that Sweden would continue to oppose American policy in Vietnam despite what he described as Washington's demand that it stop such criticism. Erlander said: "If we should normalize our relations [with the U.S.] as we have been asked to do by abandoning our criticism of the Vietnam war, it would mean a complete change in foreign policy. . . . Our position toward the Vietnam war is unchanged." Erlander made these remarks to the Foreign Affairs Council (an advisory body), which had been convened to consider the consequences of Heath's recall.

Sweden's opposition to U.S. policy in Vietnam was reiterated Mar. 16 by Sten Sundfeldt, a spokesman for Foreign Min. Nilsson. He said his country's differences with the U.S. were confined to the war. "We do not associate ourselves with other comments of anti-Americanism," he declared.

(American youths opposed to the war in Vietnam also were fleeing to France. French authorities Mar. 20 granted residence and work permits to 5 U.S. Army deserters and 4 U.S. civilians who said they had come to France to avoid the draft. All 9 identified themselves as members of a Paris-based group called the French Union of American Deserters & Draft Resisters. The French government had announced Mar. 12 that 3 U.S. soldiers who had deserted their posts in West Germany had been granted permits to remain in France.)

Protests in Other Countries

Demonstrations in protest against U.S. policy in Vietnam were held Feb. 18 in West Berlin, Rome and London.

The largest turnout was in West Berlin, where more than 10,000 persons displayed Communist and Viet Cong flags and pictures of Ho Chi Minh, Ernesto (Ché) Guevara and Lenin as they gathered in front of the Opera House to hear anti-American speeches. Demonstrators adopted resolutions calling for a campaign to persuade U.S. soldiers in West Germany to desert, for a blockade of factories producing military equipment for the U.S. and for protests against NATO bases throughout Europe.

A meeting of 3,000 antiwar demonstrators in Rome was climaxed by an attempt by 300 to 400 of the participants to march on the U.S. embassy. Police prevented the crowd from storming the building. The demonstrators later hurled rocks at the windows of an American airline office and of a shipping company office.

The London demonstration featured a silent march by more than 400 women to the U.S. embassy. Many of the marchers were dressed in black.

British Prime Min. Harold Wilson had been urged by members of his own Labor Party Feb. 6 to withdraw British support of American policy in Vietnam. A motion signed by more than 80 of the party's 327 Parliament members called on Wilson to adhere to a resolution, adopted at a Laborite conference in Oct. 1967, that had called for British dissociation from U.S. policy and had demanded that the U.S. end its bombing of North Vietnam "immediately, permanently and unconditionally."

The Feb. 18 anti-U.S. rally in West Berlin was countered by a pro-American demonstration staged in the city Feb. 21 by more than 150,000 persons. The demonstration, held in front of the City Hall, was sponsored by the city government, the major parties and labor unions. In an address to the crowd, Mayor Klaus Schutz declared: "We are linked with the American people in gratitude and friendship."

Hundreds of persons in Japan were hurt in repeated clashes Feb. 26–Mar. 31 between police and students opposing the building of an international airport and the use of a U.S. Army hospital for treating men wounded in Vietnam. The students were joined by farmers, on whose land the airport was to be built, in protesting the construction of what they called "another base for United States air strikes against North Vietnam." About 2,200 students and farmers clashed with 2,000 policemen Feb. 26 near Narita, site of the proposed new airport. 499 policemen and 61 students were injured. The farmers were supported by the students in protesting the terms offered for their land. Similar clashes involving police and leftwing students took place on the site Mar. 10 and 31; this time the students ostensibly protested the airport's presumed use by U.S. military planes. Some 350 persons were injured and 186 arrested Mar. 10 in a demonstration in which about 5,000 students took part. 43 were injured and 51 arrested in the Mar. 31 clash. Students then clashed with police Mar. 28 and 31 in protests against the treating of wounded men from Vietnam, scheduled to begin Apr. 15, at a U.S. hospital at Camp Oji in central Tokyo. In the Mar. 28 disturbance, students of the extreme leftist Zengakuren organization fought 2,000 policemen for 10 hours; 110 persons were injured and 169 students arrested. (A U.S. Army spokesman had said in Tokyo Mar. 13 that the opening of the Camp Oji hospital, which would have involved moving the facilities of the 7th Field Hospital from Johnson Air Base, had been postponed indefinitely.)

About 50,000 persons marched through London Oct. 27 in another protest against the war. The only violence occurred when some 2,000 militants, supporters of Chinese Communist Party Chairman Mao Tse-tung, broke off from the main line of the parade and headed toward the U.S. embassy. Anticipating trouble, 1,000 police had surrounded the embassy building. After an hour of speeches, some of the demonstrators clashed with police in an unsuccessful attempt to break through the cordon. 35 persons were arrested and 4 policemen were injured. More than 1,000 students had seized the London School of Economics Oct. 25 to use its buildings for possible "sanctuary and first aid" in the event that violence broke out during the antiwar march. At the conclusion of the demonstration Oct. 26, the students voted to end the occupation of the school.

One of the most violent antiwar demonstrations was staged in London Mar. 17. It climaxed with an attempt by several thousand protesters to storm the U.S. embassy. Police repeatedly clashed with the demonstrators and finally drove them off after the building had been pelted with smoke bombs, rocks and other missiles. About 20 windows were broken. Police arrested more than 300 demonstrators. About 50 persons were injured, including 25 policemen. The demonstrators had marched from a rally at Trafalgar Square, where about 10,000 persons heard speeches denouncing U.S. action in Vietnam and British support of Washington policy. Among the speakers was actress Vanessa Redgrave, who declared that "a Viet Cong victory is the only way to peace." The demonstration was sponsored by the Vietnam Solidarity Campaign, composed of about 36 leftwing groups. Participants included students from British and Continental universities. Also represented in the march was a U.S. organization in Britain called Stop-It Committee.

Index

Note: This index follows the Western usage in regard to most Vietnamese names. A Vietnamese individual, therefore, would be listed not under his family name but under the last section of his full name. *E.g.*, Duong Van Ba would be indexed thus: BA, Duong Van (not DUONG Van Ba). Exceptions are usually the cases of monks or others (*e.g.*, Ho Chi Minh) who use adopted names; such persons are generally listed under the first sections of their names (HO Chi Minh, not MINH, Ho Chi).

A

ABRAMS, Gen. Creighton W.—135, 140, 200, 208, 215, 235, 285-6
AERIAL Warfare: Bombing halts—85, 87, 213-6; curbs—90, 94, 98-9; violations—234. Cambodia—6. Laos—30-1. North Vietnam—6, 8, 57, 60, 68-9, 74-5, 79-81, 106-7, 128, 139, 156-7, 169, 201, 203; dams reported bombed—201; South Vietnam (ARVN support)—3-4, 27-8, 30, 45-6, 57, 60, 119, 187, 232, 234-5. U.S. reconnaissance flights—225, 233-4, 237; see also 'Bombing halts above
AGNEW, Spiro T.—280, 293
AIKEN, Sen. George D. (R., Vt.)—19
AIR FORCE, U.S.: Plane losses—8. Strength—59, see also AERIAL Warfare
ALBERTA, University—of (Edmonton, Canada) —155
ALESSANDRI, Federico—15
ALLIANCE of National Democratic & Peace Forces in Vietnam (ANDPF) —114, 174-5, 177, 302-4
AMERICAN Civil Liberties Union (ACLU)—311, 313
AMERICAN Federation of Labor & Congress of Industrial Organization (AFL-CIO)—301
AMERICAN Friends (Quakers) Service Committee—170

AMERICAN Humanist Association —313
AMERICAN Mobilization Committee against the Vietnam War—81
AMERICAN Society of Newspaper Editors—258
ANDUC, South Vietnam (U. S. Special Forces camp)—198
ARMY, U. S.—231-2. Casualties—3-4, 6, 32-4, 48-50, 56-60, 70, 73-5, 77-9, 82, 116-20, 127-31, 133-5, 138, 168, 185-7, 193-8, 201-3, 214, 236-7. Draft evasion & desertion —310-7. Provisional Corps—70 First Cavalry Division (airmobile) —49, 82, 119, 236. First Infantry Division—116, 195. 4th Infantry Division—32-3, 59. 5th Infantry Division—187. 9th Infantry Division —33, 43, 75, 132, 187. 11th Light Infantry Brigade—49. 25th Infantry Division—43, 77-8, 116, 168, 186, 196. 82d Airborne Infantry Division—53, 59. 101st Airborne —116, 133, 187, 194. 196th Light Infantry Brigade—129. 199th Light Brigade—43
ASHAU Valley—118-9, 128, 133, 185-7
ASIAN Development Bank—209
ASSASSINATIONS—274-5
ATTOPEU, Laos—61-2, 122
AUSTRALIA—29, 54, 94, 115

321

B

BA, Duong Van—167
BABBIDGE Jr., Homer D.—308
BAC, Vuong Van—227
BACLIEU, South Vietnam—34,49
BAITHUONG(airfield), North Vietnam
—80, 99
BALL, George W.—114, 205
BALTIMORE Sun (newspaper)—137
BAN Houi Sane, Laos—123
BANMETHOUT, South Vietnam—34,
68, 125
BAO, Maj. Nguyen—132
BARIA, South Vietnam—34
BA Thu, Cambodia—239
BATY, Donald—315
BAYH, Sen. Birch (D., Ind.)—244
BEASLEY, Pvt. Robert—316
BENCAT River, South Vietnam—44
BENTRE, South Vietnam:34. Ground
warfare 37, 49, 60, 68, 125. U. S.
aerial bombing—43
BERKELEY, Calif.—308
BERLIN, West—317-8
BERRIGAN, Rev. Daniel J.—81-2,
311-2
BERRIGAN, Rev. Philip F.—311-2
BIENHOA, South Vietnam—34
BINH, Mrs. Nguyen Thi—218
BINHSON (POW camp), South Viet-
nam—197
BIRCH, Michael Y.—125
BLACK, Capt. Jon D.—81
BO, Mai Van—16-7, 88-9
BOGGS, Rep. Hale (D., La)—285
BOSTON (U. S. cruiser)—138
BOWLES, Chester—22-5, 28, 134
BRADLEY, Gen. Omar N.—20
BRAKEFIELD, Pvt, William S.—315
BROOKE, Sen. Edward W. (R., Mass.)
—171
BROWN, George—15, 88
BROWN, Irving—301
BUDDHISTS—299-300, 303
BUNDY, McGeorge—207-8, 246
BUNDY, William P.—11,25,107,178.
Peace talks—110-1, 179
BUNKER, Ellsworth—35, 39, 105,
200, 210, 223. Peace efforts—179,
219-20. Tet offensive—50
BUNTING, Mary—307
BURMA—113-4
BURNSTEIN, Malcome S.—175
BURTON, Rep. Phillip (D., Calif.)
—285

C

CAHILL, Col. James P.—42
CAHUDOC, South Vietnam—60
CALIFORNIA—275
CALIFORNIA, University of—260
CAM, Phan Ba—304
CAMP Carroll, South Vietnam—45-6,
188
CAMAU, South Vietnam—49
CAMBODIA—63-4, 113-4. Casualties—
—29, 134, 240-1. Foreign military
aid—24. Involvement in Vietnam
war & foreign incursions—13, 22-9,
134, 238-9
CAMPUS Americans for Democratic
Action—312
CAMRANH Bay (airbase), South Viet-
nam—68
CANADA—102, 111
CANTHO, South Vietnam—34, 36,
49, 60, 68, 125, 231
CANTWELL, John L.—125
CAO Dai (religious sect)—76, 303
CAOINH, South Vietnam—60
CAREY, Rep. Hugh L. (D., N. Y.)—86
CARMICHAEL, Stokely—171
CARPENTER, Capt. Joe Victor—170
CARROLL, John S.—127
CASE, Sen. Clifford P. (R., N. J.)—251
CASUALTIES—See under ARMY,
U.S.; CAMBODIA; LAOS; MARINE
Corps, U.S.; VIET Cong;VIETNAM,
North; VIETNAM, South
CATHOLICS, Roman—14
CAU, Tran Thanh—218
CEASE-Fires—4, 241
CEAUSESCU, Nicolae—165
CENTRAL Intelligence Agency, U.S.
(CIA)—72
CHAE Myung, Lt. Gen. Shin—102
CHAMBERLAIN, Rep. Charles E.
(R., Mich.)—8
CHAMPASSAK, Sisouk Na—30-1
CHAN, Nguyen—10, 110, 154, 316
CHANH Le Quang—175-6
CHASE, William—314
CHAUDOC, South Vietnam—34
CHAUPHU, South Vietnam—49, 68
CHERNYAKOV, Yuri N.—26
CHI, Nguyen Huu—205, 308
CHICAGO—284, 287

DONGHOI (airfield), North Vietnam —75
DOUGHERTY, Most Rev. John. J. —306
DOUGLAS, Sen. Paul. H. (D., Ill.) —20
DOUGLAS, Justice Willam O—313
DOUNIS, Pvt. George—315
DOW Chemical Co.—307-8, 311
DUCLAP (U.S. Special Force Camp), South Vietnam—194
DULLES, John Foster—148
DZU, Truong Dinh—299, 301-2

E

EATON, Cyrus—165
EBERHARDT, David—311
EDMONDSON, Rep. Ed. (D., Okla.) —285
EGGLESTON, Charles R.—125
ELECTRICAL Workers Union (South Vietnam)—295
EISENHOWER, Dwight D.—20, 54, 148, 253, 291.On Vietnam war—242, 246, 281
ERLANDER, Tage—317
EVANS, Gov. Daniel J. (R., Wash.) —280-1

F

FACE the Nation (CBS-TV program) —50, 228, 243
FALK, Richard A.—175
FANFANI, Amintore—88
FEDERATED Unions for the Liberation of Vietnam—130
FERNANDEZ, Sosthene—238
5th Avenue Peace Parade Committee —309
FRANCE—102, 111
FREE Democratic Force—304
FRENCH Union of American Deserters & Draft Resisters—317
FULBRIGHT, Sen. J. William (D., Ark.)—47, 143, 171, 245. Bombing curb—96. Tonkin resolution dispute —247-8, 250

G

GALLUP Poll—41, 253
GANDHI, Indira—23

GARWIN, Richard L.—47
GENERAL Federation of Trade Unions (South Vietnam)—295
GEORGIA, University of—113
GERMANY, West (Federal German Republic),—316-8
GIAC, Thich Ho—299
GIAM, Col. Nguyen Van—132
GIAP, Gen. Vo Nguyen—45, 164
GILLIGAN, John H.—286
GIOLINH (allied base), South Vietnam —234
GLIMP, Fred L.—307
GOLDBERG, Arthur J.—88, 110
GOOD Housekeeping (magazine)—258
GOODPASTER Jr., Lt. Gen. Andrew J.—141
GOODWIN, Richard N.—286
GORE, Sen. Albert (D., Tenn.)—96, 244, 247, 285
GORSE, Georges—90
GORTON, John G.—54, 160
GOTTLIEB, Sanford—176
GOULDING, Phil—178
GREAT Britain—8, 111
GREECE—8
GREENBLATT, Robert—309
GRISWOLD, Erwin N.—312
GRIZZARD, Vernon—170
GROMYKO, Andrei A.—152, 154
GRONOUSKI, John—87
GROSSMONT College (El Cajon, Calif.)—308
GRUENING, Sen. Ernest (D., Alaska) —305
GULF of Tonkin—81, 246
GUY, Father—124

H

HABIB, Philip C.—141
HAI, Col. Tran Van—126
HAINAN Island, China—58
HAIPHONG Harbor, North Vietnam: Aerial warfare—6, 40, 68-9, 75, 79-81
HAMLINE University (St. Paul, Minn.) —272
HANLEY, William C.—308
HANOI, North Vietnam—40. Aerial warfare—8, 40, 68-9, 75, 79-81